Edward Horace Man

Aboriginal Inhabitants of the Andaman Islands

Edward Horace Man

Aboriginal Inhabitants of the Andaman Islands

ISBN/EAN: 9783337511036

Printed in Europe, USA, Canada, Australia, Japan

Cover: Foto ©Suzi / pixelio.de

More available books at **www.hansebooks.com**

ANDAM[redacted]

EDWARD[redacted]

Assistant Superintendent, Andaman [redacted]
Society; Member of the Royal [redacted]
and of the Asiatic Society [redacted]
the Scottish [redacted]

[redacted]

CONTENTS

Preface ix
Introduction .. ..

PART I.

Form and Size, 4; Anatomy and Physiology, Colour and Odour, 6; Hair, 9; Development and Decay, 11; Crosses, 12; Reproduction, 13; Abnormalities, 13; Pathology, 14; Medicine, 15; Physiognomy, 20; Motions, 21; Physical Powers and Senses, 22; Psychology and Morals, 24; Magic and Witchcraft, 26; Tribal Distribution, 30; Topography, 30; Arithmetic, [illegible]; Tribal Communities, 33; Nomadism, 35; Habitations, [illegible]; [illegible] Oaths, Ordeals, [illegible]; Laws, 42; Crimes, [illegible]; [illegible], 45; Communications, Chirography, and [illegible]

PART II.

Language, 40; Adoption, 56; Relationships, 58; Proper Names, 59; Initiatory Ceremonies, 61; Marriage, 67; Death and Burial, 73; Meetings and Partings, 79; Fire, 82; Superstitions, 84; Religious Beliefs and Demonology, 88; Mythology, 96.

PART III.

Social Relations, Education, and Infanticide, 107; Attire, 109; Tattooing, 111; Painting, 113; Shaving, 114; Deformations, 115; Weights and Measures, 115; Astronomy, 116; Trade, Exchangeable Values, and Property, 118; Agriculture, 120; Training and Domestication of Animals, 121; Food, 122; Tabu, 126; Warfare, 126; Hunting and Fishing, 136; Navigation, 146; Ornamentation, 150; Pottery, 153; Natural forms, 150; Leather-work, 158; Metallurgy, 159; Stone Implements, 159; Basket-work, 162; String, 162; Games and Amusements, 163.

APPENDICES.

	PAGE
A.—List of symbols employed to denote the sounds of the oral vowels, diphthongs, and consonants in the South Andaman language ..	174
B.—List of objects in common use among the Andamanese	175
C.—List of weights and measurements of male and female adults.. ..	188
D.—Extracts from Mr. J. E. Calder's paper "On the Native Tribes of Tasmania"	192
E.—List of ordinals	194
F.—Specimen of the South Andaman language	195
F.—(a) Philological harp	198
G.—List of possessive pronominal adjectives, as used with words denoting parts of the body (human or animal)	199
H.—List of proper names, "flower" names, and the names of the various seasons	201
I.—List of terms indicating relationship	202
K.—List of terms indicating age, &c., at various periods	207
L.—List of trees in the Andaman Islands	209
M.—Shells	214
N.—Earnings of the aborigines in the Andaman Islands	216
INDEX	217

LIST OF ILLUSTRATIONS.

		PAGE
No.	I.—Map of the Andaman Islands, illustrating distribution of the tribes	Frontispiece
"	II.—Andamanese man and woman and Nicobar youth	11
"	III.—Andamanese equipped for journey, &c...	80
"	IV.—Andamanese canoes	145
"	V.—Andamanese pottery, &c...	152
"	VI.— " "	175 to 187
"	VII.— " "	
"	VIII.— " "	
"	IX.— " "	

ERRATA.

Title page. *for* South Andaman Islands *read* South Andaman Island

Preface. p. V. *(line 2)* for 1880 *read* 1881.

p. VII. *(foot note)* *omit* a *before* communication

Introduction, p. IX *(line 16)* *insert* of *before* 93 E.

" p. XII *(foot note)* *for* Meandrina *read* Meandria

" p. XIII. *(7th line from bottom)* *for* Malaya *read* Malayan

" p. XVII. *(foot note, last line but one)* *for* seem *read* seemed

" p. XX. *(line 25)* *for* 1886 *read* 1869

" p. XXI. *(line 25)* *insert* such *before* [illegible]

" p. XXII. *(line [illegible])* *for* irresistable *read* irresistible

" p. XXVI. *(line 9 from bottom)* *for* eastern *read* southern

Page 20. *(line 8)* *for* bites *read* stings

" 182. *(line 4)* *for* jū·mu-ta- *read* jū·mu-tă

" 187. *(5th line from bottom)* *for* jū·rabuga- *read* jū·ratinga-

" 196. *(line 23)* *for* n *after* baraij *read* len

" [illegible]. *(line 17)* *for* Piar·at *read* Par·at

" 260. *(line 2 from bottom)* *for* go *read* gore

" 214, *for* Dentalism *read* Dentalium

" 222, *for* Narcondam *read* Narcoondam

E. H. M.

PREFACE.

In a paper which I was invited to read before the Anthropological Institute on 24th May, 1880, I mentioned that it was my purpose to submit to their Council a monograph then in course of preparation on the aboriginal inhabitants of the Andaman Islands which would embody the results of observations which I had made during my residence in those Islands from 1869–1880.

The exceptional advantages I enjoyed for making careful and systematic study of various matters of ethnological interest will be readily recognised when it is known that for four successive years I had charge of the "Homes" erected by Government with a view to establishing more cordial relations between the abori- [illegible] and training them, if possible, to some [illegible] in the performance of my duties, with members of the various tribes who from time to time visited the Homes, special facilities were afforded me of preparing a vocabulary[1] of the language, which eventually contained some 6,000 words, of the *bō̆jig-ngī̆ji-*, or South Andaman dialect, with numerous illustrative phrases and a comparative table of several hundred words of most of the other dialects spoken in Great Andaman. Having thus acquired a colloquial knowledge of the *bō̆jig-ngī̆ji-* language, I proceeded to collect as much information as possible in respect to the habits and customs of these savages, regarding whom only a few brief descriptive memoirs had appeared, leaving therefore a wide field for further research. In this interesting task I was greatly assisted by the excellent Manual of Anthropological Notes and

[1] This I hope to arrange for publication as soon as I can find sufficient leisure for the purpose.

Queries drawn up by a committee appointed in 1872 by the British Association for the Advancement of Science; for I was thereby enabled to work on clearly defined lines.

The value of such systematic guidance as is afforded by this Manual can only be appreciated by those who have endeavoured to collect information from savages concerning the multifarious subjects possessing interest to ethnologists. I can but express my grateful acknowledgments to Lieut.-General Pitt Rivers, F.R.S. (secretary to the committee above referred to, and one of the principal contributors to the Manual) for having made me acquainted with the volume soon after the appearance of the first edition, which fortunately was coincident with my first experiencing the need of such a work.

I think it is due to the reader as well as to myself to explain that on all points where there appeared the least risk of falling into error, by directing inquiries among those long resident in our midst, I took the precaution of substantiating my observations by seeking information on such matters from natives of distant villages who from time to time happened to visit our Settlement; but in every instance, whatever the nature of the communication or the character of my informant, I recognised the necessity and importance of testing through other channels [illegible] accuracy of every detail before finally accepting it.

During 1882[1] three evenings of the Anthropological Institute's session were devoted to the reading and discussion of portions of the paper which I had by that time prepared, and these have since appeared *in extenso* in the Institute's Journal for August and November, 1882, and February of the following year.

The division of the work into three parts[2] will thus be explained to the reader, while for convenience' sake I have, with the concurrence of the Council—to whom I am mainly indebted for the publication as a separate volume of this reprint from

[1] Viz., March 7th, April 25th, June 27th, 1882.

[2] In consequence of this arrangement it was found necessary to number the paragraphs so as to allow of references to the several sections in Parts 1, 2, and 3, the pagination of which it would have been impossible to ascertain in time for purposes of citation.

their Journal—adhered as far as possible to the original arrangement of my subject.

With the kind consent of the author[1] (Mr. A. J. Ellis, F.R.S.), and the approval of the Council of the Anthropological Institute, I am enabled to append a reprint of a valuable paper which formed part of the Presidential Address to the Philological Society (London) in May, 1882. I acknowledge with pleasure the able treatment which such an important subject as the language of these savages has met with at the hands of one so competent to deal with it, and which will, I am sure, add greatly to the value and interest of this memoir.

I have also to express my acknowledgments to the Council of the Anthropological Institute, first for obtaining the sanction of the Royal Geographical Society for the republication of the Map of the Andaman Islands, which appears in a slightly altered form as Plate I, and secondly, for permitting me to obtain copies of the plates of Andamanese objects which were published in Vols. VII and XI of their Journal, thereby enabling me to illustrate certain sections as well as Appendix B.

The photographs which appear as Plates II, III, and IV, are from my own negatives, and I can but regret that I had none better, of the requisite size, with me in England to offer the Institute.

E. H. MAN.

November, 1883.

[1] With regard to the Andamanese letters transcribed in Mr. Ellis's paper, it may be well to quote the following passage from a letter received at the time from the officer then in charge of the Homes to whom they had been forwarded for a communication to Jumbo and other aborigines at the headquarters in Port Blair: "The 'junglees' were delighted with your letter to them; Jumbo has been formally installed as Chief at Brigade Creek."

INTRODUCTION.

In considering the habits, customs, and physical peculiarities of a savage race, it is important to acquire as much information as possible regarding the land they inhabit, and also to ascertain the nature and extent of the influences exercised by, or resulting from their intercourse with other nationalities. It is therefore [illegible] to present the reader, by way of introduction, with [illegible] a few of the many points of interest con- [illegible], and referring to the writings of [illegible] Hume, Day, and other specialists for information regarding the geology, ornithology, &c., of the islands, which subjects are deemed to lie somewhat outside the scope of this volume.

The Andaman Islands, which till within the last hundred years were almost *terra incognita*, are situated in the Bay of Bengal, between the 10th and 14th parallels of N. lat. and near the meridian 93 E. of Greenwich; they comprise what are known as the Great and the Little Andamans, and, together with the Coco and Preparis Islands to the north, and the Nicobar Islands which lie to the south, form a volcanic chain extending between the province of Pegu and the northernmost point of Sumatra.

[illegible] Andaman[1] is about 140 miles long, and includes not only the three main islands known as North, Middle, and South Andaman, but also the Archipelago, Interview, Rutland, and various lesser islets adjacent to its sea-board.[2] At a con-

[1] For the possible derivation of the name "Andaman," the reader is referred to Part I, p. 2.

[2] The names of which may be ascertained by reference to the accompanying map.

b

siderable distance eastward of Great Andaman, but connected with the group, are two small uninhabited islands known as Narcondam and Barren Island, both of which contain volcanoes, though the latter only is active at the present day. To the south, and about midway between Great Andaman and the northernmost point of the Nicobar group, lies Little Andaman, consisting of a single island about 27 miles in length, and varying in breadth from 10 to 16 miles; there are also a few small islets near its coast.

None of the islands exceed 20 miles in breadth, and the area of the entire group is estimated at about 2,508 square miles, four-fifths of which are comprised in Great Andaman.

Nearly all the high land occurs in the vicinity of the east coast, shelving gradually towards the west, where few, and those but minor, elevations are to be found. The principal hills are: Saddle Peak[1] (2,400 feet) in North Andaman, overlooking Port Cornwallis; Ford's Peak (1,400 feet) on Rutland Island; and Mount Harriet (1,100 feet) in South Andaman, commanding the harbour of Port Blair.

The climate of the Andamans much resembles that of Lower Burmah, and the temperature throughout the year is very uniform; the variation in the shade during the dry season is about 22°, and averages 17° during the remainder of the year; the extreme variation throughout the twelve [illegible] estimated at 26°, viz., between 70° and 96°. The cool season [illegible] in during the last weeks of December and early part of January, and the hot season lasts through the months of March and April. The S.W. monsoon commences in the latter part of April or early in May, and usually terminates about the end of October, but on the change in the direction of the wind to N.E. [illegible] showers frequently occur for several weeks, and even, though at rare intervals, in January and February. The average number of wet days in the year is 182, and the rainfall 116 inches; the dry season is usually characterised during the first two months by strong winds from N.E., which cause sickness and prove equally prejudicial to vegetation. Although it has been ascertained that many of the most severe cyclones which have occurred in the Bay of Bengal during the past twenty-five years have had their origin in the immediate vicinity of the Andamans, only one is recorded (viz., in 1864) as having visited the islands themselves; in the same period there have been a few earthquakes, the first of which mention is made took place in August, 1868, and the next in February, 1880, from which time several slight shocks were felt until, in December (31st), 1881, another severe earthquake visited the group, the effects of which were

[1] The only ascent on record of Saddle Peak was made in February, [illegible] Major M. Protheroe, C.S.I., and other officers of Port Blair.

experienced on both the Indian and Burman coasts; another, though slighter, shock was felt on February 27th, 1882.[1]

Among the many noteworthy features of these islands are the numerous harbours in which, especially on the east coast, safe anchorage can be obtained at all seasons of the year; the most important and best known of these harbours are: Port Blair in South Andaman, and Port Cornwallis[2] in North Andaman; of both it has been said they may be classed among the finest harbours of the world, affording ample accommodation as well as shelter to even "half the British navy," in addition to which, from their central position in the Bay of Bengal, they present great advantages to vessels in need of refitting, and also as ports of refuge.

The water[3] in the harbour of Port Blair has been found to be [illegible] for its high density, as is evidenced by the rapid [illegible] of iron immersed in it: its extreme clearness has also attracted the notice of many, who have viewed through its pellucid depths the wonderful coral beds which abound in certain parts of the coast. The marvellous variety of the colouring to be found among these corals must be seen to be appreciated, but some idea of their wondrous beauty may be formed from the following extract:—"As we steamed along, visions of the splendours of the submarine world broke upon our view; . . . I feel quite unable to attempt the task of describing, much [illegible] an adequate idea of the exquisite assortment of [illegible] forms of life which were included in every [illegible] coral reefs. The most gorgeous [illegible] of vegetable and animal life afford but a poor subaërial representation of these submarine gardens."[4] But to return.

[1] On the occasion of the disastrous earthquake in the Straits of Sunda (August 26th, 1883), a report as of a distant signal gun was heard at Port Blair at about 9 P.M. of that day, followed by several similar reports at irregular intervals during the next two days. It was thought at the time that a vessel was wrecked off the coast, and the station steamer was sent out to render assistance; at 7 A.M. on Monday (27th) the sea rose and receded thrice in the course of a few minutes.

[2] This was the harbour selected in 1824 as the rendezvous of the fleet conveying the expedition under Sir Archibald Campbell to Rangoon during the first Burmese war.

[3] The supply of water from the tanks and wells in the Settlement is pronounced on medical authority to be both good and plentiful, and no diseases have ever yet been traced to the use of these waters.

[4] Vide "Jungle Life in India," pp. [illegible], by V. Ball, Esq., F.R.S. The vivid description by the same writer of a coral reef at the Nicobars (vide p. [illegible]) is so applicable also to those at the Andamans, that I feel the reader will thank me for appending it in this place:—"There are corals which in their living state are of many shades of fawn, buff, pink, and blue, while some are tipped with a magenta-like bloom. Sponges which looked as hard as stone, spread over wide areas, while sprays of coralline added their graceful forms to the picture. Through the vistas so formed, golden-banded and metallic-blue fish meandered, while on the patches of sand here and there the holothuriæ and various mollusca and crustaceans might be seen slowly crawling."

The other harbours which may be mentioned are: Stewart's Sound, Port Campbell, Port Mouat, Kyd Island Bay, Port Andaman, and the Bay between South Andaman and Rutland Island. There are besides many good anchorages, and several navigable channels have been discovered by successive commanders of the Settlement steamer, but in the absence of any other guide than Blair's old chart, which as relating to a coral-bound coast must require considerable revision at the present day, and with the knowledge that the extent of the shoals and reefs[1] is only approximately indicated in many parts, those unacquainted with the coast find it necessary to take a circuitous route and to exercise great care in proceeding from one point to another, especially on the northern and western shores, where the coral banks and reefs are known to extend as far as twenty miles seaward. Several creeks on the three main islands of Great Andaman are of a sufficient size to allow of the passage of boats for a considerable distance into the interior, and though of course these are of no little importance in opening up a country like the Andamans, they are chiefly valuable as affording a natural channel for the conveyance of produce from the extensive tracts of rich land[2] in their immediate vicinity, in lieu of the costly and indifferent land carriage which in the absence of such waterway would have to be substituted.[3]

The natural beauty of the scenery of the Andamans never fails to awaken the admiration of every visitor, and has been deservedly eulogised by various writers, one of whom (Prof. Ball) says: "Of all the places I have seen in Europe, Killarney can alone convey an idea of these scenes. The blue waters, the luxuriant emerald green vegetation down to the [illegible] coast, and the passing [illegible] nature, have their counterpart here."[4]

Various theories have been advanced with regard to the origin and affinity of the aboriginal population of the Andamans, but no certain information is obtainable in the matter. The statements of the early Arabian travellers, and also of Marco Polo, give grounds for believing that the Andamans were inhabited

[1] These are formed chiefly of *Caryophyllia*, *Madrepora*, *Porites*, [illegible], and other reef-forming corals (Kurz).

[2] By means of a comparatively light embankment, these lands are capable of cultivation to the very borders of the creek.

[3] Probably ignorance, and not disregard of these and other considerations which might be adduced, has led to the suggestion by some visitors (including [illegible] two able officers of long standing) that the bunding of the deep mouths of [illegible] creeks would prove highly advantageous by adding largely to the area of land suitable for paddy cultivation; had, however, their observations been made during the rains instead of during the dry months, their opinions would doubtless have been considerably modified.

[4] *Vide* "Jungle Life in India," by V. Ball, Esq., F.R.S., p. 362 (1880).

centuries ago by the progenitors of the present race, and afford (apart from the knowledge that the interior of the Malayan Peninsula, as well as of the Philippine Islands, has been from very distant times occupied by Negritos closely resembling if not also closely allied to the Andamanese) strong *primâ facie* evidence against the somewhat plausible tale which found credence at one time—*i.e.*, that these islands were originally peopled by a cargo of African slaves saved from the wreck of a Portuguese ship. It is surprising that this hypothesis, which has long since been disproved, should have ever been entertained, for, as Professor Owen has observed,[1] "it is to be presumed that the Portuguese would import from the Guinea coast, or other mart of Negro slaves, individuals of the usual stature, and it is incredible that their descendants, enjoying freedom in a tropical region affording such a sufficiency and even abundance of food as the Andamans are testified to supply, should have degenerated in the course of two or three centuries to the characteristic dwarfishness of the otherwise well made, strong, and active natives[2] of the Andaman Islands."[3]

The persistence with which travellers and writers, from the earliest times[4] to a comparatively recent date,[5] have maintained that these aborigines are anthropophagi would be remarkable were it not a common experience that idle tales, especially when of a prejudicial character, have always been readily accepted,

[1] [illegible] of the British Association, 1861."

[2] [illegible] in a report of a lecture delivered by [illegible] in this connection— "[illegible], whose geographical position is almost [illegible] distant extremes of the range of the woolly-haired race, may be the unchanged or little modified representatives of a primitive type from whom the African negroes on the one hand, and the Oceanic negroes on the other, have taken their origin, and hence everything connected with their history or structure becomes of the greatest interest to anthropologists" (*vide Brit. Med. Journ.*, May 3, 1879).

[3] Prior to 1879 the theories which had been advanced to account for the colonisation of the Andamans by their present peculiar inhabitants were summed up by Dr. Dobson, F.R.S., as follows:—

[illegible] present inhabitants of the Andamans are—

I. The descendants of shipwrecked negroes escaped either from some Arab slave-ship carried out of its course by adverse winds, or from a slave-ship wrecked on the Andamans on its way to the Portuguese Settlement in Pegu (Symes' "Embassy to Ava," *Calcutta Monthly Register*, 1790).

II. Aborigines not connected on any anatomical grounds with the people of any existing continent (Owen).

III. [illegible]—negroes (Huxley).

IV. Negritos or [illegible] from the Malayan Peninsula (Wallace)

V. Mincopie branch of the *Negrito* division of an original negro stock (Quatrefages).

[4] *Vide* Colonel Yule's "Marco Polo," vol. ii, p. 251.

[5] *Vide* Mouat, p. 71, and W. W. Hunter, who writes, "During the next half century (*i.e.*, from 1790) the Andamans appear in the records only as a cluster of cannibal islands" (*vide Imperial Gazetteer of India*).

whether they relate to individuals or to races; the origin of the belief in this instance may possibly be traceable to the inveterate hostility which they have manifested towards all strangers approaching their shores, but for which abundant excuse can be found in the accounts given by Capt. Miller[1] of the malpractices of the Malay and Chinese traders who visited these islands in search of *bêche de mer* and edible birds' nests.

To this belief may in all probability be also attributed the fact that these islands were avoided by most voyagers, and hence no records exist with reference to their history prior to the close of the last century, when the Honourable East India Company, recognising the advantages which the group afforded for a penal colony, sent down Lieutenant Blair (who had previously been commissioned to survey and report upon the islands) in charge of a small expedition and with instructions to provide for the reception of prisoners.

A Settlement was accordingly formed at Port Blair, then known as Port Cornwallis, where Blair displayed much energy and skill in his arrangements. After a brief residence of four years, during which the colony enjoyed excellent health, and Blair was able to report favourably of his relations with the aborigines),[2] orders were received from Calcutta for the removal of the entire establishment to the magnificent harbour in North Andaman, where it was proposed to form a Naval Arsenal. The transfer was effected in 1792, and the newly occupied station was named Port Cornwallis, while the recently abandoned Port was styled "Old Harbour," by which name it continued to be known till 1858, when, at Dr. Mouat's suggestion, it was appropriately changed to Port Blair. The new site selected for occupation, despite its apparent natural advantages, proved most unhealthy, and a year had hardly elapsed before it became evident that the change from South Andaman had been ill-advised; it was not, however, till February, 1796, that, in consequence of the continued sickness and high death rate, Government finally decided upon the abandonment of the colony, and the removal of the prisoners (numbering 270) to Penang, while the free settlers and troops were conveyed back to Bengal.

From this date the islands remained unoccupied by aliens for

[1] *Vide* Mouat, p. [illegible], and "Journ. Anthrop. Inst.," vol. xii, No. 42, p. 339.

[2] Both his account and that of Lieutenant R. H. Colebrooke, who visited the islands about the same time (if not actually in each other's company), were published, the latter appearing in vol. iv., of the "Asiatic Researches." Although the accounts furnished by them do not in all respects accord with our present knowledge of the habits of these savages, it must be borne in mind that, apart from the difficulties which attend inquiries prosecuted as were theirs, with but little or no acquaintance with the language spoken by the savages, various changes or modifications have probably occurred during the long lapse of years which may account for many seeming discrepancies.

sixty-two years, during which period all that is known regarding them or their inhabitants was derived from accounts published of casual visits paid by Government or trading vessels;[1] but as these add little to our information it is unnecessary to particularise them further than to say that they confirm the reports furnished by Colebrooke of the degraded condition of the savages and their inveterate hostility towards all strangers.

The modern history of the Andamans may be said to date from the latter end of 1857, when the scheme of founding a penal settlement and harbour of refuge in these islands, which had been under consideration for a few years, was precipitated by the events connected with the Sepoy mutiny. A Commission, composed of Dr. F. J. Mouat as President, and Dr. G. Playfair, A.M.S., and Lieutenant J. A. Heathcote, of the Indian Navy, as members, was despatched at this time with instructions to explore the coasts of these islands, to examine how far they were adapted for the establishment of a convict station, and to select a suitable site for such a Settlement.

Leaving Calcutta on the 23rd November, and travelling *viâ* Moulmein, Dr. Mouat and his colleagues reached Port Cornwallis on the 11th December; they thence visited in succession Stewart's Sound, Long Island, Barren Island, Old Harbour, McPherson's Strait, Cinque Islands, Labyrinth Islands, Port Mouat, Port Campbell, Middle Strait, and finally Port Andaman, making careful observations at each of these localities, in the course of which many adventures with the aborigines occurred, the [illegible] being at the last stage of the expedition and on the last day of the old year, when an encounter provoked by the savages took place which resulted in a few of them being killed and wounded and one being taken captive.[2] The Commission returned to Calcutta early in the new year (1858), and at once submitted their report; they advocated the selection of Old Harbour as being admirably suited for the purposes of a penal Settlement, and suggested that the name of this harbour might be appropriately changed to "Port Blair," in honour of the distinguished hydrographer.

In recognition of the excellent services performed by the Commission the special thanks of the Supreme Government were

[1] The three chief incidents recorded and mentioned by Mouat are—1. The misadventure at Port Cornwallis in 1824 of the fleet conveying the troops for the first Burmese war; 2. The visit and treacherous murder in 1839 of Dr. Helfer, a savant engaged in scientific researches; and 3. The extraordinary shipwreck in 1844 at Havelock Island of the troopships "Briton" and "Runnymede."

[2] This lad was taken to Calcutta, where he naturally excited great interest and curiosity. After a short detention he was conveyed back to the very spot which had witnessed his capture, but, owing to the kindness with which he had been treated, he appeared loth to part with his captors.

conferred upon Dr. Mouat and his colleagues for the judicious, prompt, and effectual manner in which they had carried out their instructions, and the business-like and practical shape in which they had embodied their investigations.

The Government lost no time in acting upon the recommendation of the Commission, and orders were at once sent to Captain (now General) H. Man, then on duty at Moulmein, to proceed to Port Blair and hoist the British Flag and take possession of the Andaman Islands in the name of the Honourable East India Company; before his return Captain Man was also to make arrangements for the immediate reception of a large party of convict mutineers whom it had been decided to transport thither without delay.

These instructions were duly carried into effect: the flag was hoisted on the 22nd January, and sixteen days later the first party of prisoners, numbering 200, arrived in charge of Dr. J. P. Walker, who had been appointed Superintendent of the new Settlement. During the first decade of the colony (1858–1867) the rate of mortality among the settlers was excessive, the annual average amounting to no less than 18·56 per cent., while in one year (1859) it will be seen from the annexed table to have reached the terrible figure of 63 per cent.

Year.	Death rate per cent.	Year.	Death rate per cent.
1858–59	16·00	1871–72	1·72
1859–60	63·00	1872–73	1·64
1860–61	13·40	1873–74	1·61
1861–62	14·26	1874–75	2·62
1862–63	25·59	1875–76	3·67
1863–64	21·56	1876–77	4·17
1864–65	14·64	1877–78	4·00
1865–66	6·57	1878–79	5·73
1866–67	10·56	1879–80	4·62
1867–68	10·15	1880–81	5·12
1868–69	3·9	1881–82	4·85
1869–70	2·0	1882–83	5·3
1870–71	1·2		

This extraordinary fatality was of course chiefly due to circumstances incidental to the establishment of a penal Settlement in an isolated tropical region peopled by hostile savages and covered by dense jungle largely fringed with mangrove, and rendered extremely malarious by numerous salt and fresh water swamps which are found throughout the group.

The necessity of clearing and occupying without loss of time the most commanding localities in the fine harbour of Port Blair, and reclaiming as far as possible the contiguous swamps, naturally led to much sickness, which was aggravated by various other circumstances, of which the following were doubtless the chief:—

1. Transportation of a large number of prisoners unfit either to withstand the climate or to perform the work required of them under the exceptional circumstances in which they were then placed.
2. Want of sufficient nitrogenous food.
3. Absence of a sanatarium for the recovery of invalids.
4. Employment of convict labour on works of every kind throughout the year without respect to the suitability of the season for those involving exposure to malarious influences, as evidenced by the mortality in the rains having about trebled that of the dry months.
5. Difficulties experienced by working parties in consequence of the harassing attacks of the aborigines.

The above facts being at length recognised as calling for stringent measures of reform, active remedial steps were at once taken by the then recently appointed Superintendent,[1] with the remarkable result that the death rate suddenly fell from 10·16 in 1867 to 3·9 in 1868, while an average of 1·6 in the five following years, during which vast clearings of jungle and other important works were accomplished, testified to the vigour and energy with which the wise and considerate system which had been inaugurated was carried on.

Prior to the formation of our Settlement in 1858, and for some years after, it is clearly shown, from the early records of our relations with the aborigines, that extreme jealousy and distrust prevailed among adjacent tribesmen, and even among scattered communities of the same tribe; these feelings naturally resulted in restricting intercommunication, and it is therefore not surprising to find that in many cases no knowledge was possessed regarding tribes distant only fifteen or twenty miles.[2] Of the *Ōko-jūwoi-*, *Ā·kà-kedè-*, *Ā·kà-jārò-*, and *Ākà-chāriar-* tribes, those living in South Andaman remained in ignorance till 1877, and it was not till 1879–80 that members of all the eight tribes of Great Andaman (*i.e.*, including the *Ā-kà-bal·awa-* of the Archipelago) were able to meet on friendly terms at the various Homes which had then been established for some years.

[1] Colonel (now General) H. Man.

[2] In 1876 it was found that the *bō·jig-ngi·ji·* (or South Andaman tribe) had only then recently discovered that Middle Andaman was not, as they had supposed, occupied entirely by the *Ā·kà-bō·jig-yāb-*, but that it was shared by another tribe called *Ā·kà-kōl-*; of the territory further north all they were able to say was that it was occupied by the *jā·rawa-*, a people they seem to dread equally with the natives of Little Andaman.

From the very commencement of the new Settlement, as has been stated, serious difficulties had to be contended with in consequence of the harassing attacks on our working parties by the aborigines, whose cupidity was excited by the iron tools and other implements which in their eyes presented an appearance of adaptability as weapons of the chase; the Government Gardens they likewise freely robbed, until at length stern repressive measures had to be adopted whereby they were instructed for the first time in the laws of private property. A wholesome dread of our power having been duly instilled, efforts were made by Government with a view to the civilisation of the race and the establishment of a better understanding between ourselves and the original possessors of the soil. Homes were accordingly erected in the vicinity of the harbour, where all who needed might obtain protection, shelter, food, and medicine. This step, which was deemed the best, if not the only means of furthering one of the objects which had prompted the re-establishment of the colony—*i.e.*, of reclaiming the savages from their barbarous custom of murdering all strangers who approached their shores—effected a marked improvement in our relations with the tribes in South Andaman[1] by affording them convincing proofs of our friendly intentions towards them, so that now, as Dr. Day has stated, "the convicts are left unmolested, the implements of agriculture are not stolen, the fishing stakes are left undisturbed, the gardens are no longer pillaged, runaway convicts have been recaptured, and shipwrecked sailors assisted."

It must not, however, be supposed that these beneficial results were immediately obtained, for it could hardly be expected that the aborigines should at once believe in our goodwill towards them, or forget their resentment against the people who had taken possession of their fine harbour and ousted them from many of their favourite haunts; in process of time, however, the kind and judicious treatment they consistently met with, first from Rev. H. F. Corbyn, and during ten subsequent years from Mr. J. N. Homfray, had the desired effect, and they have learned not only to regard us with favour, but also to assist us in a variety of ways.

[1] Recently (July, 1883) four men and two women were forwarded to Calcutta for the purpose of being modelled for the International Exhibition; while there they were quartered for a few weeks in the Zoological Gardens, where they attracted great crowds of Bengalis, who had never before had an opportunity of seeing the people whom they are said to regard as the descendants of the Rakshasas (!) Circumstances proved that their Port Blair training had not been lost on these representatives of their race, for on being asked by their visitors for a souvenir in the shape of a lock of their corkscrew ringlets, they promptly demanded a rupee before granting the favour; and in like manner the pleasure of witnessing an Andaman dance was not to be obtained previous to some *ik-pā·ra-* (money, lit. "slices") having been bestowed upon the performers!

To Mr. Homfray great credit is due for the zeal and energy he displayed in conciliating the members of the various tribes who visited the Homes: he spared neither time nor his private means in promoting their welfare and gratifying their wants, and so thoroughly identified himself with their concerns and interests as to gain their entire confidence and goodwill; he also acquired a fair colloquial knowledge of the South Andaman language, but abandoned an attempt he made to form a vocabulary. As Mr. Homfray's labours may be fairly said to have paved the way, and rendered easier the task of conducting ethnological and philological researches among the aborigines, it is due to his memory that this slight acknowledgment should be here made of his good services.[1]

The Homes have effected good by bringing together members of the various tribes, between whom the way has thus been paved for intermarriages, which were of course formerly of rare occurrence; tribal feuds have also here been amicably arranged, while, through visits paid to Port Blair and other Homes by members of all the Great Andaman tribes, as well as by our visits in the station steamer to the more distant encampments, the knowledge of our power, resources, and kindly intentions has spread throughout their respective territories.

It cannot, however, be contended that our attempts to reclaim the Andamanese from their savage state have produced unmixed beneficial results, for it is found that in proportion as they gain in intelligence and tractability, the more fat and indolent do they become, and having no incentive towards exertion frequently lose in great measure their quondam skill in hunting;—availing themselves of the privileges of free board and quarters, they spend their time for days together in singing, dancing, and feasting; the spirit of independence becomes thus less conspicuous, as they learn to depend upon others for the supply of their daily requirements, instead of being compelled to make such provision for themselves. There can, moreover, be no doubt that the effect of our clearances of jungle has been prejudicial to the health of the aborigines, while the excessive tobacco-smoking[2] among members of both sexes, which has been unrestricted, has seriously undermined their already enfeebled constitutions. If the evil ended here there would be ground for regret, but a graver cause exists in the deterioration which has taken place in their morals through

[1] Mr. Homfray died suddenly at Port Blair on February 25th, 1883, after twenty years' service in the Settlement.

[2] It is pitiable to notice the evident distrelish and discomfort endured by one of these savages when first given a pipe of tobacco, yet from sheer determination to share an experience which has such apparent attractions for their compatriots they willingly undergo the misery of nausea for several days till they have habituated themselves to its use.

their unavoidable contact with the alien convict population, the lamentable consequences of which will be found under the head of "Pathology."[1] So widespread is the evil influence that has been exercised, that on no point probably will future writers differ so strongly as on the social and moral virtues of the Andamanese. I wish, therefore, to make it clear to my readers that my remarks and observations on all, and especially on these points, are restricted to those communities who have been found living in their primitive state, and who may therefore be fairly considered as representatives of the race, being unaffected by the virtues or vices of so-called civilisation.

The measure of success which was considered to have attended the establishment of the Homes suggested that further good might be effected by the formation of a school or Orphanage for the education of the younger members of the aboriginal population. Accordingly in 1866 a commencement was made with a few children who had been obtained by Mr. Homfray from their guardians or relatives, and who were now placed under the care of a matron on Ross Island, where the Orphanage was opened. In 1870 two ladies from the Kidderpore Asylum (Calcutta) undertook the charge of the Orphanage, in which there were at that time more than forty children of both sexes. For some months the nature of the instruction given was of course of the simplest, comprising chiefly habits of neatness and cleanliness, the alphabet, and a little needlework and basket-making. It soon became apparent that the children possessed much intelligence and were wonderfully apt with their fingers; they were also very amenable to discipline, and proved therefore in every respect extremely interesting and promising pupils, whose chief fault was found to be the not uncommon one of want of perseverance; nevertheless, during the first year's training the baskets made by the lads and disposed of locally realised Rs. 100, while the girls earned a further sum by their needlework and fancy articles, besides which they made up the clothing for the entire party.[2]

After two or three years' labour in the Orphanage the Kidderpore ladies resigned the charge, and some difficulty was experienced in arranging for the retention of the girls; however some were finally taken by certain residents, who were desirous of training them as servants, while others were speedily married. With regard to the boys the question was less easy of solution, for it was found that those who had been taken in hand at too advanced an age began to pine for a return to their native jungles, and so intense did this desire become, that, in spite of meeting with every discouragement, they were discovered one morning to

[1] *Vide* Part I.
[2] *Vide* Appendix N.

have settled the matter for themselves by swimming away from the island.

The problem as to how the lads trained in the so-called Orphanage shall be disposed of in some profitable manner has been partially solved by training them to serve as domestic servants; but the question as to their marriage remains yet to be dealt with, for of all the girls originally trained in the Orphanage two only have continued in the Settlement, the other survivors having long since resumed the customs of their jungle homes. To encourage the marriage of the lads in question with girls brought up in the jungle, or even in one of the Homes, would probably result in re-associating, the former with those who—so strong is their general inclination towards a jungle life—would wean them from their civilised ways, thereby rendering abortive the many years' training bestowed upon them, and which has moreover unfitted them for the conditions of a savage home.

It has been ascertained that up to about the age of ten or eleven years these aborigines can hold their own with ordinary children of civilised races in respect to mental culture, but after that period further progress seems arrested. Some remarkable instances might be mentioned of boys and girls[1] who at no more than nine or ten years of age were able to read difficult passages from an Urdu book quite fluently, and explain the meaning of any word in ordinary use; it would appear, however, that, physically speaking, training has a deteriorating effect, for of all the children that have passed through the Orphanage, probably not more than ten are alive at the present time, while of those that have been married, two or three only have become parents, and of their children not one has been reared. In respect to morality, too, it must be confessed that they have suffered from contact with the convict population.

And thus, though the Orphanage, like the Homes, has not accomplished all the good anticipated by its promoters, the kindness and interest taken in their little ones have undoubtedly contributed towards strengthening the friendly relations previously established between the aborigines and ourselves.

Friendly intercourse among the tribes has been of late years further encouraged and extended by visits paid in the station

[1] One of these girls (Ruth) was highly trained by Mrs. Homfray, and is able to speak, read, and write English, as well as to converse glibly in Hindustani. As she has been with us from infancy, it is hardly necessary to say that she is ignorant of her native tongue. Ruth is also an accomplished needlewoman, and is clever at making designs; she wears the European costume, not excepting bonnets and hats. Some idea of the advance she has made on her fellow-countrymen (who are still in the stone age) may be gathered from the above statements, but further proof is found in the fact of her asking for and obtaining an English dictionary, which she says she finds "very useful" when writing her letters!

steamer to the more distant encampments by the officer in charge of the Homes[1] accompanied by males and females of the Southern tribes.[2] On these occasions dogs, iron, beads, and various other articles highly prized by the aborigines have been deposited in the huts from which the occupants had fled, or presented to such individuals as had courage to approach; stringent measures were at the same time taken to check the almost irresistable propensity of the *bōjig-ngïji-* to appropriate all portable property in the temporarily vacated camping grounds.

In these trips Little Andaman has been also visited, but all our efforts to conciliate the *jārawa-* (or inhabitants of that island) with their offshoot in South Andaman have hitherto proved fruitless. This may in part be due to the summary punishment[3] we have been compelled on two occasions to inflict for cruel murders perpetrated on inoffensive mariners; but it may also be attributable to the exclusiveness and hostility which appear as tribal peculiarities, and which are directed alike against their fellow savages and ourselves, as has been demonstrated by the terror with which they have in recent years inspired the South Andamanese, and in bygone years the Car-Nicobarese,[4] on whom they were formerly in the habit of making raids for purposes of plunder. For a long time now, however, they have desisted from these predatory expeditions, and have confined themselves[5] to the islands and localities which are regarded as their territory; but still, cases have occurred from time to time which keep alive the unpleasant conviction that any unfortunates who might be wrecked, or should venture to land on their coasts without sufficient means of self-defence, would be as mercilessly [illegible] now as at any date in their history.

The various measures already [illegible] in order to benefit the [illegible] convinced all who have come within their influence of our friendly intentions; even the distant communities of Great Andaman are now becoming as well known and as favourably disposed towards us as are our

[1] An account of one of these visits will be found in the form of a private letter which was published in "Journ. Anthrop. Inst.," vol. vii.

[2] Experience has taught us that one of the most effective means of [illegible] confidence when endeavouring to make acquaintance with these savages, is to show that we are accompanied by women, as they at once infer that whatever may be our intentions, they are at least not hostile.

[3] A further possible cause of the continued disinclination of the *jārawa-* to accept our advances is believed to be due to one or more runaway convicts, who may have succeeded in settling in their midst, and who in order to lessen their own chances of recapture and punishment, have given unfavourable accounts of us.

[4] How the *jārawa-* came to discover the distant low-lying island of Car-Nicobar is not known, but it is probably traceable to some trifling circumstance, such as the accidental drifting of a boat far out to sea.

[5] *Vide* Part I, "Tribal Distribution," p. 90, and "Communications," p. 45.

immediate neighbours the *bōjig-ngiji-*, and we have every reason to believe that crews of vessels shipwrecked on any portion of the Great Andaman coast would not only escape molestation and attack, but would receive such assistance as it might be in the power of these savages to render. That their animosity in past years was not unfounded is attested by the reports of Captain Miller and Père Barbe, both of which will be found quoted at some length in the "Journal of the Anthropological Institute" for 1882–3, p. 339.[1]

On referring to the accompanying map of the Andamans it will be seen that according to our present knowledge[2] the aboriginal inhabitants are divided into no less than nine tribes, viz.;

bōjig-ngiji-	..	South Andaman.
balawa- ..	..	Archipelago.
bōjig-yāb-		
A-kō-jūwai-	..	Middle Andaman.
A-kā-kede-		
A-kā-kōl-		
A-kā-jāro-	..	North Andaman.
A-kā-chāriar-		
jārawa- ..	..	Inhabitating Little Andaman and southern portions of Great Andaman.[4]

Although the *bōjig-ngiji-* are here shown, and in the following pages are described, as the natives of South Andaman—including Rutland and Labyrinth Island—there is no evidence to prove that they have ever been in undisputed possession of the whole of this territory; indeed, the scattered encampments of *jārawa-*, which are marked on the map as occupying certain portions within their territory give substance to the belief that before our advent they suffered from the inroads of their marauding neighbours, whose occupancy is proved to be of no recent date by the *jārawa* kitchen-middens,[5] evidently of

[1] *Vide* Part III, "Trade, &c.," p. 119.

[2] How erroneous were the views formerly held may be gathered from the following extracts :—"The Andamans . . . do not even exist in a state of [illegible]" (Figuier). "They have no tribal distinctions" (Wood). "In [illegible] Andaman there is only one tribe" (Mouat).

[3] These are the names by which they are designated by the *bōjig-ngiji-*, who, being our immediate neighbours, are the best known of all the tribes.

[4] As these communities possess many, if not all, the characteristics of the inhabitants of Little Andaman, and are presumed to have had constant communication with them in past years, they are designated by the *bōjig-ngiji-* by the name of *jārawa*.

[5] These are distinguished from those of the *bōjig-ngiji-* with readiness by members of the latter tribe, on account of the presence of the valves of certain mollusca, which they assert were never (according to tradition) considered as articles of diet by their own immediate ancestors.

remote origin, which are found in and near the harbour of Port Blair.

No one who has had the opportunity of seeing the natives of the various islands forming Great Andaman can fail to be struck with the similarity which marks their general appearance,[1] and to be convinced that, however much they may differ in many respects, they must at least claim a common origin. Any reasonable doubt on the subject has been removed by the discovery that although each of the several tribes possesses a distinct dialect, these are traceable to the same source, and are all in the same—*i.e.*, the agglutinative—stage of development; further, it has been ascertained that among all, or at least among the natives of Middle and South Andaman and the Archipelago, a coincidence of legends and customs is to be found, and that though the points of dissimilarity between the inhabitants of Great and Little Andaman are more marked, especially in regard to their weapons and implements, they are by no means such as would justify the belief that the latter are descendants of another branch of the Negrito family.

From what has been already said it will be understood that we are not yet in a position to decide whether one and the same dialect is spoken by all the communities designated as *.jārawa-*, or whether, like the people of North and Middle Andaman, they must be regarded on linguistic grounds as representing two or more tribes.

The dialects of Great Andaman may be grouped into three classes, viz.:—

I. The *.bōjig-ngĭji-* and *.bal-awa-*. [illegible]
II. The *.bōjig-yāb-*, and [illegible]
III. The [illegible] and the two tribes of North Andaman.

But it must not be supposed that the similarity between the dialect of any of these groups is so great that a knowledge of one would enable a person to converse intelligibly with members of the other tribes in the same classification, for such is not the case; now, however, that intercommunication is less restricted it is not unusual to find that members of the various communities are sufficiently acquainted with the dialect spoken by their immediate neighbours as to hold intercourse with them.

Little which throws light on their past history can be gathered from the Andamanese or from their traditions, but from a study

[1] I have been told by the *.bōjig-ngĭji-* that they can distinguish a *.bal-awa-* from members of the other tribes by his high cheek-bones, and the shape of his skull, which they describe as more dolichocephalic than those of other tribesmen; but as this tribe is now well-nigh extinct, it is impossible to determine the amount of credence which may be placed on this strange statement.

of their kitchen-middens[1] it appears that they must have inhabited these islands, and have remained in much the same state of barbarism for a very considerable period.

On the assumption that the members of these tribes lived entirely on the coast, it was till recently believed that the kitchen-middens[1] were always situated close to the sea-shore, and it was even said that the accident of their being found far inland would "indicate that some terrestrial changes in the islands have taken place." The incorrectness of this theory is beyond all question, as we have now ample evidence that not only on the coast, but also in the depth of the jungle, there are permanent encampments throughout the group, where we are assured many of these refuse heaps are to be found bearing traces which testify to the remoteness of their origin.

A change, however, appears to be gradually taking place in respect to the formation of these kitchen-middens, which is accounted for by the fact, that whereas in the olden days they were able to regard the slowly increasing heap with pride as witnessing to the success and skill in hunting and fishing of the community near whose encampment it was situated, nowadays all cause for boasting regarding their achievements is considered at an end in consequence of the material assistance they receive from the dogs we have given them, and the superiority (*sic*) of the weapons they have been able to manufacture from iron obtained from the Homes.

Various estimates have been hazarded as to the probable strength of the aboriginal population; but as no reliable data are procurable it is impossible to speak with any degree of certainty on the subject. From recent observations and the ascertained ravages of certain epidemics it seems hardly likely that the aggregate population of Great Andaman at the present day exceeds 2,000 souls, while the *jărawa*, who inhabit Little Andaman and a few localities in Great Andaman, may perchance number from 1,000 to 1,500 more; amongst these communities the effect of our occupation cannot have had, as yet, the prejudicial influence which has unhappily resulted among the tribes of Great Andaman from contact with alien races, the causes of which, being noticed elsewhere, need not here be particularised, especially as they are chiefly such as have been found to follow

[1] Col. (now Gen.) H. Man was the first to open up the kitchen-middens in and near the harbour at Port Blair, and the late M. de Röepstorff subsequently devoted some time to their examination, but it does not appear that he has left any notes as to the results of his investigations; at present all that has been published on this subject is embodied in the late Dr. Stoliczka's paper "Note on the Kjökken-möddings of the Andaman Islands" (*vide* Proc. As. Soc. Bengal, January, 1870)

ever in the wake of civilisation to the extermination of the savage race.

In closing this paper it will not, I think, be devoid of interest, even to the general reader, if I append a few particulars regarding Port Blair as the centre of the great Indian penal Settlement.

A glance at the map will show that Port Blair is situated near the south-eastern extremity of Great Andaman, and consists of a fine harbour somewhat F-shaped, which extends over seven miles in a south-westerly direction; it contains three islands, Ross, Chatham, and Viper. The first of these, containing an area of about 80 acres, is situated in a commanding position at the mouth of the harbour, and has been the site of the head-quarters of the Settlement since its re-establishment in March, 1858; the number of its residents ranges between 2,000 and 3,000, and includes the majority of the civil and military officers, the European troops, and detachments of native infantry and police; the residue consists chiefly of convicts. The Protestant church, Roman Catholic chapel, and a native Christian chapel are on this island.

The second island, Chatham, contains about 12 acres, and is situated midway between Ross and Viper, being visible to both at the bend of the harbour; its population numbers about 500, and is composed for the most part of hospital patients, convalescents, and convicts, who are employed on the steam saw-mills.

Viper, the third island, is about five miles distant by sea from Ross, from which it is hidden by the intervening hills on the so-called "mainland"; its area is slightly larger than that of Ross, but owing to its configuration is not so well adapted for building purposes; the majority of its inhabitants (usually numbering about 1,600 souls) are hospital patients, convalescents, and chain-gang prisoners, these last being confined in the only jail in the Settlement.

Mount Harriet[1] (about 1,100 feet), regarded as the sanitarium of Port Blair, is situated in a commanding position on the north side of the harbour near Chatham Island, and at the eastern extremity of a range of hills running in a northerly direction; its residents are composed of convalescents and weakly convicts and a party of police; round its base, on the western, eastern, and southern sides, various large clearings have been established, barracks and workshops erected, and cultivation and grazing carried on. Similar and more recent clearings exist between Mount Harriet and Port Mouat, where the narrow isthmus (1½ miles wide) dividing the two harbours, though so far distant

[1] It was at the foot of this hill that the late Earl Mayo, then Viceroy of India, was assassinated (when about to return to the flagship) by an Afridi convict.

from headquarters, was opened up two or three years prior to the important head-land situated between Ross and Viper Islands.

On the other side of Port Mouat, in a south-easterly direction further tracts of land have been cleared and placed under cultivation connecting that part of the Settlement with the principal clearings in Port Blair, known as the Southern District, being that portion of the mainland which lies west and south-west of Ross Island, where two-thirds of all the self-supporting prisoners and more than half the entire convict population are located.

The cultivation of paddy, sugar-cane, Indian corn, fruits, and vegetables, affords occupation to a large number (at present about 1,500) of a self-supporting population, and further industries of this nature have been opened up—chiefly by means of Government labour—by establishing plantations of cocoanut, tea, Liberian coffee, cacao, nutmeg, limes, arrowroot, *Musa textilis*, India-rubber (*Ceara* and *Hevea*), tapioca, indigo, and vanilla, all of which promise to repay well the care bestowed upon them. Cotton and tobacco have likewise been tried; the cultivation of the former was discontinued long since, apparently on account of the inability of the plants to survive the dry season without great expenditure of labour for watering; with regard to the latter, as failure was due only to ignorance of the proper method of curing the leaves, renewed experiments are being made.

The aggregate population at the present day amounts to about [illegible]; nearly four-fifths of this number, as will be shortly shown, include the convict element, which is distributed among some thirty scattered stations and a like number of villages throughout the entire cleared area; the penal Settlement is thus shown to extend all round the harbour, and to embrace the land at Port Mouat on the west coast.

Following the course of the main road, which now encircles the harbour, a distance of about forty miles would be traversed from its north-eastern extremity to its southern end opposite Ross Island; the number of roads intersecting the Settlement and connecting its various parts is of course considerable, and the importance of keeping them at all times in thorough repair is fully recognised, as is shown by the amount of labour annually devoted for this purpose. In connection with this subject it may be added that intercommunication between the most important points in the harbour has been greatly facilitated in recent years by the establishment of signalling posts at the principal police stations, so that messages can be semagraphed at any hour of the day or night, a matter of no small advantage in cases of emergency so liable to occur in a penal Settlement.

Although the aggregate of the convict population appears large and capable of ensuring a vast amount of progress in the development of the resources of the country, allowances must be made for the fact of there being but a handful of free servants and labourers in the colony, which necessitates the employment of prisoners in every department; very large deductions have, therefore, to be made on account of those who are ineligible for other than departmental or routine duty, or who from any other cause are not available for Settlement works. This will be better understood when it is explained that about 1,000 men are employed in the Commissariat, Medical, Marine, and Forest Departments; that the self-supporters and servants number about 3,000; hospital patients, the infirm and aged about 1,200; jail servants (or petty officers) about 720; those engaged in manufacturing clothing, in grinding wheat, and in miscellaneous industries 1,400; while of the remaining 4,000 about one-third are required for fixed establishments at the various stations and for conservancy arrangements, the residue being distributed among a vast number of works in all parts of the Settlement.

As in consequence of the continual drain among the self-supporting population on account of deaths and releases their numbers are but slowly increased by the addition of prisoners promoted from the labouring ranks, it must at the present rate of progress be long ere the desire can be realised of the Settlement producing the amount of its requirements even in the one item of rice, while it is certain that wheat, chenna, potatoes, and various other articles of daily consumption—for the cultivation of which the climate is ill-adapted—will always have to be imported; but as a set-off against these it may not be in vain to hope that the day will come when the surplus produce of our cocoanut, tea, Liberian coffee, cacao, nutmeg, and other plantations, together with our exports of timber, will afford substantial compensation by the sums realised in the Indian and home markets. The present average annual cost to Government of every transported convict is believed to amount to about Rs. 105. In proportion as the measures taken to develop the resources and increase the revenue of the Settlement mature, this heavy charge may be reasonably expected to diminish to a material extent.

PART I.

Derivation of name "Andaman"—Origin of the Race—Form and Size—Anatomy and Physiology—Colour—Odour—Hair—Development and Decay—Crosses—Reproduction—Abnormalities—Pathology—Medicine—Physiognomy—Motions—Physical Powers and Senses—Psychology and Morals—Magic and Witchcraft—Tribal Distribution—Topography—Arithmetic—Etymology—Tribal Communities—Nomadism—Habitations—Government—Covenants, Oaths, Ordeals—Laws—Crimes—Narcotics—Cannibalism—Communications—Chirography and Drawing—Swimming.

MUCH interest has for many years been manifested by ethnologists and others concerning the origin and affinities of the Andamanese, and efforts have been repeatedly made to obtain fuller and more reliable information regarding them, but various causes have hitherto militated against the success of these endeavours. The most important of the many obstacles to be surmounted has been, undoubtedly, ignorance of the language, whereby their biographers—being precluded from correcting by personal intercourse with the aborigines, the current misstatements, based on hearsay, or on the hasty observations of earlier travellers—were betrayed into the repetition of many erroneous assertions as to the social habits and customs which prevail among these tribes: now, however, this difficulty has been practically overcome, and we are in a position to substantiate our inquiries, and to speak on most points with a confidence hitherto impossible. But before we touch upon the physical characteristics and culture of the race, let us glance back for a moment to our earliest information as to the islands, and to the probable origin of the name "Andaman."

In the records of certain Arabian travellers of the ninth century we appear to find the first mention that is made of these islands being inhabited by negritos, and Marco Polo, some four hundred years later, bears out their statement, while it would seem that the islands themselves were known to Ptolemy, who speaks of a group in the Bay of Bengal as *Insulæ bonæ fortunæ*.

As regards the derivation of the name "Andaman," there seems to be some uncertainty. Colonel Yule, in his well known work on Marco Polo, mentions that, to his knowledge, Nicolo Conti, who calls it the "Island of Gold," is the only person who has attempted to give it a meaning. Colonel Yule's suggestion is that Angamanain (the name used by Marco Polo) is an Arabic (oblique) dual indicating "The Two Andamans," viz., The Great and The Little, while the origin of the name (Angaman) may be traced to Ptolemy's reference to these islands, which he describes as those of *Good Fortune*, Ἀγαθοῦ δαίμονος, whence may have sprung the forms Agdaman, Angaman, and ultimately Andaman.

With regard to the origin of the race, many conflicting opinions have, from time to time, been entertained; but, from the knowledge we now possess, the questions raised on the following points may, I think, be considered as more or less satisfactorily set at rest, viz.:—

I. That they are Negritos, *not* Papuans.[1]

II. That they are the original inhabitants, whose occupancy dates from pre-historic times; and that racial affinity—if there be any—may possibly some day be found to exist between them and the Semangs of the Malayan Peninsula,[2] or the Aëtas of the Philippine Islands.[3]

III. That all the tribes, as at present known to us, undoubtedly belong to the same race, and are of unmixed origin, the differences which occur among them being attributable as much to their constitutional peculiarities of jealousy and distrust in all dealings with strangers as to the natural barriers

[1] Figuier speaks of them as "pure Papuans, whose isolated position has kept them from intermixture with other races."

[2] *Vide* Wallace's "Malay Archipelago," 2nd Ed., vol. ii, pp. 278-79, and "Journ. Indian Archipelago," vol. iv, p. 427.

[3] If similarity of moral and social characteristics afforded a sufficient basis in ethnological researches among races not otherwise widely distinguished, a theory of affinity between the extinct negroid race of Tasmanians and the Andamanese might be regarded as not altogether untenable, for the descriptions given of the former by some writers are found applicable in many particulars to the race under consideration; notably is this the case in the account given by Mr. J. E. Calder, which I have deemed of sufficient interest in this connection to make a somewhat lengthy extract, and this will form the subject of one of the Appendices. (*Vide* Appendix D.)

presented by their densely wooded and hilly country, which facts have combined to isolate the various communities, and to check freedom of intercourse among them; further, in the case of Little Andaman, it may fairly be assumed that the peculiar bee-hive form of their huts, as well as certain modifications of their domestic habits and customs, have been borrowed from their neighbours, the Car Nicobarese, upon whom, in the last century, they made some hostile raids.

IV. That, in spite of all our endeavours to protect them, contact with civilisation has been marked with the usual lamentable result of reducing the aboriginal population; indeed, the death-rate, among those within the area of our influence, during the past twenty years has so far exceeded the birth-rate, as to compel the belief that before many decades have passed, the race, at least that portion of it which inhabits Great Andaman, will be well-nigh extinct.

In view of their probable early extermination, and the rapidity with which they are being meantime reduced to the standard of civilised manners, it seems very desirable that, ere it be too late, all possible information respecting their habits, customs, physical characteristics, etc., should be obtained, more especially as many of the errors which, excusably enough, found their way into the early accounts, having been allowed to pass unchallenged, are accepted as trustworthy, and false ethnological theories are built on these most imperfect bases.

Almost all accounts which have been written regarding these islanders speak of them as *Mincopies*, in explanation of which it is asserted that it is thus "these people style themselves;" but this is far from being the case, for not only is the name, or any at all resembling it, unknown to the *bōjig-ngiji-*,[1] *i.e.*, the inhabitants of South Andaman, but the other six tribes with which we are acquainted are in a like state of ignorance as to its origin and significance. The only sounds at all approximating it in the South Andaman dialect at the present day being *min kaich!* (come here!) and *kámin kápi!* (stand here!). The former of these being in common use may have given rise to the term (*Mincopie*) as a nickname, to which, indeed, it may possibly have borne a more striking similarity of sound in the language spoken at the period when this name was first adopted; for each generation cannot fail to produce changes more remarkable, and even of greater importance in the phonology of an unwritten language, such as this, depending as

[1] For the list of symbols adopted for denoting the sounds in this language see Appendix A; this list has been finally adopted in accordance with the kind advice of Mr. A. J. Ellis, F.R.S., whose valuable assistance I would here again gratefully acknowledge.

it must entirely on the delicacy of ear, and correctness of individual articulation.

The following remarks, except where otherwise specified, must be understood as referring to the eight tribes of Great Andaman, for the continued and inveterate hostility with which the inhabitants of Little Andaman, known as *járawa-*, have hitherto met all our advances and attempts to establish an *entente cordiale* has rendered it extremely difficult to obtain, much less substantiate, any information concerning them.

Form and Size.—1. Those of my readers who have studied the various accounts which have appeared regarding the physical characteristics of the Andamanese cannot fail to have been struck with their divergence. For the sake of others, however, to whom the race is comparatively unknown, it is necessary that I should here quote, on the subject of their form and size a few writers, commencing with the Mahomedan travellers of the ninth century, already mentioned, who stated that "their complexion is black, their hair frizzled, their countenance and eyes frightful, their feet very large and almost a cubit in length, and they go quite naked;" while Marco Polo (cir. 1285) appears to have been still less favourably impressed, for he says "the people . . . . are no better than wild beasts, and I assure you all the men of this island of Angamanain have heads like dogs, and teeth and eyes likewise; in fact, in the face, they are all just like big mastiff dogs!" Next we find Colonel Colebrooke, towards the close of the last century, describing "their limbs as ill-formed and slender, their bellies prominent, and, like the Africans, as having woolly heads, thick lips, and flat noses." In opposition to the foregoing we have Dr. Mouat, than whom no better judge could be desired, giving it as his opinion, that "they are the most perfectly formed little beings in existence. In proportion to their size, their general framework is well constructed, and their limbs present a remarkably good muscular development, and . . . . the whole form is as elegant as that of any European," in which opinion he is supported by the eminent craniologist, Dr. J. Barnard Davis, recently deceased, who, after careful study of a number of Andamanese skulls and skeletons, affirmed that they were "most beautifully proportioned."[1]

2. From my own observations I would remark, that though it is quite true that there are found among them individuals whose "abdomens are protuberant,[2] and whose limbs are dispropor-

[1] A peculiarity which I have observed is that the males have in many cases as marked a bend in the small of the back as the females. (*Vide* figure on the left of group in Plate III, Fig 1.)

[2] "From childhood they cram their stomachs with an immense amount of bulky food in a short period, and they do literally 'swell visibly' after their

tionately slender," such persons no more represent the general type of the race, than the sickly inmates of a London hospital can be regarded as fair specimens of the average Englishman; in point of fact the remark which is commonly made by strangers who see them for the first time, is, "how well these savages are developed." In confirmation of this I would refer you to the photographs, and table of weights and measurements of forty-eight male, and forty-one female adults, which I have prepared,[1] being persuaded that more correct information can be obtained by such means than from any verbal description, however minute and careful.

3. Although the Mahomedan travellers, a thousand years ago, described their feet as "very large, and almost a cubit in length," my observations and measurements go to prove that their feet, as well as their hands and ears, are small and well-shaped; the heel in some cases projects slightly, but never to the extent peculiar to negro races.

4. Dr. Dobson, in his valuable paper "On the Andamans and Andamanese" (published in the Anthropological Institute's Journal, vol. iv, p. 464), alleges the existence of a "remarkable contrast between the size of the males and females;"[2] but the example, which he cites in proof, of *mai'a .bō̆'ra* and his wife, was quite exceptional, for this man, whom we nicknamed "Moriarty," like many of the Andaman chiefs, was as much above, as his ebon consort was below, the ordinary stature of the race. From the illustrations and lists of measurements, to which reference has already been made, it will be found that the average height of the men is 4 feet 10¾ inches, and of the women 4 feet 7¼ inches,[3] while their average weight is 98¾ lbs. and 93½ lbs. respectively—results which cannot be said to indicate a striking disparity between the sexes.

meals. This distended abdominal condition is noticeable in children of both sexes; but as the lads grow up, they take more exercise, and their abdominal, as well as other muscles, become firmer and retain the mechanical distension of the belly. With the women it is different; these latter influences do not exist. . . . ." ("Remarks on the Aborigines of the Andaman Islands," by Surgeon E. S. Brander, late 2nd Medical Officer, Port Blair.)

[1] *Vide* Appendix C.

[2] The following extract from an article in the *Bombay Gazette* of 2nd August, 1881, by an officer stationed for about a year at the Andamans, will show what opposite conclusions are arrived at by those who are content to trust to the accuracy of their individual judgment without reference to actual measurements:—"The women . . . are on the whole bigger than the men, who are, however, particularly well made."

[3]

				ft. in.
Maximum height of the males measured was				5·4½.
"	"	females	"	4·11¼.
Minimum	"	males	"	4·6½
"	"	females	"	4·4.

5. The old statement, so often repeated, that their stature never exceeds 5 feet, must also be noticed, as the list in question shows that fourteen of the forty-eight males who were measured were slightly above that height. I would add, that on a visit paid to North Andaman, about two years ago—by Colonel Cadell, V.C., the present Chief Commissioner—an *Akà-chàriàr-* was seen whose height was estimated at about 5 feet 8 inches; but this must be regarded as very remarkable and exceptional, for the tallest specimen of the race, that had till then been met with, was a chief standing 5 feet 4½ inches.

6. In consequence of their early marriages, the cares of maternity, and the nature of the duties which devolve upon them, the women soon lose the graceful figures which many of them possess in their youth, and they often, in their maturer years, become so obese as to be objects of wonder to Europeans.[1]

Anatomy and Physiology.—1. With the view of forming some idea of the average temperature and rates of pulse and respiration per minute, five youths, fair representatives of the race, were examined, with the following results:—

No.	Age.	Temperature under the axilla.*	Rate per minute		Remarks.
			of pulse.	of respiration.	
1	22	96·9	88	19	The subjects were at rest and in the shade, and had not eaten for several hours previously. * The bulb was left undisturbed for five minutes.
2	20	97·9	92	22	
3	19	97·8	84	24	
4	18	97·9	84	25	
5	17	98·3	76	20	

Colour.—1. Their skin is naturally smooth, and greasy to the touch, and there is little or no hair or down over the surface,[2] and, with regard to its colour, by the aid of reflected light it has been found that not only are there several shades of colour among this race, ranging between bronze or dark copper colour, sooty, and black, but also that in individuals the complexion of the face and body are different. The distinctions are, however, so slight as to be unnoticed by the people themselves.

2. The results of careful observation go to prove that these

[1] Surgeon Brander, in the paper referred to in the preceding footnote, remarks, that "this condition, I should think, is induced partly by the absence of any proper abdominal support during pregnancy, and is partly due to the distension their stomachs habitually undergo after food."

[2] Even under the axilla it is rarely found, and then only very scantily, but a certain amount of tufted hair is not wanting about the genitals.

variations in colour are not confined within certain tribal limits, but are alike found in all, whether living inland or on the coast; and it would therefore appear that the cause is not attributable to diet, habits, or, indeed, to any external circumstance.

3. The opinion expressed on this subject by Dr. Mouat was that "their hue is remarkably black and lustrous;" while Surgeon-Major Hodder[1] describes them as "extremely black, more so than the African negro, and some have a dull leaden hue like that of a black-leaded stove." In this latter remark I fully concur; indeed, the simile strikes me as an exceedingly happy one, and as exactly expressing the predominating colour of their skin.

4. On examining a number of individuals, and comparing the colour of their skin and eyes with the standard tables prepared by the late M. Broca, it was found that the skin of the face and shoulders of the majority corresponded most nearly with No. 42, the variations tending towards 27 and 28, while that of the trunk, in the generality of cases, agreed with No. 27, and in certain others with No. 49. The prevailing hue of the eyes was found to be most closely represented by No. 16, one exception, which had to be classed under No. 1, being found among those tested.

Odour.—1. The ammoniacal, rancid, goat-like exhalations of the negro are not found among them, and the peculiarity of odour which attaches to their persons is chiefly due to the unguent, called *kòiob-da*,[2] composed of red oxide of iron mixed with either turtle or pig's fat, with which they delight to paint themselves. When in health, and under ordinary circumstances, their breath is sweet.[3]

Anatomy and Physiology (*continued*).—2. Their powers of abstinence from solid food have never, to our knowledge, been severely tested; but it has been noticed that, on rare occasions, when forced to make a long day's journey through the jungles without a halt, they are in the habit of binding a strip of bark or other substance round their waists, to reduce, as much as possible, the inconvenience and pain which are caused by what they consider a long fast. Whether in exercise or repose they

[1] *Vide* "Pall Mall Budget," 20th April, 1877.

[2] Substantives, adjectives, and many adverbs have the termination "da," which, as mentioned in my previous paper, I believe to be traceable to the defective or partially obsolete verb, *ré'ke*, to be; it is dropped before prepositions and in construction generally, but is usually heard when the word occurs alone. Hence, when I write a hyphen at the end of an Andamanese word, I shall mean that in its full form it has *da*.

[3] It is, nevertheless, commonly noticed, that after feasting on turtle and certain kinds of fish, they are unpleasant neighbours, their breath and hands being then highly odoriferous.

cannot apparently abstain from food without inconvenience for more than eight hours at a time.

3. When exerting themselves in any way they perspire freely, which may account for their inordinate thirst. So great, indeed, is their inability to endure any privation in respect to drink, that they seldom leave home on the shortest expedition, whether by land or sea, without providing themselves with one or more bamboo vessels, called *gōb-*, containing a supply of fresh water.

4. Loss of sleep they can bear well only when under the influence of strong excitement, as in turtle hunting, or at festive gatherings, where singing and dancing are kept up for many successive hours;[1] they have even been known to spend forty-eight hours at such times without taking any rest.

5. What little cool weather there is in the latitude of their islands, during December and January, they dislike extremely; in striking evidence of this they are found, as I will elsewhere mention,[2] unconsciously concurring with the great Italian poet in depicting the region of punishment, for the souls of the wicked, as one of intense cold. After this, it will appear somewhat strange to say that, in spite of their aversion to what they consider cold weather—which never registers less than 63° F. on the highest elevation in South Andaman—they are careful, during the hot season, to avoid any lengthened exposure to the direct rays of the sun, and endeavour to lessen the discomfort caused by the heat by smearing their persons with a white-wash of common white clay and water.[3] It has long been erroneously believed that they have recourse to this expedient in order to allay the inconvenience which they would otherwise suffer from the bites of mosquitoes and other jungle pests; but the true reason for the practice is, I am well assured, that which I have above given, for the various insects which might annoy them are, for the most part, kept away by the smoke of the hut fire, beside which a great portion of their time is spent when at rest, or when engaged in any sedentary occupation.

6. The voices of the men are usually clear without being deep, while those of the women, especially when raised, are very shrill.

7. The mucous membrane of the mouth is stained with pigment to a greater degree than was found to be the case with such of the natives of India as were compared with them.

8. The general excellence of the teeth strikes one as remark-

[1] *Vide post* "Games and Amusements," paragraph 22.

[2] *Vide post* "Religious Beliefs, &c.," paragraph 25.

[3] I would here draw attention to the fact, that while the object in smearing themselves with *tā-* wash is to keep themselves as cool as possible, they often daub their bodies with *kōi'ob-* after sundown for the opposite reason, *i.e.*, for the sake of warmth.

able, for not only are no precautions taken for their preservation, but they are used roughly, small bones being broken by them, and food commonly eaten at almost boiling point. The grinding surface of the molars is generally much abraded: five or six tubercles are occasionally observed in the posterior molars, but are not all marked with equal distinctness; in some cases, indeed, they are scarcely distinguishable. The crowns of these teeth frequently present one long and comparatively even surface, and the peculiarity is of course due to the practice above referred to, of grinding hard substances with them. The canines are not longer or more prominent than the other teeth; caries appear to be rare, except with those well advanced in years. The front teeth of the lower jaw are generally the first cut: the first dentition is completed apparently at an earlier age than is usual among ourselves.

Hair.—1. Dr. Allen Thomson, F.R.S., who has kindly examined some of the hair microscopically, gives it as his opinion that the form of the transverse section is *oval*. Having, however, only a small quantity at his disposal, he has not been able to make a sufficient examination as yet, so he adds that, "it may be that some sections are oblique, but a number are certainly transverse, and none of them have a circular outline." In appearance it is extremely frizzly and seems to grow in spiral tufts,[1] but examination proves that the roots are uniformly distributed over the scalp: it is fine in texture and fairly abundant, but lustreless, and seldom more than two or three inches long, or five inches if the actual length when untwisted be measured; in a few instances it has been found to be eight or ten inches long, but the ends were matted, dead-like, and easily broken.

2. The majority of the women every week or ten days shave their heads almost entirely, leaving only two narrow parallel lines of hair, termed *gōr-*, from the crown to the nape of the neck. The *gōr-* is never allowed to exceed one-eighth of an inch in length; therefore, as they have no means of clipping it, it is constantly shaven off, and a fresh *gōr-* is made with the hair which has grown since the last operation.[2]

[1] Just two years ago it was pointed out by Dr. J. Barnard Davis, F.R.S., that the delicate ribbon-like hair of these islanders is exactly similar to that of the now extinct race of Tasmanians ("Journ. Anthrop. Inst.," vol. ii, p. 100).

[2] I would here call attention to some errors of the artist by whom Dr. Mouat's book was illustrated. He has represented the men as shaven and the women with their curly wigs intact, whereas it is the latter only who as a rule shave their heads; and they do not go about entirely nude, but wear leaves, as will be explained in another place (*vide post* "Psychology and Morals," paragraph 6, and "Attire," paragraph 3). They are further incorrectly represented in the same plate as using a gipsy's tripod for cooking purposes.

3. Though many of the men were and are in the habit of having their heads shaved like the women, the style of hair-dressing most affected by them before our arrival left only a circular patch of hair, about six or eight inches in diameter, like a skull cap, on the top of the head. Of late, however, they have indulged in many fanciful modes, such as shaving a piece about two or three inches broad between the forehead and the nape of the neck, or making a large tonsure. From this it will be seen that the Andamanese cannot be instanced as a tribe that "goes bald always," as has been asserted.[1]

4. Men will sometimes shave each other's heads, but only when the services of a woman are not available; for it is one of the duties of the fair sex in these tribes to act as barbers, regarding which fact I shall have occasion to make further reference in subsequent sections.[2]

5. When, in consequence of its having attained an unusual length, the hair is found to be oppressively hot and difficult to clean, it is shaved off entirely or in part, clipping, as already mentioned, being impracticable, owing to the lack of a suitable instrument. On these occasions the eyebrows are generally removed, which explains Dr. Day's remark, that "they [illegible] have eyebrows."

6. With the exception of the eyelashes and eyebrows, which are of slight growth, hair is only occasionally seen on the face, and then but scantily and in patches on the upper lip and chin, where it has a tendency to grow in spiral tufts: as it is esteemed a decoration it is never shaved or depilated.

7. It has been rumoured[3] that there are tribes of a long-haired race on Interview and also on Rutland Islands; but, with regard to the former, none of the Northerners who have been to Port Blair have possessed this characteristic, or will allow that it is to be met with amongst their communities, while our relations with the inhabitants of the latter enable us to contradict the assertion, which, indeed, can only be explained by supposing that runaway convicts, who have frequently escaped thither, must have been mistaken for aborigines.

8. That baldness has been known among them may be assumed from their having a word in their language to express it, but such cases would appear to be of very rare occurrence since none have come under my notice.

9. It has been asserted that "they are in the habit of dyeing their hair with red ochre;" but, whatever may have been the custom in former times, this is certainly not now the case, as

[1] *Vide* "Anthropology," p. 236, by Dr. E. B. Tylor, F.R.S.
[2] *Vide post* "Social Relations, &c.," paragraph 3, and "Shaving," paragraph 2.
[3] "Encycl. Brit."

PLATE II.

Fig. 1.—Andamanese Man and Woman, showing Profiles.

Fig. 2.—Andamanese Chief, with Bow and Arrows.

they never intentionally interfere with the natural colour, but some of the pigment, *kòiob-*, with which they so frequently paint their persons sometimes accidentally adheres to their curly wigs, these being often used for wiping or drying their hands.

10. The colour of the hair among different individuals varies between black, greyish-black, and sooty, the last perhaps predominating; it is apparently uninfluenced by, and does not correspond with, the hue of the eye or skin; it commences to turn grey about the fortieth year, but the number of those who exceed that age being small, white hair is seldom seen.

Development and Decay.—1. The average length of life, owing to excessive infant mortality as well as to the small number that attain old age, can hardly be reckoned as much, if at all, beyond 22 years. Not more than three generations of the same family have ever been known to be alive at the same time.

2. Fifty years is believed to be the extreme limit of age among them, and the majority of those who attain it are women.

3. Judging from those whose births have been registered by us, it would seem that physical development takes place at a late age as compared with natives of India, the males not attaining puberty till about the 16th year, and the females not before the 15th,[1] while the maxima of stature and bulk are not reached till two or three years later; should the opinion thus formed be confirmed by further observations, the fact will serve to weaken the theories that have been advanced by some anthropologists to account for the phenomenon hitherto assumed to be of universal application, that "the period of immaturity is curtailed in inverse proportion to the approximation to the equator or the polar circle;"[2] but, as the same writer goes on to say, "probably the latitude of the abode has no reference to this phenomenon; it may more probably have some connection with the darkness of the skin."

4. Among the Andamanese, when the head is in the customary position, the line taken by a horizontal plane drawn through the *meatus auditorius* would, in most cases, pass through the apex of the facial angle, or, in exceptional cases, somewhat lower. I cannot entirely concur in the opinion expressed by Dr. Brander regarding the variety of the facial type found among them, as he says that "some faces seem to resemble the Negraic, some the Malayan, and some even the Aryan in character;" it is, however, a curious physiognomical fact, of which there can be little or no question, that a remarkable diversity in this respect *does* exist among them, though it is

[1] The extreme ages for child-bearing appear to be 16 and 35 years.
[2] Peschel.

hardly sufficient to admit of the inference, which might be drawn from the passage just quoted, and on which the incorrect theory might be based, as to their being of mixed descent. I would add that I observed, like Dr. Brander, that these differences are more noticeable among the males than among the females of the population.

CROSSES.—1. In a footnote to his interesting paper on the Andamanese, Dr. Day mentions that "some have entirely smooth hair," and he suggests the probability of a portion of the race being of African origin or of mixed African descent.

2. With the exception of three children of mixed parentage,[1] none of whom survived more than seven or eight years, no examples are known of the existence of a cross-breed among these tribes; and, as none but these three children have been known to have had other than the frizzly hair which is one of the distinctive characteristics of the race, I have no doubt that Dr. Day either observed, or was informed of, the peculiarity occurring in their case, and his remarks must, therefore, be taken as applying only to them.

3. Not only would it have been impossible for us to have continued so long in ignorance of the existence of any individuals of this race who differed so widely from their fellow countrymen as to have smooth hair, but additional evidence is afforded by the denial of the Andamanese to every inquiry instituted on this point.

4. Another statement has been published which is also calculated to mislead; it is as follows:—"I agree with Mr. F. Day that the chief of Rutland Island is probably a native of India."[2] The chief here referred to, by name *maia .Bí·ela*, but generally called by us *mámai .Bí·ela*[3] (*vide* Plate II, fig. 2), was one of the best known, as he certainly was the most useful of all our aboriginal acquaintances. He was not only a thorough, though superior, specimen of the race, but his parents were so well known to be of pure Andamanese blood that his intimates were surprised to learn that a doubt regarding the purity of his descent should even for a moment have been entertained, and certainly I, and others who have for many years been associated with the man and his friends, see no grounds for regarding their statements on this point with the least suspicion.

5. Judging from the exceptional cases above mentioned of a cross-breed occurring among them, it seems improbable that the existence of a mixed race in their midst would be tolerated, for all three of the children met their death by violence or neglect,

[1] Hindoo fathers and Andamanese mothers.
[2] Dr. Dobson.
[3] He died of measles in April, 1877.

not at the hands of their mothers, but of the male members of the tribe.

Reproduction.—1. Marriages never take place till both parties have attained maturity, and generally not till a few years later; the usual age of the bridegroom varies from 18 to 22, and of the bride from 16 to 20. The result of inquiries tends to show that there is a slight predominance of female over male births; three or four is the average number of children born of the same parents. The largest family known consisted of six, three only of whom attained maturity.[1]

2. Twins are rare, and as no instance can be recalled of both surviving infancy, notwithstanding all possible care being bestowed on them, they are not favourably regarded. No case of triplets has been known to occur. Births out of wedlock are considered discreditable, and in the one known instance of the kind, the parents were married immediately after the event; no difference was made in the treatment which the child received.[2]

3. The limited fecundity of the women may in some measure be due to the circumstance that they never wean their babies, so long as they are able to suckle them, and it not unfrequently happens that the two youngest children are seen together at their mother's breast.[3]

4. The ill success in rearing their offspring is doubtless owing in great part to the injudicious management and petting which each of the mother's friends considers right to bestow on the infant. It is looked upon as a compliment for every woman who may be nursing, to relieve the mother of this duty at frequent intervals; it is, therefore, no matter of surprise that the little one ails and dies.

5. The proportion of deaths from violence and accident, is believed to amount to four or five per cent.

6. Barrenness is rare, as are also cases of stillborn children. No drugs or other contrivances are employed in order to increase or limit reproduction.

Abnormalities.—1. Excessive development of fat about the gluteal region is frequently observable among the adult women.

[1] It is said that more children are born during the rains than at any other season of the year.

[2] *Vide post* "Marriage," paragraph 6.

[3] On this subject Dr. Brander remarks as follows:—

"They mostly possess considerable mammary development, and the glands in many cases seem to be in a chronic state of functional activity. This may be due to the late period to which they suckle their young (even to three or four years), or to another purpose to which the milk is applied. . . ." (*vide post*, "Shaving.") [As will be seen from Plate II, fig. 1, the mammæ are pyriform rather than spherical; with the advance of years they become flaccid and elongated.]

Dr. Dobson, in noticing a marked case of this kind, drew attention to the fact of its differing from steatopyga, thereby distinguishing them in this respect from Hottentots.

2. Albinism and polydactylism are unknown, and only one case of erythrism, and that of a faint type, has been observed, or is known to the natives of our acquaintance.[1]

3. No instance appears of obliquity of vision, of cleft palate, absence of teeth, or of supernumerary teeth, and only one of prognathism[2] and hare-lip respectively. Cases of "Darwin's point" in the ear are constantly met with.

Pathology.—1. No idiots, maniacs, or lunatics have ever yet been observed among them, and this is not because those so afflicted are killed or confined by their fellows, for the greatest care and attention are invariably paid to the sick, aged, and helpless. Two or three cases of hunchback and lateral curvature of the spine have come under notice, but instances of the kind are evidently very rare.

2. It has often been observed, that though the Andamanese waste away very rapidly in sickness, they regain flesh with equal facility when convalescent; but, nevertheless, they possess so little vital power, that they readily succumb to diseases against which others usually struggle successfully;[3] indeed, they appear to suffer as much, if not more, than individuals of alien races from the febrile disorders—mainly attributable to malaria, so prevalent throughout these islands—which frequently lay the foundation of chest complaints, from which they rarely recover.

3. Pulmonary consumption and other forms of pectoral disease are among the chief causes of mortality among these tribes.[4] These disorders do not appear to be confined to, or to be more prevalent in, certain districts, but there is little doubt that they have been most frequent amongst those living in the homes provided for their benefit in and near our settlements in South Andaman.[5]

[1] In no other particular does this case appear to differ from the rest.

[2] As Professor Owen, F.R.S., truly remarks, "their prognathism is not more than is found in most of the Southern Asiatic peoples, and, indeed, in the lower orders of men in all countries, and may be due or relate to the prolonged sucking of the plastic infant." (*Vide* "Brit. Assn. Reports," 1861.)

[3] This not only refers to maladies introduced by the alien population, such as measles, venereal diseases, &c., but to those complaints from which they suffered prior to the establishment of the settlement.

[4] In reference to complaints of this nature, it may interest some to know that Dr. De Jongh's cod liver oil was largely used in the homes, and with considerable benefit to the patients, several recoveries having resulted therefrom. From inquiry it would seem that cases of constipation are comparatively rare, and that diarrhœa is almost the habitual state of their excretory functions.

[5] As this circumstance was traced to the system of giving them clothes to be worn at our various stations, and when visited by Europeans, it was deemed advisable to modify the regulation and to supply them only with drawers, leaving the upper part of the body exposed. A marked improvement in the general health resulted from this change.

4. Epilepsy is a recognised form of malady, and is considered as peculiar to certain individuals, but the fits are not regarded in a superstitious light. Cutaneous diseases of a scaly character occasionally occur, but do not appear to be of a serious kind. Leprosy is as yet unknown among them. The physical pain caused by injuries seems less acute than that suffered under similar circumstances by Europeans, and all wounds, as a general rule, heal rapidly.

5. A few years ago (1877), an epidemic of ophthalmia occurred, principally among the people of South Andaman, and, during the few months it lasted, about fifty persons were attacked, many of whom suffered entire or partial loss of sight. The origin of the outbreak was obscured in doubt, and it does not appear that the disease was previously known to the aborigines.

6. They have never yet been afflicted with small-pox, and only once with measles, viz., in 1877, when it was computed that nearly 20 per cent. of the sufferers, who comprised a large proportion of the population, succumbed. This disease was introduced by a batch of convicts from Madras, who, in spite of all the precautions that were taken, communicated it to others in the settlement, from whom it spread to the Andamanese. The contagion extended to the people of Middle and North Andaman, but only those patients who were living within a few miles of our settlement could be attended to by our medical officers; the treatment to which the remainder had recourse, was that commonly adopted among them in fever cases.[1] The ravages committed by this epidemic among the unfortunate aborigines can only be compared, though on a small scale, to the effects of a similar outbreak among the Fijians, shortly after the annexation of their islands to the British Crown.[2]

[1] *Vide post* "Medicine," paragraph 2.

[2] Before leaving this part of my subject it is necessary to mention that, within the last eight years, they have been visited for the first time by that terrible scourge, syphilis, the introduction of which was traced to a few Indian convicts whose duties brought them much in contact with the aboriginal inmates of the homes; the ravages already committed have been most lamentable, and there seems now no hope of checking its spread throughout the various islands forming Great Andaman: this is due to a few of the original sufferers having refused to submit to the system of segregation which was determined upon at the principal home at Viper Island, where all those who were known to be affected were placed in a separate building. Although allowed every indulgence short of liberty to associate with those who were in health, a few of them found the restraint too irksome, and effected their escape one night by swimming from the island, and to them have been traced many fresh cases that subsequently occurred in various jungle encampments. Had it not been for this it might have been possible to confine the disease to those first affected (then numbering about 80), for after their isolation from the rest, no fresh cases occurred at Viper. Thus, unhappily, this terrible malady has now extended over a very considerable area, probably not less than two-thirds of Great Andaman. The rapid spread of the contagion has been greatly attributable to the almost universal practice which prevails

Medicine.—1. The diseases most common among these tribes are:—

1st, malarial fever (*did'dirya-*).
2nd, catarrh (*ngō'rab-*).
3rd, coughs (*ō'day-*).
4th, rheumatism (*mōl-*).
5th, phthisis.
6th, pneumonia.
7th, heart disease.[1]

2. In febrile complaints the treatment adopted by those living in the interior, and less frequently by the coast dwellers,[2] is the following:—A bed is made for the patient of the leaves of the *Trigonostemon longifolius* (*gū'gma-*), and his body is rubbed with these leaves, which are sometimes first boiled, while he sniffs at some crushed pieces of the same; after a time *chā'laga-*[3] is given him to drink, and then with some of their patent ointment, *kōi'ob-*,[4] which is not used internally, as has been supposed,[5] the upper lip is painted and also the neck, if the invalid be married. When the fever is accompanied by pains in the chest or head, a *chāu'ga-tā-*[6] is tied tightly round the part affected, as this is believed to act as a charm, internal pains being always ascribed to the malign influence of evil spirits. During the course of the fever, the patient is constantly rubbed with *gū'gma-* leaves by one or more friends, who insist also upon his swallowing large quantities of *chā'laga-*; scarifying is never practised at such times. As only a small proportion of cases of this kind have a fatal result, great faith is placed in the treatment above described, and, at all events, it is certain that no injurious effects are caused by it.

3. The first half of the rainy season is usually the most sickly time with them, as with ourselves, in regard to fever and bowel

among the women of suckling each other's infants; in fact many parents have thus become tainted with the disease, the characteristics of which have in almost every case been most strongly marked, presenting an interesting study to the medical officers who have had charge of the patients. Great benefit was derived from the treatment and remedies (mercury and iodide of potassium) usually employed in Europe, but time alone will show how far our efforts will avail to prevent the disease from infecting the entire population, if, indeed, it do not, as in certain parts of Australia, lead to the early extermination of the race.

[1] Because of the insidious nature, and (to them) mysterious origin, of the last three named diseases, they say that either *Ē'rem-chāu'gala* has shot the sufferer, or *Jū'rua-win-* has speared him: regarding these evil spirits further reference will be found at "Death and Burial," paragraph 25, and "Religious Beliefs and Demonology," paragraphs 13 and 14.

[2] The reason for this will be found under "Tribal Communities," paragraph 5.

[3] *Vide* Appendix B, No. 69.

[4] *Vide* Appendix B, No. 60.

[5] *Vide* Mouat, p. 306.

[6] *Vide* Appendix B, No. 44.

affections. Those natives who have been long with us, have great faith in our medicines, especially in the efficacy of quinine for curing fever, from which, as exposure is very trying to their constitutions, they suffer greatly when living in the clearings we have made at Port Blair.

4. For a cold in the head they merely remain at home and nurse themselves, crouching over the fire; for a cough, sea-water is often drunk, or they will chew the thick portion of the long leaves of a plant called *jini-* (of the *Alpinia* species), and when the bitter juice has been extracted and swallowed, tie the chewed fibre round the neck; if benefit be not derived from this, they then take a piece of the upper portion of the stem of the *Calamosagus laciniosus*, called *pōr-*, and, removing the bark, chew the rest, and swallow the sap. Many cures having been attributed to the wonderful properties of the two descriptions of *chā'nga-*, one or two quarts daily are prescribed to the unhappy patient, until the cough leaves him.

5. In cases of rheumatism and paralysis, a *chāu'ga-tā-* is tied round the parts affected, and *chā'nga-*, moist as found, is rubbed into them: if no relief is experienced within a day or so, warm water is poured over the suffering members, which are then shampooed; should no improvement result, even after these measures, recourse is had to scarification; this is done with a quartz or glass flake, by a woman, generally the wife or one near of kin to the sufferer. It has been noticed that but few of those who have been attacked by rheumatism in the jungle ever regain the full use of their limbs.

6. In phthisis, or when any internal organ is diseased, steps are taken by the friends of the patient to defeat the machinations of the evil one, to whom the victim's sufferings are attributed; to this end, one or more *chāu'ga-tā-* are first fastened tightly over the seat of pain, a lump of black beeswax, *tōbul-pid-*,[1] is then held over a fire till it begins to melt, when it is instantly applied, being passed rapidly over the flesh; the wax which adheres is not removed, but wears off in a few days. The patient is also subjected to pressure with the hands by a relative or friend of the same sex, while an attendant frequently sucks the skin. Scarification is the *dernier resort* when the bad symptoms increase.[2]

7. Every attention is paid to the wants and wishes of the sick, and the friends do all in their power to effect recovery, but no charms, excepting the *chāu'ga-tā-*, are employed in the hope of

[1] *Vide* Appendix B, No. 67.

[2] As many bad cases of lung disease among those in the homes have been successfully treated with cod liver oil, they have now great faith in that medicine.

averting or curing illness; after recovery, no ceremonies of purification take place.

8. With respect to these necklaces of human bones, it should be stated that it is not considered necessary that the bones used for this purpose should have belonged to an adult, those of a child or of one long since dead, are considered equally efficacious; the belief is that they cure diseases, and shield the wearer in some measure from the machinations of evil spirits, through the intervention of the disembodied spirit, who is supposed to be gratified by, and aware of, the respect thus paid to his memory. Loose teeth, obtained from human skulls and jaw bones, are sometimes strung together as necklaces, or, if too few for such a purpose, they are included among the pieces of bone which are broken up to form the *châuga-tâ-*; turtle bones are also sometimes added under similar circumstances.

9. The skull and jawbone are carried, either separately or together, merely as mementoes, and are not accredited with any peculiar virtues.

10. During pregnancy, the women eat in moderation, but delight in as great a variety of food as possible, telling their husbands day by day what to procure for them;[1] they are also in the habit of taking as much active exercise as possible, as they believe it conduces to an easy *accouchement*, and the same reason is given for the custom, common among them, of consuming small quantities of *tâ'la-ōg-*[2] from time to time; but this practice may be traced with more probability to the fact that the appetite of persons in an anæmic condition is generally fanciful and depraved, such substances as "lime, chalk, or slate pencil being sometimes greedily devoured by them."

11. When about to be confined, the custom is for the husband, and some of the woman's female friends, to attend on her; she is placed in a sitting posture, the left leg is stretched out, and the right knee brought up, so as to enable her to clasp it with her arms. Her husband supports her back and presses her as desired, while her female friends hold a leaf screen, *kâ'pa-pi'tnga-* over the lower part of her person, and assist her, to the best of their ability, in the delivery and in the removal of the after-birth; the umbilical cord is severed by means of a *Cyrena* shell (now a steel blade is often used), and when the infant has been washed in cold water, its skin is gently scraped with the shell. Publicity is not courted on these occasions, as has been asserted,[3] but all, save those whose services are required, continue their occupations as usual. Soon after the delivery, some warm

[1] Further allusion to this subject will be made under "Tabu."
[2] *Vide* Appendix B, No. 58.
[3] *Vide* Mouat, p. 304.

water is given to the woman to drink; she is also fed with meat-gravy, and the water in which shell or other fish have been boiled; after a time, should she desire it, fish, shell-fish, yams, or fruit are given her, but no meat.[1] During the first two or three days, she remains in a sitting posture, propped up by articles arranged so as to form a couch. As might be supposed, from the active habits and unsophisticated manners of these people, their women rarely suffer much during labour and child-birth; in fact, no instances of difficult delivery are known.[2]

12. For ear-ache, head-ache, and tooth-ache, recourse is had, in the first instance, to the *chá·nga-tá-*, then to scarification, should the pain continue and cause swelling.

13. In cases of skin disease, they afford relief, at least from irritation, by applying to the parts affected a large smooth stone previously warmed over a fire.

14. When a wound is inflicted by a thorn, stone, shell, &c., hot water is poured over it from a *Cyrena* shell, which is then heated and applied to the part as hot as it can be borne; or, if the injury be slight, sea-bathing is prescribed, as it is said to expedite the healing process. In treating a boil, they scarify all round the swelling in order to reduce the inflammation, and afterwards bathe it with *chú·lnga-* "lotion." This substance is also taken internally when suffering from dysentery, while for diarrhœa they swallow small quantities of a whitish clay, called [illegible].

15. The *larvæ* of bees found attached to honeycombs is eaten to correct constipation, or, if in season, the fruits of two trees, *ó·ropa-* and *chôb-*, which are much relished, and not without reason.

16. Their method of treating a case of epilepsy is to sprinkle the patient with cold water, and then to scarify his brow.

17. When bitten by a snake (especially a venomous one), if they succeed in killing it, they cut it open, and apply the kidney fat to the wound, rubbing it in for some time; should they fail in capturing the reptile, a ligament is tied above the bite, and the surrounding flesh is scarified. Deaths from snake bites, though not unknown, are rare. The late chief of the Middle Strait community died in a few hours from the bite of a certain tree snake called *lā·ga-jō·bo-*,[3] in September, 1878, and another

[1] During menstruation they abstain from pork, *Paradoxurus*, turtle, honey, and yams, and live upon certain varieties of fish, sour fruits, iguanas, and prawns.

[2] The custom known by the name of *couvade*, or the paternal lying-in, is quite unknown among the Andamanese.

[3] This snake is said to be the most deadly, after which the *lā·raba-* and *wā·ra-jō·bo-* are the most dreaded. The last appears to be the *Ophiophagus elaps*. Further allusion to the *lā·raba-* and the *wā·ra-jō·bo-* will be made under "Superstitions."

case of a similar kind occurred a few years since in McPherson's Strait. When bitten by a centipede on the leg or hand, urine is applied; less inconvenience seems to be caused by these injuries to the Andamanese than to the natives of other countries, although the insects are here larger than in many districts, measuring sometimes as much as eight inches. The scorpions, on the other hand, are small and comparatively innocuous; no attention is therefore paid to the bites they inflict.

18. Elephantiasis appears never to have occurred among them; but since seeing cases of this complaint among the Nicobarese, they have given it a name, *lá·pi-*, from *lá·pike*, to swell (as a bruise).

19. Bandages of leaves are applied to gunshot wounds, ulcers, fractures, sprains, or bruises.

Physiognomy.—1. When an Andamanese is in good spirits, his eyes sparkle and the surrounding skin is slightly wrinkled, while the corners of the mouth, which is partially opened, are drawn back; if he be in low spirits the eyes are directed to the ground, the forehead is transversely wrinkled in the centre, and the lips are closed, but the corners of the mouth are not depressed; under the influence of great grief the nostrils are observed to dilate.

2. In thinking deeply, or while endeavouring to understand the construction of some object, the eyes are fixed intently on it, and a slight elevation of the lower lid is noticeable.

3. Astonishment is expressed by the eyebrows being raised, the mouth opened a little and covered with the left hand, while the right hand is brought smartly to the left side just above the heart; a man will also, on being reminded of an unintentional omission to fulfil some promise, act either in this manner, or he will slap his thigh and then place the hand over his opened mouth. Women show their surprise (and also joy) by striking the thigh, which is raised for the purpose, with the open hand. To this practice may be attributed the mistaken notion entertained by an early writer,[1] that "their salutation is performed by lifting up a leg and smacking with their hand the lower part of the thigh."

4. Indications of slyness, guilt, and jealousy can be detected in the eye only.

5. Disgust is shown by throwing the head back, dilating the nostrils, drawing down the corners of the mouth, and slightly protruding the lower lip: no expiration is, however, made.

6. Shame is evinced by the head being averted, the eyes lowered, and the hands raised so as to conceal the portion of the face exposed to view.

[1] *Vide* Colebrooke.

7. Defiance is expressed by raising and slightly averting the head, and slowly uttering the word *ártá·lög-ba*, which is equivalent to "try it on."

8. Women and children, when too frightened to run away, throw themselves on their faces on the ground and raise shrill cries, while men, under similar circumstances, show their alarm by falling backwards, with their hands uplifted, and their eyes rolling. Laughter is sometimes carried to such an extreme as to bring tears.

9. When very angry a man does not stamp his foot, but he places his left hand, palm uppermost, between his teeth, and glares fiercely at some object on the ground *near* the offender; he, at the same time, raises some weapon with his right hand, and utters, as well as the position of the other hand permits, words of terrible import.

10. A man, if threatening another, does not clench his fist, but will seize some weapon or missile, and express his intention of inflicting an injury with it.

11. A dogged or obstinate expression is indicated by averting the head, closing the lips, lowering the eyes, as if ignoring the presence of others, and frowning slightly.

12. When sneering, the teeth are clenched, the upper lip slightly curled, and the eyes are fixed on some object *near* the person addressed.

13. Children, when sulky, behave much as those in other lands, for they pout, frown, and utter noises which betoken discontent.

14. When a man wishes to show that he cannot prevent something being done, or cannot himself do something, he averts his head and pouts his lips, but does not shrug his shoulders.

15. In beckoning, the head is nodded vertically and a hand outstretched, the fingers with the knuckles uppermost being waved towards himself.

16. In affirmation the head is nodded vertically, in negation it is shaken laterally.

[illegible].—1. The attitudes of these savages are usually easy; the body when in motion is fairly balanced, the leg, if standing, is straightened; the foot is usually evenly planted, with the toes turned slightly outward; when stalking game they go on tip-toe, but, as a rule, the gait is energetic only under momentary excitement. The average length of a man's pace on level ground is 29–30 inches, and of a woman's about 24 inches. The arms (which they swing when walking) are habitually held with the palms turned inward. If pointing to any object, they usually do so with one finger, and not with the open hand.

2. In climbing up a rope or large creeper they proceed hand over hand with great rapidity, assisted by the big and second

toes of each foot; if a tree is branched they will scramble up it almost as quickly as if scaling a ladder, and though when "swarming" a mast or cocoa-nut tree they clasp the trunk in the usual manner with the arms and legs, their movements are more rapid, and they are less easily fatigued, than are the generality of natives of India; in descending also they display the same activity.

3. I have observed a peculiar trick among young men and women, after a lengthened rest or after engaging in some sedentary occupation, of twisting their bodies from side to side in order to stretch the muscles of the back. In doing this they produce a succession of sounds like that caused by cracking the joints of one's fingers.

4. Their favourite position in taking temporary rest after any violent or prolonged exertion is the ordinary Oriental posture between sitting and standing, *i.e.*, squatting on their heels; if very much exhausted they either sit or lie down.

5. The usual attitude in sleep (*vide* Plate III, fig. 2) is to lie on one side, preferably the right, with the knees bent so as to allow of the hand of the upper arm being placed between the thighs and the other hand under the head, which is raised on some impromptu pillow, such as a bundle or a roll of sleeping mat.

6. Many are able to shut one eye without closing the other, but they do not appear to possess the power of moving the ears or scalp. They can extend one finger without opening the hand. No tricks of sleight of hand are known to or attempted by them.

7. Much use is made of the feet in holding and picking up light objects, and the great toe is in a considerable degree opposable. When a heavy load has to be moved they prefer pushing to dragging it.[1]

Physical Powers and Senses.—1. Though for a short distance heavier loads are often borne, the maximum of a man's burden is about 40 lbs.; this he will on occasion carry for as much as 15 miles through the jungles between sunrise and sunset, a distance rarely exceeded in one day under any circumstances, or for more than two or three days in succession. This has been particularly remarked when they have been in pursuit of runaway convicts, for, if they fail in coming up with them within the third day, they are wont to take a long rest, unless strong inducements are offered by way of inciting them to further efforts.

[1] They do not understand, or, at least, do not carry into practice, the principle of pushing or dragging a weight *simultaneously*, whether in silence or to the sound of the voice.

2. Unlike the natives of India, the men allow scarce any weight to rest on the head; the entire strain is thrown on the shoulders and back by passing the cord to which the load is attached across the chest. As this mode would with women be attended with inconvenience on account of the *chip-*,[1] besides causing injury to the breasts, the cord is in their case brought over the head,[2] and the back is bent in order to reduce the pressure.

3. In his account of a visit to the Nágá Hills, about ten years ago,[3] Mr. S. E. Peal makes allusion to the "peculiar noise, like a whistle or note on a flute, clear and plain, and seeming to come from the chest, made by Nágánis when carrying loads and distressed." The same peculiarity is noticeable under similar circumstances among the Andamanese of *both* sexes.

4. Running is seldom practised by them except for a short distance, when hunting, &c., and four or five hundred yards appears to be the greatest extent of ground they can cover without halting or slackening speed. Though in running or walking on a good road they are generally passed without difficulty by natives of India, their superiority in the jungles is at once manifest when the beaten track is left; and in the ease and rapidity with which they are able to bound over rocks, fallen trees, mangrove roots, and other obstacles, few, if any, would care, or be able, to compete with them.

5. Both coastmen and "junglees" are, as a rule, gifted with extremely keen sight. It was, however, found impossible to gauge their powers by the test papers[4] in consequence of their inability to count; but many satisfactory proofs of their acuteness of vision have been afforded, as, for instance, by the manner in which, while coasting along the shore or when threading their way through the jungle, they detect birds or other objects, so hidden by the dense foliage of their forests as to be hardly distinguishable, even when pointed out, to more than ordinarily sharp-eyed Europeans and others.

6. The inland tribes have especially keen scent, and are able from an almost incredible distance to specify, and direct their steps towards, any particular tree that may happen to be in blossom; their sense of taste is also strongly developed, enabling them to discriminate between the various flowers from which the bees have produced their honey.

7. On the other hand, while the coastmen are not deficient in

[1] *Vide* Appendix B, No. 24.

[2] A peculiarity in the conformation of the female skull due to this practice will be hereafter noted, under the heading of "Deformations," paragraph 3.

[3] *Vide* "Journ. Asiat. Soc. Bengal," vol. xli, part 1, 1872.

[4] Viz., those used in the Army for recruiting purposes.

these points, they are found to surpass the natives of the interior in their sense of hearing, which is so acute that they commonly spear turtles on the darkest nights, though able to direct their aim only by the slight sound made by the animal when rising to the surface to take breath. "*ng'ab-mū'lwa-*" (you deaf person!) is a term of reproach often applied by the coast people to those dwelling inland, in allusion to the admitted inferiority of the latter in this respect.

Psychology and Morals.—1. It has been remarked with regret by all interested in the race, that intercourse with the alien population has, generally speaking, prejudicially affected their morals; and that the candour, veracity, and self-reliance they manifest in their savage and untutored state are, when they become associated with foreigners, to a great extent lost, and habits of untruthfulness, dependence, and sloth engendered.

2. Though there are some grounds for the opinion hitherto held regarding their fearlessness, our more recent relations with them prove that the surprising courage and apparent utter recklessness of life which they manifested in their early encounters with us were due rather to their ignorance of, and disbelief in, any foe more powerful than themselves, or with means of destruction more deadly than their own. Probably nothing short of despair or uncontrollable rage would ever induce any of them to make an attack in which they have not a decided advantage, real or imaginary. All is regarded as fair in war, and cunning and treachery are considered worthy of commendation; in short, the high type of courage common among most civilised, and a few savage, nations appears to be totally lacking among the Andamanese; nevertheless, those who evince courage are much admired, and poltroons are objects of general ridicule.[1] When apprised of the existence of danger, they usually evince extreme caution, and only venture upon an attack when well assured, that, by their superior numbers, they can put the enemy to flight, or will be able, by stealth, to surprise and overpower him.

3. At the same time certain traits which have been noticeable in their dealings with us would give colour to the belief that they are not altogether lacking in the sense of honour, and have some faint idea of the meaning of justice. An amusing incident is related by Dr. Day on this point. It appears that on a certain

[1] Their conduct on occasions of personal risk is, however, generally governed by the consideration that "discretion is the better part of valour," and that

"He who fights and runs away,
May live to fight another day."

They thus resemble the South Sea islanders spoken of by Sir J. Lubbock who, "though not cowards, regard it as much less disgraceful to run away from an enemy with whole bones than to fight and be wounded."

occasion "they brought in some escaped convicts, whom, however, they first plundered, besides removing every bit of iron from the boat in which they had escaped. On being taxed with this they at first pleaded surprise, then said they would make restitution, and brought a canoe as an exchange for the mischief they had done to the government boat. At first this was not quite understood and the canoe was sent back, but they returned it next day, explaining that they desired it to be kept as a reimbursement for the injury they had done to the government boat, so no longer considered the canoe theirs."

4. As another example of the same kind:—when the present penal colony at Port Blair was first established, the aborigines were observed to refrain from shooting at any of the chain-gang prisoners, evidently judging that they at least could not be voluntary invaders of their territory, and to confine their hostility to the petty officers and others not in chains, till these at last, finding themselves in constant danger, sought and obtained permission to carry on their duties in fetters.[1]

5. Much mutual affection is displayed in their social relations, and, in their dealings with strangers, the same characteristic is observable when once a good understanding has been established.

6. It is a noteworthy trait, and one that deserves high commendation, that every care and consideration are paid by all classes to the very young, the weak, the aged, and the helpless, and these, being made special objects of interest and attention, invariably fare better in regard to the comforts and necessaries of daily life than any of the otherwise more fortunate members of the community.

7. Andamanese children are reproved for being impudent and forward, but discipline is not enforced by corporal punish-

[1] It may not be unworthy of notice to record here yet another instance of generosity of disposition displayed by one of these savages. In January, 1877, a party of 24 *Bhīl* convicts effected their escape: all but some 11 or 12 were soon re-captured. Those still at large proved desperate, showing by their murderous assault on some aborigines, who had unconsciously approached their hiding place in the jungle, that they were prepared to resist capture at all hazards. The chief "*māiola*" *Bī'ala* (*vide* Plate II, fig. 2) thereupon headed a party of his tribe and some policemen, and, in spite of the parched condition of the soil—it being then late in February—succeeded in tracking the runaways, who had penetrated several miles into an unfrequented part of the jungle. Refusing to surrender themselves they were attacked, with the result that all were either captured or shot down. On being asked by the Chief Commissioner what reward would be most acceptable for the service the aborigines had performed on this occasion, *Bī'ala* replied that he would prefer to anything else that the Chief Commissioner should remit the remaining portion of the six months' sentence passed on four members of a Middle Andaman tribe, who, a few months before, had been convicted of shooting, at Kyd Island, some Chinamen engaged in collecting edible birds' nests. The prisoners were almost unknown to *Bī'ala*, and their release, therefore, could no more have concerned him personally than did their punishment. His request was granted

ment; they are early taught to be generous and self-denying, and the special object of the fasting period, regarding which I shall hope to speak to you on another occasion, seems to be to test the fortitude and powers of endurance of the lads and lasses before entering upon the cares and responsibilities of married life. The duties of showing respect and hospitality to friends and visitors being impressed upon them from their early years, all guests are well treated; every attention is paid to their wants, the best food at their host's disposal is set before them, and, ere they take their leave, some tokens of regard or goodwill are bestowed, or, to speak more correctly, interchanged. Strangers visiting an encampment for the first time are welcomed if introduced by some mutual friend.[1]

8. It has been observed by ethnologists who have described certain other primitive races, that modesty and morality are not dependent on, or to be gauged by, the amount of covering which is deemed requisite by either sex. The Andamanese present another instance in point; and in the esteem in which they hold these virtues, and the self-respect which characterises their intercourse with each other, may even be said to compare favourably with that existing in certain ranks among civilised races.[2]

9. In the manufacture of their weapons, utensils, and other articles, they habitually display a remarkable amount of perseverance and industry, spending hour after hour in laboriously striking pieces of iron with a stone hammer for the purpose of forming spear or arrow-heads, or in improving the shape of a bow, &c., even though there be no necessity, immediate or prospective, to stimulate them to such efforts. The incentive is evidently a spirit of emulation, each one priding himself on being able to produce work which will excel, or at least compare not unfavourably with, that of his neighbours.

10. Selfishness is not among their characteristics, for they frequently make presents of the best that they possess, and do not reserve, much less make, weapons, &c., of superior workmanship for their own private use; at the same time it must be

[1] On seeing a stranger at a gathering, it would be asked: *ŏl mij'a!* (who is he?) or, if the visitor be senior to the inquirer, *ŏl mij'ola!* (who is that elder or chief?)

[2] Women are so modest that they will not renew their leaf aprons in the presence of one another, but retire to a secluded spot for this purpose; even when parting with one of their *bōd-* appendages to a female friend the delicacy they manifest for the feelings of the bystanders in their mode of removing it almost amounts to prudishness. Coarse conversation appears to be of rare occurrence and to meet with little or no encouragement. Remarks on the personal appearance or peculiarities of friends or blood relatives are considered harmless, but if made in reference to a wife or husband would be regarded as indelicate and objectionable, and resented accordingly.

confessed that it is tacitly understood that an equivalent should be rendered for every gift.

11. Like the Papuans they are merry, talkative, petulant, inquisitive, and restless. Their speech is rapid, with a constant repetition of the same idea, and a joke, if not played in too practical a form, is highly appreciated.

12. When out of temper with any one they never defame his relatives or use improper expressions, as is so common a practice among natives of India, but merely indulge in mild terms of abuse, such as the following:—

ngab-tad·inga tâ·paya! (You liar!)
ngūn-lâ·maya! (You duffer!)
ngūn-jā·bagya! or *ng'ab-mūgutigpī·chaya!* (You fool!)
ngī-chô·na! (You long head!)
ngig-chô·ronga-lâ·nta! (You long nose!)
ngig-pâ·namaya! (You sunken-eyed one!)
ngid-kī·nabya! or *ngī-gō·robya!* (You skin and bone!)

A quarrel, as may be supposed, generally results from this style of address.[1]

13. With the exception of those who have lived with us away from their friends from birth or early childhood, not a case can be cited in which a preference is not manifested for a jungle life, even after a sojourn of many years at the Orphanage or Homes at Port Blair.

14. Opportunities for comparing the mental capacity of the children with those of other races have been few, but these have tended to show that, up to the age of 12 or 14, they possess quite as much intelligence as ordinary middle-class children of civilised races when competing in subjects in which they have been instructed in common; but the precociousness of intellect which has so often been remarked in the very young does not appear to be long maintained. Dr. Brander, who was for some time in charge of the Andaman Hospital, gave it as his opinion, that as a race "they are not deficient in brain power; it rather lies dormant and unused in their savage state;" and he mentions the case of an aboriginal patient of 12 years of age, who had been educated in the Ross Orphanage School, and who, in spite of his tender years, could yet read English and Urdu fluently, as well as speak and write in both these languages, retaining also a knowledge of his mother tongue. He had, besides, acquired a fair knowledge of arithmetic. I may add that this is not an exceptional case, for I could instance others, and one lad in particular, who was his superior.

15. More lengthened observations than have hitherto been

[1] *Vide post* "Laws," paragraph 1.

possible are required before we can speak with certainty regarding the extent, limits, and conditions of heredity among this race; but it has been noticed that, as a general rule, they have excellent memories, especially on those subjects in which the intellects of their ancestors have been consciously or unconsciously exercised or cultivated in the savage state. The following passage will afford an illustration of the intelligence displayed by these people on such subjects. It is taken from the late Mr. Kurz's Report on the Vegetation of the Andaman Islands:—"While I was in the Andamans I was in the habit of consulting people (convicts) from the most different parts of India for the native names of the plants. As a general result, I may state that the Burmans were best acquainted with the flora of the Andamans, but they are by no means equal to the Andamanese in accuracy and certainty of determination. While the Burmans were obliged continually to cut into the bark to recognise the trees, the Andamanese readily gave their names, and I could rely upon their statements, which was not the case at all with those of the Burmese."

16. Instances have been observed among them of individuals possessing strong wills and vivid powers of imagination: as a race they do not appear to be subject to trances, illusions, or somnambulism, but, like many other savages, they place implicit faith in dreams, shaping their conduct in superstitious conformity to the warning or advice supposed to have been conveyed therein.

Magic and Witchcraft.—1. There are, however, certain individuals in these tribes, known as *ōko-paiad-* (*lit.*, a dreamer), who are credited with the possession of supernatural powers—such as second sight, expressed by the term *ār-tā-mūgu-lā-rabanga-*,—and of a mysterious influence over the fortunes and lives of their neighbours. It is thought that they can bring trouble, sickness, and death upon those who fail to evince their belief in them in some substantial form;[1] they thus generally manage to obtain the best of everything, for it is considered foolhardy to deny them, and they do not scruple to ask for any article to which they may take a fancy.

2. These quasi-seers are invariably of the male sex, and it sometimes even happens that a young boy is looked upon as a "coming" *ōko-paiad-*, their position being generally in the first instance attained by relating an extraordinary dream, the details

[1] This reminds one somewhat of the disease makers of Tanna (New Hebrides), who are supposed to cause disease and death by burning *nahak* (rubbish, principally refuse of food), and who are propitiated by continual presents. The practice of burning beeswax, in order to cause annoyance to an enemy, will be mentioned under "Superstitions," paragraph 13.

of which are declared to have been borne out subsequently by some unforeseen event, as, for instance, a sudden death by accident.

3. In order to maintain his status it is necessary for an *ôko-paiʹad-* to give fresh evidences of his powers from time to time, for, so long as his companions have faith in him, he is the constant recipient of presents of all kinds, which are unblushingly given[1] and accepted as bribes to curry favour.

4. Sometimes, owing to the multiplicity of these gifts, it is inconvenient to the *ôko-paiʹad-* to take charge of them; he then enters into an arrangement with the donors that such articles as he does not at present need shall be available for his use or appropriation whenever he may require them; hence many individuals possess property which is said to be *rôʹdare* (i.e., bespoken) by a certain seer, and which is, therefore, not available for presentation to anyone else.

5. If a disaster occur which they think might have been averted had the *ôko-paiʹad-* chosen to exercise his powers, they are said sometimes to conspire to kill him, but so greatly is he feared that not a single instance is known of anyone having ventured to carry such a plan into execution.

6. The position and influence possessed by a seer are not affected by his falling ill, but if some serious misfortune occur to him, such as the death of a child, it is looked upon as a sign that his power is waning, or that he has at least lost a portion of it; they, however, continue to stand in awe of him unless, as time passes, he fails to afford further proof of his supposed superiority. His wife enjoys no distinction, nor is she treated with more respect and consideration than any other woman of the like age in the tribe.

7. The *ôko-paiʹad-* is credited with the power of communicating in dreams with the invisible powers of good and evil, and also of seeing the spirits of the departed, or of those who are ill. On the occurrence of an epidemic in an encampment, he brandishes a burning log, and bids the evil spirit keep at a distance; sometimes, as a further precaution, he plants stakes a few feet high in front of each hut, painted in stripes with black beeswax (*tôʹbul-pîd-*), the smell of which being peculiarly offensive to this demon, called *êrem-chàuʹgala*, insures his speedy departure from their midst.

8. Though we may be disposed to question the belief of the *ôko-paiʹad-s* themselves in the supernatural powers they profess to possess, it is quite possible that they, like sorcerers in other

[1] Especially is this done by those advanced in years for fear of their end being hastened by the *ôko-paiʹad-* whom they fail to propitiate.

savage tribes,[1] imagine themselves gifted with superior wisdom, and can hardly be blamed if they endeavour to turn their talents to account by imposing a little on the credulity of their neighbours.

Tribal Distribution.—1. The inhabitants of these islands are divided into at least nine tribes,[2] linguistically distinguished, even if we reckon as one those communities to which I have already alluded under the title of *jär·awa-*, among whom it is not improbable further divisions and dialects may eventually be discovered. The conjecture that they are one is merely based on the assertions of the people of South Andaman, and on the circumstance that all the weapons, utensils, huts, &c., of the *jär·awa-*, which we have been able to examine, appear to be constructed invariably on the same model, while all such members of the various scattered communities as we have had the opportunity of observing, resemble each other in abstaining from the practice, so general among all the eight Great Andaman tribes, of shaving their heads and tattooing their persons. Still, these outward similarities are manifestly insufficient, affording as they do mere negative evidence, whereas our present knowledge, so tardily acquired, of there being inland communities, called *ĕ·rem-tă·ga-*, dwelling in the heart of South and Middle Andaman, who are allied in all respects, save in their mode of life, with the *āryŏ·to-*, or coast communities of their respective tribes, would seem to justify the belief that hereafter the aborigines of Little Andaman will be found to present not only distinctions of this nature but differences also of dialect, as is the case with the inhabitants of both North and Middle Andaman, which are known to be divided into no less than six tribes.

2. As to the numerical strength of these several tribes it is impossible to speak with any degree of certainty, for, as you are aware, there is no part of the country which is not covered with jungle, more or less impenetrable to any but the aborigines themselves, while their capacity for estimating and expressing numbers is wholly inadequate to assist us in forming any conclusions on the subject. The surmise that the entire group contains about 4,000 souls is based on the calculation that the *bō·jig-ngī·ji-* tribe with whom we are most intimate do not at the present day exceed 400, though at the time of our advent in 1858, they are believed to have numbered about 1,000.

Topography.—1. The chief geographical landmarks of these islands are:—

1st. *Saddle Peak*, a massive hill rising to the height of

[1] *Vide* Lubbock, "On the Origin of Civilisation," &c., 4th Ed., pp. 350–1.

[2] For the names of the various tribes, and the localities they occupy, the reader is referred to the accompanying map.

2,400 feet, situated in North Andaman, and visible at a distance of 60 miles.

2nd. *Narcondam*,[1] a small hilly island, containing an extinct volcano, with an elevation of 2,330 feet, lying about 70 miles east of North Andaman.

3rd. *Barren Island*, 75 miles S.S.W. of *Narcondam*, and about 42 miles east of the nearest island of the Great Andaman group, from no portion of the coast of which is it visible. It contains an active volcano, the height of which is about 1,015 feet.

2. Until recent years[2] the first only of these was known to the aborigines, probably owing to the circumstance that they, at least the natives of Great Andaman, have never been seen to venture far out to sea in their frail and clumsy canoes. The name borne by this hill is *Pū·luga lā·kā bang-* (*lit.* Creator his mouth), referring apparently to its size and inaccessibility, and to a large ravine running down its side. There is also a belief that Saddle Peak was the place of *Pū·luga-'s*[3] residence prior to the deluge.

3. The formation of rocks, valleys, hills, &c., they attribute to the will of *Pū·luga-*, but they assign the sources of the streams containing oxide of iron, *kōi·ob-chū·luga-*, and the olive-coloured mineral, *chū·luga-*, to the action of a poisonous snake, called *lō·raba-*, well known to them.[4]

4. The names they give to the natural forms of land and water are as follows:—

Cape (point)—*tōla-chō·ronga-* [*chō·ronga-* = nose].
Isthmus—*tō·to-lī·rnab-* [*lī·rnab-* = waist].
Mountain—*bō·roin-*.
Valley—*pā·rag-*.
Strait—*tog-pā·rag-*.
Coast (shore)—*tōgō·ra-* [*gō·ra-* = strong].
Fore-shore—*kē·wad-* and *bō·roga-*.
Island—*tā·rchō·na-*.
Islet—*tōt-kai·cha-*.
Harbour—*ēlā·rū·la-*.
Bay—*kō·bungo-*.
Creek—*jīg-*.[5]

[1] The probable derivation of this name will be given in Part II.

[2] Since amicable relations have been established with the South and Middle Andamanese, several members of these tribes have visited Barren Island by accompanying us in the station steamer. The name by which it is now known to them is *mōla-tā·rchō·na-* (*lit.*, Smoke Island), in allusion to the smoke which is almost always to be seen rising from the volcano, and which they account for by saying that it must be due to a fire which *Pū·luga-* kindled.

[3] *Pū·luga* represents to them The Creator. *Vide* "Religious Beliefs, &c.," paragraph 7.

[4] *Vide post* "Superstitions," paragraph 21.

[5] The legendary belief regarding the formation of creeks will be found under "Mythology."

ARITHMETIC.—1. The utter hopelessness of obtaining from the aborigines any correct idea of the population of the tribes individually and collectively will be readily understood when it is stated that the only numerals in the language are those for denoting "one" and "two," and that they have absolutely no word to express specifically any higher figures, but indulge in some such vague term as "several," "many," "numerous," "innumerable," which seem to convey to their minds an approximate idea of the number intended, but fail to satisfy the requirements of the statistician.[1]

2. When anxious to express a certain small number with exactness, as, for example, nine, the nose is tapped with the tips of the fingers in successive order, and, commencing with the little finger of either hand, "*ū·ba-tū·l-*," (one) is said; with the next finger "*ī·kpō·r-*" (two), after which with each successive finger "*an-ká·*" (and this) is uttered. When the forefinger of the second hand is reached both are held up, and, the thumb of the second hand being clenched, the necessary number of digits is exposed to view, whereupon the word "*ārdū·ru-*" (all) is pronounced.

3. If ten be the number in question—and this is the highest numeral they attempt to indicate by this or any other method—on reaching the thumb of the second hand, both hands, before being held up, are brought together and then is said, as in the former case, "*ārdū·ru-*."

4. To express "one," they hold up the forefinger of either hand and utter the word *ū·ba-tū·l-* or *ū·ba-dō·ga-*; to denote "two" they hold up the first two fingers and say "*ī·kpō·r-*."

5. The toes are never used in counting, nor are pebbles, grains, or notches in a stick ever so employed. When it is stated that only the more intelligent are in the habit of computing by even the primitive method I have here described, it is somewhat remarkable to find that their system of denoting ordinals is more comprehensive, as will be seen by reference to Appendix E.

6. Before their comparatively recent acquaintance with us, they had not the faintest knowledge of the existence of even the

[1] With regard to human beings, to express a small number, say, from 10 to 20, *ārdū·ru-* would be used, while a somewhat greater number would be implied by the use of *jeg-châr-* (*lit.*, collected body), and a still greater assemblage, say of 50 persons, by *jī·baba*, beyond which number *at-ū·baba*, would be used. These words may be translated in a rising scale as follows:—

ārdū·ru-, several; *jeg-châr-*, many; *jī·baba*, very many; *at-ū·baba* (or *ū·baba*), innumerable.

As regards animals and inanimate objects the words *ārdū·ru-* implying many, and *at-ū·baba* (or *ū·baba*), innumerable, are generally used, and sometimes *jī·baba*, denoting very many.

neighbouring coast of Burmah, much less of the world at large, and consequently imagined that their islands formed almost the entire terrene area, and that they themselves comprised the bulk of the inhabitants.

7. The few voyagers who from time to time ventured near their shores were regarded as deceased ancestors, who, by some dispensation, had been permitted to re-visit the earth, and who were supposed to live on some small island in the vicinity of their *ē·rema-*, *i.e.*, world. In confirmation of this may be cited the name by which natives of India are to this day called, viz., *chāu·gala* (*lit.* departed spirits).

Etymology.—1. From the following list of some of the numerous encampments of the natives of South Andaman,[1] it will be observed that the names are usually derived from some circumstance peculiar to the spot, or from some tree overshadowing the site:—

.tá-bō·roga-, coral (*tá-*), shore (*bō·roga-*).

.tigbang-, rock-hole, there being at that place a hole in a large rock through which a canoe can pass.

.tôramū·gu-.[2] West (island).

.yū·kala-chàng-, grassy (*yū·kala-*), camp (*chàng-*).

.Dū·mla-paicha-ông-, anchorage (*ông-*), in neighbourhood (*paicha-*), of the (*la*), *Dūm-* tree.

.Lā·kera-lar·nga-, a row (*lar·nga-*) of *Lā·kera-* trees.

.ā·rāla lâr chū·lnga-, the spring (*chū·lnga-*), at the (*lâr*, *lit.* of the) *.ā·rāla-* tree (*Pandanus verus*).

.chē·la-dō·k·nga-, the dragging (*dō·knga-*) of the ship (*chē·leua-*). A ship was once wrecked there.

.būd lōt dog·ranga-. Defeat camp; the defeat (*dog·ranga-*) at the (*lōt*, *lit.* of the) camp (*būd-*). There was once a severe fight there.

2. There are a few place-names which are unintelligible to the present inhabitants, *e.g.*, *.lū·rua-*, *.kū·rubūn-*, though it is believed that they conveyed a meaning to former generations. Many of the names show an old, but unmistakable form of the present language, while others, again, might be judged to be of recent adoption, but they are not so in point of fact.

Tribal Communities.—1. It is no matter of surprise that, during the *first* years of our present occupation, when our acquaintance with the aborigines was so limited, we should

[1] A fairly complete list of the names of these encampments, and the meanings of the greater number of them, will be found in a short paper, entitled "Note on two Maps of the Andaman Islands," by E. H. Man and R. C. Temple, which was published in the "Journal of the Royal Geographical Society," 1880.

[2] *Vide* "Astronomy," paragraph 5. (*West*, the disappearing face place.)

D

have failed to learn that there are permanent encampments and kitchen-middens in the heart of the jungles of Great Andaman; but, since it has been recently asserted in a paper[1] by one of the officers long resident at Port Blair, that, to quote his words, "No tribe of Negritos in the same stage of existence . . . . as the Andamanese could exist in the Andaman jungles," it is very necessary to expose his error, for repeated inquiries and personal observation prove the accuracy of the account given by one of the inhabitants of the interior of Middle Andaman, named *Wōi*, that during the entire year the jungles afford them ample sustenance.[2]

2. All the tribes with which we are acquainted possess terms denoting—1, a coastman; 2, a fisherman; 3, a creek man; and 4, a jungle-man; the two former being applied to those living by the shore, *ārya·to-*, and the two latter to those living inland, *ē·remtā·ga-*, whose subsistence depends on the spontaneous products of the jungle, which they all agree in describing as amply sufficient for the support of many times their present population.

3. The coastmen are divided into two classes, viz., those who are chiefly employed in constructing canoes, turtle-lines, &c., and those who are engaged in fishing and turtling, but each acquires a certain knowledge of the duties of the other, and also of hunting the *Sus Andamanensis*: in the latter accomplishment, as well as in finding their way through trackless portions of the jungle, they are naturally surpassed by the natives of the interior, who display in these, as in other respects, all the dexterity and intelligence peculiar to savages similarly situated in other tropical regions.[3]

4. Although these two distinct sections (*ārya·to-* and *ē·remtā·ga-*) still exist in a measure among the *bōjig-ngī·ji-*, as among the people of Middle Andaman, many of their more marked characteristics have become so blended or modified, in consequence of the establishment of the homes, that it is difficult in many cases to determine to which class certain individuals originally belonged. This, it will be understood, is because those of the *ē·remtā·ga-*, who have accompanied parties of the coastmen in

[1] *Vide* "Proceedings Asiat. Soc. Bengal," July, 1876.

[2] With reference to the above, Mr. W. T. Blanford, F.R.S., remarked at the meeting at which the paper in question was read, that "it is very difficult for a civilised human being to understand how savages live, or even to conceive what a marvellous variety of animal and vegetable productions, on which savage man, at any rate, can subsist, are to be found in the forests of all tropical regions." He added, that it was his belief that "man could certainly find food wherever monkeys could exist."

[3] *Vide* "Physical Powers and Senses," paragraphs 5 and 6, and "Communications," &c., paragraphs 4 and 6.

fishing and turtling expeditions, at one or other of the homes, for several years, have become sufficiently skilled in these pursuits to escape the ridicule of the genuine *āryō'to-*, while these in their turn have made themselves almost as well acquainted with the interior of the jungles as were the original occupants, from whom they are, therefore, scarcely distinguishable.

5. It will be of interest to note in this place the nicknames employed by the "junglees" and the coastmen when quizzing each other, as they serve to indicate the peculiarities which are held to be their distinguishing characteristics. The *ē'remtā'ga-* sometimes chaffingly address an *āryō'to-* as *ēr-chā'tā'kanga-*,[1] i.e., one who loses his way; *ēr-lō'inga-ba*, i.e., one who cannot find his way in the jungle; or, *ūn-pāg-ī'kanga-ba*, i.e., one who cannot follow tracks; while the terms which the coastmen will, under similar circumstances, employ towards the jungle men are *ab-mū'lon-* and *gū'gma-tōng'-*, the first implying a deaf person, for only the practised ear of an *āryō'to-* can judge of the distance of a turtle so correctly as to be able to harpoon it in pitch darkness; the second meaning "leaf of the *Trigonostemon longifolius*," in allusion to the practice, current among the inland tribes,[2] of using these leaves for the cure of fever, but to which the *āryō'to-* rarely have recourse, as they believe the scent prevents turtles from approaching a canoe in which there are any persons who have recently employed this remedy.

6. The intermingling of the members of the inland and coast communities in and near our settlement has naturally resulted in such a marked modification of many of the characteristics which distinguish them in their primitive condition that, for reliable information respecting the same, it is necessary to seek among the more distant encampments, where similar influences have not as yet been at work.

7. Amongst those who have now for some years resided at the principal home at Port Blair, there is a young *ē'remtā'ga-*, named *Wōi*, of the *ōko-jū'wai-* tribe, who, till the end of 1875, had been living in the depths of the Middle Andaman jungle, and who then, with a few others of his village, received a message from *mai'a Jīpa*, chief of *bārid'kābil-*, an encampment on the coast, inviting them to accompany him in a trip he was about to make, by way of Port Mouat, for the purpose of seeing the officer in charge of the home, and procuring some presents from him. *Wōi* and his friends gladly availed themselves of the opportunity of visiting what must have been to them a new

[1] By way of mock respect *mai'a* (i.e., Mr.) is occasionally prefixed to these epithets when used in this way.

[2] *Vide* "Medicine," paragraph 2.

world: on their arrival at Viper Island, they saw, for the first time, Europeans, and a mode of living of which they could have previously formed no idea. *Wōī*'s companions returned to their tribe after spending a few months with us, but he, having lost his heart to one of the South Andaman houris, was without difficulty induced to remain behind, and settle down in our midst as a married man. As he speedily acquired a knowledge of the *.bōjig-ngīji-* dialect, we were enabled to question him on various points, besides those referred to in the statement which forms one of the appendices to this volume,[1] and thus learned much that was before unknown concerning the habits of the inland branch of the *.ōko-jū'wai-* tribe: the information thus obtained, when compared with the result of our own observations of the customs and mode of living of the communities in the vicinity of our settlement, afforded convincing proof of the universality of the customs and practices of the respective classes of *aryō'to-* and *ē'remtā'ga-* throughout Middle and South Andaman.

8. In Dr. Mouat's book mention is made of the capture of a youth, nicknamed "Jack," after a hostile encounter with some of the natives of Interview Island, from which circumstance it may be inferred that the lad belonged to the *.ākā-kedē-* tribe, only one member of which had, till 1879, stayed amongst us, and he is an *ē'remtā'ga-*, who had travelled out of curiosity as far as Middle Strait, and from thence had been persuaded by the chief of that district to accompany him to Port Blair. He proved himself very intelligent and active in all jungle accomplishments, but was entirely ignorant of fishing and turtling After remaining with us a few months he was taken (in March, 1879), at his own request, to a point on the north-west coast of Middle Andaman, and landed with a heap of presents: his home, he informed us, was situated midway between that place and the east coast.

Nomadism.—1. Nomadism appears to be almost, if not entirely, confined to the *aryō'to-*, and even among them there are hamlets which are only abandoned temporarily, as with the *ē'remtā'ga-*, in consequence of a death, or of a *jeg-* (*i.e.*, "corroboree"), at some neighbouring encampment.

2. The nature of the temporary migrations which take place among the *ē'remtā'ga-* during the dry season, as well as of those necessitated by a death, will be explained in subsequent sections. In the case of the *aryō'to-*, migrations are occasioned by a variety of circumstances, as, for instance, fishing operations being rendered impossible by a change in the wind, the

[1] *Vide* Appendix F, a free translation of which will be found in "Journ. Anthrop. Inst.," vol. xi, pp. 290–2.

suitability of a particular spot for fishing and turtling during certain phases of the moon, on account of the character of the foreshore, or the configuration of the coast, and the hope of meeting with better luck elsewhere—to these might be added the love of a change, and the prospect of seeing some of their friends; but it must not be supposed that a long journey is thereby involved, the move being generally made to a spot only a mile or two further on, and thus, by short stages, they sometimes proceed along the entire coast-line of their tribal territory, spending a few days or weeks at each halting place, according to the special attractions it may happen to possess in affording good sport on land or sea, or in supplying a rich harvest of fruit, honey, &c.

3. The necessity of a migration is also frequently forced on them by the consequences of their neglect to sweep away the refuse of their meals, it being regarded by these *insouciant* and unclean creatures as not worth their while to take so much trouble, when only a short stay is contemplated.

4. That the necessity for observing *some* sanitary measures has long since been recognised by the Andamanese is evident from the existence of numerous kitchen-middens throughout their territory, many of which are doubtless of remote origin. These refuse-heaps are still in course of formation by communities living at a distance from Port Blair, and are invariably found near camping grounds which have been, or are still more or less, permanently occupied. In those sites, where they are not seen, evidence is at once afforded of the temporary nature of the occupancy: the rubbish and refuse of food in these latter places is only swept aside if the ground be needed for a dance, wedding, or other ceremony, so that injury may not befall the revellers through inadvertently treading on a bone, stone, or shell. Crows, hermit-crabs, and, of late years, dogs, are the principal scavengers of these ill-ordered and dirty habitations, the two former performing their useful office as soon as a migration takes place.

Habitations.—1. We will now pass to the consideration of the three varieties of huts which are commonly met with in the permanent and temporary encampments throughout the territory of the eight Great Andaman tribes, and which are known as *châng-tē·pinga-*, *châng-tô·rnga-*, and *châng-dat·anga.*

2. To commence with the *châng-tē·pinga-*, which is made by men, and erected in all permanent encampments as being the most durable. No particular kind of wood is used for the posts, which are four in number, two in front and two in rear, the former varying from six to nine feet in height, and the latter from two to three feet; upon these, slender rafters and two light transverse poles are secured, so as to form the framework of

the roof, which is thatched with palm leaves of the variety called *chá·ngta-*. These are neatly plaited together, and fastened with cane, *pī·dga-*, and then placed in rows and tied, so that, when complete, the whole forms a capital roof impervious to the heaviest shower of rain.

3. The second variety, *chàng-tō·rnga-*,[1] are erected when temporary homes are required, which will last for a few months, as during the period of mourning;[2] they are made by men, and differ only from the *chàng-tē·pinga-* in being generally somewhat smaller, and less neatly thatched; another variety of palm leaf, called *ām-*, is sometimes substituted for the *chá·ngta-*.

4. The *chàng-da·ranga-*, or the third variety, being only intended to serve as shelter during a halt or short visit, is constructed in a yet more simple manner. The duty of erecting dwellings of this class devolves on the women, and from the following description it will be seen that the labour required is not excessive: two slender posts, about five feet long, are driven into the ground about five or six feet apart, and connected by means of a light pole or stick, which is secured to their upper ends. The roof is then formed by placing, stem downwards and firmly fixed in the ground, large palm leaves, which are made to overlap each other in such a way as to provide a fairly rain-proof shelter for one or two persons.[3] The leaves used for the purpose are either the *chá·ngta-*, *kā·pa-*, or *ā·pura-*.

5. Above the small fire, without which no hut is complete, a small wooden platform or shelf, called *chá·pa lē tā·ga-*, or *yāt lēt tā·ga-*, is placed on one or more sticks. On this they deposit their spare food, so that it may be preserved by the smoke from the attacks of insects, &c.[4] By way of adornment, trophies of the chase, such as the skulls of pigs,[5] turtles, dugongs, &c., are suspended from the front of the roof.[6]

6. It seems desirable to draw attention to the following passage in Dr. Dobson's paper, lest, if left unnoticed, some misapprehension should arise on the subject. He states that "the Andamanese, at least the inhabitants of the southern island, erect no kind of house whatever . . . . When walking along the beach in the vicinity of Port Mouat,

[1] This variety is shown in Plate III, fig. 2.

[2] *Vide post* "Death and Burial," paragraph 4.

[3] Similar leaf shelters are erected by the Puris. *Vide* E. B. Tylor's "Anthropology."

[4] *Vide post* "Food," paragraph 31.

[5] This style of decoration is now-a-days falling into disuse, especially in South Andaman, for, with the assistance of dogs, hunting is much less arduous now than formerly, and a large collection of pig skulls is, therefore, easily obtained by the least skilful among them.

[6] Figuier speaks also of "large dried fish tied in bunches" being similarly treated, but no ground for such a statement can be discovered.

I have often come across one of their temporary habitations, which consists of a hole scooped out in the sand, beneath an over-hanging rock, large enough to contain a single person." As these savages are *never* in the habit of sleeping on the sand, or in holes scooped in the ground, but on a mat, or leaves spread under one or other of the three varieties of huts described above, it is difficult to account for what Dr. Dobson saw, unless they were the resting places of ticket-of-leave fishermen or convict runaways. No other explanation than this could be given when some aborigines, and an experienced attendant at the homes, were questioned by me on the subject. One other solution only is possible, and that is, that the "holes scooped out in the sand" were the result of a game of mock burial, which, as I shall mention under "Games and Amusements," is rather a favourite recreation of the *bōjig-yâb-* children.

7. The majority of the Great Andaman huts[1] partake of the character of a lean-to, the only respects in which the three varieties differ being[2] size and durability. They are found either standing alone, or, as is more especially the case in permanent encampments, so joined together as to form (at least, in their owners' eyes) a commodious as well as a weather-proof dwelling; and, constructed, as they usually are, in well-sheltered localities, away from the prevailing wind, they fulfil all the requirements of a savage home.

8. Permanent encampments vary in size, and consist of several huts, which in all are rarely inhabited by more than from 50 to 80 persons, though they are capable of affording accommodation, of a kind, to a much larger number if necessity arise as happens not unfrequently when festive tribal gatherings are arranged in honor of a wedding or other occasion of rejoicing.

9. The permanent encampments of the *bōjig-yâb-* are established in those sites which offer special advantages for fishing and turtling at all seasons. Wherever there is a fine stretch of sandy beach, with an extensive foreshore, they will be invariably found, for, at such places, throughout the year the women are able at low tide to catch fish in pools with their hand-nets, and to collect large quantities of shell-fish; while, during the flood

[1] One of the huts in the *jârawa-* territory, between Port Blair and Port Campbell, when visited a few years ago, was found to measure 60 feet × 48 feet; and Mr. Homfray, in 1867, described the huts at Little Andaman as capable (*more Andamanico*) of accommodating 100 persons, being 50 feet in diameter and 30 feet in height. The leaf employed by this tribe for thatching purposes appears to be invariably the variety called [illegible], and not the *chàd·ngâ-*.

[2] The largest hut of the ordinary type is rarely found capable of accommodating more than six persons. Sometimes these huts are placed together so as to resemble small sheds, but as this has hitherto been seen only in or near South Andaman, it is possible that the form of our barracks gave rise to the idea.

tides, the men enjoy exceptional facilities for shooting fish and harpooning turtles, &c.

10. Although the sites selected for occupation are usually well-sheltered, it is not always found possible in tempestuous weather, even in the dense jungle which covers every portion of their country, to obtain shelter sufficient to allow of their huts being so placed as to face inwards towards the *bū·lum-*, or dancing ground. The primary consideration being naturally to secure as much comfort as possible, the sloping roof is at such times presented towards the prevailing wind.

11. The following diagram will give a general idea of the plan commonly adopted in laying out an encampment consisting of several huts, though the form depends much on the nature of the ground, and on the relative position of the surrounding trees, for they do not consider it worth their while to fell these, or to clear away anything but the lightest brushwood for the mere purpose of providing space for their huts, and dancing ground. Another point to be taken into account is the possibility of accidents being caused by falling branches, and, therefore, when erecting their frail dwellings, they are careful to guard against this danger as far as possible, and so much judgment do they display in the matter that accidents of this nature are comparatively unknown.

a. Married persons.[1]

b. Bachelors.[1]

c. Spinsters.[1]

d. Public cooking place.

e. Dancing ground (*bū·lum-*).

Government.—1. The entire country is apportioned among the various tribes, and the territory occupied by each is considered the common property of all its members, and not as belonging exclusively to the chiefs.

2. Their domestic polity may be described as a communism modified by the authority, more or less nominal, of the chief. The head chief of a tribe is called *mai·a-igla·-*, and the elders, or sub-chiefs, *i.e.*, those in authority over each community, consisting of from 20 to 50 individuals, *mai·ola*.

3. The head chief, who usually resides at a permanent

[1] Even at the homes they are careful to maintain this order, viz.: of placing the bachelors and spinsters at either end of the building, and the married couples in the space between.

encampment, has authority over all the sub-chiefs, but his power, like theirs, is very limited. It is exercised mainly in organising meetings between the various communities belonging to his tribe, and in exerting influence in all questions affecting the welfare of his followers. It is the chief alone, as may be supposed, who directs the movements of a party while on hunting or fishing expeditions, or when migrating. It is usually through his intervention that disputes are settled, but he possesses no power to punish or enforce obedience to his wishes, it being left to all alike to take the law into their own hands when aggrieved.

4. The *āryō'to-* and *ĕremtā'ga-* in each tribe have their own head chief, who are independent the one of the other.

5. As might be assumed from the results of observations made of other savage races, whose sole or chief occupation consists in hunting or fishing, the power of the chiefs is very limited, and not necessarily hereditary, though, in the event of a grown-up son being left who was qualified for the post, he would, in most instances, be selected to succeed his father in preference to any other individual of equal efficiency.

6. At the death of a chief there is no difficulty in appointing a successor, even if he leave no son, for there is always at least one who is considered his deputy or right-hand man. As they are usually, on these occasions, unanimous in their choice, no formal election takes place; however, should any be found to dissent, the question is decided by the wishes of the majority, it being always open to malcontents to transfer their allegiance to another chief, since there is no such thing as forced submission to the authority of one who is not a general favourite.

7. Social status being dependent not merely on the accident of relationship, but on skill in hunting, fishing, &c., and on a reputation for generosity and hospitality, the chiefs and elders are almost invariably superior in every respect to the rest. They and their wives are at liberty to enjoy immunity from the drudgery incidental to their mode of life, all such acts being voluntarily performed for them by the young unmarried persons living under their headship.

8. Though females, like minors (that is to say youths under 18), cannot be chiefs, the former have a similar position relatively among the women, to that held by their husbands among the men of the tribe. A chief's wife enjoys many privileges, especially if she be a mother, and in virtue of her husband's rank rules over all the young unmarried women and such also of the married ones as are not senior to herself. Should she become a widow she continues to exercise the same rights, unless she re-marries, when her social status depends on that of

her husband. In the event, however, of the widow of a chief being young and childless, she returns to the home of her maiden days, and is in a measure lost sight of, as she sinks to her former position.

9. It is believed by the people themselves that the system above described has prevailed among them from a remote period.

Covenants, Oaths, Ordeals.—1. No forms of covenant are to be traced in their dealings with one another, nor is there to be found among them anything of the nature of an oath or of an appeal to a higher power—as Heaven or the Sun—to punish breach of faith, or to bear witness to the truth.

2. They are in too primitive a state to possess any form of trial, or even to have any belief in the efficacy of an ordeal for discovering a guilty person; nor does it appear that any such practice existed in times past.

Laws.[1]—1. Justice, as I have already said, is administered by the simple method of allowing the aggrieved party to take the law into his own hands, which he usually does, either by flinging a burning faggot, or discharging an arrow, at, or more frequently *near*, the offender, while all who may be present lose no time in beating a retreat, and—taking with them as much of their property as their haste will allow—remain in concealment until sufficient time has elapsed for the settlement of the quarrel. When such an affair seems imminent, and likely to be serious, friends often interpose, seize the disputants, and remove their weapons, which are not restored so long as there appears any risk of their misusing them.

2. Should a man kill his opponent nothing is necessarily said or done to him, though it is permissible for a friend or relative of the deceased to avenge his death; in most cases, however, the murderer succeeds in striking such terror in the minds of the community that no one ventures to assail him or even to express any disapprobation of his conduct while he is within hearing: as conscience, however, makes cowards of us all, the homicide, from prudential motives, not unfrequently absents himself till he is assured that the grief and indignation of his victim's friends have considerably abated.

3. These remarks do not now-a-days apply, to the same extent, to those living near us, for the terror inspired by the punishments inflicted in all cases of murder brought to our notice has resulted in materially diminishing crimes of this nature among them. In May, 1880, an Andamanese youth was hanged

[1] As regards laws (!) relating to inheritance, information will be found in a subsequent paper, under the heading of "Property," paragraph 3.

at Port Blair for the murder of one of his countrymen. He had previously, in 1878, been sentenced to imprisonment for the murder of two children of his tribe, and he committed his last crime soon after his discharge. This has hitherto been the only occasion on which any of these savages has suffered the extreme penalty of British law. It may be added, that this last step was not taken until the unhappy wretch, as well as all his fellow-countrymen in South Andaman, had been repeatedly warned that no other than a capital sentence would in future be passed on those convicted of murder.

4. It is by no means an uncommon occurrence for a man, or even a boy, to vent his ill-temper, or show his resentment at any act, by destroying his own property as well as that of his neighbours, sparing only the things belonging exclusively to the chief, or other head man. The amount of damage done at such times, to canoes and other articles of more or less value, will often give occasion for several weeks' employment in repairing and replacing to himself and his companions; but as these outbreaks are looked upon as the result of a temporary "possession," and the victim considered, for the time being, dangerous, and unaccountable for his actions, no one ventures to offer any opposition, or impose any restraint upon him.

5. Women, when in a rage, occasionally act in a similar manner towards one of their own sex, or even to all the females of the encampment, injuring or destroying their nets, baskets, and other articles; at other times they will seize a burning log, and, banging it furiously on the ground, vent their feelings by some such exclamation as *ngig mū'gu ji'-bagile!* (May your face become hideous!); or they will struggle and fight till they are forcibly separated by the wife or daughter of their head man. They do not, however, attempt to settle their differences with the stronger sex, but leave it to their husbands or male relatives to obtain redress for their real or fancied grievances.

6. When a chief or elder so far forgets himself as to lose his temper, those of his own standing betake themselves to their huts, while the other members of the community, male and female, beat a hasty retreat to some secluded spot, for no one would venture to find fault with one in authority, and with some reason, for little or no harm usually results to the community, while his own reputation is sure to suffer. Should he, however, wantonly cause loss or injury to any of his people, they would be pretty certain to take an early, though secret, opportunity of repaying him in kind.

Crime.—1. That outcome of civilisation, suicide, is unknown among them; but, since they have seen cases of self-murder among the alien population, they have coined a lengthy com pound word (*ō·yun-tē·mar-tō'liganga-*) in order to express the nature of the act.

2. That they are not entirely devoid of moral consciousness may, I think, in some measure, be demonstrated by the fact of their possessing a word, *yū·bda-*, signifying sin or wrong doing, which is used in connection with falsehood, theft, grave assault, murder, adultery, and — burning wax (!),[1] which deeds are believed to anger *Pū·luga-*, the Creator, of whom more will be said hereafter.[2]

3. Cases of adultery in their own villages are said to be of rare occurrence. If detected, the injured husband would probably inflict condign punishment on the guilty parties, but at the risk of retaliation on the part of the male offender and his friends; there appears, however, to be an understanding, that the greater the provocation offered the less is the risk incurred of the injured person or his friends avenging the wrong, but no appeal to the chief for redress is ever made.

4. If an offence, such as an assault or theft, be committed by one or more members of another tribe during a visit or by stealth, it is regarded as premeditated, and generally resented as a tribal affair, resulting in a feud and more or less bloodshed.

5. Intercourse with Europeans and other foreigners has, it must be confessed, unhappily opened their eyes to the existence of some vices of which they had formerly no knowledge;[3] notably is this the case with regard to drunkenness, for, being, till the time they made our acquaintance, "blessed in the ignorance of spirituous liquors," they had no conception of its effects, and, to express an inebriate, have invented a word (*lē'lēkunga-*) signifying "staggerer." It must, however, be added, that in consequence of the extreme partiality for rum and other intoxicating drinks which they manifest, much care has to be taken to prevent them from gratifying the easily acquired taste.

Narcotics.—1. Prior to our advent they were also entirely ignorant of narcotics in any form; but one of the evil results of their intercourse with us has been the introduction of the practice of smoking, and so rapidly have they (both men and women) acquired the habit, that, when at a distance from the homes and unable to obtain tobacco, they have been seen to fill their short clay pipes, which, it is scarcely necessary to say, have been obtained from us, with *pān* leaves rather than endure entire deprivation.

[1] *Vide* "Journ. Anthrop. Inst.," vol. xi, p. 288, and *post*, "Superstitions," paragraph 13.

[2] *Vide post* "Religious Beliefs," paragraph 8.

[3] The crimes of abduction, rape, seduction, unnatural offences, &c., appear never to have been committed among them.

2. I have used the word "evil" advisedly, for there can be no doubt, from observations extending over many years, that the result of their excessive indulgence in smoking has been seriously to impair their constitutions. The attempts that have been made to check the mischief have hitherto failed, as it has been found difficult, if not impossible, to induce them to do a stroke of work without the accompaniment of the "fragrant weed."

Cannibalism.—1. The early stories regarding the prevalence of cannibalism among these savages do not at the present day require refutation.[1] No lengthened investigation was needed to disprove the long credited fiction, for not a trace could be discovered of the existence of such a practice in their midst, even in far-off times.

2. It is curious, however, to note, that while they express the greatest horror of the custom, and indignantly deny that it ever held a place among their institutions, a very general belief has been entertained by the tribes living in South and Middle Andaman as to its prevalence in other races, and even among their own countrymen inhabiting North and Little Andaman; and to this cause is chiefly ascribed the dread which they and their fathers have, from a distant period, evinced of their neighbours, and the animosity displayed towards strangers who have approached or landed on their shores; but these sentiments are now confined to those individuals who have had but scant opportunity of becoming acquainted with ourselves and other aliens, or with the results of the visits paid by us to the dreaded *yĕrewa*- and *jārawa*- territories.

Communications, Chirography, and Drawing.—1. The density of the Andaman jungles, and the unsuitability of their canoes for long expeditions by sea, would of themselves be serious hindrances to free intercourse between the various tribes, even were there not the further difficulty—due in great measure to the above circumstances—of difference of language to contend with.

2. There are no marked boundaries between the various tribal districts, but a general understanding exists between neighbouring tribes regarding the limits of their respective domains, which are usually defined by such natural barriers as a range of hills, a creek, or even a belt of dense jungle. So careful are they to respect these boundaries, that, before even travelling through, and particularly before hunting or fishing in, the territory of a

[1] Papuans being regarded as such inveterate anthropophagi, ethnologists will probably agree in considering that the non-existence—nay, even horror—of this custom among the Andamanese furnishes an important item in the array of facts which militate against the theory held by some that the latter form a branch of the great Papuan family.

neighbouring tribe, an express invitation or permission is required, unless, indeed, the party entering happens to be accompanied by one or more members of the district visited, or when, from long and friendly intercommunication, a right of way has been tacitly sanctioned. In cases where there has been a breach of this observance sharp retribution has generally followed, causing sometimes serious loss of life, and resulting in a long-standing tribal feud.

3. Those communities of *ē-rem-tâ'ga-* and *âryô'to-*, living within a few miles of each other and speaking the same dialect, arrange from time to time large gatherings—generally numbering about a hundred persons[1]—for purposes of barter, or for the celebration of some particular event. Though not unfrequently on these occasions old enmities are healed and friendships formed, fresh tribal feuds and personal quarrels sometimes originate in consequence of a misunderstanding or dispute over some comparative trifle.[2]

4. There are numerous paths intersecting each territory, the result of continuous traffic over the same ground. When, for some reason, a new course is taken through the jungle, the route is indicated to those following by bending the twigs of the brushwood in a *reverse* direction at intervals along the track. This is especially the case during the dry season, when, owing to the parched condition of the soil, there is some difficulty in distinguishing footprints.[3]

5. No marks on rocks, trees or other objects, made for purposes of record, are believed by them to exist, and, with the exception of the supposititious hieroglyphics,[4] hereafter to be mentioned, nothing of the nature of writing is to be found among these tribes, nor have they any method of recording the name and exploits of a deceased chief or other individual who may have gained distinction during his life, save the narration—more or less garbled—of the same by their admiring descendants. The messenger who conveys intelligence to a distant encampment bears no outward token with him to testify to the authenticity or character of the communication he has to make.

6. Although no method of signs exists, such as tying knots in a string, making notches in a tally, or figures on wood, bark, or stone, they have means of distinguishing arrows and spears belonging to one another, by certain differences peculiar to each

[1] It is believed that no larger number than 300 has ever been assembled at one time in any place in our vicinity, at least since our advent.

[2] *Vide post* "Games and Amusements," paragraphs 24 and 37.

[3] No prejudice exists in respect to crossing water, going by certain paths, or handling particular objects, excepting the *Asadendrum paniculatum*. *Vide post*, Part III, "String," paragraph 3.

[4] *Vide* "Mythology," paragraph 29.

individual in the method of tying and knotting the string employed in the manufacture of these missiles;[1] these, however, are often so slight that, even when pointed out, they are scarcely to be detected by a stranger, unless he be one who has bestowed careful attention to the subject.

7. In their savage state they never attempt to represent any object, and, though they do not appear to possess any natural taste for drawing, they differ from the Australians[2] in the intelligence they display in recognising any familiar form depicted in a sketch; and while no such method for indicating the situation of any place is known or employed among themselves, some of them are quick in understanding a chart of their own country, and are able to point out the sites of their various encampments.

8. It is hardly necessary to state that they have nothing answering to mile-stones or roadside marks. Swamps are never crossed, but in all cases avoided by circuitous routes; experience seems to have taught them the natural line of fords from salient to salient banks, and, when a creek has to be crossed, they always avail themselves of the advantages thus afforded, even making a detour in order to do so.[3] This applies, however, to those occasions when they are not heavily laden, or are carrying articles liable to be damaged by immersion, or which would hinder them from swimming.

Swimming.—1. With the exception of some of the *ē̆rem-tá·ga-*,[4] a knowledge of the art of swimming is common to members of both sexes; the *children* even, learning almost as soon as they can run, speedily acquire great proficiency. In this accomplishment the Andamanese greatly surpass the majority of Europeans, but it is probable that, in competition with an experienced English swimmer, their best men would be distanced in the first few hundred yards, it being not so much for speed, as for the length of time they can remain in the water, that they are remarkable.

[1] With reference to this circumstance, it may be mentioned that, a few years ago (1876), five aborigines, concerned in the murder near Kyd Island of some Chinese traders with whom they had had a dispute, were discovered by means of the arrows found on the spot, as these were identified by some of their acquaintances then living at Port Blair.

[2] Brown. [From remarks, however, contained in a recent article, entitled "The Indo-Chinese and Oceanic Races," by Mr. A. H. Keane, which appeared in "Nature" (Jan. 6th, 1881), it would appear that the low estimate of the Australian intellect formed by certain ethnologists is not shared by all, and "many instances are given of their skill even in drawing, a capacity for which was wholly denied them."]

[3] Wells are not dug, but when encamping, whether for days or months, care is always taken that the spot selected be near some fresh-water stream.

[4] The reason of this is obvious, as it is known that the majority of the creeks are fordable in many places within three miles of the coast, even in the rainy season, and, therefore, the necessity of acquiring the art of natation has never been experienced by those permanently resident in the interior.

2. The "frog-stroke" is the one in general use; in diving,[1] they invariably leap *feet* foremost into the water, and their skill in recovering any small object which has been thrown into the sea, or which is lying at a considerable depth, equals that displayed by Somali boys.

3. The younger people delight in disporting themselves in the sea, and in displaying their skill in capturing a harpooned turtle or fish by diving after it; but, while they surpass most races in this respect, they are by no means equal to the astounding feat of catching fish—not to mention any larger than themselves—by merely plunging into the sea after them, as was alleged by the ex-sepoy convict, *Dúdhnáth*, in one of his many Munchausen-like statements. His allegation, according to Dr. Mouat, was that he had "seen three or four of them dive into deep water, and bring up in their arms a fish six or seven feet in length, which they had seized." A well-known work having been lent me in which the Andamanese are referred to, I took advantage of an opportunity to show them some of the illustrations, amongst others one in which two of their race are represented as rising to the surface with an enormous fish in their arms, while a third person, standing on the shore, is endeavouring to despatch it by repeated blows with a log. Great was the amusement of my Andaman friends, and also of those natives of India, who, from long residence among them in the homes are well aware of the degree of skill they are capable of manifesting in their various pursuits, to learn the wonderful prowess attributed to them, and a hearty laugh was indulged in at the artist's expense, who, however, it will be seen from the foregoing, did not draw entirely upon his fertile imagination for the incident.

[1] Since my return to the Andamans in September, 1882, by way of testing their powers of remaining under water, I timed three *áryôto-* youths, who were instructed to do their best to distinguish themselves. One reappeared above the water after an interval of forty seconds, and made excuses for himself, while the other two remained down for fully seventy seconds, and could doubtless have held out longer had any sufficient inducement been offered them by way of reward.

PART II.

Language—Adoption—Relationships—Proper Names—Initiatory Ceremonies—Marriage—Death and Burial—Meeting and Parting, &c.—Fire—Superstitions—Religious Beliefs and Demonology—Mythology.

BEFORE we enter upon the consideration of the marital relations customs, superstitions, traditions, and beliefs of these aborigines, I wish to say a few words in reference to the dialects or languages spoken by the various tribes, more especially the language spoken by the *.bō̆jig-ngī́ji-*, or South Andaman tribe. As I shall presently show, the people themselves have a legend[1] to account for the linguistical distinctions existing in their midst; but, on a subject of such importance as the origin of an unwritten language, the traditions current among the savages who speak it have rarely, if ever, I believe, been known to throw any light.

Language.—1. A few short lists of Andamanese words have been prepared from time to time, commencing, I think, with Colebrooke, who visited the islands nearly a century ago; but

[1] *Vide post* "Mythology," paragraphs 14 and 22.

owing to a variety of circumstances, not the least of which was the absence of any system of representing the sounds in the language—each author having chosen to employ a phonetic code best understood by himself and capable of varying interpretation by others—the result has been, to say the least, unsatisfactory, and the words for the most part are, in their printed form, either wholly unrecognisable by the people themselves, or possess a meaning differing very much from that given.

2. I do not make these remarks with a view of depreciating the efforts of others, for I fully recognise the difficulties with which they had to contend, and am aware that these exceeded any I have had to overcome, consequent on the improved relations which have subsisted between ourselves and the aborigines in recent years.

3. It must also be borne in mind that time necessarily works vast changes in all savage languages, which depend so entirely upon the oral correctness of the whole population for their accurate transmission.

4. As my knowledge of the other dialects is not as yet sufficient for me to be able to describe them comparatively at any length—leisure having failed me to obtain more than a few hundred words of five of the seven remaining tribes of Great Andaman—I wish it to be understood that, except where otherwise stated, my remarks refer to the *.bō'jig-ngī'ji-*, or South Andaman dialect.

5. The Andamanese are, as a rule, very conservative, and prefer to coin from their own resources rather than to borrow from aliens, words expressing ideas or objects which are new to them. To give only one of many examples:—having themselves no forms of worship, they had no word for "prayer," but since seeing the Mahomedans at their daily devotions, and learning that they are addressing an Invisible Being, they express the act by a compound word, *ā'rlalik-yā'b-*, signifying "daily repetition" (viz.: *ā'rla-* daily, and *ik-yā'b-* repetition).

6. They have also a distinct poetical dialect, and in their songs subordinate everything to rhythm, the greatest liberties being thereby taken not only with the forms of their words, but even with the grammatical construction of the sentences. For instance the chorus of one of their songs runs thus:—

chā'klā yā lak'a mā'j'rā!

which means "who missed the hard (backed) turtle?" the prose construction of the sentence being *mā'ja yā'dī chē'balen lā'kāchī're?* It will be at once noticed how great is the difference between the two versions, for in this, as in most of their songs, the words in their poetic form are so mutilated to suit the metre as to be scarcely recognisable; indeed, it not unfrequently happens that the composer of a new song has to explain its meaning in the ordinary vernacular to his chorus[1] as well as to the audience in general.

7. It may perhaps interest some of my readers to see a comparative table which I have prepared of the various forms of the possessive pronominal adjectives in most frequent use among five of the eight tribes of Great Andaman:

	.Bō'jig-ngī'ji-	*.Bō'jig-yā'b-*	*.A'kà-kō'l-*	*.Ako-jū'wai-*	*.Bal'awa-*
my ..	*dī'a-* ..	*li'ya-* ..	*li'ya* ..	*li'ya* ..	*deg'e.*
thy ..	*ngī'a-* ..	*ngī'ya-* ..	*ngī'ya* ..	*ngī'ya* ..	*ngeg'e.*
his ..	*ī'a-* ..	*ī'ya-* ..	*ī'ya* ..	*āi'ya* ..	*eg'e.*
our ..	*mē'ta-* ..	*mī'ya-* ..	*mī'ya* ..	*mī'ya* ..	*mai'tat.*
your ..	*ē'ta-* ..	*ngūrdī'ra- li'ya-* ..	*ngūrdī'ra- lī'ya* ..	*ngarnkā'par- lī'ya* ..	*ngō'tat.*
their ..	*ō'nta-* ..	*nō'ngtō'le- li'ya-* ..	*ō'nūtō'le- abo-li'ya* ..	*nard'ngūiok- li'ya* ..	*ē'tat.*

8. There are in each dialect several other forms of possessive pronominal adjectives, each of which must be used with its own class of nouns, but I do not now purpose entering into particulars regarding them. The form which, roughly speaking, is of general application among the *bō'jig-ngī'ji-* is, as I have just shown, that of *dī'a-*, *ngī'a-*, &c. Ex.:—*dī'a kā'rama-*, my bow; *mē'ta yā'dī-*, our turtle; the exceptions to its use being, (*a*) those nouns denoting human objects, (*b*) those indicating the various parts of the body,[2] and (*c*) certain other nouns denoting degrees of relationship. To be as brief as possible, I will give but one or two examples of each.

(*a*)

dī'a-, my..	*mē'tat*, our	Ex. *dī'a ābō'la-*, my man.
ngī'a-, thy	*ē'tat*, your	*mē'tat ai-pail-*, our women.
ī'a-, his	*ō'ntat*, their	
l'ī.a-, ——'s	*l'ō'ntat*, ——s'	

[1] I cannot here enter into particulars regarding their songs and choruses, an account of which will be hereafter given under "Games and Amusements."

[2] For a complete list of these *vide* Appendix G.

(*b*)

I. Used with words indicating the head, brain, occiput, scalp, neck, nape, chest, lung, heart, &c.

dōt, my	*mō'tot*, our	Ex.: *dōt chē'ta-*,
ngōt, thy..	*ngō'tot*, your	my head.
ōt, his	*ō'tot*, their	*ō'tot lō'ngota-*,
l'ōt, ——'s	*l'ō'tot*, ——s'	their necks.

II. Used with words indicating the hand, finger, wrist, knuckle, nail, foot, toe, heel, ankle, &c.

dōng, my	*mōi'ot*, our	Ex.: *ngōng tō'go-*,
ngōng, thy	*ngōi'ot*, your	thy wrist.
ōng, his	*ōi'ot*, their	*ōi'ot pāg-*,
l'ōng, ——'s	*l'ōi'ot*, ——s'	their feet.

III. Used with words indicating the shoulder, arm, breast, face, temple, cheek, nose, ear, eye, gum, tear, tooth, &c.

dīg, my	*mit'ig*, our	Ex.: *ngīg tō'go-*,
ngīg, thy	*ngit'ig*, your	thy shoulder.
īg, his	*it'ig*, their	*mit'ig tāg-*,
l'īg, ——'s	*l'it'ig*, ——s'	our teeth.

(N.B.—The words for eye, eye-lid, and eye-lash, generally take the abbreviated form, *dĭ*, *ngĭ*, *ĭ*, *mit'i*, *ngit'i*, *it'i*.)

IV. Used with words indicating the body, back, spine, thigh, calf of leg, elbow, knee, rib, stomach, spleen, liver, shoulder-blade, &c.

dab, my	*mat*, our	Ex.: *dab chā'u-*,
ngab, thy	*ngat*, your	my body.
ab, his	*at*, their	*at pā'rēlā-*,
l'ab, ——'s	*l'at*, ——s'	their ribs.

V. Used with the words indicating leg, hip, loin, bladder, &c.

dar, my	*mar'at*, our	Ex.: *dar chāg-*,
ngar, thy	*ngar'at*, your	my leg.
ar, his	*ar'at*, their	*ar'at chā'rag-*,
l'ar, ——'s	*l'ar'at*, ——s'	their hips.

VI. Used with words indicating mouth, chin, lip, throat, palate, tongue, gullet, jaw-bone, collar-bone, breath, &c.

dá·kà, my	*mak·at*, our	Ex.: *ngá·kà bang-*,
ngá·kà, thy	*ngak·at*, your	thy mouth.
á·kà, his	*ak·at*, their	*ak·at ĕ·kib-*,
l'á·kà, ——'s	*l'ak·at*, ——s'	their jaw-bones.

VII. Used apparently only with the word indicating waist.

dó·to, my	*mó·to*, our	Ex.: *dó·to kī·nab-*,
ngó·to, thy	*ngó·to*, your	my waist.
ó·to, his	*ó·to*, their	*mó·to kī·nab-*,
l'ó·to, ——'s	*l'ó·to*, ——s'	our waists.

(*c*)

I.

dab, my	*mat*, our	Ex.: *dab mai·ola*,
ngab, thy	*ngat*, your	my father.
ab, his	*at*, their	*dab ĕ·tinga-*,
l'ab, ——'s	*l'at*, ——s'	my mother.

II.

dá·kà, my	*mak·at*, our	Ex.: *dá·kà bàm-*,
ngá·kà, thy	*ngak·at*, your	my younger brother.
á·kà, his	*ak·at*, their	
l'á·kà, ——'s	*l'ak·at*, ——s'	

III.

dar or *dár*, my	*mar·at*, our	Ex.: *dar ó·dire*,
ngar or *ngár*, thy ..	*ngar·at*, your	my son.
ar or *ár*, his	*ar·at*, their	
l'ar or *l'ár*, —— 's ..	*l'ar·at*, ——s'	

IV.

dai, my	*mē·tat*, our	Ex.: *dai ik·yá·te-*,
ngai, thy..	*ē·tat*, your	my wife.
ai, his	*ó·ntat*, their	*ó·ntat pail-*,
l'ai, ——'s	*l'ó·ntat*, ——s'	their wives.

V.

ad, my	*mē·tat*, our	Ex.: *ad ik·yá·te-*,
ong, thy	*ē·tat*, your	my husband.
ó, his	*ó·ntat*, their	*ē·tat bū·la-*,
l'ó, ——'s	*l'ó·ntat*, ——s'	your husbands.

VI.

ad-en, my	*am-et*, our	Ex.: *ad-en ib·bare*, my elder brother.
ang-en, thy	*ang-et*, your	*ang-et ib·bare-pail-*, your elder sisters.
á-en, his	*á-et*, their	
l'á-en, ——'s	*l'á-et*, ——s'	

VII.

döt, my	*mō·tot*, our	Ex.: *döt chā·tinga-*, my adopted son.
ngōt, thy	*ngō·tot*, your	
ōt, his	*ō·tot*, their	
l'ōt, ——'s	*l'ō·tot*, ——s'	

VIII.

dob, my	*mob·et*, our	Ex.: *dob aden·ire*, my step-son.
ngob, thy	*ngob·et*, your	
ob, his	*ob·et*, their	
l'ob, ——'s	*l'ob·et*, ——s'	

9. Lieutenant R. C. Temple, in his Notes on my translation of the Lord's Prayer into *.bōjig-ngōji-* quotes some of the remarks made by Dr. Caldwell on the Australian languages, which he considers can with perfect truth be applied to the Andamanese dialects. The grammatical structure exhibits a general agreement with the languages of the Scythian group; in both we find the use of postpositions instead of prepositions; they also agree in the formation of inceptive, causative, and reflective verbs by the addition of certain particles to the root, as well as generally in the agglutinative structure of words and their position in a sentence.

10. In the same work, six sentences in *.bōjig-ngōji-* and *.bōjig-yá·b-*,[1] such as would occur in daily conversation, are given as examples to illustrate the diversity of speech in two adjacent tribes. Only three out of some thirty words are there

[1] Or, in the language of that district, *.pú·chik-wār-*. Both *yáb-* in South Andaman, and *wār-* in South of Middle Andaman, signify "language." As will shortly be explained under "Mythology," the belief held by all, or the majority of the tribes of Great Andaman, is that the *.bō·jig-yá·b-* is the original language spoken by their remote ancestors, and from which the various other existing dialects have sprung. The word *bō·jig* is used in a special sense to denote "our," or "our style of." Ex.: *.bō·jig-ngō·ji-* (the South Andaman tribe's name for itself), literally, *our friends*; *.bō·jig-yá·b-* (their name for the tribe on their northern border), literally, *our language*; *mī·a ngen bō·to bō·jig kā·rama mā·are?* Who gave you that *bō·jig* (*i.e.*, our style of) bow? [As shown in Appendix B, item 1, this term is used to distinguish the description used by the five tribes occupying Middle and South Andaman and the Archipelago, from the bows of the *.yā·rawa-* *i.e.*, the three North Andaman tribes), and the *.jā·rawa-*.]

shown to be the same in both languages, while they differ in *every inflection*, from which fact it will readily be understood that, apart from the great difficulties of inter-communication, the task of acquiring a knowledge of the dialects of the remaining eight tribes must be one involving considerable sacrifice of time and labour, such as, I fear, it is hopeless to expect any government officer, unless specially deputed for the work, will be able to accomplish during his term of service.

11. Before concluding this part of my subject I will add an extract from a letter received in August, 1881, from my friend and fellow-worker in this branch of my studies, Lieutenant R. C. Temple (cantonment magistrate at Ambála), which he authorises me to publish as embodying his opinion after a careful study of the vocabularies and other data which I have collected and forwarded to him: "The Andaman languages are one group; they are like (*i.e.*, connected with) no other group; they have no affinities by which we might infer their connection with any other known group. The word-construction (the etymology of the old grammarians) is two-fold, *i.e.*, they have affixes and prefixes to the root of a *grammatical* nature. The general principle of word-construction is agglutination pure and simple. In adding their affixes they follow the principles of the ordinary agglutinative tongues; in adding their prefixes they follow the well defined principles of the South African tongues. Hitherto, as far as I know, the two principles in full play have never been found together in any other language. Languages which are found to follow the one have the other in only a rudimentary form present in them. In Andamanese both are fully developed, so much so as to interfere with each other's grammatical functions. The collocation of the words[1] (or 'syntax,' to follow the old nomenclature) is that of the agglutinative languages purely. The presence of the peculiar prefixes does not interfere with this; the only way in which they affect the syntax is to render the frequent use possible of long compounds almost polysynthetic in their nature, or, to put it another way, of long compounds which are sentences in themselves, but the construction of these words is not synthetic but agglutinative, and they are *as words* either compound nouns or verbs taking their place in the sentence, and having the same relation to the other words in it as they would were they to be introduced into a sentence in any other agglutinative language. There are of course many peculiarities of grammar in the Andamanese group, and even in each member of the group, but these are only

[1] For an example of this the reader is referred to "Wō'i's statement," which will be found in Appendix F.

such as are incidental to the grammar of the other languages, and do not affect its general tenor. I consider, therefore, that the Andamanese languages belong to the agglutinative stage of development, and are distinguished from other groups by the presence in full development of the principle of prefixed and affixed grammatical additions to the roots of words."

12. As it is my intention to arrange and publish at an early date the results of my study of the various Andamanese dialects, I will not detain the reader with any further remarks on the subject. I have the less scruple in here dealing cursorily with this important point, as I have been so fortunate as to interest no less an authority than Mr. A. J. Ellis, F.R.S., who—after examining my vocabulary, containing probably about 6,000 words,[1] with examples of their use, together with a copious treatise on the grammar prepared by Lieutenant Temple from my notes[2]—incorporated a valuable paper on the South Andamanese language in his annual presidential address, which was delivered before the Philological Society on the 19th May, 1882.[3]

Adoption.—1. I have already pointed out several instances in which we find, on closer acquaintance with the race, that mistaken views have been entertained, and that both astonishment and merriment were evoked from the aborigines by the narration of certain of the habits and customs attributed to them, especially in connection with their social and marital relations.

2. It is generally admitted that one of the surest tests of a man's character may be found in the treatment women meet with at his hands; judged by this standard these savages are qualified to teach a valuable lesson to many of the fellow-countrymen of those who have hastily set them down as "an anomalous race of the most degraded description."

3. In a previous section I have mentioned that self-respect and modesty characterise their intercourse with one another, and

[1] And yet we find it stated by Figuier that "language is extremely limited among them;" and by Surgeon-Major Hodder that it "consists of a few words, and these sound harsh and explosive, and are principally monosyllables;" but it will be sufficient to refer to Mr. Ellis's interesting digest of the Andaman MSS. above mentioned, and to Wōi's statement (Appendix F), to disprove the assertions of these writers.

[2] I would take this opportunity to express my acknowledgments of the great assistance afforded me by Mr. Temple in my philological researches. The result of his study of my vocabulary and notes on the Andamanese languages during a little over two years, is comprised in a large number of MSS. on the Grammar (above referred to) which, from lack of leisure, he has been compelled reluctantly to return to me for completion.

[3] A reprint of which instructive report is, with the kind permission of the author, appended to this monograph.

that the young are early instructed in the duties of hospitality, while the aged, the suffering, and the helpless are objects of special attention; that their moral code is not confined within these limits will be seen as I proceed.

4. The curious, but by no means uncommon,[1] savage custom of adoption prevails among them, from which, however, it must not be inferred that love of offspring is a characteristic in which they are at all deficient, for this is far from being the case.

5. It is said to be of rare occurrence to find any child above six or seven years of age residing with its parents, and this because it is considered a compliment and also a mark of friendship[2] for a married man, after paying a visit, to ask his hosts to allow him to adopt one of their children. The request is usually complied with, and thenceforth the child's home is with his (or her) foster-father (*mai-ōt-chā'tuga-*): though the parents in their turn adopt the children of other friends, they nevertheless pay continual visits to their own child, and occasionally ask permission (!) to take him (or her) away with them for a few days.

6. A man is entirely at liberty to please himself in the number of children he adopts, but he must treat them with kindness and consideration, and in every respect as his own sons and daughters, and they, on their part, render him filial affection and obedience.

7. It not unfrequently happens that in course of time permission to adopt a foster-child is sought by a friend of the *soi-disant* father, and is at once granted (unless any exceptional circumstance should render it personally inconvenient), without even the formality of a reference to the actual parents, who are merely informed of the change in order that they may be enabled to pay their periodical visits.

8. Foster-parents constantly manifest much opposition to any desire they may observe on the part of the lads they have brought up, to make a home for themselves, for the selfish reason that they are useful in a variety of ways, above all, when they have acquired skill in hunting, turtling, &c.; over the maidens little or no restraint is imposed, as their marriage entails but a trifling loss in a material sense on those who have reared them.

9. Human nature, however, is the same all the world over, and boys will be boys even in the Andaman jungles, so it is not surprising that, in spite of all the precautions taken by their

[1] *Vide* Lubbock, "On the Origin of Civilisation," &c., p. 98.

[2] Whether this be the true explanation of its object and origin or not, there can be little doubt that it has the effect of greatly extending the intercourse between the members of the various encampments.

seniors, a good deal of flirtation, and often something more, is carried on by the young people without arousing any suspicions as to their sentiments for one another, until the affair has become too serious to be broken off, and has to end, sooner or later, in their marriage and start in life on their own account. In some cases, when the guardians have reason to believe that a lad has, notwithstanding his assurances to the contrary, a *sub silentio* attachment, they adopt the following method for testing the truth of his asseveration; on a given day it is arranged by the friends of the suspected couple that they shall (without the knowledge of either) be painted respectively with the red oxide of iron unguent, *kòi·ob-*, and the white clay *tá·la-òg-*, for, as they would not meet till night-fall, the risk of their discovering the trap laid for them is reduced to a minimum, while a glance on the following morning would suffice to betray them if guilty, and the guardians' object would be attained, for, from shame at his secret being known, and his falsehood exposed, the youth feels in honour bound to break off his connection with the girl, at least for some time.

Relationships.—1. In all the relations of life the question of propinquity is, in their eyes, of paramount importance, and marriage is only permissible between those who are known to be not even distantly connected, except by wedlock, with each other; so inexorable, indeed, is this rule, that it extends, and applies equally, to such as are related merely by the custom of adoption to which I have just referred.

2. A first cousin, actual or by adoption, is regarded as a half-brother or half-sister, as the case may be, and nephews and nieces almost as sons and daughters, while the terms used to denote a grandfather, grandmother, grandson, and grand-daughter are equally applied to indicate respectively a grand-uncle, grand-aunt, grand-nephew, and grand-niece.

3. Parents, when addressing, or referring to their children and not using their names, employ distinct terms, the father calling his son *dar ō·dire*, *i.e.*, he that has been begotten by me, and his daughter *dar ō·dire-pail-*; while the mother makes use of the word *dab ē·tire*, *i.e.*, he whom I have borne, for the former, and *dab ē·tire-pail-* for the latter; similarly, friends in speaking of children to their parents say respectively, *ngar ō·dire*, or *ngab ē·tire* (your son), *ngar ō·dire-pail-*, or *ngab ē·tire-pail-* (your daughter).[1]

4. Uncles and aunts on the father's are not distinguished from those on the mother's side; relationships are traced in both lines, and the system with reference to either sex is identical.

[1] Foster-parents employ the terms *dòt ekà·taga-* and *dòt ekà·taga-pail-* in referring to their adopted son and daughter respectively.

5. In consequence of the shortness of their lives, their ignorance of any method of maintaining accurate records, and last, not least, the unavoidable complications arising from their system of adoption, it naturally follows that they fail in tracing, and therefore in recognising, relationships beyond the third generation.

6. In addressing a senior male relative, the term *mai'a* or *mai'ola* is employed; if of equal standing, and a father, the same; but if not a parent, the term *mar* is prefixed to his name; if junior, he would be addressed by his name only. The same system applies to the females, with whom *chāna'*[1] or *chā'nola* takes the place of *mai'a* and *mai'ola*, and the "flower" name, to which I can now make but a brief allusion,[2] the place of *mar;* these terms, *mai'a, chāna,* &c., are equivalent to Mr., Sir, Mrs., Madam, &c.[3] Sir John Lubbock, in his well known work "On the Origin of Civilization,"[4] points out the existence of a similar custom among the *Telugus* and *Tamils.*

7. In a table I have prepared,[5] and which I believe to be fairly complete, there are about sixty terms, exclusive of equivalents, employed to denote the various degrees of relationship recognised by this race. It will there be seen that, as among the Australians near Sydney, mentioned by the Rev. W. Ridley,[6] brothers and sisters speak of one another by titles that indicate relative age; that is, their words for brother and sister involve the distinction of elder or younger, while a like system is adopted in respect to half-brothers, half-sisters, cousins, brothers-in-law, and sisters-in-law.

8. In addressing the relatives of a wife or husband, or a brother's wife, or sister's husband—provided such be senior to the speaker—the term *mām*[7] is used.

9. A man or woman may not marry into the family of their brothers- or sisters-in-law, but there is no rule against a man marrying a girl bearing the same name as himself, either in another tribe or in his own community, the *only* bar being that of consanguinity or adoption.

10. The nearest of kin to a widow or widower are, (1) the grown-up children, (2) the parents, and (3) the brothers and sisters.

Proper Names.—1. One of the alleged[8] peculiarities of the

[1] Not "*Chaunah*," as given by Dr. Day.

[2] *Vide* next section, paragraph 9.

[3] "According to Williams ('Fiji and the Fijians') their (*i.e.*, the Fijian) languages contain expressions which exactly correspond to the French *Monsieur* and *Madame*." (Peschel, p. 246.)

[4] *Vide* 4th edition, p. 164.

[5] *Vide* Appendix I.

[6] *Vide* "Journ. Anthrop. Inst.," vol. ii, p. 266.

[7] This term is likewise employed in addressing a chief.

[8] *Vide* Tickell.

Andamanese is that they have no proper names, whereas their system of naming is, on the contrary, somewhat elaborate, and commences even prior to the child's birth.

2. When there is reason to expect an increase to the family,[1] the parents decide what name the child shall bear; as a compliment they not unfrequently select one which is borne by a relative, friend, or chief; and, since all their proper names[2] are common to both sexes,[3] no difficulty arises on this score.

3. In illustration of this let us suppose the name chosen in advance to be *.dō·ra*; should the infant prove to be a boy he is called *.dō·ra-ō·ta-*, or, if a girl, *.dō·ra-kā·ta-*. These terms (*ō·ta-* and *kā·ta-*[4]) are used only during the first two or three years, after which, until the period of puberty, the lad would be addressed as *.dō·ra-dā·la-*, and the girl as *.dō·ra-pō·ilola* until she arrived at womanhood, when she is said to be *ōn-lā·wi-* or *ā·kā-lā·wi-*, and receives a "flower" name[5] as a prefix to her proper or birth name. By this method they are apparently able to determine when their young women become marriageable. There are eighteen prescribed trees[6] which blossom in succession, and the "flower" name bestowed in each case is taken from the one which is in season when the girl attains maturity; if, for example, this should be about the end of August, when the *chā·langa-* (*Pterocarpus dalbergioides*) is in flower, *.dō·ra-pō·ilola* would become *.chā·gara*[7] *.dō·ra*, and this double name would cling

[1] When near her delivery a woman will sometimes be heard saying (assuming the name chosen for the yet unborn child to be *.wō·loga*): *.wō·loga dak-ē-jūlike*, Wō·loga is fidgetting me, or *.wō·loga dab-ngō·lowake*, Wō·loga is clawing me, or, *.wō·loga ō·to-yārke*, Wō·loga is ready. [During the period of pregnancy, both the woman and her husband are spoken of as *pīj-jō·bag-*, which signifies "bad hair;" the only explanation offered for the adoption of such a term is that it is in allusion to the fœtus.]

[2] These number forty. (*Vide* Appendix H.)

[3] A man calls a male namesake { if his senior, *mai'a ting·la.* / if his equal or junior } *mar ting·la.*
" " female " *chān ting·la.*
A man (or woman) calls a child of either sex bearing the same name } *dal ot-ting-ō-te-yā·te-* (my-name-which-who).
A woman calls a male namesake { if her senior, *mai'a* (his name) *ting·la.* / if her equal or junior } *mar* (his name) *ting·la.*
" " female " if her senior, *chān ting·la.*
" " " " if her equal or junior } (her name) *ting·la.*

[4] Signifying respectively the genitals of the male and female.

[5] Dr. Day writes: "Girls arriving at a marriageable age wear certain flowers to distinguish themselves by"; but, as a fact, the flower is neither worn nor gathered.

[6] Names of these will be found in Appendix H.

[7] Euphonic corruption of *.chā·langa-*.

to the girl until she married and was a mother,[1] then the "flower" name would give way to the more dignified term *chā'na* (madam or mother) *.dō'ra*; if childless, a woman has generally to pass a few years of married life before she is called *chā'na*,[2] after which no further change is made in her name.

4. In consequence of this system, as it rarely happens that in one community two women are found bearing the same "flower" *and* birth names, there is little chance of confusion arising.

5. Since no equivalent custom exists with regard to men,[3] nicknames are given which generally indicate some personal peculiarity, as, for instance, *.bī'a-pdg-* (*Bī'a-*, foot, he having large feet), *.bal'a-jū'bo-* (*Bal'a-*, snake, he having lost a hand from a snake-bite), *.pū'nga-dā'la* (*Pū'nga-*, good-looking), and so on. All these names cling to the bearer for life, especially if they refer to some physical deformity.

6. Seniors often address young married persons in a (to us) strange fashion, *i.e.*, calling the husband by the wife's name and prospective designation; for example, in speaking to a man whose name is *.ī'ra*, and who had married a woman called *.tū'ra*, they would say *chā'na .tū'ra*; if the wife were *enceinte* the child's name would be used beforehand to denote its parents; thus, assuming *.wō'loga* to be the name of the yet unborn child, the father would be called by that name, and the expectant mother *.wō'loga-bŭd-*[4] until after the birth of the infant, when, for several months, the former would still bear the same appellation among his seniors, but would receive from his juniors the more dignified title of *mai'a .wō'loga*; while the latter would be addressed by her seniors as *.wō'loga-ō'ta-* (or *kō'ta-* in the case of her child being a girl), and by her juniors as *chā'na .wō'loga-ō'ta-* (or *kō'ta-*).[5]

Initiatory Ceremonies.—1. On or soon after reaching puberty, the fast[6] which has been kept during the few previous years (or in some cases, months) is broken; and instead of the affix *dā'la*, the prefix *gū'ma'*[7] (denoting in this connection a neophyte or

[1] From the account given under "Marriage," paragraph 4, it will be inferred that in many cases she has not long to wait.

[2] *Vide* section on "Relationships," paragraph 6.

[3] In a few cases nicknames are bestowed on women.

[4] *bŭd-* signifies house, habitation.

[5] For further information on the subject of proper names and terms applied to men and women, *vide* sections on "Relationships" and "Initiatory Ceremonies," and Appendices I and K.

[6] *Vide* section on "Tabu."

[7] In Dr. Day's paper the following passage occurs:—"The youthful swain eats a peculiar kind of ray-fish termed *goom-dah*, which gives him the title to the appellation of *goo-mo*, signifying, 'a bachelor desirous of marrying.' Girls arriving at a marriageable age . . . . (*vide* footnote 5 on previous page). Before marrying, young men take a species of oath, after which they sit very still for several days, scarcely taking any food." Plausible as this explanation

novice) is attached to the boy's birth-name; he is also addressed as *mar*[1] *gū·ma* (master novice) if senior to, and alone with the speaker: this term *gū·ma* is retained until the lad is married and is a father, after which *mai·a*[2] (Mr.)—or, if a chief, *mai·ola*—is adopted in its place, and by this title he would be known for the rest of his life. A young chief, however, attains the honorary designation of *mai·a* as soon as the novitiate terminates.[3]

2. The *ā·kà-yā·p-*, or fasting period (during which turtle, honey, pork, fish, and a few other favourite articles of food[4] are *choses défendues*), commences between the 11th and 13th year, and varies in length from one to five years; it is observed by both sexes, but lasts longer in the case of girls, with whom, indeed, it is not terminable till some time after matrimony. As an *ā·kà-yā·b-* makes up for these restrictions by eating a larger quantity of other food, he (or she) does not ordinarily suffer in physique during the probationary period. It does not rest with the youth or maiden to determine when he, or she, will resume eating the various articles above mentioned, but with the chief, who decides when each individual's powers of endurance and self-denial have been sufficiently tested. Exceptional cases are cited in which the probationer has expressed a desire to prolong the time of abstinence, it being a cause for boasting when the average period has been exceeded.

3. As at present understood, the *ā·kà-yā·p-* is regarded as a test of the endurance, or, more properly speaking, of the self-denial of young persons, and as affording evidence of their fitness and ability to support a family. It is divided into three periods: 1st, the *yā·di-* (turtle) *gū·mul-*; 2nd, the *ā·ja-* (honey) *gū·mul-*; and 3rd, the *reg-jī·ri-* (kidney-fat of pig) *gū·mul-*.[5]

4. When the youth is permitted, and agrees, to break his turtle fast, a feast is arranged by his friends, consisting entirely of that delicacy. The chief, or headman present, first boils in a pot (*būj-*[6]) a large piece of turtle-fat, which, when sufficiently cool, he

may appear, there is no connection between *gūm-*, a ray-fish, and *gū·ma* (a youth who has undergone his probationary fast); moreover, as mentioned in a foregoing section (*vide* "Proper Names"), marriageable young women do not derive their "flower" names in the manner here described; in point of fact, no such custom as "wearing flowers" is practised by any class.

[1] *Vide* section on "Relationships," paragraph 6.

[2] As with the term *chā·na* among women, the title is not bestowed for several years if there be no child.

[3] Both before and after the *ā·kà-yā·p-* the individual is said to be *bī·lìga-*.

[4] These comprise the flesh of the iguana and paradoxurus, the larvæ of the Great Capricornis beetle (*ōi·yum-*), and a smaller insect called *bū·tu-*.

[5] It will thus be seen that the *gū·mul-* answers very much to the Australian "born," or ceremony of initiation into the privileges of manhood, spoken of by the Rev. W. Ridley in his Report on Australian Languages and Traditions (*vide* "Journ. Anthrop. Inst.," vol. ii, p. 269, 1873).

[6] *Vide* Appendix B, item 18.

pours over the head of the lad, who remains seated and perfectly still in the midst of his friends while the oil streams over his body. The men present remove any ornaments that he may be wearing, and rub the grease into his person; the women and children meantime occupy themselves with crying, the idea being that, after abstaining from turtle for a long time, madness, illness, or even death, may result from partaking of it again.[1] After this the novice, who may not wash off the oil with which he has been anointed at least until late on the following day, is fed with the flesh of the turtle,[2] of which a certain quantity is reserved for his consumption on the ensuing two or three days, and the remainder is distributed among those assembled. He is then led to his hut and directed to sit cross-legged on a spot covered with leaves of the *Myristica longifolia*, with a support behind him against which he may lean. The turtle flesh, previously cooked and set apart for him, is deposited at his side, and one or more of his friends take it by turns to sit with him, it being their duty to enjoin silence, to supply his wants, and to prevent him from falling asleep by singing from time to time as the night wears away. The following morning his mother, sister, and other female relatives, come and weep[3] over him, and paint, first, his ears and the adjoining parts with *pā·tŭ-tăla-ŏg-*, and afterwards his entire person with alternate stripes of this compound and *tā·la-ŏg-*. Some large leaves[4] made into two broom-like bundles are placed in his hands, and other leaves are placed in his waistbelt. Thus provided he rises and dances frantically,[5] swinging his arms at the same time, for an hour or more, while the women, who are seated with legs outstretched, keep time for him by slapping the hollow between their thighs with the palm of the right hand, which is held at the wrist by the other hand; the males look on, or, if they have gone through the ceremony themselves, accompany him in his performance.

5. After an hour or so, when, fatigued with his exertions, the youth stops dancing, the *yā·dī-gŭ·mul-* is considered at an end, and the new *gŭ·ma* mingles with his friends, who, nevertheless,

[1] The same reason is given for the silence which the neophyte has to observe during this ceremony, as well as at the *ō·ja-gŭ·mul-* and *ŏg-jĭ·ri-gŭ·mul-*.

[2] He is then said to *gŭ·mul ŏdŏ·ke* (or *gŭ·mul lĕ·ke*), *i.e.*, to eat, or devour, the *gŭ·mul-*.

[3] The reason given for this demonstration of grief is that the youth has now entered upon an important epoch in his life, and is about to experience the trials and vicissitudes incidental thereto.

[4] The leaves of the *Myristica longifolia* (*bŭ·rema-*) are usually selected on these occasions, apparently because this tree is associated with turtle-hunting, paddles being made of the wood.

[5] The step is a peculiar one, and is only seen on these occasions: the performer keeps his heels together and stamps on the ground, at the same time he swings his arms violently, holding in his hands the two leaf brooms.

continue to watch him carefully for two or three days, lest harm should result from his recent feast, and also because they think evil spirits are not unlikely to do him some injury by taking advantage of his supposed helpless condition to make him deaf, or cause him to forget his way, and thus meet the fate which, on the faith of their traditions, they believe to have overtaken two of their antediluvian ancestors.[1]

6. All that has been said of youths in respect to the *yâ·dī-gŭ·mul-* applies equally to young women, except that matrons remove the novice's ornaments, and all but one or two of her *bōd-s* (waistbelts[2]), and her *ō·bunga-* (leaf apron[3]), which are left for the sake of decency. As, while performing the concluding dance, some difficulty is experienced in regard to the *ō·bunga-*, girls are provided on these occasions with a more substantial apron of leaves, so that the feelings of the most prudish are not violated.

7. The origin of the term *gŭ·mul-lē·ke* is obscure, and inquiries have failed to elicit any satisfactory explanation regarding it; the literal translation is "rainy-monsoon devour-does," and though the *yâ·dī-gŭ·mul-* is always celebrated at that season of the year, the term is also applied to the honey feast, which can only take place during the dry months. The same equivalents are found in the other tribal dialects, so that the peculiarity is not confined to the *.bō·jig-ngi·ji-*. The only reasonable explanation offered is that the expression is in allusion to the sweaty (*gŭ·mar-*), or rain-like (*yŭm-*), appearance of the novice when the melted fat or honey has been poured and smeared over his person.

8. Lengthened intercourse with the alien population in their midst has naturally led to their occasionally betraying some indifference in regard to customs, such as that above described; especially is this the case with those who have been brought up in the orphanage at Ross Island. A few years ago one of these youngsters, who had been named Martin, refused to accede to the wishes of his friends in the jungle home to which he had returned, and persisted in partaking of the articles of food proscribed to all of his age; as he happened shortly after to fall sick and die, they were fully persuaded that he had incurred his fate by failing to comply with the ancient rites and ceremonies as handed down by their fathers.

9. On the conclusion of the *yâ·dī-gŭ·mul-*, the youth is said to be an *d·kà-gŭ·mul-*, and, as before stated, is addressed as *gŭ·ma*; but this is not the case with the girl, possibly because she, at

[1] *Vide post* "Mythology," paragraph 25.
[2] *Vide* Appendix B, item 25.
[3] *Vide* Appendix B, item 79.

this period of her life, receives a "flower" name,[1] and does not, therefore, require any additional designation to denote that she has attained maturity. If more than one become *gū·ma* on the same day they call each other *gū·ma l'arjō·pinga-.*[2] After the *yā·dī-gū·mul-* turtles' eggs and the kidney-fat of the ray-fish and turtle may, at the bidding of the chief, be again eaten by the novice, and in the first ensuing dry season edible roots, and the heart of the *Caryota sobolifera* may be added to the bill of fare without further ceremony than the observance of strict silence on the first occasion of partaking of them.

10. Between the *yā·dī-gū·mul-* and the *ā·ja-gū·mul-* no fruit may be eaten by the novices, who have, moreover, to abstain till after the *reg-jī·ri-gū·mul-* from pig's flesh of any kind.

11. When the honey fast is to be broken, a quantity of honey-combs, according to the number assembled, are on the appointed day procured: the *ā·kà-yā·b-* being placed in the midst of the group, the chief or other elder goes to him with a large honey-comb wrapped in leaves; after helping the novice to a large mouthful, which he does by means of a bamboo or iron knife, he presents the remainder to him, and then leaves him to devour it in silence: this he does, not, however, by the ordinary method, for it is an essential part of the ceremony that he should not use his fingers to break off pieces, but eat it bear-fashion, by holding the comb up to his mouth and attacking it with his teeth and lips.[3] After satisfying his present requirements, he wraps what is left of the comb in leaves for later consumption.

12. The chief then takes another comb and anoints the youth by squeezing it over his head, rubbing the honey well into his body as it trickles down. The proceedings at this stage are interrupted by a bath, in order to remove all traces of the honey, which would otherwise be a source of considerable inconvenience by attracting ants. Beyond the observance of silence, and continued abstention from *reg-jī·ri-*, the youth is under no special restrictions, being able to eat, drink, and sleep as much as he pleases.

13. Early the following morning the lad decorates himself with leaves of a species of *Alpinia*, called *jī·ni-*,[4] and then, in the presence of his friends, goes into the sea (or, if he be an *ēre·m-tā·ga-*, into a creek) up to his waist, where, locking his thumbs

[1] *Vide ante* "Proper Names," paragraph 3.

[2] *arjō·pike*, to share, or to be a partner with another.

[3] This mode of eating is termed *pai·ke* (to use the lips), from *pai-*, the lip.

[4] This plant is selected because it is associated with honey-gathering; its bitter sap, being extremely obnoxious to bees, is smeared over their persons when taking a comb, and enables them to escape scot free with their prize (*vide post* "Food," paragraph 35).

together, with open hands he splashes as much water as possible over himself and the bystanders, occasionally ducking his head under the surface as well. This is considered a safeguard or charm against *snakes*, and the on-lookers cry "*ô·to-pal·ike, kĭ·nig wd·ra-jō·bo lŏ·tike* (Go and splash yourself, or *Wd·ra-jō·bo*[1] will get inside you), for they imagine that unless they go through this splashing performance, this snake will by some means enter their stomachs and so cause death.

14. The only difference between the sexes with respect to the *ô·ja-gū·mul-* is that with females it cannot take place until after the birth of the first child; they are also required to abstain from honey during each subsequent pregnancy; in their case, too, a chief or elder (preferably a relative) officiates, and not a woman.

15. A year is generally allowed to elapse between the *yâ·di-gū·mul-* and the *reg-jĭ·ri-gū·mul-*. When this final step is determined on, the friends and relatives of the *â·kà-yâ·b-* start on a pig hunt, and, if unsuccessful, the *gū·mul-* has to be postponed, for, in the case of a young man, it is necessary that the ceremony be performed with a boar, while for females a sow must be procured.

16. When all is ready, and the party assembled, the chief presses the carcass of the boar heavily on the shoulders, back, and limbs of the young man as he sits on the ground,[2] silent and motionless, this is in token of his hereafter becoming, or proving himself to be, courageous and strong. The animal is then cut up, and when the fat has been melted, as in the previous cases, it is poured over the novice, and rubbed into his person; he is then fed with *reg-jĭ·ri-*, and if he makes signs for water it is given him, but, until the following day, he may not utter a word, rise, or even sleep. Two or three friends generally remain with him to attend to his requirements, which he makes known to them by gestures.

17. In the morning fresh leaves of a tree called *reg lâ·kà chāl-* —the fruit of which is much eaten by the *Sus And.*—are brought, and a quantity of them are placed in the hands of the youth, and some more in his waistbelt; he then rises and, as at the turtle feast, dances until fairly exhausted. During the month following the *reg-jĭ·ri-gū·mul-*, the young persons are called *â·kà-gō·i-*, *i.e.*, "one commencing to eat."

18. It should be added that, whatever may have been the intention and practice in former years, it is not necessary at the present day for a youth to undergo these several ordeals before

[1] This is believed to be the *Ophiophagus elaps*.

[2] In the case of the woman, the carcass of the sow is not pressed in this manner on her limbs or body.

he is permitted to marry:[1] although many remain single until they have undergone these various rites, it is considered almost as binding on those who marry before doing so, to comply with these time-honoured usages at some early opportunity.

Marriage.—1. It has been asserted that the "communal marriage,"[2] system prevails among them, and that "marriage is nothing more than taking a female slave,"[3] but so far from the contract being regarded as a merely temporary arrangement, to be set aside at the will of either party, no incompatibility of temper or other cause is allowed to dissolve the union, and, while bigamy, polygamy, polyandry, and divorce are unknown, conjugal fidelity till death is not the exception, but the rule, and matrimonial differences, which, however, occur but rarely, are easily settled with or without the intervention of friends.

2. It is undoubtedly true that breaches of morality have occasionally taken place among a few of the married persons who have resided for any length of time at Port Blair, but this is only what might be expected from constant association with the Indian convict attendants at the various homes; justice, however, demands that in judging of their moral characteristics we should consider those only who have been uninfluenced by the vices or virtues of alien races.

3. As in various other savage tribes, unchastity[4] is apparently universal among the unmarried of both sexes, and is indeed so entirely disregarded that no reproof is administered, even by the nearest relatives, to those who offend in this manner; notwithstanding this laxity, the girls are strikingly modest and child-like in their demeanour, and when married are good wives and models of constancy, while their husbands do not fall far short of them in this respect. It should, however, be mentioned, that the freedom which exists between the sexes prior to wedlock, is confined to those who are not within the prescribed limits of affinity, as their customs do not permit of the union of any who are known to be even distantly related;[5] the fact of our allowing first cousins to marry seems to them highly objection-

[1] They think highly of a man who defers marriage until he is of full age, and the reverse of a youngster who rushes into matrimony before attaining the mature (!) age of eighteen.

[2] "So absolutely closely allied are the Andaman Islanders in their moral as well as physical life to the lower animals, that it is said by an eminent scientific voyager (Sir Edward Belcher) that the man and woman remain together until the mother ceases to suckle the child, after which they separate as a matter of course, and each seeks a new partner" (Brown).

[3] *Vide* Wood.

[4] "A great many races of mankind are quite indifferent to juvenile unchastity, and only impose strict conduct on their women after marriage" (Peschel).

[5] "It is precisely nations in the most primitive stage which have the greatest abhorrence of incestuous marriages" (Peschel).

able and immoral, which is turning the tables on us with a vengeance.[1]

4. In consequence of the lax code of morality prevailing among the unmarried, it not unfrequently happens that a marriage is brought about by the circumstance of the young woman being found *enceinte*. When this is the case, the guardians ascertain from her companions or herself who is the cause of her being in such a condition, and, whether it is an easy matter or not to decide this question with certainty, there never appears to be any difficulty in persuading the youth whom she names as her lover to become her husband. It thus happens that children are very rarely born out of wedlock.

5. Parents and foster-parents have the power of betrothing their children in infancy, and though subsequently, during childhood, they may be parted, the contract must be fulfilled soon after they attain a marriageable age; it is even alleged that, like the Yorubas,[2] the Andamanese look upon a girl betrothed by her parents as so far a wife that with her prematrimonial unfaithfulness is accounted a crime.

6. As soon as the betrothal has been agreed upon, the girl is taken to the hut of her future father-in-law, or foster father-in-law, and the children remain together for several months, in order that the fact of their engagement may become generally known; after this the girl returns to her old home, or is adopted by one of her father's friends. Should either of the betrothed pair die young, the survivor is not called upon to take any part at the obsequies, and is at liberty to form another alliance.

7. Until a man attains middle age he evinces great shyness in the presence of the wife of a *younger* brother or cousin, and the feeling is invariably reciprocated; it is, however, otherwise in the case of the elder brother's (or cousin's) wife, who, moreover, should she be many years his senior, receives from him much of the respect accorded to a mother. In the first of the above cases all communications are made through a third person, though under no circumstances would marriage be permissible between them; while in the latter it is almost obligatory, unless the disparity between the ages be very great.

8. It is not customary for lovers to intimate their desire of being married, but it is the duty of the guardian, or, in the case of widows and widowers, of the chief of the community, to

[1] On reference to Appendix I, it will be found that the terms which are used to denote *half-brother* and *half-sister*, are also employed to denote male and *female cousins*, showing how close they regard the relationship.

[2] Farrer's "Primitive Manners and Customs," p. 201.

arrange matters for those between whom he observes there is something more than a passing attachment.

9. Although nearly all marriages are brought about by one or other of the above-mentioned modes, it remains to be added that an individual is now and then met with who is regarded as married though he (or she) has not conformed with the prescribed ceremony; this occurs when a bachelor or widower is found asleep in one of the huts occupied by unmarried females; he and the woman beside whom he was seen are then said to be *tigmil·nga-*, which means that their union has been contracted irregularly. In such cases no ceremony or entertainment takes place, for a certain amount of discredit attaches to a couple thus united; but if their after conduct towards each other be considered satisfactory no unpleasant allusions are made to the past.

10. As they have no idea of invoking the aid or blessing of a Supreme Being, nothing of a religious character attaches itself to the marriage ceremony, which may be briefly described as follows:—On the evening of the eventful day[1] the bridal party assemble at the chief's hut or in one of those occupied by unmarried women. The bride (whether spinster or widow) sits apart, attended by one or two matrons, and the bridegroom takes his place among the bachelors until the chief, or elder, approaches him, whereupon he at once assumes a modest demeanour and simulates reluctance to move; however, after a few encouraging and re-assuring remarks he allows himself to be led slowly, sometimes almost dragged, towards his *fiancée*, who, if she be young, generally indulges in a great display of modesty, weeping and hiding her face, while her female attendants prepare her by straightening her legs; the bridegroom is then made to sit on her thighs, and torches are lighted and brought close to the pair that all present may bear witness to the ceremony having been carried out in the orthodox manner, after which the chief pronounces them duly married, and they are then at liberty to retire to the hut which has been previously prepared for their occupation.

11. Unless they have made arrangements to settle[2] elsewhere,

[1] I can find nothing to account for the statement, which appeared in Dr. Day's paper, to the effect that they "pass their marriage day staring at one another."

[2] From the fact that, sometimes from choice, and sometimes in compliance with the wishes of the bride—should she belong to another tribe—they settle down in another community, it has been inferred in Dr. Day's account that it is customary to spend the honeymoon away from their friends, but such is not the case. The same writer further states that "on the bridegroom's return to the tribe with his bride, *Jowlyo*, crying and dancing are kept up with great spirit." The word here intended is evidently *abjad·i-jô'g-*, but it means *spinster*, the word for *bride* being *ab-l'rôbil-pail-*.

the newly married couple do not leave the encampment in order to get food, or anything else that they may require, as their friends consider it a duty or privilege to supply all their needs until the shyness, consequent on the marriage, has worn off.

12. Wedding presents being as much *de rigueur* among these savages as in Mayfair, the happy pair invariably find themselves enriched by their relatives and acquaintances with the various articles of ordinary use, such as nets, buckets, bows, arrows, &c., in honour of the event.

13. On the morning following the marriage the bridegroom's mother, or other near female relative, decorates his person by painting him with *td·la-ög-*, while the bride is similarly ornamented by her friends. It often happens that a young couple will pass several days after their nuptials without exchanging a single word, and to such an extent do they carry their bashfulness that they even avoid looking at each other: in fact their conduct would lead a stranger to suppose that some serious quarrel had caused an estrangement.

14. When a few days have elapsed, and they are in some measure accustomed to the novelty of their position, they enter upon the duties of life, and conduct themselves like their neighbours: the marriage is then celebrated by a dance, in which all, save the bride and bridegroom, take part.

15. A certain amount of jealousy usually exists between young people during the first year of their married life;[1] indeed, complete confidence and genuine affection are never entirely established until they become parents or, at least, till the wife is found to be *enceinte*, and even their relationship to each other is not regarded as being so close *prior* to the birth of a child as it is *after* that event. Confirmatory evidence on this point will be given when describing the funeral rites,[2] where it will be noticed that the survivor of a childless couple is not looked upon as chief mourner.

16. There is no prohibition against second marriages, but greater respect is entertained for those who show their love and esteem for the deceased by remaining single and leading chaste lives (*ō·yun-tē·mar-bar·minga-*). It is by no means unusual for a man, even though he be young at the time of his wife's death, to remain a widower[3] for her sake for many years, or even till death;

[1] It often happens that a man will not at first allow his wife to leave their hut at night for any purpose unless he accompanies her, professedly to protect her from dangers, spiritual and temporal, but in reality to satisfy himself that she has not made an assignation.

[2] *Vide* "Death and Burial," paragraph 20.

[3] It must, however, be admitted that as their customs allow of a widow or widower consorting with the unmarried of the opposite sex, a single life is not of necessity a virtuous one, or evidence of constancy and devotion to the memory of the dear departed.

but widows generally marry again when the prescribed term has passed : this is not altogether due to inconstancy on the part of the fair (!) sex, but to the custom, to which allusion has before been made, which all but compels a bachelor or widower to propose to the childless widow of his elder brother or cousin (if she be not past her prime),[1] while she has no choice beyond remaining single or accepting him ; should she have no younger brother-in-law (or cousin by marriage), however, she is free to wed whom she will.[2]

17. A young widow who is childless usually returns to the home of her girlhood, but, if elderly, she lives in one of the huts set apart for spinsters, and those who, situated like herself, are eligible for matrimony ; during the period of her widowhood it devolves on one of her senior male relatives to act as her guardian ; it is not considered decorous that any fresh alliance should be contracted until about a year has elapsed from the date of bereavement.

18. In the case of a widow who has children, it is customary for her to remain in the same community and keep house for her family ; during widowhood—if her husband had been a chief or elder—she continues to enjoy the privileges accorded her in his lifetime. Should she re-marry and her husband happen to be a bachelor, or widower "without encumbrances," it is usual for him to join her community, and live in her hut, but if they both have families it becomes a matter of arrangement between them which establishment shall be given up.

19. Some idea of the erroneous views formerly held respecting their marital relations will be gathered from the following extracts :—(*a*) "There is promiscuous intercourse save with the parent, which only ceases in regard to the woman when she is allotted as wife to a man, but is retained as the prerogative of the male sex."[3] (*b*) "Marriage, as we understand the word, is unknown to them, and there seem to be few restrictions of consanguinity, a mother and her daughter being sometimes the wives of the same husband."[4] A similar statement appears in Dr. Brown's work, and the source of both is probably to be found in the following passage in Dr. Mouat's book, in which he publishes several extraordinary stories told by an escaped

[1] It should be added that marriage with a deceased wife's younger sister is equally a matter of necessity on the part of a *childless* widower.

[2] A case of this kind came under my notice where a young man living at one of the homes was reluctantly married to the widow of an elder brother, or cousin, who was considerably his senior, and innocent of any attractions. This *mariage de convenance* proved by no means a happy one, though, so far as could be judged, neither had any just cause of complaint against the other.

[3] *Vide* Mouat.

[4] *Vide* Wood.

convict Sepoy, named *Dúdhnáth*,[1] who had apparently spent about thirteen months with the aborigines, during the first two years of our settlement at Port Blair (1858-59):—"A man named *Pooteeah*, who doubtless considered him (*Dúdhnáth*) a desirable match, offered to bestow upon him, in what they called wedlock, his daughter *Hessa*, a young woman of twenty years of age, whose attractions were doubtless regarded as considerable among her native tribe, and a mere girl named *Zigah*, a daughter of *Hessa*, who, in that eastern part of the world, was considered quite old enough[2] for the state of marriage. As they were by no means troubled with an uneasy amount of virtue they made no objection to being assigned to the Brahmin soldier in the most unceremonious manner. The two, mother and daughter, at once recognised him as their husband." . . . . .

20. The main feature of interest in this story is, however, somewhat marred when it is discovered that the woman (*.lī·pa*[3]), who was well known to us for many years subsequent to the establishment of the homes, was a girl of not more than seventeen at the time of *Dúdhnáth*'s escape, and that she had never been a mother prior to her marriage with him.[4] The child (*.yē·ga*, not *Zigah*) was merely living under *Lī·pa's* protection, and was employed, like all children, in helping to supply the wants of her guardians. The fact of child marriages—not to mention bigamy and concubinage—being quite unknown among them, affords additional support to this statement, which is the result of careful inquiry.

21. *Dúdhnáth* being of course aware of the ignorance which prevailed at the time regarding the habits and customs of the Andamanese, appears to have availed himself of the opportunity thus afforded him of drawing largely on his imagination, probably with the object of exciting as much interest as possible in his adventures, and perhaps also of amusing himself with the wonder created by his narrative. Some of his unrecorded[5] stories seem, however, to have been still more

[1] Of all who absconded on this occasion it appears that he was so fortunate as to be the only one who was spared by the aborigines, his companions being shot down as soon as they were discovered.

[2] *Vide ante*, "Development and Decay," paragraph 8, and "Reproduction," paragraph 1.

[3] This was her name. There is no name at all resembling *Hessa* in the language (*vide* Appendix H).

[4] In his report for the month of December, 1866, the officer in charge of the Andaman homes stated that on *Dúdhnáth's* desertion of her "she was called *Mada*, which signifies a deserted bride, or a woman that has lost her husband while young, and before becoming a mother." [N.B.—*.mā·da* (not *Mada*) is one of the twelve "flower" names borne by all young women (married and single) until they become mothers (*vide* "Proper Names," paragraph 8, and Appendix H.)]

[5] "Our friend the Sepoy tells some remarkable exploits of the Mincopie in

highly coloured, and failed, therefore, in imposing on the almost excusable credulity which existed at a time when next to nothing of a trustworthy nature was known concerning these savages.

22. With regard to a deceased husband's property, the widow disposes of everything, which she does not require for her personal use, among his male relatives.

23. It seems superfluous to add that no such custom as *suttee* prevails or has ever been known to exist among them.

Death and Burial.—1. Amongst other erroneous opinions held regarding these tribes is that which declares that "no lamentation is publicly made at death," whereas, in point of fact, the demonstrations of grief on such occasions are generally excessive, and are shared, in a greater or less degree, by every member of the community in which the melancholy event occurs.

2. In the case of an infant, the parents and relatives remain weeping for hours beside the corpse; afterwards they smear their persons with a wash composed of *ōg-* (the common olive-coloured clay) and water, and, after shaving their heads, place a lump of the same, called *dē·ru-*, just above their foreheads,[1] where it hardens, and is left, much to the individual's discomfort, until the expiration of the days of mourning;[2] should it fall off in the meantime it is renewed.

3. The burial usually takes place within 18 hours of the decease, which time is spent by the mother in painting the head, neck, wrists, and knees of her dead child with *kōiob-* and *tâla-ōg-*; she also shaves off the hair, and folds the little limbs so as to occupy the least possible space,[3] the knees being brought up to the chin and the fists close to the shoulders; the body is then enveloped in large leaves, called *kd·pa-*,[4] which are secured with cords or strips of cane. The father meantime employs himself in digging a grave with an adze (*wō·lo-*[5]), in the place where his hut fire usually burns; when all is prepared the little head is uncovered, and the parents gently blow upon the face

fishing, which, as they seem to indicate a Munchausen-like faculty of exaggeration in the narrator we decline to repeat" (Mouat).

[1] This applies to men, for women usually place the *dē·ru-* on the top of the head. It is worn by neither sex until after they have attained maturity, and only for a father, mother, husband, wife, brother, sister, son, or daughter, the *ōg-* wash alone being deemed sufficient "mourning" in the case of other relatives or friends.

[2] The term *ō·ko-ōg-* is therefore applied to mourners, since they are prohibited from the use of *kōi-ob-*.

[3] "If we knew no further details as to the opinions of the intellectually gifted Hottentots, formerly so greatly underrated, it would be enough that, previous to burial, they place the body of the deceased in the same position which it once occupied as an embryo in the mother's womb" (Peschel).

[4] *Vide* Appendix B, item 74.

[5] *Vide* Appendix B, item 15.

two or three times in token of farewell;[1] then, replacing the leaves, they put the corpse into the grave in a sitting posture, and fill in and level the earth; next, having procured a quantity of the young leaves of the common jungle cane, they split them and make long fringe-like wreaths, called *á·ra-*,[2] which they fasten to the trees surrounding the hut, or encircling the entire camping ground, the object being to apprise any stranger or friend who might chance to visit the spot, that a death has recently occurred, and that they would therefore do well to keep away.

4. After suspending the *á·ra-* the fire is rekindled and the mother places a shell containing some of her own milk beside the grave, obviously in order that the child's spirit, which is believed to haunt its late home for a few days, may not lack nourishment. All in the encampment then pack up those things which are mostly needed and depart to some other camping ground,[3] generally not less than two or three miles distant, where they at once construct huts, usually of the description called *chàng-tô·rnga-*,[4] to serve as shelter during the mourning period, which as a rule lasts about three months; and during which the parents and relatives, naturally enough, refrain from taking any part in the festivities occurring among their neighbours. While mourning it is customary for the *ĕrem-tâ·ga-* to abstain from pork, and for the *âryô·to-* to deny themselves turtle as well as other luxuries, in token of the sincerity of their grief, but they never mutilate themselves by cutting off joints of their fingers, &c., as do the Hottentots and the Papuans of the Fiji Islands, nor have they, as has been erroneously asserted in Dr. Day's paper, daily, during periods of deep sorrow, to throw honey-comb, if obtainable, into the fire.[5]

5. At the expiration of the time mutually agreed upon, they all return to the deserted encampment and remove and destroy the *á·ra-*. The parents then exhume the remains, which are taken by the father to the sea-shore, or the nearest creek, there to be cleansed[6] from all putrefying matter: this done, he brings

[1] *Vide* ceremony at parting (*post*, "Meeting and Parting," paragraph 6).

[2] *Vide* Appendix B, item 73.

[3] Similarly do the Koi-Koin (Hottentots) "break up their kraals after every case of death, to avoid the proximity of the grave" (Peschel).

[4] *Vide* "Journ. Anthrop. Inst.," vol. xi, p. 281, and *ante*, "Habitations," paragraph 8.

[5] The practice here referred to is evidently that of burning beeswax (not honey-comb), the object of which will shortly be explained under "Superstitions," paragraph 14, and is not that here stated.

[6] This repulsive duty is always performed by one of the near *male* relatives of a deceased person. Dr. Day was led to believe that "the extraction of the skull and bones, it is considered, requires great skill and courage," but experience and the statements of all those aborigines who have been questioned on the subject, do not bear out this view.

the skull and bones back to his hut and breaks up the latter into small pieces suitable for necklaces.[1] The mother, after painting the skull with *kòi·ob-*, and decorating it with small shells attached to pieces of string, hangs it round her neck with a netted chain, called *rāb-*.[2] After the first few days her husband often relieves her by wearing it himself. Infants' skulls, being fragile, are generally preserved carefully from risk of injury by being entirely covered with string, but (except temporarily as when travelling, fishing, &c.) these souvenirs are not carried about in a basket. The next few days are spent by the mother in converting the bones into necklaces, called *chàu·ga-tá-*, and when several have been made, she and her husband pay visits to their friends, among whom they distribute these mementoes, together with any of the pieces that may remain over, in order that they may make additional necklets for themselves.

6. Before this distribution takes place, it should be mentioned that the mourners remove from their heads the lump of clay placed there on the day of the child's death; the wife also paints her husband's neck, waist, wrists, and knees with *kòi·ob-* and further adorns him with a stripe of the same compound from his throat to his navel, and afterwards decorates herself in a similar manner.

7. All due preparations having thus been made, the friends assemble round the hut to pay their final visit of condolence; whereupon the bereaved father sings some old song of his, which he last sang, perchance, with his little one alive and well in his arms, on which all except himself express their grief and sympathy by breaking out into loud lamentations. The chorus of the song is chanted by the women while the parents perform a dance which goes by the name of *ri-tō·latnga-* (*lit.*, the shedding of tears); when wearied with their exertions they retire to their hut, and cease from any further display of sorrow, whereupon their friends generally take up and continue the melancholy dance and song for many hours, the women being then joined by the men, who, till this stage of the proceedings, have merely acted the part of spectators. It should be explained that the character of this dance does not differ from that which is customary at a wedding or other occasion of rejoicing, except in the doleful appearance of the performers.

8. On the death of an adult and others, the relatives (as in the case of an infant) smear themselves with *ōg-* and place a lump of the clay on their heads, where it must remain until the *ri-tō·latnga-*; any necklaces, waistbelts, &c., which the deceased was wearing are removed; women then paint the

[1] *Vide* Appendix B, item 44.
[2] *Vide* Appendix B, item 42.

corpse, whose limbs are folded and enwrapped in the manner above described.

9. What the true significance of this practice may be is not quite clear, as such of the aborigines as have been questioned assert that it is merely for convenience in removal; but since the custom is also observed in infant burials which, as I have mentioned, take place in the very hut wherein the death occurred, it seems probable that a deeper meaning underlies the act; and the real reason may be that which Peschel supplies in his reference to the Hottentots, who observe the same custom, *i.e.* "that the dead will mature in the darkness of the earth in preparation for a new birth."[1]

10. As it is not customary for females to attend the funeral, when *their* part is done, they gently blow upon the face, and take their last farewell look.

11. None save infants are buried within the encampment, all others being carried to some distant and secluded spot in the jungle, and there interred or placed upon a "machán," or platform; it is generally arranged beforehand which of these two methods shall be employed, but the latter is considered the more complimentary, apparently because it involves a little more labour.[2]

12. Arrived at their destination, the corpse, which has been carried by one of the men on his back, is put down, while the final preparations are being made. A spot is selected where there is a boulder or large tree,[3] to mark it, and there, if a grave has been decided on, they dig a hole about 4 or 5 feet deep, with an adze (*wō̆lo-*), into which the body is lowered in a sitting posture, facing the east; all present then raise the leaf covering the head, and take leave of their friend by blowing upon his face. Before the grave is filled in the cords or canes are cut, the object being to hasten the process of decomposition by loosening the leaves; a fire is lighted over the spot and a *gōb-*,[4] or nautilus shell, filled with water, as well as some article which belonged to the deceased, is placed beside it: then the surrounding brushwood for some little distance is cleared away, and *ā'ra-* are suspended between the trees in the manner and for the purpose before stated.

13. Should it, however, have been determined to dispose of the corpse by the alternative method, a small stage is constructed

[1] This singular practice also prevailed amongst the ancient Peruvians (*vide* "Anthropology of Prehistoric Peru," by T. J. Hutchinson, "Journ. Anthrop. Inst.," vol. iv, p. 447, 1875).

[2] Old persons are generally buried.

[3] They never wittingly use the same tree or spot a second time, and are careful to remember those which served on a former occasion.

[4] *Vide* Appendix B, item 82, and "Journ. Anthrop. Inst.," vol. xi, p. 269.

of sticks and boughs, about 8 to 12 feet above the ground, generally between the forked branches of some large tree,[1] and to it the body is lashed. The head is raised slightly, looking eastward, and, though the position of the arms is not altered, the cords are loosened to allow of the legs being straightened, after which the leaves are re-adjusted, so as to cover the entire form, in order to protect it from the attacks of hawks, crows, and vermin.

14. Two reasons are given for the practice of placing the corpse with the face towards the rising sun: one being that dissolution may thereby be hastened, the other that *jer'eg-* or Hades, whither the souls of the departed flee, is situated in the east.

15. The mourners take a last farewell in the manner before described, and fulfil the remaining duties, as related in the former case. The spirit of the deceased being supposed to haunt not only the spot where he has been buried, but also the encampment where the death occurred, the community migrate temporarily to another camping ground immediately after the return of the funeral party, leaving the dve- to witness to casual visitors of the cause of their absence.

16. When the period of mourning has expired, the men who assisted in the funeral rites return to the place of burial, destroy the dve-, and remove the remains of the deceased to the sea-shore, or to a creek, where the bones are cleaned and afterwards conveyed to the old encampment, whither they all return and restore their camp to its normal condition.

17. As all that has been related regarding the distribution of the bones of a child and the subsequent dance applies equally to all cases, further account of these ceremonies here is unnecessary; for fuller information anent the manufacture of the necklaces, &c., the reader is referred to an interesting paper by Dr. Allen Thomson, F.R.S., which will be found in the Journal of the Anthropological Institute for 1881.[2]

18. Although in the majority of cases the display of grief is thoroughly sincere, there is no doubt that they hope, by testifying to their sorrow in the various ways mentioned, to conciliate the spirits of the departed, and to be by them preserved from many misfortunes which might otherwise befall them.[3]

19. In the case of a young married couple who are childless, if either die, the survivor is not the chief mourner, and does not even assist at the obsequies, which are performed solely by

[1] They are careful not to select a fruit-tree, or one used for the manufacture of their canoes, bows, and other implements.

[2] *Vide* "Journ. Anthrop. Inst.," vol. xi, p. 295.

[3] *Vide post* "Religious Beliefs, &c.," paragraph 24.

the relatives of the deceased, one of whom subsequently takes possession of the skull, and wears it until he (or she) chooses to part with it, or is asked to do so by another member of the family. It should here be stated that it is by no means obligatory upon the survivor of an elderly couple, or any relative, to carry the bones or skull of the deceased for a lengthened period:[1] except in the event of marrying a brother, sister, or cousin of the deceased, these relics can be given at any time to a friend who may ask for them; thus it not unfrequently happens that the remains of one who was a chief or a favourite in his day, are scattered far and wide among his admirers, but when in course of time they get mislaid or broken, the owner is often easily reconciled to his loss, or makes it good by procuring similar mementoes of another and more recently departed friend.

20. It may be said that as a rule no adult is without at least one *chàu'ga-tà-* (*i.e.*, a human bone necklace), and the skulls, which are generally to be found in every encampment, are worn by each in turn, if only for a few hours.

21. The only difference made on the occasion of the death of a chief, his wife, or one of his near relatives, is that *all* the men and lads of the encampment smear themselves with *ōg-*, and attend the funeral; the relations alone, however, are the mourners during the succeeding weeks or months which intervene before the *tī-lō'lakngs-*, though, as a token of respect for the deceased, and of sympathy with the mourners, other members of the tribe often abstain from some favourite article of food, and take no part in festivities during the same period.

22. If a member of another tribe happen to die while on a visit, the body would be disposed of in one of the modes I have endeavoured to describe, after which intimation would be sent to the friends of the deceased, so that they might know where to seek for the skeleton when the time for disinterment should arrive.

23. The body of an enemy, stranger, or captive child would be thrown into the sea, or buried *sans cérémonie*, as the bones would never be in request.

24. A sudden death is at once attributed to the malign influence of *ĕrem-chàu'gala*, if the deceased had been recently in the jungles, or to *jū'ru-win-*, if he had been on the sea; in either case one of the male relatives of the victim, representing the feelings of the community, approaches the spot where the body

[1] I mention this more especially as the erroneous statement made by some early writer, that "a widow wears her husband's skull suspended round her neck for the rest of her life," has been repeated in more recent accounts, and hitherto remains uncontradicted.

is lying, and shoots several arrows in rapid succession into the surrounding jungle, only taking care to avoid injury to the by-standers, and then, seizing a pig-spear, *ĕr-dū'tnga-*,[1] if *Ērem-chàu'gala* be the demon suspected, or a turtle-spear, *kowaia l'ōko dū'tnga-*,[2] if it be *jū'ru-win-* who is accounted guilty, he pierces the ground all round the corpse, hoping thereby to inflict a mortal injury upon the unseen enemy; while so engaged he vents his grief and indignation in no measured terms of imprecation.

25. When a death which is attributed to *Ērem-chàu'gala*'s malignity occurs so late in the day that the burial has to be deferred till the following morning, those who are not mourners sing in turns throughout the night, in the belief that this demon will thus be deterred from doing any further harm in the encampment.

26. At death they say that *Ērem-chàu'gala* and his sons feast upon the blood and soft tissues of all who die on land, and that their leavings, excepting of course the bones, are disposed of by worms, *wĕn-*, but *jū'ru-win-* is supposed to consume every portion of those who fall into his clutches.

Meeting and Parting, &c.—1. Contrary to the customs of most races, no salutations[3] pass between friends, even after a more or less lengthened separation, such as rubbing noses, kissing[4] shaking hands, &c.; but on meeting they remain silently gazing at each other for, in our eyes, an absurdly long time—unless of course one or both be hurried; the younger then makes some commonplace remark which apparently has the effect of loosening their tongues, for they at once commence hearing and telling the news.[5]

2. Relatives, after an absence of a few weeks or months, testify their joy at meeting by sitting with their arms round each other's necks,[6] and weeping and howling[7] in a manner which would lead a stranger to suppose that some great sorrow had befallen them; and, in point of fact, there is no difference observable between their demonstrations of joy on these occasions and those of grief at the death of one of their

[1] *Vide* Appendix B, item 9.

[2] *Vide* Appendix B, item 10.

[3] *Vide* Colebrooke and Anderson.

[4] Kisses are considered indicative of affection, but are only bestowed on infants.

[5] One might imagine that the writer of the article entitled "Chippers of Flint", which appeared in "Cornhill" (vol. xli, p. 200), had heard of or witnessed a rencontre of this description, but had not watched its progress, or he would not have spoken of this race as "all but speechless."

[6] *Vide* Plate III, fig. 2.

[7] This custom resembles that which exists among New Zealanders under the name of the *Tangi*.

number. The crying chorus is started by women, but the men speedily chime in, and groups of three or four may thus be seen weeping in concert until, from sheer exhaustion, they are compelled to desist; then, if neither of the parties are in mourning, a dance is got up, in which the females not unfrequently take part, but the style of their performance differs from that of the males.[1]

3. A husband who is *childless*, and has been absent from his home for some time, on his return to the encampment visits first a blood relation (if any), and when *they* have wept together he goes to his own hut, not in order to shed more tears, but to see and talk to his spouse. The same remark applies to a wife similarly circumstanced. But in the case of married couples who are *parents*, the meeting takes place first between them; the wife hangs round her husband's neck sobbing as if her heart would break with joy at their re-union; when she is exhausted with weeping, he leaves her, and, going to one of his relations, gives vent to his pent-up feelings of happiness by bursting into tears.

4. It is usual for friends at meeting to give each other something which may happen to be in their hands at the time, and these gifts are regarded as tokens of affection.

5. Strangers introduced by mutual friends are always warmly welcomed by the whole community: they, in common with all guests, are the first attended on, the best food in the encampment is set before them, and in every way they are well treated; presents also are often given them, especially when about to take their leave.

6. "Speed the parting guest" is an axiom upon which these people invariably act: the departing visitor is accompanied by his host to the landing-place, or, at all events, some distance on his way; when bidding each other farewell the guest takes the hand of his host and blows upon it; when the compliment has been returned, the following dialogue ensues:—

Departing visitor: *kam wai dōl.* I am off (*lit.*, Here indeed I).

Host: *ō, ū·chik wai òn; tain ŭ·lik kach òn gē·te!* Very well, go; when will you come again?

Departing visitor: *ñgī·tek dō·ngat mīn l·ke.* I will bring away something for you one of these days.

Host: *jō·bo la ngōng chā·pikok!* May no snake bite you!

Departing visitor: *wai dō ēr-yē·lepke.* I will take good care of that (*lit.*, I will be watchful).

Afterwards they again blow upon each other's hands, and part.

[1] *Vide post* "Games and Amusements," paragraphs 27 and 30.

PLATE III.

FIG. 1.—ANDAMANESE EQUIPPED FOR JOURNEY.

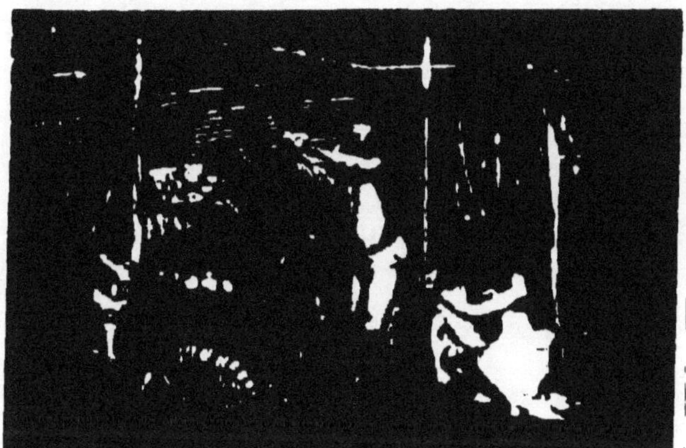

FIG. 2.—ANDAMANESE SHOOTING, DANCING, SLEEPING, AND GREETING.

shouting invitations and promises for a future date until beyond earshot.

7. When nearing home, after an unusually successful hunting or fishing expedition, the men raise a shout[1] of triumph in order to apprise their friends of their good fortune, and the women take up the cry and express their delight by yelling[2] and slapping their thighs; but when the encampment is entered, these sounds of rejoicing almost invariably cease for a while, and, after depositing their spoils, the hunters remain speechless for some time ere recounting their adventures and exploits: for this strange practice they appear unable to account.

8. No matutinal greetings pass between friends or between husband and wife, and inquiries relating to health are unusual unless addressed to an invalid.

9. When a man is thirsty and wishes also to wash his hands, he first, if alone, stoops down and drinks from the stream, or raises the water to his lips in a leaf or vessel; then, filling his mouth with water, he squirts it over his hands, using his unkempt locks as a towel. Should any one else be present, he would pour the water over his friend's hands as well, not from his mouth, but from a leaf.

10. They do not bathe daily, but at irregular intervals, when oppressed with the heat, or when, from some cause, as, for instance, in gathering honey,[3] their persons become sticky and unpleasant, and ablutions, consistently with comfort at least, cannot be dispensed with. It will be understood that these remarks apply to the *ĕremtâ'ga-*, rather than the *ar-yâ'to-*, who, from the nature of their pursuits, are on the whole fairly clean.[4]

11. During the hot weather they smear their bodies with common white clay, called *ōg-*,[5] dissolved in water, and avoid, as far as they are able, any lengthened exposure to the direct rays of the sun. If compelled to leave the shelter of the jungle, they are in the habit of holding a large leaf screen, *kâ'pa-jâ'tnga-*,[6] over their heads as a protection (this is also done during a shower); should they be travelling by boat they lessen the discomfort caused by excessive heat by pouring water over themselves, or by plunging overboard and swimming alongside the canoe for some part of the way.

[1] There is a specific term for this description of shouting, viz.: *ki-rĭ-bâ-ke*, while that of the women in answer thereto is called —

[2] *rī·moke.*

[3] *Vide* Appendix H (*lot'a-châ-da-*, lit., dirty body).

[4] They never allow vermin to breed on their persons — in fact, such a thing could not possibly occur, owing to the constant shaving of the head, painting of the person, and, in the case of the *ar-yâ'to-*, immersion in the sea while fishing and turtling.

[5] *Vide* Appendix B, item 80.

[6] *Vide* Appendix B, item 74.

FIRE.—1. It would seem that the Andamanese, like the quondam aborigines of Tasmania, have always been ignorant of the art of producing fire.

2. The assertion[1] that these tribes when first discovered, assuming that this refers to either the second or ninth century,[2] were ignorant of the use of fire may or may not be correct; but if any faith can be placed in the traditions held by them on the subject, their acquaintance with it dates from no later period than the Creation![3]

3. The most satisfactory conjecture as to the source whence they first obtained fire appears to me to be based on the fact of there being two islands attached to the group, one of which (Barren Island) contains an active volcano, and the other (Narcondam Island[4]) a now extinct one.

4. Being strangers to any method of producing a flame, they naturally display much care and skill in the measures they adopt for avoiding such inconvenience as might be caused by the extinction of their fires.

5. Both when encamped and while journeying, the means employed are at once simple and effective. When they all leave an encampment with the intention of returning in a few days, besides taking with them one or more smouldering logs, wrapped in leaves if the weather be wet, they place a large burning log or faggot in some sheltered spot, where, owing to the character and condition of the wood invariably selected on these occasions, it smoulders for several days, and can be easily rekindled when required. Decayed pieces of the *Croton argyratus*, and two species of *Diospyros*,[5] and a fourth, called by them *chòr-*, but not yet identified, are chiefly used as fuel. As may be inferred, all labour of splitting and chopping is saved, as it is only necessary

[1] *Vide* Brown.

[2] *Vide* Part I (commencement).

[3] *Vide post* "Mythology," paragraphs 5 and 6.

[4] Regarding this island, which is sometimes shown as Narkandam, Colonel Yule, in his "Marco Polo," writes as follows:—

"Abraham Roger tells us that the Coromandel Brahmins used to say that the *Rakshasas* or Demons had their abode 'on the Island of Andaman, lying on the route from Pulicat to Pegu,' and also that they were man-eaters. This would be very curious if it were a genuine old Brahminical *Saga*; but I fear it may have been gathered from the Arab seamen. Still it is remarkable that a strange weird looking island, which rises, covered with forest, a steep and regular volcanic cone, straight out of the deep sea to the eastward of the Andaman group, bears the name of *Narkandam* in which one cannot but recognise नरक. (*Narak*), 'Hell.' Can it be that in old times, but still contemporary with Hindu navigation, this volcano was active, and that some Brahmin St. Brandon recognised in it the mouth of Hell, congenial to the Rakshasas of the adjacent group?"

Colonel Yule adds: "I cannot trace any probable meaning of Andam, yet it looks as if *Narak-andam* and *Andam-án* were akin."

[5] Bastard ebony or marble wood.

to beat a log of this description on a stone or other hard substance a few times before it breaks up into as small pieces as are needed.

6. In each hut that is occupied there is invariably a fire, the object of which is to keep the owner warm, to drive away insects, and to cook food, while the smoke is useful in preserving the store of provisions, which are placed about two feet above it for that purpose.[1]

7. Council fires, or fires burnt on special occasions, are not among their institutions; even the household fire is not held sacred, or regarded as symbolical of family ties, and no rites are connected with it; there are no superstitious beliefs in reference to its extinction or pollution, and it is never employed literally or figuratively as a means of purification from uncleanness, blood, death, or moral guilt.

8. Fires are generally kindled by fanning the embers with a frond of the *Asplenium nidus* (*pd'tla-*), and they are extinguished by pressing the burning logs against some such object as a tree, canoe, or stone.

9. Reference must here be made to the mis-statement which has found its way into several papers concerning the existence of so-called "oven-trees" among the Andamanese. The belief appears to have originated in the practice which prevails among them of taking advantage, during brief halts, of the natural shelter afforded by the peculiar formation of the roots of the *Pterocarpus dalbergioides*, and trees of the *Ficus* genus, so common in these islands, and which, extending like buttresses on all sides of the trunk, are, especially when roofed over with a light thatch such as these people are accustomed to make in a few minutes, capable of accommodating small parties suddenly overtaken by a storm, or needing a temporary resting-place: the traces of fires lighted by successive parties against these trees, and the hollows thus caused, having been noticed, the opinion was formed, and, without sufficient corroborative evidence, promulgated, that they were "purposely charred," and that "great pains is taken in their preservation."[2] As a matter of fact, the Andamanese no more employ oven-trees than do the gypsies in Bulgaria, alluded to by General Pitt-Rivers, F.R.S.,[3] who, using constantly the same trees, have formed a semi-cylindrical chimney, which might reasonably be regarded, by one unacquainted with their habits, as an attempt to form an oven.

10. While it is the women's business to collect the wood, the duty of maintaining the fires, whether at home or while travelling

[1] *Vide ante* "Habitations" paragraph 5.
[2] *Vide* Mouat, pp. 308–9.
[3] *Vide* Journ. Anthrop. Inst., vol. xi, pp. 273 and 290 (Appendix I).

by land or sea, is not confined to them, but is undertaken by those of either sex who have most leisure or are least burdened.

11. Probably nothing introduced by us so impressed them with the extent of our power and resources as *matches*; that we should be able to produce fire with such ease and by such means was not unnaturally regarded as evidence of our being superhumanly gifted.

Superstitions.—1. Fire is supposed to possess the power of driving away evil spirits: when, therefore, at night they hear in imagination the approach of the dreaded *Ērem-chàugala*,[1] they throw burning logs into the jungle surrounding the encampment. Again, should any of the community have occasion to leave their huts at night, no matter how short the distance, he (or she) invariably takes some fire as a protection against any demons that may be in the vicinity; a torch is also taken if it be very dark at the time.

2. Of darkness they assert that it was instituted on account of the misconduct of two of their ancestors, as will shortly be mentioned.[2]

3. From fear of displeasing *maia Ōgar-*[3] (Mr. Moon), during the first few evenings of the third quarter, when he rises after sundown, they preserve silence, cease from any work on which they may be engaged—even halting should they be travelling—and almost extinguish any light or fire which they may be burning. This is owing to the belief that he is jealous of attention being distracted to other objects than himself at such a time, or of any other light being employed than that which he has been graciously pleased to afford so abundantly. By the time the moon has ascended a few degrees, however, they restore their fires and resume their former occupations, as they consider they have then sufficiently complied with *maia Ōgar-'s* wishes and requirements. The glowing aspect of the full moon on its first appearance above the horizon is supposed to indicate that *maia Ōgar-* is enraged at finding some persons neglecting to observe these conciliatory measures; there is also an idea that, if he be greatly annoyed, he will punish them by withdrawing or diminishing the light of his countenance.

4. Regarding meteorolites they appear to possess no superstition. Shooting stars and meteors they view with apprehension, believing them to be lighted faggots hurled into the air by *Ērem-chàugala* in order to ascertain the whereabouts of any unhappy wight in his vicinity; if, therefore, they happen to be away from

[1] *Vide post* "Religious Beliefs, &c.," paragraph 12.

[2] *Vide post* "Mythology," paragraph 31.

[3] Singing, dancing, and thumping on the sounding board at that hour are, however, not displeasing to him.

their encampment when the phenomenon occurs, they invariably secrete themselves, at the bottom of a boat, for example, if fishing, and remain silent for a short time before venturing to resume their interrupted employment.

5. Between dawn and sunrise they will do no work, save what is noiseless, lest the sun should be offended, and cause an eclipse, storm, or other misfortune to overtake them. If, therefore, they have occasion to start on a journey or hunting expedition at so early an hour, they proceed as quietly as possible, and refrain from the practice, observed at other periods of the day, of testing the strength of their bow-strings, as the snapping noise caused thereby is one of those to which the sun objects.

6. They invariably partake of a meal soon after rising, as it is believed that no luck can attend any one who starts to his day's work on an empty stomach.

7. They dare not use the wood of the tree called *ul·aba-* (the bark of which supplies the fibre used in making harpoon lines and turtle nets) for cooking turtle, for, as will be found elsewhere,[1] this is an act so abhorrent to *maia ō·gar-* that he visits the offenders with summary and condign punishment.

8. In tempestuous weather the leaves of the *Mimusops Indica* are constantly thrown on the fires, as the popping sounds thus produced are thought to have the effect of assuaging *Pū·luga-*'s fury and causing the weather to moderate.

9. When they see a dark cloud approaching at a time when rain would prove very inconvenient, as when hunting, travelling, &c., they advise *Pū·luga-* to divert its course by shouting "*Wā·ra-jōbo kō·pke, kō·pke, kō·pke*" [*Wā·ra-jōbo*[2] will bite, bite, bite (you)]. If in spite of this a shower falls they imagine that *Pū·luga-* is undeterred by their warning.

10. This practice of menacing *Pū·luga-* is probably that to which Colonel Symes alluded when he wrote that "they confess the influence of a malignant Being, and, during the south-west monsoon, when tempests prevail with unusual violence, they deprecate his wrath by wild choruses."

11. Storms are regarded as indications of *Pū·luga-*'s anger; winds are his breath, and are caused to be blown by his will; when it thunders *Pū·luga-* is said to be growling at something which has annoyed him; and lightning, they say, is a burning log flung by him at the object of his wrath.

12. There is an idea current that if during the first half of the rainy season they eat the *Caryota sobolifera*, or pluck and eat the seeds of the *Entada pursaetha*, or gather yams or other edible

[1] *Vide post* "Mythology," paragraph 32.

[2] This snake, as already mentioned under "Medicine," appears to be the *Ophiophagus elaps*.

roots, another deluge would be the consequence, for *Pū'luga-* is supposed to require these for his own consumption at that period of the year; the restriction, however, does not extend to the *fallen* seeds of the *Entada pursætha*, which may be collected and eaten at any time with impunity.

13. Another of the offences visited by *Pū'luga-* with storms is the burning of beeswax,[1] the smell of which is said to be peculiarly obnoxious to him. Owing to this belief it is a common practice secretly to burn wax when a person against whom they bear ill-will is engaged in fishing, hunting, or the like, the object being to spoil his sport and cause him as much discomfort as possible; hence arises the saying among them, when suddenly overtaken by a storm, that some one must be burning wax.

14. The rainbow is regarded as *E'rem-chàu'gala*'s dancing or sounding board, which is only visible at certain times; its appearance is said to betoken approaching sickness or death to one of their number, and is, therefore, inauspicious.[2]

15. There are no superstitions anent hills, valleys, rocks, &c., which, as stated in my last paper,[3] *Pū'luga-* is believed to have formed for some purpose of his own. The formation of creeks is attributed to a fortunate accident, the account of which being connected with their traditions must be reserved for that section.[4]

16. They imagine earthquakes to be caused by some mischievous male spirits of their deceased ancestors, who, in their impatience at the delay in the resurrection, combine to shake the palm-tree on which they believe the earth to rest, in the hope thereby of destroying the cane bridge[5] which stretches between this world and heaven, and alone maintains the former in its present position. These selfish spirits are, however, said to be careful never to indulge in such practices during the dry months, as they imagine that, in consequence of the surface of the earth being then much cracked with heat, there would be considerable risk of its tumbling about their ears and crushing them instead of toppling over in one solid mass. They are said, therefore, never to play at earthquakes except during, or shortly after, the rainy season. But for the intervention of female spirits, who do their utmost to dissuade or prevent their male companions from continued enjoyment of this dangerous pastime, they are persuaded that there would be much cause for alarm on every occurrence of an earthquake.

17. They believe that every child which is conceived has had a

[1] *d'ja-pid-* (*vide ante* "Death and Burial," paragraph 4, footnote).

[2] The Chippeway Indians call it the dancing spirit (*vide* "Travels in the Interior of North America," by Maximilian, Prince of Wied).

[3] *Vide ante* "Topography," paragraph 3.

[4] *Vide post* "Mythology," paragraph 12.

[5] *Vide post* "Religious Beliefs, &c.," paragraph 25.

prior existence, but only as an infant. If a woman who has lost a baby is again about to become a mother, the name borne by the deceased is bestowed on the fœtus, in the expectation that it will prove to be the same child born again. Should it be found at birth that the babe is of the same sex as the one who died, the identity is considered to be sufficiently established, but if otherwise the deceased one is said to be under the *râu-* (*Ficus laccifera*) in *chā·itā·n-* (Hades).[1]

18. They have no peculiar ideas in reference to yawning, hiccoughing, spitting, or eructating, and hissing[2] is unknown.

19. To sneeze is auspicious, and therefore regarded with favour. When any one sneezes the bystanders ask, "Who is thinking of you?" to which the person replies by naming some absent friend, or, should he be alone when he sneezes, he says, "Here I am at —— " (naming the place).

20. If they have a dream which they regard as bad, as, for instance, that a canoe was dashed on a reef, or that an accident occurred while pig-hunting, or even if, when awake, they hear two canoes bumping against each other while at anchor, they consider it essential to accept such as a warning, and act accordingly, viz., by taking steps to incur no risk of a misadventure: this is generally accomplished by remaining at home for two or three days.

21. A small striped snake, called *ld·rabe-*, is supposed to produce the streams of the red oxide of iron, *kòi·ob-chŭ·lugu-*, and olive-coloured clay, *chŭ·lugu-*, so much employed by them; the ground for the belief is the alleged fact that this snake, when disturbed, ejects from its tail a whitish fluid, which is of a deadly nature. They declare that the poison is such that it cannot be removed by washing or other means, and that it causes intense pain to the victim, who invariably dies within a few hours.

22. There is a small bird, not yet identified, called by them *pĭ·chrō·l-*, the meeting with which is looked upon as ominous of an approaching death in their midst. When a woodpecker is heard tapping on a tree he is said to be giving warning of the approach of *ū·chu-*,[3] so they proceed in fear and trembling until the danger is supposed to be past. The notes of the *pai-* and *ràtegi-* (two birds not yet identified) are regarded as a sign that there are enemies in the vicinity. When, therefore, either of these are heard, they at once retrace their steps, if they happen to be on the move, or, should they be in an encampment, they

[1] *Vide ante* "Proper Names," paragraph 1, and *post* "Religious Beliefs, &c.," paragraphs 22 and 23.

[2] This is accounted for by the absence of sibilants in their language (*vide* Appendix A).

[3] A legendary elephant, to be spoken of under "Mythology," paragraph 30.

temporarily vacate their huts and remain on the alert with their weapons ready for immediate use. The cry of another bird, called *chē̆ra-*, informs them of the approaching visit of a friend. Finally, if while travelling they hear the cawing of a crow, they say they must be near some occupied, or recently abandoned encampment. This belief is doubtless traceable to the fact that these birds are among the principal scavengers of their camping grounds.

23. It has been noticed that they will never whistle between sunset and sunrise, and the reason they give is that this sound, more than any other, attracts *ĕrem-chàugala* during those hours. When animals behave in an unaccountable manner, especially at night, it is said to be because they see this demon.

Religious Beliefs and Demonology.—1. I have several times mentioned the Supernatural Beings, *Pŭluga-* and *ĕrem-chàugala*, and must now enter more into detail regarding the beliefs held by the Andamanese concerning these and other spirits.

2. Though no forms of worship or religious rites are to be found among them, yet are there certain beliefs regarding powers of good and evil, the Creation, and of a world beyond the grave, which show that even these savages have traditions more or less approximating the truth, but whence derived will ever remain a mystery.

3. It is extremely improbable that their legends were the result of the teaching of missionaries or others who might be supposed to have landed on their shores in by-gone years; for not only have they no tradition of any foreigners having settled in their midst and intermarried with their ancestors, or even of having so far established amicable intercourse as to be able to acquire a knowledge of any one of their languages, but our own records, so far from differing from theirs on these points, tend clearly to show that, from the earliest times till so recently as 1858, these islanders have been more or less universally regarded as cannibals, in consequence of which they were much dreaded by all navigating the adjacent seas. The persistency with which they resisted with showers of arrows all attempts to land on their shores,[1] precludes the belief that any one, prior to our settlement,[2] would from choice have visited these islanders in the vain hope of reclaiming them from their savage state, and in order to teach them the Biblical, Mahomedan, or other versions of the Creation, Fall, Deluge, &c.; while it may surely be

[1] The probable cause of their hostility will be explained in a later section (*vide post* "Trade, &c.," paragraph 1).

[2] In 1870 an orphanage was established at Ross Island (Port Blair) for children of the aborigines, but it is very doubtful whether even the more intelligent of the inmates have obtained, much less retained, more than an elementary knowledge of the outline of the truths of Christianity.

assumed that if any shipwrecked persons had ever been cast on their coast, they would, in the improbable event of their lives being spared, have left some traces of the fact, such as might be looked for among the customs, in the culture, or physical characteristics of these savages, but these are vainly to be sought in any section of the race.

4. Moreover, to regard with suspicion, as some have done, the genuineness of such legends as those in question argues ignorance of the fact that numerous other tribes,[1] in equally remote or isolated localities have, when first discovered, been found to possess similar traditions on the subjects under consideration.

5. Further, on this subject as well as on all others in which there appeared any risk of falling into error, I have taken special care not only to obtain my information on each point from those who are considered by their fellow-tribesmen as authorities, but who, from having had little or no intercourse with other races, were in entire ignorance regarding any save their own legends: I have, besides, in every case, by subsequent inquiry, endeavoured to test their statements, with the trustworthiness of which I am thoroughly satisfied. I may also add that they all agree in stating that their accounts of the Creation, &c., were handed down to them by their first parent *Tōmo-* (Adam), and his immediate descendants, while they trace all their superstitions and practices to the "days before the Flood!"

6. I shall presently speak of the legends current anent the Creation, and also the Fall and Deluge: the latter will there be seen to have been, *selon eux*, consequent on the former.

7. In spite of their knowledge of, or belief in, a Supreme Being,[2] whom they call *Pūluga-*, they live in constant fear of certain evil spirits, whom they apprehend to be ever present, and on the watch to do them some bodily injury.

8. Of *Pūluga-* they say that—

I. Though His appearance is like fire, yet He is (now-a-days) invisible.

II. He was never born and is immortal.

III. By him the world and all objects, animate and inanimate, were created, excepting only the powers of evil.

IV. He is regarded as omniscient while it is day, knowing even the thoughts of their hearts.

V. He is angered by the commission of certain sins,[3] while to

[1] A story of the Fall occurs in the myths of the Eskimo, the South Sea Islanders, the Zulus, the Australians and the New Zealanders (*vide* "Biblical Traditions and Savage Myths."—*St. James' Gazette*, July 14th, 1881.)

[2] *Vide* Mouat, pp. 303–4.

[3] *Vide ante* "Crimes," paragraph 2.

those in pain or distress he is pitiful, and sometimes deigns to afford relief.

VI. He is the Judge from whom each soul receives its sentence after death, and, to *some* extent, the hope of escape from the torments of *jer·eg-l̄ar-mū·gu-* (regarding which anon) is said to affect their course of action in the present life.[1]

9. *Pū·luga-* is believed to live in a large stone house in the sky, with a wife whom he created for himself; she is green in appearance, and has two names, *chān·a .au·lola* (Mother Fresh-water Shrimp), and *chān·a .pā·lak-* (Mother Eel); by her he has a large family, all, except the eldest, being girls; these last, known as *mō·ro-win-* (sky spirits or angels), are said to be black in appearance, and, with their mother, amuse themselves from time to time by throwing fish and prawns into the streams and sea for the use of the inhabitants of the world. *Pū·luga-*'s son is called *.pij-chō·r-*: he is regarded as a sort of archangel, and is alone permitted to live with his father, whose orders it is his duty to make known to the *mō·ro-win-*.

10. *Pū·luga-* is said to eat and drink, and, during the dry months of the year, to pass much of his time in sleep, as is proved by his voice (thunder) being rarely heard at that season; he is the source whence they receive all their supplies of animals, birds, and turtles; when they anger him he comes out of his house and blows, and growls, and hurls burning faggots at them—in other words, visits their offences with violent thunderstorms and heavy squalls; except for this purpose he seldom leaves home, unless it be during the rains, when he descends to earth to provide himself with certain kinds of food; how often this happens they do not know since, now-a-days, he is invisible.

11. *Pū·luga-* never himself puts any one to death, but he objects so strongly to seeing a pig badly quartered and carved that he invariably points out those who offend him in this respect to a class of malevolent spirits called *.chōl-*, one of whom forthwith despatches the unfortunate individual.

12. *Pū·luga-* has no *authority* over the evil spirits, the most dreaded of which are *ē·rem-chāu·gala*, *jū·ru-win-*, and *.nī·la-*; they are self-created, and have existed from time immemorial. The first of these, the evil spirit of the woods, has a numerous progeny by his wife *chān·a .bad·gilola*, who remains at home with her daughters and younger children, while her husband and grown-up sons roam about the jungles with a lighted torch

[1] It is from regard to the fact that their beliefs on these points approximate so closely to the true faith concerning the Deity that I have adopted the English method of spelling all equivalents of "God" with an initial capital.

attached to their left legs, in order that the former may injure any unhappy wights who may meet them unprotected,[1] and in the dark; he generally makes his victims ill, or kills them by wounding them internally with invisible arrows,[2] and, if he is successful in causing death, it is supposed that they feast upon the raw flesh;[3] *.ĕrem-chàugala*, indeed, appears to be to the Andamanese much what "*Arlak*"[4] is to the aboriginal Australian: in both cases these evil spirits are represented as afraid of light; *.ĕrem-chàugala* is said to be also afraid of, or to avoid, the demon *.nī'la-*.

13. This spirit, *.nī'la-*,[5] is supposed to live in ant-hills, and to have neither wife nor child; he is not regarded as such a malevolent personage as *.ĕrem-chàugala*, and, though he is always armed with a knife, he rarely injures human beings with it, or, when he does do so, it is not in order to feed upon their bodies, for he is said to eat earth only.

14. As regards *jū'ru-win-*, the evil spirit of the sea, they say that he too is invisible, and lives in the sea with his wife and children, who help him to devour the bodies of those who are drowned or buried at sea; fish constitute the staple of his food, but he also occasionally, by way of variety, attacks the aborigines he finds fishing on the shores or by the creeks. The weapon he uses is a spear, and persons who are seized with cramp or any sudden illness, on returning from, or while on the water, are said to have been "speared" by *jū'ru-win-*. He has various submarine residences, and boats for travelling under the surface of the sea, while he carries with him a net, in which he places all the victims, human or piscine, he may succeed in capturing.

15. Besides these three chief demons, there is a company of evil spirits who are called *.chōl-*, and who are much dreaded. They are believed to be descendants of *mai'a .chōl-*,[6] who lived in antediluvian times. They generally punish those who offend them by baking or roasting pig's flesh, the smell of which is particularly obnoxious to them, as it is also to *Pūluga-*, who, therefore, often assists them in discovering the delinquent; the same risk does not attend *boiling* pork,[7] which the olfactory nerves of the fastidious *.chōl-* are not keen enough to detect.

[1] *Vide ante* "Superstitions," paragraph 1.

[2] *Vide ante* "Medicine," paragraph 1 (foot-note), and "Death and Burial," paragraph 24.

[3] *Vide ante* "Death and Burial," paragraph 26.

[4] *Vide* Wood, "Natural History of Man," p. 93.

[5] Cases have been cited of persons who have been found stabbed, whose deaths are attributed to *Nī'la*; the possibility of the individuals in question having been murdered is scouted.

[6] *Vide post* "Mythology," paragraph 83.

[7] *Vide post* "Food," paragraph 27.

16. While the Andamanese say that they are liable to be struck by *.ērem-chàugala* or *jūru-win-* at any time or in any place, the *.chōl-* strike those only who offend them, and that during the day while they are stationary, this being necessitated by the distance from the earth of their abode, whence they hurl their darts: an invisible spear is the weapon they always use, and this is thrown with unerring aim at the head of their victim, and is invariably fatal. As these demons are considered especially dangerous on the hottest days, they are apparently held accountable for the deaths from sunstroke which happen from time to time.

17. The sun, *chāna .bōdo-*, is the wife of the moon, *maia .ōgar-*, and the stars, *chāto-*, which are of both sexes, are their children: the latter go to sleep during the day; the whole family have their meals near *Pūluga-*'s house, but never enter it; *chāna .bōdo-* is like fire and covered with thorns, but *maia .ōgar-* is white skinned, and has two long tusks[1] and a big beard; their home is situated somewhere below the eastern horizon, and while the former, after setting, rests till dawn, the latter, probably in consequence of the cares of his numerous family, is obliged to keep very irregular hours. During their passage under the earth to their home, they are believed to afford the blessing of light to the unfortunate spirits in Hades, and also, while sleeping, to shed a "dim religious light" over that region: it is by *Pūluga-*'s command that the celestial bodies, while crossing the sky, bestow their light.

18. The phenomena of the waning and waxing of the moon is explained by saying that they are occasioned by "his" applying a coating of cloud to his person by degrees, after the manner of their own use of *kòiob-* and *tà·la-ōg-*,[2] and then gradually wiping it off.[3]

19. Reference has already been made to their superstition regarding the cause of a lunar eclipse, but in case *maia .ōgar-* should be so ill-advised as permanently to withhold his light or render himself in other ways still more disagreeable, whenever the moon is eclipsed some persons at once seize their bows and twang them as rapidly as possible, thereby producing a rattling sound as if discharging a large number of arrows, while others commence at once sharpening their *rā·ta-*.[4] Of course this hostile demonstration is never lost upon the moon, who does not venture to hurt those who show themselves ready

[1] The horns of the crescent moon.

[2] *Vide* Appendix B, items 58 and 60.

[3] "The Eskimo say that the sun, which they regard as feminine, smears the face of her brother, the moon, with soot, when he presses his love upon her" (*vide* Peschel, p. 256).

[4] *Vide* Appendix B, item 2.

to give him so uncomfortable a reception. Their immunity from harm on these occasions has given rise to some joking at the expense of the luminary in question, for, during the continuance of the eclipse, they shout in inviting tones to the hidden orb as follows :—*ō·gar-, ta den bal·ak ban lē·be ng'ī·dō·ati! dō·ati! dō·ati!*" (O moon, I will give you the seed of the *bal·ak!* show yourself! appear! appear!)

20. This seems to explain the custom which Colonel Symes describes as adoration to the sun and moon, for, as has been stated, no traces of worship or forms of religion, in the common acceptation of the term, exist among these tribes.

21. A solar eclipse alarms them too much to allow of their indulging in jests or threats, &c.: during the time it lasts they all remain silent and motionless, as if in momentary expectation of some calamity.

22. The world, exclusive of the sea, is declared to be flat and to rest on an immense palm-tree (*Caryota sobolifera*) called *bā·rata-*, which stands in the midst of a jungle comprising the whole area under the earth. This jungle, *.chā·itā·n-* (Hades), is a gloomy place, for, though visited in turn by the sun and moon, it can, in consequence of its situation, be only partially lighted: it is hither the spirits (*chāu·ga-*) of the departed are sent by *Puluga-* to await the Resurrection.

23. No change takes place in *.chā·itā·n-* in respect to growth or age; all remain as they were at the time of their departure from the earth, and the adults are represented as engaged in hunting, after a manner peculiar to disembodied spirits. In order to furnish them with sport the spirits of animals and birds are also sent to *.chā·itā·n-*, but as there is no sea there, the *chāu·ga-* of fish and turtle remain in their native element and are preyed upon by *jū·ru-win-*. The spirits (*chāu·ga-*) and souls (*ōt-yō·lo-*) of all children who die before they cease to be entirely dependent on their parents (*i.e.*, under six years of age) go to *.chā·itā·n-*, and are placed under a *rāu-*[2] (*Ficus laccifera*) on the fruit of which they subsist. As none can quit *.chā·itā·n-* who have once entered, they support their stories regarding it by a tradition that in ages long past an *ōko-paiad-*[3] was favoured in a dream with a vision of the regions and of the pursuits of the disembodied spirits.

24. Some of their legends, as will be seen elsewhere,[4] appear to bear out the doctrine of the transmigration of souls, as

[1] This is said derisively, for, although these seeds are largely consumed by the pigs, the aborigines themselves do not consider them fit for food.

[2] *Vide ante* "Superstitions," paragraph 17.

[3] *Vide ante* "Magic and Witchcraft," paragraph 1.

[4] *Vide post* "Mythology," paragraphs 15, 16, 29.

certain of their ancestors (*.tô·mola*) are stated to have vanished from earth in the form of various kinds of animals and fish. The spirits of those not thus transformed, although in Hades, are believed occasionally to assist them in performing tasks of unusual difficulty; and it is thought that all the departed are to some extent conscious of what transpires in the world they once inhabited, and are able to promote the welfare of those who bear them in mind.[1]

25. Between the earth and the eastern sky there stretches an invisible cane bridge (*pī·dga-lâr-châu·ga-*) which steadies the former and connects it with *jer·eg-* (paradise); over this bridge the *souls* (*ōt-yō·lo-*) of the departed[2] pass into paradise, or to *jer·eg-lâr-mū·gu-*, which is situated below it: this latter place might be described as purgatory, for it is a place of punishment for those who have been guilty of heinous sins, such as murder. Like Dante, they depict it as very cold, and therefore a most undesirable region for mortals to inhabit. From all this it will be gathered that these despised savages believe in a future state, in the resurrection, and in the threefold constitution of man.

26. In serious illness the sufferer's spirit (*châu·ga-*) is said to be hovering between this world and Hades,[3] but does not remain permanently in the latter place until some time after death, during which interval it haunts the abode of the deceased and the spot where the remains have been deposited.[4] In dreams it is the soul which, having taken its departure through the nostrils, sees or is engaged in the manner represented to the sleeper.

27. The Andamanese do not regard their shadows[5] but their *reflections* (in any mirror) as their souls. The colour of the soul is said to be red, and that of the spirit black, and, though invisible to human eyes,[6] they partake of the form of the person to whom they belong. Evil emanates from the soul, and all good from the spirit; at the resurrection they will be re-united and live permanently on the new earth, for the souls of the wicked will then have been reformed by the punishments inflicted on them during their residence in *jer·eg-lâr-mū·gu-*.

28. The future life will be but a repetition of the present, but all will then remain in the prime of life, sickness and death will be unknown, and there will be no more marrying or giving in

[1] *Vide ante* "Medicine," paragraph 8, and "Death and Burial," paragraph 16.
[2] Their *spirits* (*châu·ga-*) pass to *.chā·itān-* (*vide* paragraphs 22 and 23).
[3] *Vide* Journ. Anthrop. Inst., vol. xi, p. 289.
[4] *Vide ante* "Death and Burial," paragraphs 6 and 15.
[5] As is believed to be the case among certain races, *e.g.*, the Benin negroes.
[6] Save those of the *ôko-paiʼad-* (*vide ante* "Magic and Witchcraft," paragraph 7).

marriage. The animals, birds, and fish will also re-appear in the new world in their present form.

29. This blissful state will be inaugurated by a great earthquake,[1] which, occurring by *Pū'luga-'s* command, will break the *pī'dga-lâr-chàu'ga-* and cause the earth to turn over: all alive at the time will perish, exchanging places with their deceased ancestors.[2]

30. There is no trace to be found of the worship of trees, stones, or other objects, and it is a mistake to suppose[3] that they adore or invoke the celestial bodies. There is no salutation, dance, or festival of any kind held in honour of the new moon: its appearance does not evoke anything more than an exclamation such as *yēlo! ōgar l'àulō'atire.* (Hurrah! there's the moon.)

Mythology.—1. In other sections mention has been made of *Pū'luga-*, the Creator of all, and it has also been stated that no reason is given for the formation of the earth's surface, except that it was according to His will, and the same hypothesis is held to account for the varying seasons.

2. Until recent years it was supposed[4] that the Andamanese were without traditions, and had no idea of their own origin, but since we have been enabled to become better acquainted with them it has been ascertained that such is not the case. While I have been extremely careful as to the source whence I obtained my information, I would at the same time mention that much that is found under these last headings has been obtained from the older and more intelligent members of distant communities, and is probably little, if at all, known to many of the rising generation in our immediate vicinity.

3. Certain mythic legends are related to the young by *ōko-paiʹad-*s,[5] parents, and others, which refer to the supposed adventures or history of remote ancestors, and, though the recital not unfrequently evokes much mirth, they are none the less accepted as veracious. The personages figuring in these tales are believed to be real and historical, but, beyond the fact of a very general acceptance and agreement of the traditions respecting them, no satisfactory traces are to be found of their existence except in the lively imaginations of their descendants.

4. There are a few discrepancies in their accounts of the

[1] *Vide ante* "Superstitions," paragraph 16.

[2] Whether the fate of the former is irrevocably fixed is not explained, but with these, as with other savages, it is in vain to expect them to understand the logical conclusions to which their beliefs tend.

[3] *Vide* statements of Symes, Brown, Grant, and Anderson; *vide* also *ante* "Superstitions," paragraphs 9 and 10.

[4] *Vide* Mouat, p. 349.

[5] *Vide ante* "Magic and Witchcraft," paragraph 1.

creation and origin of the human species, but in the main features all are agreed. The following tradition appears to be the most generally received, and, as far as possible, it is given in the words in which it was first taken down:—

5. In the beginning, after the world had been made, *Pū·luga-* created a man whose name was *.tō·mo-*;[1] he was black, like the present inhabitants, but much taller and bearded. *Pū·luga-* showed him the various fruit-trees in the jungle, which then existed only at *.wōtăemi·i-*[2] (the "Garden of Eden"), and, in doing so, told him not to partake of certain of them during the rains: he then taught him how to obtain and use fire; this he did by first stacking in alternate layers two varieties of wood known as *chōr-* and *bĕr-*, and then bidding *chāna .bō·do-* (Mother Sun) to come and sit on or near the pile until she had ignited it, after which she returned to her place in the sky. *.tō·mo-* was then taught how to cook pigs, which were easily caught, as they had in those days neither ears nor noses.

6. Another version relates that *Pū·luga-* came with a spirit or angel called *lach·i*[3] *.pū·nga .ā·blola* to instruct *.tō·mo-*, who, at his direction, prepared a pyre and then struck it, on which the fire was kindled, and *pū·nga .ā·blola* proceeded to teach him how to cook food.

7. About the origin of the first woman, whose name was *chāna .ē·lewadi*, there is a diversity of belief: according to some, *Pū·luga-* created her after he had taught *.tō·mo-* how to sustain life; others say that *.tō·mo-* saw her swimming near his home and called to her, whereupon she landed and lived with him; while a third story represents her as coming pregnant to Kyd Island, where she gave birth to several male and female children, who subsequently became the progenitors of the present race.

8. These legends ascribe the name *.tō·mola* to all the descendants of their first parents until the period of the Deluge. *.tō·mo-* had two sons and two daughters by *chāna .ē·lewadi*; the names of the former were *.bī·rola* and *.bō·rola*, and of the latter *.rī·ela* and *.chō·rmila*.

9. As time went on, the pigs multiplied to such an extent that they became a nuisance, so, with woman's ready wit, *chāna .ē·lewadi* drilled holes in their heads and snouts, thereby giving them the powers of hearing and smelling, and enabling them to avoid danger and procure food for themselves. *Pū·luga-* then covered the whole land with jungle, into which the pigs

[1] The name of the first man among the Brazilians was *Tamoi* (*vide* Tylor's "Anthropology").

[2] Situated about long. 92° 52', and lat. 12° 18'. Some assert that this event occurred at *.tō·lo-kōt·ima-*, which is in the same district.

[3] *lach·i* is applied to deceased persons, and answers to "the late."

wandered in various directions.[1] But this change was found to have its disadvantages, as it became next to impossible to catch the now wily *sus*. *Pū·luga-*, however, again came to the rescue, and taught *.tō·mo-* how to construct bows and arrows, and to hunt, after which he taught him to manufacture canoes and harpoons, and to fish. On a subsequent visit[2] he instructed *chān·a .ē·lewadi* in the art of basket and net-making, and in the use of red ochre (*kō·iob-*) and white clay[3] (*tā·la-ōg-*), and thus by degrees he imparted to their first parents a knowledge of the various arts which have ever since been practised among them.

10. *.tō·mo* and *.ē·lewadi* were also told that, though they were to work in the wet months, they must not do so after sundown, because by doing so they would worry the *bū·tu-*,[4] which are under *Pū·luga-*'s special protection. Any noise, such as working (*kō·pke*) with an adze, would cause the *bū·tu-*s' heads to ache, and that would be a serious matter. During the cold and dry seasons work may be carried on day and night, as the *bū·tu-* is then seldom seen, and cannot be disturbed.

11. As soon as the first couple were united *Pū·luga-* gave them the *.bō·jig-yā·b-* dialect, which is the language spoken to this day, according to their belief, by the tribe inhabiting the south and south-eastern portion of Middle Andaman, in which district *.wōtaemi-* is situated. It is, therefore, regarded as the mother tongue, from which the dialects of the various other tribes have sprung.

12. The canoes used in those days are said to have had no outriggers, and were made by scooping out the trunk of the *Pandanus*, which is believed to have been much larger than it is now-a-days, and well adapted for the purpose.

13. The formation of creeks is attributed to a fortunate accident: it happened that one day *.tō·mo-* harpooned a large fish, called *kō·ro-ngid·i-chāu-*, which had a projecting snout wherewith it lashed the shore in its frantic efforts to escape; so violent were the blows that the land was broken each time they fell, a result which proved of great benefit and service to the redoubtable harpooner and his descendants.

14. *.tō·mo-* lived to a great age, but even before his death his offspring became so numerous that their home could no longer accommodate them. At *Pū·luga-*'s bidding they were furnished with all necessary weapons, implements, and fire, and then

[1] Another version states that *.tō·mo-* caused the jungle to spring up beyond *.wōtaemi-* by stringing flies on a number of arrows, and shooting them off, whereupon they turned into trees, and soon spread over the country.

[2] In those days *Pū·luga-* lived at Saddle Peak (*vide ante* "Topography," paragraph 2), and being so near, used often to pay them a visit.

[3] *Vide post* paragraph 27, and Appendix B, items 58 and 60.

[4] *Vide post* "Food," paragraph 18.

scattered in pairs all over the country. When this exodus occurred *Pū·luga-* provided each party with a distinct dialect.[1]

15. After the dispersion of the surplus members of his family, *.tō·mo-*, one day while hunting, fell into a creek called *.yūr·a-tig-ĵig-*, and was drowned. He was at once transformed into a cachalot (*.kā·ra-dū·ku-*), and from him have sprung all the cetaceans of this class.[2] *chāna .ē·lewadi-*, ignorant of the accident that had befallen her husband, went in a canoe with some of her grandchildren to ascertain the cause of his continued absence; on seeing them, *.kā·ra-dū·ku-* upset their skiff, and drowned his wife and most of her companions. She became a small crab, of a description still named after her, *ē·lewadi-*, and the others were transformed into iguanas.[3]

16. Consequent on the disappearance of *.tō·mo-* and his wife, the duties of headship over the community at *.wōtdem·i-* devolved upon one of their grandchildren, named *.kō·lwōt-*, who was distinguished by being the first to spear and catch turtles. The *.tō·mola* remained on the islands long after *.tō·mo-*'s transformation, but after *.kō·lwōt-*'s death, according to one legend, they grew disobedient, and as *Pū·luga-* ceased to visit them, became more and more remiss in their observance of the commands given at the Creation. At last *Pū·luga-*'s anger burst forth, and, without any warning, he sent a great flood which covered the whole land,[4] and destroyed all living. Four persons (two men, *.lō·ralola* and *.pō·ilola*, and two women, *.kā·lola* and *.rī·malola*), who happened to be in a canoe when the catastrophe occurred, were able to effect an escape. When the waters subsided, they found themselves near *.wōtdem·i-*, where they landed and discovered that every living thing on earth had perished; but *Pū·luga-* re-created the animals, birds, &c. In spite of this, however, they suffered severely, in consequence of all their fires having been extinguished, and they could devise

[1] It would almost seem that, without straining the legend to suit facts, we might discern in this a faint echo of the Biblical account of the confusion of tongues and dispersion at Babel.

[2] They consider that the whale is evil disposed towards them, and attribute their occasional non-success in catching turtles to his influence. *.kā·ra-dū·ku-* is also accused of inciting sharks and other large fish to attack them.

[3] Another version of this story is, that wearied with an unsuccessful day's hunting, *Tō·mo-* went to the shore where he found a *chi·di-* (*Pinna*) shell-fish; while playing with it, it fastened on him, and he was unable to free himself until a *bat·an-* (*Paradoxurus*) seized the *chi·di-* and liberated him at the expense of one of his members. Shortly after he saw his wife and some of their children coming after him in a canoe; unwilling that they should become aware of the misfortune which had befallen him, he upset the canoe, drowning its occupants and himself. He then became *.kā·ra-dū·ku-*, and the others *.dā·ku-*, which are now very plentiful in the jungles.

[4] Some modify this statement by saying that Saddle Peak, where *Pū·luga-* then dwelt, was not submerged.

no means of repairing their loss. At this juncture one of their recently deceased friends appeared in their midst in the form of a bird named *Lū·raṭūt-*.[1] Seeing their distress he flew up to *mŏ·ro-*, the sky, where he discovered *Pū·luga-* seated beside his fire; he thereupon seized[2] and attempted to carry away in his beak a burning log, but the heat or weight, or both, rendered the task impossible, and the blazing brand fell on *Pū·luga-*, who, incensed with pain, hurled it at the intruder; happily for those concerned, the missile missed its mark and fell near the very spot where the four survivors were deploring their condition. As *Lū·raṭūt-* alighted in their midst at the same moment, he gained the full credit of having removed the chief cause of their distress.[3]

17. Being relieved from anxiety as to their means of subsistence, *Lŏ·ṭola* and his companions began to entertain sentiments of anger and resentment against *Pū·luga-* for his wholesale destruction of their friends, and, accordingly, when they met him one day at *Tō·lo-kōt·imi-*, they determined to kill him, but were deterred from their purpose by *Pū·luga-* himself, for he assured them that, whereas he was as hard as wood and could not be injured by their arrows, any attempt they might venture to make on his life would cause him to destroy them all. Having reduced them to submission by these assurances, *Pū·luga-* explained that they had brought the Deluge upon themselves through their wilful disobedience of the strict injunctions he had laid down, and which had always been observed by their forefathers, and he intimated that a repetition of their transgressions would inevitably lead to their utter destruction.

18. This is said to be the last occasion on which *Pū·luga-* rendered himself visible, or held any communication with them, but the warning he then gave them has not been forgotten, and the islanders are to this day strict in their observance of his commands.

19. Another legend regarding the origin of the Deluge states that one day, at the commencement of the rainy season, a *Tō·mola* named *Bĕ·rebi-* came to visit *Lŏ·ṭola*'s mother, *chāu·a Ērep-*, with the express intention of seeing her son, of whom he

[1] A small variety of kingfisher.

[2] The myth of Prometheus will recur to the reader.

[3] Since that day till the present time, they say they have never been without fire, thanks to the precautions they employ to guard against its extinction. I would add that when first making my investigations on this subject some six years ago, I was led to believe that this kingfisher is regarded by the present inhabitants with a certain amount of veneration (*vide* "The Lord's Prayer in the South Andaman dialect," p. 49), but I have since been assured that such is not the case.

was extremely jealous. When he appeared, *.bē·rebi-* treacherously bit him in the arm, but his teeth became fixed in the flesh and he was therefore unable to detach himself from his victim, whose friends promptly avenged his murder, and disposed of the corpses by throwing them into the sea.[1] The bereaved mother, in her rage, grief, and despair, committed various acts, against which *.tō·mo-* had been warned by *Pū·luga-*, and while so doing incited others to follow her example by the following words:—

ē,ē,ē, dĭ·a rā-gū·mul lab dā·la,
ē,ē,ē, ngū·l kā·ja pĭj pū·gnīken,
ē,ē,ē, ngūl chō·akan tŏ·aiken,
ē,ē,ē, ngūl bad·rato ā·ka-kolā·ken,
ē,ē,ē, ngūl gō·no bō·angken,
ē,ē,ē, ngūl tōng chad·ra bō·angken,
ē,ē,ē, ngig ā·rĭdī pū·laijoken.

The translation of which is:—

"ē, ē, ē,[2] (sobbing)—My grown-up handsome son,
Burn the wax,[3]
Grind the seed of the *chā·kan-*,[4]
Destroy the *bā·rata-*,[5]
Dig up the *gō·no-*,[6]
Dig up the *chā-ti-*,[6]
Destroy everything."

Thereupon *Pū·luga-* was exceeding wroth, and sent the flood which destroyed all living things with the exception of two men and two women.

20. This tradition is preserved in the following lines:—

Kē·ladōnĭ ĭbā·jĭ lār chō·ra,
Rā-gū·mul abgō·rka en ighod·ĭkĭ,
Rā-gū·mul lĕ ligra bō·arnga,
Rā-gū·mul abgō·rka.
Tod·lo ā·rbo eb dā·kan choar·po.

The meaning of which is:—

"Bring the boat to the beach
I will see your fine grown-up son,

[1] *.bĕ·lwĕ·ĭ-*, after death, was transformed into a species of tree lizard, which is still named after him, and *.bē·rebi-* became a fish called *kē·ngo-*, which is armed with a row of poisonous barbs on its back.
[2] Exclamation indicative of grief.
[3] *Vide ante* "Superstitions," paragraph 12.
[4] The *Entada pursætha*.
[5] The *Caryota sobolifera*.
[6] Two varieties of edible roots much relished by them after the rains.

The grown-up son who threw the youths (into the sea),[1]
The fine grown-up son,
My adze is rusty, I will stain my lips with his blood."

21. In this, as in all their songs and chants, a good deal is left to the imagination, but from the explanations which have been given by the aborigines, the following appears to afford some light on the subject:—*.bĕ·rebi*, being jealous of the renown *.kō·lwōt-* had won for himself by his numerous accomplishments and great strength, took advantage of meeting him and his mother one day on the water to ask them to let him enter their boat. On their complying with his request, he provided himself with a rusty adze and a hone, and joined them; approaching near to *.kō·lwōt-*, he put down the adze and hone, remarking on the rusty condition of the former; then taking *.kō·lwōt-* by the arm he sniffed it from the wrist to the shoulder, as if admiring the development of the muscles; while doing so he muttered the threat of staining his lips with blood, which he shortly after fulfilled in the manner already described.

22. *lach·i*[2] *.lō·ralola*, the chief of the survivors from the Deluge, gave, at his death, the name of *.chāu·ga-tā·banga-*[3] to their descendants. When, for the second time in their history, their numbers had increased to so great an extent that it became impossible for them to remain together in one spot, an exodus, similar to the first, took place; each party, being furnished with fire and every other essential, started in a different direction, and on settling down adopted a new and distinct dialect. They each received a tribal name, and from them have sprung the various tribes still existing on the islands.

23. The *.chāu·ga-tā·banga-* are described as fine tall men with large beards, and they are said to have been long-lived,[4] but, in other respects and in their mode of living they did not differ from the present inhabitants. The name seems to have been borne till comparatively recent times, as a few still living are said to remember having seen the last of the so-called *.chāu·ga-tā·banga-*.

24. After the Flood the *Pandanus* was found to have deteriorated so greatly as to be unfit for its former uses; their canoes were consequently thenceforth made by scooping the trunks of the *Sterculia villosa*, and other trees of a similar description.[5]

25. The story regarding certain *.lō·mala*, who failed to

[1] Literally, *caused them to flee into the sea* (*vide post* paragraph 29).
[2] Signifying "the late," or "deceased."
[3] *i.e.*, the big-bodied.
[4] The Andamanese attribute the present increased rate of mortality to the jungle clearances we have made.
[5] The native names of which are *bī·ja-*; *maū·-*; *yī·re-*; and *kī·tan-*.

observe the rules laid down for neophytes, states that, on the day after they broke their fast of *reg-jī·ri-*[1] (kidney fat of pig), they left the encampment without giving notice of their intention to their friends, and the result was that, when they were missed and searched for, it was found they had gone to the shore to fish, and had there met a sad fate; the body of one was discovered adhering to a large boulder, and turned into stone, while the other, likewise in a state of petrifaction, was standing erect beside it.

26. *mai'a .dū·ku-*, who appears to be identical with *.tō·mo-*,[2] is said to have been the first to tattoo himself. One day, while out on a fishing expedition, he shot an arrow; missing its object it struck a hard substance which proved to be a piece of iron, the first ever found. With it *.dū·ku-* made an arrow-head and tattooed himself, after which he sang this ditty:—

> "*Tōng mā lir pī·renga ! tōng yī·tiken ! tōng yī·tiken ! tōng mā lir pī·renga ! tōng yī·tiken !*"

the interpretation of which is, "What can now strike me? I am tattooed! I am tattooed!" &c. (*Da capo*).

27. It would seem that after the Deluge they had to feel their way again to the necessary arts and manufactures in which *Pū·luga-* had vouchsafed to instruct their first parents:[3] especially is this declared to be the case with the pigments used in painting their bodies, one of which, viz.: *tā·la-ōg-*,[4] is said to have been accidentally re-discovered by a *.tō·mola* female, named *chān'a .chā·rid-*, while she was engaged in searching for the much relished edible root known as *gō·no-*; another woman, *chān'a .tē·lin*, is credited with finding, about the same time, *kō·iob-chū·nga-*.[5] Like true daughters of Eve they were not long at a loss in turning their knowledge to some (?) profitable account.

28. Another of their antediluvian ancestors was famous for propagating yams. This was *mai'a .bū·rodg-*, who, in shooting an arrow, struck the creeper belonging to the favourite variety called *gō·no-*; his curiosity being excited he dug up the root, and tasted it: the result being satisfactory, he informed his friends of his discovery, and they all feasted upon it; when they had had sufficient, he scattered the remains in different directions; this

[1] *Vide ante* "Initiatory Ceremonies," paragraph 5.

[2] *.dū·ku* is also credited with having, like Pygmalion, created a woman! The Andamanese Galatea (*chān'a .tol-kal'at-chā·pa-* or *chān'a .boi'ea-*) was made out of *chā·pa-* (firewood), and in due course became her creator's wife. The legend does not explain how she was endued with life, but relates that at death she became a Paradoxurus.

[3] *Vide ante* "Mythology," paragraph 9.

[4] *Vide* Appendix B, item 58.

[5] *Vide* Appendix B, item 63.

apparent waste so angered his mother that, on pretence of shaving him, she split his head open with a piece of quartz. After his death it was found that the act for which he suffered had tended to the spread of the plant which is now plentiful.

29. To explain the origin of certain fish, they say that one day before the Deluge, *maia kō·lwō·t-* went to visit an encampment of the *tō·mola* situated in the Archipelago. While engaged in his song,[1] the women, through inattention to his instructions, marred the effect of the chorus, so, to punish them, he seized his bow, whereupon the whole party in terror fled in all directions; some escaping into the sea were changed into dugongs, porpoises, sharks, and various other fish which till then had not been seen.[2]

30. Only two geological legends have hitherto been discovered: the one refers to a large block of sandstone lying at *.wō·tdem·i-*, and the other relates to two boulders of elephantine proportions, situated within a mile of the same place, which convey the idea that they once formed part of a narrow neck of land which jutted out into the sea, but which has been gradually demolished by storms and by the action of the waves. The belief current regarding the first is that the deep incisions visible on its surface are hieroglyphics inscribed by *.tō·mo-*, the first man, giving a history of the Creation, which event, as already mentioned, is believed by all the tribes of our acquaintance to have occurred at this very spot *.wō·tdem·i-*. The art of deciphering the supposed record has, it is said, been lost for many ages, and no attempt is made to assign a specific meaning to any of the marks which form the mythical inscription. Many of the legends regarding their ancestors picture the scene of their exploits at *.wō·tdem·i-*; hence the special interest of the spot to all the tribes of Middle and South Andaman and the Archipelago. In regard to the two boulders, tradition declares that one day, in the years before the Deluge, *maia dū·ku-* and some of his friends, seeing two animals swimming near the shore, shouted to them, whereupon they came out of the water and showed themselves to be two enormous creatures such as had never before been seen or dreamt of by

[1] *Vide post* "Games and Amusements," paragraph 22.

[2] The following is a list of *.tō·mola* who were transformed into animals, birds, or fish:—

.kā·ra-dū·ku- (whale),
.dū·ku- (iguana),
.kō·lwadi- (small species of crab),
.tegbū·l- (dugong),
.kō·lwō·t- } (tree lizards),
.ā·ga- }
.kōi·an- (paradoxurus),
.ī·d- (rat),
.tū·ratāt- (a variety of kingfisher),
.mū·rud- (pigeon),
.ā·ep- (parrot),
.tē·liu- (jungle fowl),
kā·ka- (crow),
.ōdā·lab- (heron),
.kad·gi- (fish eagle),
.chū·ag- (porpoise),
and various other fish.

the *ṭō·mola*, who were so terrified that they fled precipitately; *dū·ku-* with difficulty escaped, but a few of his companions were less fortunate, being captured and devoured by these monsters, who are known by the name of *ū·chu-*. Consternation filled the minds of the scanty population then inhabiting the "world," when their deliverance was unexpectedly and speedily effected by the *ū·chu-*, who, in attempting to ford the shallow water near *wō·tāemi-*, stuck fast in the deep mud, and, being unable to extricate themselves, met a lingering death.[1]

31. The manner in which the world was illuminated at the beginning is not clearly to be ascertained from their legends, for one story states that the sun and moon were subsequently created at *ṭō·mo-*'s request, as he found that, under the then existing circumstances, it was impossible to catch fish by night or to hunt by day; while, in direct disagreement with this, another story tells us that night was a punishment brought upon mankind by certain individuals who angered *Pū·luga-* by killing a caterpillar. The tale informs us that the sun, one day, burned so fiercely as to cause great distress. Two women named *chāūa ṭī·mi-* and *chāūa jūr·a-ngūd-*, became exceedingly irritable, and while in this unhappy frame of mind they discovered a caterpillar (*gū·rug-*), and a certain plant called *ū·tura-*. By way of venting their spleen, one crushed the hapless grub, and the other destroyed the plant. These wanton acts so displeased *Pū·luga-* that he determined to punish them, and to teach them to appreciate the privilege of daylight, which they had hitherto uninterruptedly enjoyed. He accordingly visited the earth with a long-continued darkness, which caused every one much inconvenience and distress. At last their chief, *maia kō·lwōt-*, to whom reference has already been made, hit upon a happy expedient of inducing *Pū·luga-* to restore the former state of things by trying to assure him that they were quite unconcerned, and could enjoy themselves in spite of light being withheld from them. To accomplish this, he invented the custom of dancing and singing, the result of which was that *Pū·luga-*, finding that they had frustrated his intention, granted, as a first concession, alternate periods of day and night, and subsequently, moved by the difficulties often occasioned by the latter, created the moon to mitigate their troubles. It is in this way that they account for the fact of the same word being used to denote a *caterpillar* and *night*.

32. With regard to the *ū·uba-*, which tree they value greatly, in consequence of the fibre produced from its bark being

[1] The name *ū·chu-* has accordingly been given to the two boulders. On first seeing the elephants which have been introduced by Government at Port Blair, the aborigines at once called them *ū·chu-*, in allusion to this legend, and it is the name ever since adopted by them in speaking of these animals.

used in the manufacture of their turtle-harpoon lines, nets, &c., it is said that *Pū·luga-* commanded *.tō·mo-* never to make use of it as fuel when cooking a turtle, though he might burn it when pigs or other animals were being prepared for food; a warning was also given him that a severe punishment would follow disobedience in this particular, for the males found transgressing would have their throats cut, while the females would be deprived of their breasts; if the offence were committed by day, the carrying out of the sentence rested with *chāna .bōdo-*, or, if by night, with *mai·a .ōgar-*. On one occasion, at night, shortly before the Deluge (when the *.tō·mola* appear to have been a very depraved set), they were guilty, among other enormities, of disregarding this injunction, whereupon *mai·a .ōgar-* descended and inflicted the threatened penalty.

33. The legend regarding the origin of the evil spirits known as *.chōl-* is as follows:—Their ancestor, *mai·a .chōl-*, one day stole a pig which had just been captured by *mai·a .kōl·wōt-*, and climbed up into a gurjon-tree with his prize. Now *mai·a .kōl·wōt-* was remarkable for his great strength, and being enraged, determined to revenge himself; he thereupon planted a number of spikes all round the tree in which the thief had taken refuge, and then proceeded to force it into the ground. On finding that, if he remained where he was, he must inevitably be buried alive, *mai·a .chō·l-* sprang off the tree, and thereby met a more terrible fate, for he was impaled on the spikes, and perished miserably. His disembodied spirit did not pass to *.chā·itā·n-* (Hades), but took up its abode on the invisible bridge, where, by *Pū·luga-'s* orders, numbers of his descendants were afterwards sent to join him, in the form of black birds with long tails.

34. Another curious fable is told to account for a drought from which their early ancestors suffered: it relates that once upon a time, in the dry season, a woodpecker discovered a black honeycomb in the hollow of a tree; while regaling himself on this dainty he observed a toad eyeing him wistfully from below, so he invited him to join the feast; the toad gladly accepted, whereupon the woodpecker lowered a creeper, giving instructions to his guest to fasten his bucket (*dā·kar-*[1]) thereto, and then to seat himself in it, so that he might be drawn up. The toad complied with the directions, and the woodpecker proceeded to haul him up; but just when he had brought him near the comb he mischievously let go the creeper, and his confiding and expectant guest experienced an unpleasant fall. The trick so exasperated him

[1] *Vide* Appendix B, item 13.

that he at once repaired to the streams far and near in the island and drained them, the result of which was that great distress was occasioned to all the birds, as well as to the rest of the animate creation. The success of his revenge so delighted the toad that, to show his satisfaction, and to add to the annoyance of his enemies, he thoughtlessly began to dance, whereupon all the water flowed from him, and the drought soon terminated.

These are among the best known and most important of their legends, but the list is by no means exhausted, others having been narrated to me which space forbids me to include at the present time, as many subjects of more importance yet remain to be considered in connection with the occupations, &c., of their daily life.

PART III.

Social Relations, Education, Infanticide—Attire—Tattooing—Painting—Shaving—Deformations—Weights and Measures—Astronomy—Trade, Exchangeable Values, and Property—Agriculture—Training and Domestication of Animals—Food—Tabu—Warfare—Hunting and Fishing—Navigation—Ornamentation—Pottery—Natural Forms and Miscellaneous Manufactures—Leather-work—Metallurgy—Stone Implements—Basket-work—String—Games and Amusements.

Social Relations, Education, and Infanticide.—1. Although it is true that the performance of most of the domestic duties falls to the lot of the women and children, it would be a great mistake to suppose that any compulsion is used by the head of the family; he usually leads quite as active a life as any of the females, and often shares certain of their labours, when necessity arises in consequence of sickness or other cause. As I have already stated,[1] it is quite incorrect to say of these savages that with them "marriage is nothing more than taking a female slave," for one of the most striking features of their social relations is the marked equality and affection which subsists between husband and wife;[2] careful observations extending over many years prove that not only is the husband's authority more or less nominal, but that it is not at all an uncommon occurrence for Andamanese Benedicts to be considerably at the beck and call of their better halves: in short, the consideration and respect with which women are treated might with advantage be emulated by certain classes in our own land.

2. The duties of the husband,—varying in the case of his being an *ĕrem-tá-ga-* or an *ár-yŏ-to*—consist chiefly in hunting, fishing, turtling, collecting honey, &c., constructing canoes, building the better kinds of huts,[3] and manufacturing the bows, arrows, and other implements needed in his various pursuits; he must also assist his wife in looking after the children, in keeping up the fire, and in providing the materials

[1] *Vide* "Marriage," paragraph 1.

[2] It has been correctly stated that "their mutual intercourse is courteous and genial, and the affection between parents and children is peculiarly tender" (Peschel, p. 148).

[3] *Vide ante* "Habitations," paragraph 2.

required in making their various weapons, utensils, &c.; but though he has no hesitation in sharing and lightening his wife's labours up to this point, it is only in cases of stern necessity that he will condescend to procure either wood or water for the family requirements; the supply of these essentials of daily life being considered as peculiarly feminine duties and derogatory to the lords of creation.

3. Every woman is supposed to be a proficient in shaving,[1] tattooing,[2] and scarifying; she has also to prepare the *kòi·ob-*, *tá·la-ōg-*, and *kà·ngatá-bŭj-*,[3] which are needed on so many occasions. The erection of the *chàng-da·ranga-*,[4] and the manufacture of personal ornaments,[5] and various other objects in constant use,[6] is also confined to the fair (!) sex, and when to these are added their daily duties of procuring certain kinds of food, cooking, and providing the water and fuel required for the family, it will be seen that the Andamanese materfamilias—who has not several children old enough to give her material assistance—has her time fully employed, or at least sufficiently so to prevent her getting into much mischief.

4. It is the duty of those men and women who remain at home to attend to the sick, infants, and others who are in a dependent position, to look after the fires in the various huts, and, of course, if needs be, to protect the property of absentees: for all those who are not physically incapable are supposed to employ themselves in some way, either for their own benefit or that of the community to which they belong.

5. It is customary for every family to maintain a supply of provisions in excess of its own requirements for the use of friends who may chance to visit the encampment; but in the storage of their food—owing probably to the ease with which it is generally procured—much is often wasted which might without difficulty be preserved. The seeds of the *Artocarpus chaplasha*, and of a species of *Semecarpus*, are alone kept for any length of time. The manner in which this is effected will be described in the section treating of "Food."[7]

6. Migrations and other events affecting the movements of a whole community are arranged by the chief and elders; women in such matters are not consulted, though while on the march it is they who are expected to carry the heaviest loads: this

[1] *Vide ante* "Hair," paragraph 4, and *post* "Shaving," paragraph 2.
[2] *Vide post* "Tattooing," paragraph 3.
[3] *Vide* Appendix B, items 60, 58, 62.
[4] *Vide ante* "Habitations," paragraph 4.
[5] *Vide post* "Attire," paragraph 1.
[6] In Appendix B will be found detailed the various objects manufactured by both men and women.
[7] *Vide post* "Food," paragraph 22.

arises from no want of consideration for the weaker vessel, but simply because, if unnecessarily encumbered, the men would be unable to shoot or pursue any animal which might cross their path.

7. Such training as the children receive is undertaken by their parents or guardians; in the case of boys it consists merely in providing them with miniature weapons suitable to their age, and instructing them in their use: as they advance in years they accompany the men in their hunting and fishing expeditions, and, being by nature intelligent and emulous, they speedily acquire sufficient skill to enable them to afford material assistance to their elders.

8. The girls, similarly, are taught by their mothers, or other female guardians, how to fulfil the various duties which are regarded as essentially pertaining to their sex, and which I have described in the foregoing.

9. It seems hardly necessary to add that the unnatural custom of infanticide is unknown to the Andamanese,[1] and though the mortality among infants is excessive,[2] it is traceable to no want of affection, but to the injudicious treatment and lavish attentions bestowed upon the little ones by their ignorant though well-intentioned elders.[3]

10. For the better security of their babies, when travelling, women are in the habit of hanging round their necks a string the ends of which have been previously fastened to the infant's wrists; the child being then placed in a *chip-*,[4] cannot by any accident meet with a serious fall.

Attire.—1. Madame de Staël speaks of certain children being "*vêtu du climat;*" the same expressive remark may be applied to the Andamanese, for no clothing, as we understand the word, is worn by either sex; there are, however, certain so-called ornamental circlets, garters, bracelets, cinctures, and necklaces of bones,[5] wood, or shell, which are its substitute[6] and serve to

[1] The birth of a girl is usually as gratifying to the parents as that of a boy.

[2] *Vide ante* "Reproduction," paragraph 4.

[3] Dr. Day has correctly stated that "men and women seem equally fond of carrying the babies about; all pet them; when they cry for anything, they give it; and over-kindness early consigns the little one to the grave."

[4] *Vide* Appendix B, item 24.

[5] As far as we at present know, the *jâr'awa-* do not wear necklaces of bone, or the skulls of their deceased relatives. The males of this tribe wear round their heads, waists, knees, and arms, fringes of string attached to a cord or cane, which are called by the *.bô'jig-ngi'ji-*, *bĕ'ria-* (*vide* Plate IX, figs. 13, 13*a*, 13*b*).

[6] The relatives of a deceased person will commonly wear such of the ornaments as are in good condition, "in memoriam;" this is not, however, a distinguishing peculiarity, or one confined to savages.

remove in some measure the impression that they are naked;[1] these appendages are not worn as symbols of rank or (if we except the *rō·gun-*) of status, and their manufacture devolves always upon the females of the community.

2. When fully attired[2] the men are seen with peculiar shredded bunches of *Pandanus* leaves attached to their knees and wrists (termed *tā-chō·nga-* and *tō·go-chō·nga-*), and a folded Pandanus leaf round their heads (called *ijī-gō·nga-*[3]), which, as well as the belt (*bōd-*[4]), is common to both sexes; if, however, they (*i.e.* the men) were denuded of one and all, they would be in no way distressed, and in point of fact, often, as while hunting, when perfect freedom of action is needed, they strip themselves of all except the *bōd-*, or other still lighter cincture, in which are inserted any portable objects, such as arrows and knives, that might be required at a moment's notice during the chase.

3. It is otherwise with women, who never[5] appear without an *ō·bunga-*,[6] or small apron of leaves, which is kept in position by the lowest *bōd-*; while men are usually content with one *bōd-* women almost invariably wear four or five, and have been seen with as many as eight round their waists: in addition to the *ō·bunga-* and *bōd-s* married women[7] wear the *rō·gun-*.

4. It seems probable that Colonel Colebrooke's remarks on the want of decency shown by the Andamanese women referred to the *yĕ·rewa-*,[8] or to the tribe we now know as *jār·awa-*[9] for they alone answer to his description in going about perfectly nude: all my experience tends to prove that the females of the tribes of South Andaman are strikingly modest; indeed so particular are they

[1] As has been remarked by Peschel of other black-skinned races, their "dark colour almost removes the impression of nudity."

[2] All ornaments are made by women, whether for themselves or their relatives. Sometimes at a "*jeg-*" (*vide* Games and Amusements) females exchange their girdles (*bōd-s*) and necklaces as keepsakes.

[3] They wear no head covering, but carry a large leaf screen (*kā·pa-jā·nga-*) as a protection against sun and rain.

[4] For a complete list of personal ornaments, *vide* Appendix B, items 25 to 43.

[5] "Nudity prevails among both sexes of the Australians, the Andaman Islanders, sundry tribes on the White Nile, the Red Negroes of the Soudan, and the Bushmen, all of which tribes have as yet no sense of shame" (Peschel, p. 173).

[6] A description of these cinctures, aprons, &c., will be found at Appendix B, items 25 to 43.

[7] During pregnancy loose *bōd-s* (*bōd-lār-gō·rob-*) are worn by women in lieu of the ordinary kind, which are tight fitting; the *rō·gun-* is also discarded when it becomes inconvenient: after the birth of the child both these cinctures are resumed, the former being fastened as tightly as possible for several days.

[8] *Vide* Appendix B, item 79 and footnote.

[9] The *jār·awa-* women have hitherto been seen with only armlets and cinctures of string, to which a few short fibres were attached, obviously only for ornamental purposes.

in this respect, that they will not remove or replace their *ō·bunga-*[1] in the presence of any person, even though of their own sex.[2]

Tattooing.—1. With regard to the practice of tattooing,[3]—so general among the eight tribes[4] of Great Andaman, and which, as Peschel remarks, "is only another substitute for raiment"—it has been erroneously asserted that its object is to "harden the skin against the stings of mosquitoes, sandflies, &c., and also for jungle travelling;" but so far from any such benefit being derived therefrom the aborigines aver that the skin becomes more sensitive after undergoing the ordeal, which is considered, primarily, as ornamental, and secondly, as proving the courage of the individual, and his (or her) power of enduring pain.

2. There are no special ceremonies connected with the operation, which, except in the northern tribes, is almost invariably performed by women, who, however, receive no remuneration, but rest satisfied with the honour of being considered competent to fulfil the task; all the sex are not equally skilled, and therefore, those who have gained distinction by former successes are, it may be said, the recognised practitioners, though no special status, or profit, in a material sense, is gained thereby.

3. Very few children[5] of either sex are allowed to remain untattooed after about the eighth year, and the final operation is often not attempted until the sixteenth or eighteenth year, the process being carried on gradually during the intervening period.[6]

4. The instrument used on these occasions is a flake of quartz, or, now-a-days, glass,[7] which is not "inserted in a stick," but held between the forefinger and thumb; the markings are found chiefly on the back, shoulders, nape of the neck, chest,

[1] The *ō·bunga-* is first worn by girls when they are about five or six years of age.

[2] *Vide ante* "Psychology and Morals," paragraph 8, and footnote.

[3] The legend explaining its supposed origin has been given in Part II (*vide* "Mythology," paragraph 86).

[4] So far as our present knowledge enables us to say, the *jār·awa-* do not tattoo or shave themselves (*vide* "Tribal Distribution," paragraph 2).

[5] Even in the homes the practice is still observed, and one strong-minded youth, *Ira-jē·do-*, who has hitherto declined to undergo the operation, which he has ventured to stigmatise as unnecessary, has earned for himself the (to them) unenviable designation of "*ab-ŭ·te-*," *i.e.*, the "untattooed."

[6] The arms are generally the first part tattooed, and this is accomplished *prior* to the probationary period; the back is ornamented *during* the continuance of the fast and the chest, belly, legs, &c., *subsequently*. Sometimes an *ā·kā-kī dōba-*, *i.e.*, a youth about 11–12, requests that he may be tattooed on his back and on the nape of his neck *before* attaining the usual age; such a request from a lad is considered manly, and, indeed, almost heroic, for ordinarily the painful operation is postponed until some years later.

[7] *Vide post* "Stone Implements," paragraphs 6 and 7.

sides, abdomen, and also on the upper part of the feet and back of the hands.

5. Cicatrices are often observed on the persons of both sexes, but these are due to scarification (*tū·pke'*), or some accidental circumstance whereby the cut has been obliterated, or has failed to heal in the same manner as the others forming the design.[1]

6. The *A'kà-chà'riàr-*, *A'kà-jūr'o-*, *A'kà-kedè-*, and *ó'ko-jū'wai-*[2] are most given to tattooing their persons, and may be specially distinguished by three rows of cuts down the back and chest: these latter marks are ordinarily much fainter than the former. Though women do the greater part of this work, the three lines down the back are almost exclusively made by some male friend with the *ē·la-*,[3] or pig arrow; except the three lines in front, the women of these tribes have no special marks, but are covered, like the females of South Andaman, with small raised cuts, which are inflicted by their own sex, with the ordinary glass or quartz flake, and not with the *ē·la-*.

7. The *A'kà-bò-* differ from the four tribes just mentioned, only in that they omit the centre row of the three down the back.

8. The *bō'jig-ngi'ji-*, *bō'jig-yàb-*, and *bal'awa-* are covered with plain tattooing consisting merely of perpendicular and horizontal incisions all over[5] the person, thus:

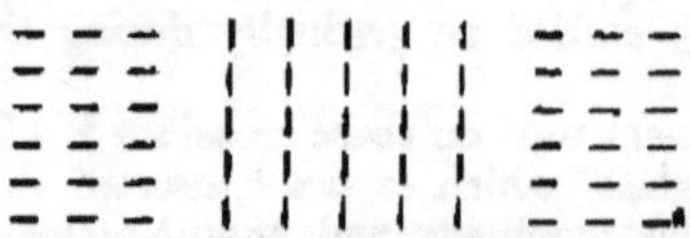

9. There is no distinction made in the mode of tattooing a chief's child and the other children of the tribe; the marks have no special significance, being merely regarded as ornamental;

[1] *Vide ante* "Medicine," paragraphs 5, 6, 12, 16 and 17.

[2] They are not raised by producing "proud" flesh.

[3] Among these tribes the first and most severe operation consists in making the three rows down the back; during the time the wounds take to heal, the patient abstains from pork, in the belief that his recovery will thus be expedited.

[4] *Vide* Appendix B, item 5.

[5] The special poss. pron. denoting the various parts of the body are also used, in connection with tattooing, to express the particular limb or member to which reference is intended; thus:—

ót-yi·tinga-	tattooing on	chest or neck.
ig-yi'tinga-	„	arm, shoulder, or breast.
ór-yi·tinga-	„	leg.
ab-yi'tinga-	„	back body, or thigh.
ông-yi'tinga-	„	foot or hand.
á'kà'yi·tinga-	„	side.

[6] *Vide* Plate II, fig. 1. Where, however, it will be seen that they do not quite attain to the regularity in marking here represented by the printing press.

no coloured pigments or other preparations are rubbed into the wounds, which are left to heal of themselves: before leaving this subject I would mention that the face is never tattooed.

Painting.—1. Besides the permanent tattooing decorations, these savages employ three kinds of pigments for the further adornment of their dusky persons; and from the mode of their application it can be at once ascertained whether the individual be sick, or sorry, or whether he has taken, or is about to take, part in a merry-making.

2. No distinction with regard to rank or sex is made in the designs executed, yet, though these are not very numerous, no two persons are ordinarily painted exactly in the same way, as the pattern traced may be in one case on the chest, in another on the arm, in a third on the face, and so on; a temporary restriction is, however, laid upon the unmarried, who are not permitted to use the paint to their necks, either by way of ornament, or to relieve their pains.[1]

3. We have seen that according to their traditions[2] this was one of the arts in which *Pū'luga-* instructed their first parents, and though temporarily lost after the Deluge it was revived by the accidental re-discovery of the necessary pigments: it may, therefore, be reasonably inferred that the practice is a very ancient one among these tribes.

4. The materials used are *ŏg-*, *tā'la-ŏg-*, and *kōi'ob-*, which are applied, respectively, as a wash and in designs, more or less minute, with the nail or the tips of the fingers.

5. The first (*ŏg-*), is a pale "whitish-grey" clay,[3] which is mixed with water and smeared thickly over the entire person with the palms of the hand, to denote mourning;[4] a lump of the same compound (*del'a-*) is also placed on the head at these times: hence the term *ā'kà-ŏg-*, a mourner.

6. After eating pork or turtle they are also in the habit of smearing *ŏg-* over their bodies with their fingers, in the belief that it affects their breath, and that evil spirits will be unable to detect, and therefore will not be attracted to, them by the savoury smell of the food of which they have partaken. Again, when heated by travelling, or by hunting or dancing, they have recourse to the same wash, but in these cases it is applied thinly.[5]

[1] *Vide ante* "Medicine," paragraph 2.

[2] *Vide ante* "Mythology," paragraphs 9 and 27.

[3] "I may remark that the natives far West . . . . . when mourning for the dead, paint the whole of the body of a white or yellow colour; while in the East of New Guinea the natives *for a similar event* paint themselves with black" (*vide* paper by Signor S. M. D'Albertis: "Travels in New Guinea," Journ. Anthrop. Inst., vol. vi, p. 215.)

[4] *Vide ante* "Death and Burial," paragraph 2.

[5] *Vide* "Anatomy and Physiology," paragraph 5.

7. *tá·la-ōg-* is a pure white clay, which, being comparatively scarce, is more prized than *ōg-*, and consequently more sparingly used; it is applied ornamentally, usually with the nail of the forefinger, in fine tattoo-like patterns, to the cheeks, body and limbs; the designs are invariably executed by women, who, when adorning their relatives[1] for a *jeg-* or other festivity,[2] vie with one another, both as regards the variety and the neatness of their work.

8. *kòi·ob-* consists of burnt yellow ochre mixed with the melted fat of the pig, turtle, iguana, or dugong, and occasionally with oil obtained from a species of almond called *ē·mej-*; this unguent is much used[3] in decorating both the living and the dead[4] and is also employed as a remedy in certain forms of suffering;[5] but it is never applied to the person when in mourning, or, as has been so often asserted, in order to protect the body from the stings of insects.[6]

9. Both *tá·la-ōg-* and *kòi-ob-* are used to adorn their weapons and the various utensils, &c., in daily use.

10. With *kòi·ob-*, of course, no delicate patterns can be worked, but rough zig-zags and stripes are made with the finger tips all over the body: judging from the appearance of a person who had been shortly before painted with *kòi·ob-*, one might easily suppose that the unguent had been smeared over his person, but this is not the case, for it is always applied in some sort of design, which, however, is speedily effaced, as the heat of the body causes the oleaginous pigment to liquify.

Shaving.—1. Under an earlier section[7] shaving was necessarily, to a great extent, included; it remains, however, to be here added, that it is commenced at a very early age: indeed, within a few hours of its birth the Andamanese baby has its head shaved and painted with *kòi·ob-*,[8] while its diminutive face and body are adorned with a design in *tá·la-ōg-*:[9] this latter, as may

[1] These substances are not employed with a view of improving the texture of the skin; they never stain their nails or apply cosmetics to their eyes to increase their lustre.

[2] Though *tá·la-ōg-* is never used by mourners on their own persons it is always applied, as is *kòi·ob-*, to a corpse before it is interred (*vide ante* "Death and Burial," paragraph 3).

[3] The *jár·awa-* are believed to use *kòi·ob-* only for the ornamentation of their implements and weapons.

[4] *Vide ante* "Death and Burial," paragraphs 3 and 8.

[5] *Vide ante* "Medicine," paragraph 2.

[6] It may, however, be said to be used also as a perfume, for it is often applied to the upper lip after a feast on pork or turtle, as the odour of the unguent at such times is apparently particularly agreeable to them. This act of painting the upper lip with *kòi·ob-* is termed *a·kan-iṭ·edamlike*.

[7] *Vide ante* Part I, "Hair," paragraphs 2, 3, and 5.

[8] *Vide ante* "Painting," paragraph 7.

[9] *Vide ante* "Painting," paragraph 6.

be supposed, is soon obliterated, and requires therefore to be constantly renewed.

2. Only in very exceptional cases, when the services of a woman are not obtainable, will men consent to operate upon one another, for among these savages shaving is regarded as essentially a feminine occupation:[1] the instrument used for this purpose is effective, if rude, and consists merely of a flake of quartz, or now more generally of glass; the manner in which these primitive razors are made is described under "Stone Implements."[2]

3. Previous to shaving an *infant*, the mother usually moistens the head with milk which she presses from her breast, but when operating upon bigger children and adults, water only is used.

Deformations.—1. Unless tattooing can be so regarded, these savages do not intentionally produce any deformities, or practice artificial deformations in any way.[3] No attempt is made to alter the shape of the nose by flattening or pinching it, nor is the cartilaginous septum ever perforated for the purpose of inserting ornamental bars or rings.

2. In this, as in many other respects, the Andamanese differ greatly from their neighbours, the Nicobarese, who not only flatten the occiputs of their children in infancy, but, from the period of puberty, blacken their teeth,[4] and perforate the lobes of their ears to such an extent as to enable them, by the time they are full grown, to insert a wooden cylindrical instrument three-quarters of an inch thick.

3. There is, however, a deformity of the skull observable in most Andamanese women, but it is caused unintentionally, and arises from the practice, to which allusion has already been made,[5] of placing the cane or cord by which a load is borne across the anterior portion of the cranium: this habit, especially when commenced at an early age, cannot fail to produce a more or less deep indentation.[6]

[1] *Vide ante* "Social Relations," paragraph 2.

[2] *Vide post* "Stone Implements," paragraph 4.

[3] Mutilation, such as the amputation of a part, or whole, of the fingers, which is practised among certain African tribes, is quite unknown to this race, as are also the customs of circumcision and castration.

[4] "Men and women use so large a quantity of betel-nut lime and betel-leaves that their teeth are as black as ink, and the space between them being filled with that matter they appear as a solid piece, much like the horn inserted in the jaws of the tortoise" (*vide* "Notice of the Nicobar Islands," by the Rev. P. Barbe).

[5] *Vide ante* "Physical Powers and Senses," paragraph 2.

[6] So strongly marked is the deformation in most cases, that the late Dr. J. Barnard Davis, being unaware of its true cause, in a letter to me on the subject, wrote as follows:—"The skull shows unmistakably that she has been subjected to the same barbarous treatment which the women among Australians have to submit to: every Australian woman's skull that I have

Weights and Measures.—1. When speaking of their physical powers I stated that 40 lbs. is ordinarily the maximum of a man's burden; but this is, of course, only an approximate estimate, for among these savages there is no recognised standard of weights or measures, corresponding to the nail, finger-joint, thumb, span, or pace.

2. In referring to the size, shape, or weight of a small object, they would, if possible, liken it to some seed, such as that of the *Entada pursætha*, or fruit, such as mangosteen, jack-fruit, or cocoanut; of larger weights they would say, "as much as" or "more than one man could carry" or "lift;" for expressing capacity or quantity they would say "a bucketful," "basketful," "handful," "canoe-load," as the case might be.

3. There is no prescribed or uniform size for any mat, tool, weapon, or utensil, the dimensions of each and all being dependent on the will of the maker, and on the material at his disposal.

4. No tallies are kept of numbers of articles, nor are counters such as seeds, stones, &c., employed in counting.

5. In speaking of a short distance, as, for example, 50 yards, they would compare it to "a bowshot," but in describing the distance of a certain spot it would be defined as equal to that separating two places, well known to the speaker and the person addressed; any distance over 15 miles would be said to "exceed a day's journey."

Astronomy.—1. It has been stated by Dr. Day that the Andamanese "divide the day into three portions, sunrise, mid-day, and sunset, recognising no subdivisions;" this is, however, incorrect, for though they are naturally content with a, to us, rough method of reckoning time, there are no less than thirteen periods of the day and night distinguished by definite terms, viz.:—

wā·ngala-, the first appearance of dawn.
ela-wā·nga-, between dawn and sunrise.
bō·do-la-dō·atinga-, sunrise.[1]
lū·li-, or *di·lma-*, from sunrise to about 7 a.m.
bō·do-la-kā·galnga-,
bō·do-la-kā·ynga-, or } forenoon.
bō·do-chā·nag-,
bō·do-chā·n-, noon.

met with has borne ineffaceable marks of injuries from which the living woman has suffered during her lifetime. And this is clearly the fate of the Mincopie woman also."

[1] Although they are aware of the variation in the sun's position at the same hour at different seasons they do not take the fact into consideration.

bō·do-la-lō·ringa-, from noon till 3 p.m. } afternoon.
bō·do-lār-dī·yunga-, or, *dār-dī·yunga-*, } from 3 p.m. till 5 p.m. } afternoon.
dī·la-, from 5 p.m. till sunset.
bō·do-la-lō·tinga-, sunset.
elā·kā-dā·urya-, twilight.
elār-yī·tinga-, after dark till midnight.
gū·rug-chāu-, midnight.

2. Of the property of the sun-dial they possess no knowledge, nor can they indicate short intervals of time, such as fractions of an hour, save by some such vague term as—"wait a little" (*tō·laba !*), "it will soon be finished" (*kaw·ya !*), "it is close at hand" (*tari lag·iba !*).

3. As they have no method of numeration, it of course follows that they are unable to denote the number of lunations occurring during a solar year, which with them consists of three main divisions, viz.: *pī·par-*, the cool season; *yē·re-bō·do-*, the hot season; and *gū·mul-*, the rainy season. These again are subdivided into twenty minor[1] seasons, named, for the most part, after various trees which, flowering at successive periods, afford the necessary sources of supply to the honey bees that are so numerous in these islands.

4. They have distinct terms for indicating the four phases of each lunation, i.e.:

ō·gar-dē·reka-yabā·-, new moon (lit., moon-baby-small);
ō·gar-chā·nag-, first quarter (lit., moon-big);
ō·gar-chāu-, full moon (lit., moon-body);
ō·gar-kī·nab-, last quarter (lit., moon-thin);

and that they further recognise the influence of this luminary upon the tides may be gathered from their words denoting high and low tide at full and new moon, viz.:

ō·gar-kā·la-,[2] high tide at the springs at full moon.
yē·char-kā·la-,[3] high tide at the springs at new moon.
ō·gar-pā·di-,[4] low tide at the springs at full moon.
yē·char-pā·di-, low tide at the springs at new moon.
tārbō·rong-kā·la-, flood tide at full and new moon (in the evening) from 3 to 9 p.m.
gū·mul-kā·la-, flood tide at full and new moon (in the morning) from 3 to 9 a.m.
ē·a-bū·nga-, or *kā·la-bū·nga-*, flood tide.

[1] *Vide* Appendix H.
[2] Lit., moon-tide.
[3] Lit., dark-tide.
[4] *pā·di* does not apparently occur alone, or in connection with any other word: its meaning may, therefore, be inferred from the context.

el-a-ĕrnga-, or *kā'la-ĕrnga-*, ebb tide.
wō'ro-, neap tide.
tō'ya-,[1] low tide at daybreak.

5. The four cardinal points of the compass are distinguished; the names indicating these are not derived from prevalent winds, but, as far as the east and west are concerned, have reference to the sun, the word for the former signifying "the appearing face place" (*eldrmū'gu-*), and for the latter "the disappearing face place" (*tār-mū'gu-*); the term for south is the "separate place" (*el-iglā'-*), while the meaning and derivation of that denoting north (*elār-jana-*) is unknown to the present inhabitants.

6. For the winds, too, they have distinctive names, viz.:

chāl-jō'tama-, north-west wind.
Pū'luga-tā-, north-east wind (lit., "The Creator His wind").
dĕ'ria-, south-west wind.
chī'la-tā-, south-east wind.

Of these the second (*Pū'luga-tā-*) only, now-a-days, possesses any special significance; it is called "The Creator's (or God's) wind," because it proceeds from that part of heaven where the connecting bridge[2] between this world and the next is supposed to be situated.

7. They identify three forms of clouds, and indicate them thus:

tō'wia-, cumulus.
ara-mū'ga-bar'nga-, stratus.
yūm-li-dī'ya-, nimbus.

8. Of all the stars and constellations Orion's belt alone is found to bear a name (*bē'la-*), but this is not to be wondered at, as they never venture upon any distant voyages, and do not therefore experience any necessity for studying the bearing of the various planets and constellations at different seasons, or for distinguishing them by name. Their astronomical observations have, however, extended to the discovery of the milky way, which they call *ig-yō'lowa-*[3], and poetically describe as the road used by the angels (*mō'rowin-*).[4]

Trade, Exchangeable Values and Property.—1. It is evident, from the accounts of various writers, that for many years prior to our present occupation, these islands were visited by trading vessels manned by Malays, Burmese, and Chinese, who were *said* to traffic with the Andamanese for edible birds'-nests and *bêche de*

[1] *Vide post* "Hunting," paragraph 39 (footnote).
[2] *Vide ante* "Religious Beliefs," &c., paragraph 23.
[3] The Chippeways call the milky way "the path of the ghosts" (*vide* "Travels in the Interior of North America," by Maximilian, Prince of Wied).
[4] *Vide ante* "Religious Beliefs," &c., paragraph 8.

mer;[1] but it seems more than probable that they obtained their supplies without any assistance from the aborigines; their visits, were, moreover, in later years attended with considerable risk, owing to the malpractices of some of the traders in kidnapping such of the race as they could entice on board their vessels, for the purpose of carrying them away into captivity.

2. Even at the present day, with the exception of procuring turtles, shells, honey, bows, arrows, and a few other articles which are sold, for their own benefit, by the inmates of the homes in and near the harbour, to visitors and residents at Port Blair, the natives attempt nothing in the way of trade, and this much is only done by dint of constant inducements being offered in the shape of presents of tobacco, files, &c.[2]

3. Of our imports they prize chiefly:—dogs, iron, bottles, tobacco, pipes, and matches, all of which have for many years past been freely distributed among the coast people throughout Great Andaman, by whose means they have, doubtless, either by barter or in the form of presents, reached many of the communities inhabiting the interior.[3]

4. In respect to barter, in their transactions with each other, some weapon, utensil, or other common article, such as *kòi'ob-*, or *tá'la-ög-*[4] (used for painting[5] their persons and for general decorative purposes), serves as the medium of exchange.

[1] Captain J. H. Miller, in a communication to the Nautical Magazine, 1842, says: "The islands in the west side of the Andamans are frequented during the fine season, from December to April, by a mixed and mongrel race of Malays, Chinese, and Burmese fishermen for *bêche de mer* and edible birds'-nests, who are of very doubtful honesty; and it is necessary to take a few muskets and cutlasses, just to show them that you are prepared for mischief in case of need. These fellows are also 'fishers of men,' and to their evil deeds much of the hostility of the islanders may be attributed; they carry off children, for whom they find a ready market as slaves in the neighbouring countries. I have been told that formerly they were friendly, and assisted these fishermen, until a large party was invited on board a junk or prow (the Chinese got the blame of it), and after being intoxicated, were carried off and sold at Acheen; and the practice is still carried on by these fellows, who land and carry them off whenever they can catch them. The Andamanians have retaliated fearfully whenever any foreigner has fallen into their power, and who can blame them?" (Sailing Directions for the principal ports in the Bay of Bengal, by W. H. Rosser and J. F. Imray).

"Formerly, both Malays and Burmese procured at the Andamans a considerable quantity of these nests: collecting them themselves, or receiving them from the islanders in exchange for their tobacco, &c." ("Notice of the Nicobar Islands," by the Rev. P. Barbe).

[2] Spiritous liquors would serve as the most powerful medium in this respect, but, in view of the certain and great mischief which would result from gratifying their innate liking for alcohol, it has been rarely given and then only in small quantities medicinally, or by a few persons who are indifferent or ignorant as to its ill effects.

[3] *Vide* Part I.

[4] *Vide* Appendix B, items 60 and 55.

[5] *Vide ante* "Painting," paragraphs 7, 8, 9, and 10.

5. They set no fixed value on their various properties, and rarely make or procure anything with the express object of disposing of it in barter. Apparently they prefer to regard their transactions as presentations, for their mode of negociating is to *give* such objects as are desired by another in the hope of receiving in return something for which they have expressed a wish, it being tacitly understood that, unless otherwise mentioned beforehand, no "present" is to be accepted without an equivalent being rendered.

6. The natural consequence of this system is that most of the quarrels which so frequently occur among them originate in failure on the part of the recipient in making such a return as had been confidently expected.[1]

7. All iron-pointed weapons, tools, or shell ornaments are eagerly accepted by the *ĕrem-tâ'ga-* in exchange for such things as are more easily procured by them than by the *âryô'to-*;[2] for instance, an adze would generally be considered worth two ordinary bows, or a bundle of wooden-pointed arrows; or a man might undertake to make a canoe or bucket for one who would give him an adze.

8. But little care is taken of the utensils, weapons, canoes, &c., in daily use, and consequently new ones are often required, the old, when no longer serviceable, being thrown aside; as all their possessions consist of goods which need to be more or less frequently replaced, it is hardly necessary to explain that there is no accumulation of the labours of former generations; hence also it arises that they are not tied by any laws of inheritance: more as a matter of sentiment than for any other reason, the nearest of kin takes possession of all the effects left by a deceased person, and as often as not they are distributed ere long among such friends as may be in need of any of the articles in question.

9. The weapons, tools, and other property pertaining to one member of a family are regarded as available for the use of his or her relatives, but such articles as a cooking-pot, canoe, or sounding-board, when not required by the owner, are looked upon somewhat in the light of public property by members of the same community; in short, the rights of private property are only so far recognised that no one would without permission appropriate or remove to a distance anything belonging to a friend or neighbour.

Agriculture.—1. Before the arrival of strangers in their midst,

[1] *Vide post* "Games and Amusements," paragraph 37.

[2] Further mention of this will be made at "Games and Amusements," paragraph 24. As will there be explained, the occasions on which they usually barter are when they meet for a *jeg-* at some permanent encampment.

the Andamanese were entirely ignorant of agriculture, and to this circumstance is primarily to be attributed their degraded condition, while it also affords evidence of the same.

2. Notwithstanding the ample opportunities that they have now had of observing the benefits derived from cultivation, and though they undoubtedly prefer such products to the spontaneous vegetation of their jungles, they still consider that the exertion necessary to obtain the former far outweighs every advantage; in short, it is their opinion, that "*le jeu ne vaut pas la chandelle.*"

3. We must not, however, lose sight of the fact that as they have hitherto seen only prisoners engaged in tillage, they cannot but be strengthened in the objections entertained by most savages to all such labour, regarding it as a degrading occupation, and fit only for such as have forfeited their freedom.

4. Further, to quote from Peschel, "it must be remembered that hunting affords supreme enjoyment, and that agriculture has nothing to offer in compensation for the excitement and delights of the chase."

Training and Domestication of Animals.—1. Prior also to our occupation of these islands, the Andamanese, as will have been already inferred,[1] possessed no dogs, and it was some time (1865) before they became aware of their usefulness in the chase; but now that the intelligence of certain breeds has been proved, they prize them highly, and eagerly accept any we have to give them; at the same time, though treated with every intentional kindness, and allowed to sleep, and even to eat and drink out of the same vessel as their masters, the training to which the dogs are subjected is very severe, and their attenuated condition bears witness to the state of semi-starvation in which they are commonly kept in order to render them the more keen in hunting. The custom of summoning dogs by whistling has of course been borrowed from ourselves, as is also the practice of naming them; "Jack" or "Billy"[2] are the names generally bestowed by these people upon their canine companions, whom also they address as *ligala* (children), and who in their turn seem greatly attached to their new owners, and testify their affection by attacking all strangers, not being aborigines, who approach the encampment to which they belong.

2. It is regarded as a good omen to meet certain birds, while of others the contrary belief is held;[3] the absence of migratory

[1] *Vide ante* "Trade, Exchangeable Values, &c.," paragraph 3.

[2] They sometimes nickname them as follows:—*bí'bi-bal-ratnga-* (lit., dog-mottled), *bí'bi-ngol-ronga-* (lit., dog-beggar), *bí'bi-tel-ik-ponga-* (lit., dog-bone-crusher), *bí'bi-tel-ik-ráwa-* (lit., dog-yellow), *i.e.*, according to any peculiarity that may distinguish them.

[3] *Vide ante* "Superstitions," paragraph 22.

species at certain seasons is now accounted for by saying that they are visiting some of the adjacent isles.

3. Of mythological animals,[1] such as dragons and unicorns, they have no knowledge, nor do they venerate or regard as sacred any quadruped, bird,[2] or fish, even though the names of several are identical with those borne, according to tradition, by their antediluvian ancestors,[3] who are supposed to have been transformed into, or to have assumed the forms of, such creatures. Beyond the instances already mentioned, no trace can be found of a belief in transmigration, and, now-a-days at all events, the souls of animals and men are not considered by these savages as interchangeable.

4. The names of four animals only appear to have originated in their cries, viz.: *dū·ku-* iguana, *wū·rud-* pigeon, *bī·bi-* dog, *rō·go-* pig; of these the dog only is trained, or in any way domesticated, and they do not, as has been supposed, keep poultry.[4]

FOOD.—1. Among the many erroneous statements regarding the life and habits of these islanders, none seem at the present day so devoid of foundation as that which declared that they are constantly reduced to want and even to starvation.[5]

2. It has been conjectured by some writers that these savages "glean a miserable subsistence," judging, it would seem, merely from the fact of their eating the larvæ of beetles,[6] and certain other articles, the predilection for which seems, to civilised palates, equally revolting;[7] but evidence is not wanting to disprove this assumption, for during the season, when such things are obtainable, they may frequently be seen enjoying a handful of cooked larvæ when a quantity of pork or turtle is lying beside them, and, if questioned, they declare that they regard the former as dainties (*á·kd-rá·rnga-*), and eat them as

[1] The legend regarding the *ö·ko-* can hardly be included in this category (*vide ante* "Mythology," paragraph 29).

[2] *Vide ante* "Mythology," paragraph 16 (footnote 3).

[3] *Vide ante* "Mythology," paragraph 29 (footnote 2).

[4] "They have no dogs nor any domestic animals, unless indeed their poultry may be regarded as such" (Lubbock, "Prehistoric Times," 4th edition, p. 450).

[5] "In tempestuous weather they are reduced to the utmost want, feeding on rats, lizards, and snakes, and perishing when these resources fail" (Grant). "In the jungles, beyond a few berries and the wild hog, there was no food to be found" (de Röepstorff).

[6] The Loobais, however, appear to be even less fastidious, for they are said to "eat everything that flies, runs, crawls, or creeps, as well as the grub in its ante-natal tomb" ("On the Loobais or Kookees," *vide* Journ. Anthrop. Inst., March, 1872).

[7] "Nor are civilised Europeans justified in shuddering . . . . when they themselves do not shrink from the trail of snipe, nor from lobster and crayfish, although the latter, as water scavengers, act both as grave-digger and grave" (*vide* Peschel, p. 150).

such, not because they find any difficulty in procuring other food.[1]

3. Both *ăryŏ·to-* and *ĕrem-tă·ga-* find ample[2] provisions for their simple wants in their immediate surroundings, without exerting themselves to any great extent, and their eagerness in the chase is induced almost as much by actual love of sport as by the necessity of obtaining food: were this not the case they would hardly be found spending so much time in dancing and singing, in personal decorations, and in the preparation of their meals, while they reject with aversion anything that has become at all tainted. Further, it may be fairly estimated that one-third of the food daily consumed by them consists of edible roots, fruits, and honey, and the remaining portion of the flesh of one or more of the following, viz.: pig, paradoxurus,[3] iguana, turtle, fish, and molluscs, with rare additions of pigeons and jungle fowls;[4] Flying-foxes, bats, rats, sea- (not land-) snakes, the larvæ of the Great Capricornis beetle (*Cerambyx heros*) called *bĭ·yum-*,[5] as well as two other insects, called *bŭ·tu-* and *pĕ·rigi-*,[6] are, it is true, also eaten, but they are partaken of by way of variety, and the latter are regarded as luxuries (*ā·kà-rĭ·raga-*, tid-bits) to supplement (not substitute) other fare.[7]

4. The Andamanese are nominally content with two meals a day, viz.: breakfast (*ā·kà-nă·-*) and a heavy supper (*ā·kan-pō·lugaga-*) after sun-down; they will, however, often help themselves to small quantities of food from time to time in the course of the day when engaged on any work; and, when leaving on a

[1] "It cannot be wondered at that these savages love the unfettered life of their own wild jungles, where their simple wants are easily supplied—a lean-to serving them for quarters, and food such as they are accustomed to being found in great abundance. Nothing comes amiss to an Andamanese maw; roots, wild fruits, berries, crabs, clams, fish, wild pigs, and turtle are all ravenously devoured, and a glance at the well-nourished bodies of men, women, and children amply convinces one that they do not starve" (*vide* "Bombay Gazette," 2nd August, 1881: "The Andamans, our Indian Penal Settlement;" *vide* also paper by Professor Owen, F.R.S., "On the Psychical and Physical Characteristics of the Mincopies," Report of British Association, 1861 p. 2[illegible].)

[2] *Vide* "Tribal Communities," paragraph 2, and Appendix F (*Wō·i's* statement).

[3] It is presumed that Dr. Day refers to this animal when he states that "they eat cats," for they do not appear ever to have had any fancy for the flesh of *pŭ·shi*, the name they have adopted for the domestic cat, from the English "pussy."

[4] *Vide* "Tabu," paragraph 2 (footnote).

[5] Probably the "fat grub, about three or four inches long, much relished by the natives" (Australians), mentioned by Mr. H. W. Bates, in his "Illustrated Travels," is identical with the *bĭ·yum-*.

[6] The *bŭ·tu-* is found in rotten logs of jungle trees, especially the *Dipterocarpus lævis* (*ā·rain-*), *Gluta longipetiolata* (*jĭ-*), and *Chickrassia tabularis* (*ă·ra-*).

[7] Their fancy for grubs does not extend to the *Teredo navalis*.

day's hunt, they usually provide themselves with some fire and a *gōb-*[1] of food, which they warm up and enjoy about midday:[2] no difference is made between the sexes, but all fare alike.

5. The average amount eaten by an Andamanese adult appears to exceed that of a native of India, and to average three or four pounds daily, while, like many other savages, after a successful hunt, or on some special occasion, when dancing is carried on through the entire night,[3] the consumption of food is surprising, and has, in some instances, been estimated at upwards of ten pounds of pork, or turtle, in the twenty-four hours, helped out by mouthfuls of some one or more of the delicacies above enumerated.[4]

6. As may be assumed from foregoing sections, caste distinctions are unknown; while, however, all members of a family take their meals together, a married man is only permitted to eat with other Benedicts and bachelors, but never with any women save those of his own household, unless indeed he be well advanced in years. Bachelors as well as spinsters are required to take their meals apart with those of their respective sexes.

7. Their mode of eating meat is to cram a large piece into the mouth, and then to cut off whatever is in excess[5] with a bamboo or cane (now-a-days generally a steel) knife. The same custom, carried to a more disgusting extreme, is found among the Esquimaux.[6] Speaking generally of the Andamanese it may be said that water is their only beverage, for though the aborigines in the vicinity of Port Blair have acquired a strong liking for rum, &c., they have not been permitted to gratify it; if very thirsty while on a fishing expedition, and all the fresh water supply be exhausted[7] the *drydʼto-* pour water over their

[1] *Vide* Appendix B, item 83.

[2] This applies to the meat of the turtle, pig, iguana, and paradoxurus; the remains of a feast of fish, shell-fish, and prawns are not warmed up a second time; a further distinction is made in the case of turtles' eggs, the three insects mentioned in paragraph 3, edible roots, and such fruits as are cooked (*vide post* paragraph 14), for these are left to cool before they are eaten.

[3] *Vide* "Games and Amusements," paragraphs 21 and 22.

[4] *Bêche de mer* and edible birds'-nests, so highly esteemed by some, and of which large supplies are obtainable along their coasts, are not regarded by the Andamanese as fit for food.

[5] For the following note, which refers to a similar practice among the Napo-Indians of South America, I am indebted to Mr. W. L. Distant:—"In eating meat (usually monkey, sea-cow, and peccari) we observed that they did not tear or bite it, but, putting one end of a long piece in the mouth, cut off what they could not get in, as Darwin noticed among the Fuegians" (Jas. Orton: "Andes and the Amazon," p. 169).

[6] *Vide* Lubbock's "Prehistoric Times," p. 496.

[7] They will now-a-days occasionally assuage their thirst, when away from home, by cutting off a piece of ground rattan (*bōl-*); this practice is only known to the people of South Andaman, and has been borrowed from the Burmese convicts.

heads or jump overboard, and even at times try to alleviate their sufferings by swallowing salt water.[1]

8. In opening certain shell-fish[2] the adze is not employed, but one of the valves of the *Cyrena* is dexterously inserted between the lips, which are thus forced apart, after which the fish is killed with a knife or bladed arrow, and boiled; the *Tridacna crocea* and *Tridacna squamosa* are opened by inserting a piece of wood as a wedge between the valves,[3] afterwards the fish is despatched by stabbing it with an arrow point or blade; the various *Arca* species and the *Mytilus smaragdinus* are, however, not so treated, but are placed among a heap of burning logs for a few moments, the object being merely to part the valves, which would otherwise be a matter of some difficulty: when this is accomplished the shells are removed by means of the bamboo tongs (*kai-*[4]), and their half-cooked contents are transferred to a pot[5] (*bûj-*) in which a little water has been placed; after being boiled a short time the gravy and flesh are eaten with the help of the shells. In former times oysters were eaten *cooked*,[6] but now their consumption appears to be confined to the inhabitants of North (and possibly also Little) Andaman: they give no reason for this change, but it may be due to their having occasionally suffered by feasting unconsciously on the poisonous, or at least indigestible, variety so commonly found in the mangrove swamps.

9. Dr. Day remarked that the mullet was their favourite fish, and "one day, having placed a quantity of different species before them, they helped themselves in the following order: . . . . *Chorinemus*, *Platycephalus*, horse-mackerel or *Caranx*, *Chrysophrys calamara*, and lastly *Tetrodon*, or frog-fish, which latter has generally the credit of being poisonous." My experience is that there are apparently no fresh-water, and but few salt-water, fish[7] which they will not eat.

10. It is a mistake to suppose that pigs were ever scarce in these islands, for though it was formerly more difficult than at the present day to shoot them, there is no lack of evidence to

[1] *Vide* note "Medicine," paragraph 6.

[2] Viz., those of the *Pinna* and *Cyrena* species.

[3] This is only attempted when they succeed in surprising the fish before it has time to close its valves.

[4] *Vide* Appendix B, item 80.

[5] *Vide* Appendix B, item 18. [Note.—Water is boiled in a *bûj-* by the ordinary process, and not by heated stones being dropped into it.]

[6] That Europeans should swallow these molluscs *raw* is a matter of considerable surprise to them.

[7] They prefer the fleshy part of the head to any other portion. To cut up a fish is termed *ôd-lûa*, while to remove its head, tail, and entrails is styled *ered'gi*.

prove that they are, and always have been, fairly numerous.[1] The pig hunts are most frequent during the rains, not only because these animals are then more plentiful and in better condition, but because it is no longer the *ráp-wáb-*, or season of abundance of jungle fruit and honey; from this, however, it must not be inferred that scarcity is then experienced, for those who choose to help themselves need never be in want.

11. During the cool season, *pá'par-wáb-*,[2] the people themselves are alleged to become noticeably thinner: this they attribute not to a deficiency of food, but to the meagre condition of the pigs, which are then breeding, and to the fact that the edible roots (or yams), and other fruits then in season are not fattening. There are six varieties of esculent roots, viz.: the *gō'no-*, *chá'ti-*, *kád-*,[3] *bō'to-*, *mal'ag-*, and *tāg'i-*, which are eaten alone (preferably cold), and not with meat; their chief difference consists in the extra care in preparation which some require, in consequence of their very acrid flavour.

12. The *gō'no-* is cooked in three ways: (*a*) it is placed on the fire in the condition in which it is found until it is soft, when it is freed from the burnt earth and eaten; (*b*) the root, after being washed, is cut up into small pieces and boiled in a pot; and (*c*) after being washed and cut up, the pieces are wrapped in large leaves and baked on burning logs.

13. The *chá'ti-* is cooked in the first of the above-mentioned methods, or by surrounding it with hot stones,[4] and covering the whole with leaves and weights, in order to confine the heat as much as possible.

14. The *kád-* is first cooked as found, the skin is then peeled off, and a number of thin slices are cut and placed in water for a couple of days, so as to lessen the bitterness of its flavour; afterwards it is either baked in leaves or boiled, as already described in speaking of the *gō'no-*.

15. The other three varieties are never boiled, but are placed on the fire without leaves, and the outer skin is removed before they are eaten.

16. The seed of a species of sea-weed, known to them as *tō'no-tòng-*, on which turtles and dugongs feed, and which can only be obtained in small quantities, is carefully cooked and eaten as a relish.

[1] In his examination of a kitchen-midden near Port Blair harbour the late Dr. Stoliczka recorded that "the large number of bones of the Andaman pig is remarkable."

[2] This is the period between the rains and the dry season, and lasts about ten weeks, between the middle of November and the middle of February.

[3] The *gō'no-*, *chá'ti-*, and *kád-*, are very plentiful during the cool season, and are much relished.

[4] *Vide post* "Stone Implements," paragraph 1.

17. The fruit of three varieties of mangrove,[1] known to them as *jū·mu-*,[2] *ngā·tyn-*, and *bā·loga-*, are occasionally eaten, but only by way of change; they are prepared like the *kā·d-* (*vide* above).

18. The following table contains a fairly complete list of the different kinds of food eaten by the Andamanese during the varying seasons of the year; their ordinary diet, as will be gathered from the foregoing, consists of pigs,[3] paradoxurus, iguanas,[4] eggs of the hawkbill turtle, turtles, shell and other sea-fish and prawns, with occasional treats of dugong and porpoise,[5] and for married persons certain birds, already named: the fruit of the *Pandanus* and black honey must also be added, besides which, during the dry season, fresh-water fish, shell-fish, eggs of the green turtle, honey, the bee-bread, and that portion of the comb in which the larvæ are found, as well as the *Caryota sobolifera*, yams, and numerous fruits, about to be named, are eaten with great relish; while during the rains they vary their fare with preserved seeds of the *Artocarpus chaplasha*, *Semecarpus*,[6] and the fallen seeds of the *Entada pursætha*,[7] with three grubs, viz.: the *bū·tu-*, *pī·rigi-*, and the larvæ of the Great Capricornis beetle (*bī·yum-*), and certain fruits. Although on one occasion I saw a man (a member of the *A·kà-bea·a-* tribe) actually eat an *bī·yum-* alive (!) their usual practice is to collect a quantity of the above-named insects and to wrap them up in leaves and place them on the burning embers, turning the bundle from time to time, so that its contents may be thoroughly cooked, whereupon, in the case of the *bū·tu-*, after breaking off the tails, they are consumed with evident gusto.[8]

19. The native names[9] of most of the fruits in season during the dry (*a*), wet and cool (*b*) months are:—

[1] Some terrible calamity, such as another Deluge, would result, so they say, from any one rashly presuming to taste the fruit of a certain species of mangrove, called *tō·kal-*.

[2] *Bruguiera gymnorhiza.*

[3] Not only are the sows eaten when with young, but even their unborn litter is not rejected.

[4] Iguanas and paradoxuri are in better condition during the rains, and are consequently more eaten at that season.

[5] There are special restrictions connected with eating both the dugong and porpoise for the first time (*vide post* "Tabu," paragraph 8).

[6] *Vide* paragraph 32.

[7] *Vide ante* "Religious Beliefs, &c.," paragraph 12.

[8] The *bī·yum-* is found in newly fallen logs, and they say that they do not treat it like the *bū·tu-*—viz., in breaking off its tail—because it does not live in such rotten Gurjon trees.

[9] The botanical names of most of these, as well as of many others, will be found in Appendix L.

(*a*)

*‡*ŭm'dag-*, *‡*ŏ'tŭl-* } either cooked or uncooked.

dŏ'gota-
jŏ-
ŭ'dala-
kŏ'tu-
§*chŏ'kan-*
**bŏ'to-kŏ'ko-kŭ'ra-*
§*pŭ'lia-*
§*pŭ'lain-*
**pi'dga-*
§*gel'dim-*
**ŏ'ria-tŭl-*
*†§*chŏ'rij-*
kăr'ega-
dŏ-
§*ŭgē'bēr-*
§*ŏ'mej-*
**eng'ara-*
§*lō'gaj-*

(N.B.—The best fruits, and those which are most abundant, are in season during these months and at the commencement of the rains.)

(*b*)

†*ŏ'ropa-*
§*pŏ-*
*†*kai-*
†§*kai'ta-*
†*chŏb-*
†*ŏ'dorma-*
**ŏ'bnga-*
§ { *jŭ'mu-*, *ngŏ'tya-*, *bŏ'taga-* }
**bŏ'pa-*
pi'cha-
§*pai'la-*
**bŏr'ŏl-*[1]
§* *jang'ma-*[2]
**jŭ'ni-*
†*pŭ'la-*
**pŏr-*
**dŏ-*
*†*mŏ'lain-*
tŏ'tia-
**eng'ara-*

During the *pŏ'par-wŏ-* (cool season) and *gŏ'rŏ-bŭ'do-* (dry months) the six varieties of edible roots mentioned above (*vide* paragraph 11) are also eaten.

(It will be understood that those fruits that are unmarked in the above list are eaten in the ordinary way).

20. Many fruits they merely suck for the sake of the flavour;[3] others are eaten with fine wood-ash,[4] taken from the hut fires *in lieu of sugar*, to diminish their extreme acidity,[5] while a few are cooked,[6] and the stones of several[7] are cracked for the sake of their kernels. The favourite fruits are *dŏ'gota-*, *ŏ'ropa-*, *kŏn-*, *chŏb-*, *jŏ-*, *pŏ-*, *kai'ta-*, *kăr'ega-*, *chŏ'kan-*, *jŭ'mu-*, *ngŏ'tya-*, *bŏ'taga-*, *ŭgē'bēr-*, *pŭ'lia-*, and *pŭ'lain-*.

21. The fruit of the *ŭgē'bēr-*, *chŏ'kan-*, *pŭ'lia-*, *pŭ'lain-*, *pai'la-*, *gel'dim-*, *lō'gaj-*, and the seeds of the three above-named varieties of mangrove (*i.e.*, *jŭ'mu-*, *ngŏ'tya-*, and *bŏ'taga-*), are freed from their husk or rind and boiled in water until quite soft; when cold they are cut in slices, and left to soak for two days or more in salt or fresh water, after which they are baked in leaves, or again boiled in a *bŭj-*.

22. The Andamanese are, now-a-days at least,[8] extremely particular over the cooking of their food, and will not eat certain

[1] This is a small yellow fruit, the seed of which, after being sucked, is broken, and the outer portion eaten while the kernel is thrown away.

[2] This is a small red fruit, about the size of a bean or filbert, containing one stone; it is wrapped in leaves and baked, because they say that if eaten uncooked it would cause them to forget their way in the jungle, as well as entire loss of memory on all points.

[3] These are marked in the preceding paragraph by a *.

[4] Their immunity from scurvy may not improbably be due to the chemical combination of the acid, contained in many of the fruits, with the potash of the burnt wood.

[5] These are marked in the preceding paragraph by a †.

[6] These are marked in the preceding paragraph by a §.

[7] These are marked in the preceding paragraph by a ‡.

[8] They are very expert in spearing their fish, which they consume in a half-cooked state (Anderson); Symes also writes that "they throw the food on the fire, and devour it half broiled."

fruits and vegetables, much less fish, flesh, or fowl that is raw,[1] or, as far as I could ascertain, even underdone.[2]

23. On ordinary occasions the meals are prepared by these estimable wives in the absence of their lords, but when their labours in procuring wood and water are exceptionally heavy, as on gala days, or after a very successful hunt, the cooking is performed in the special fire-place[3] set apart for the purpose in each community, by some male volunteer, who, when the meat is partly done, distributes[4] it among those present, leaving them to complete over their own fires the necessary preparation of their several shares.[5]

24. Sometimes it happens that the animal is cut up and distributed without being even partially cooked, but the person undertaking this duty is under a tacit obligation to help the slayer of the animal and himself to the last two portions.

25. Small pigs, if caught alive, are sometimes kept and fattened up (*chi'lyuke*) for slaughter;[6] with these, as with others killed while hunting, the same system is observed: the entrails, lungs, liver, kidneys, &c., are first removed (*jō-do-lōi'chrake*), and replaced by leaves (*koktā'r-rā'mke*), to which they set fire—care is always taken to select such as, being entirely free from scent and taste, will not affect the flavour of the meat—the object of this is that all parts may be equally heated when the carcase is placed on the burning logs, where it is left, not until thoroughly

[1] A recent writer (*vide* "Bombay Gazette," May 24, June 7, July 1, July 5, August 2, 1881), in giving an instance of the skill of these savages in shooting fish, affirms that he observed "that most of these fish were just scorched on hastily-lit fires and devoured at once half raw, care being taken that the children present (there were no women) had their full share of the spoils." I am, nevertheless, sure that he is mistaken in supposing that the fish were otherwise than thoroughly cooked, for besides having made close observations myself at the homes, on the point in question, I have made careful inquiries of the aborigines, who assure me (as do also the Hindustani attendants, who have paid numerous visits to the tribes in Middle Andaman) that they never eat fish, flesh, or vegetable until it is thoroughly cooked.

[2] Exception, however, must be made in regard to turtles' eggs, which are eaten with other food or alone, as the case may be, and which, though preferred soft boiled, are sometimes eaten raw: they are among the articles of food prescribed to an *ā'kà-yàb-*. Dr. Day says he has seen them "cook a prawn by placing it inside the bowl of a pipe which they had been smoking!"

[3] This is generally an open space at one end of the encampment. [The [illegible] have a separate hut, which is used exclusively for cooking purposes.]

[4] The "cook" is under an obligation to taste a morsel before all present; should the chief happen to be there he receives the first and lion's share; after him all the men are helped, and then the women and children, while the remainder falls to the share of the distributor.

[5] During the process of cooking all that the Andamanese Soyer requires in the way of impediments are a skewer, [illegible], and a pair of bamboo tongs, *kai-* (*vide* Appendix B, items 70 and 80.)

[6] If the pig should die a natural death while being thus kept it would be eaten, unless visibly diseased.

cooked, but until the bristles have been singed and the skin dried sufficiently to allow of the dirt adhering to it being scraped off; this done, the remains of the charred leaves are removed, and the tendons at the joints being severed (*pū·nuke*), the carcass is cut up (*wā·ratke*) and distributed; while thus engaged, the operator not unfrequently helps himself to choice morsels which he may chance to find done to a turn, as his perquisite. The lining and flesh of the stomach are usually first disposed of;[1] the skin of the entrails, after being thoroughly cleansed, is also frequently consumed.

26. From the account given under "Initiatory Ceremonies"[2] it will be seen that the kidney-fat and omentum (*reg-ji·ri-*) are considered as luxuries from which the young of both sexes must abstain during a certain period. The lungs, liver, and eyes are also eaten, and they are quite of a mind with the Chinese in their estimation of "crackling"[3] (*ōt-ā·gam-*, also *ōt-gō·ma-*), which they consider one of the choicest parts, and enjoy so much that they are even willing to run the risk of offending the *chāl-*[4] by baking their pigs, rather than eat them boiled.

27. When, from some circumstance or other—such as possibly a death from sunstroke[5]—the dread of these demons is paramount, and they boil their pork, it has been observed that, as their pots are small, they remove each piece when partially cooked to make room for others, which afterwards, in the same way, are in turn replaced until thoroughly done; the reason given is that the flavour of the whole animal is thus equally distributed in every portion. On other occasions when the pig is not broiled whole on burning logs, or apportioned among the several families of the community for cooking in their own huts, the flesh is baked in leaves by means of heated stones (*lā-*), which are placed between alternate layers of the meat; in every case the chief concern appears to be that the whole should be so wrapped in leaves that none of the juices be dried up, though every portion be thoroughly well done.[6]

[1] Experience and inquiries have alike failed to find an explanation of the following peculiar statement made by Dr. Day:—"The children and weakly persons eat sucklings, the bachelors and spinsters use those of medium size, whilst adults prefer the stronger boar."

[2] *Vide* paragraphs 15–17.

[3] The skin of the iguana is also eaten, but that of the *paradoxurus* is thrown away.

[4] *Vide ante* "Religious Beliefs, &c.," paragraph 16.

[5] *Vide ante* "Religious Beliefs, &c.," paragraph 16.

[6] In this respect they differ much from the Australians, who "never take the trouble to cook their food, but merely tear off the interior skin of the animal and, after holding the body over the fire for a few minutes, eagerly devour it in its uncleaned state, and frequently eat so voraciously as to be in a state of inactivity and torpor for several hours afterwards" ("A Ride across the Frontier of Victoria," by P. H. Eagle).

28. For brains and marrow they have a great *penchant*, and, in order to extract the latter, will often crush the smaller bones with their teeth, while they break up the larger ones with a stone hammer.

29. The blood of the turtle only are they careful not to spill,[1] and this, though not preferred to the flesh, is considered a dainty, and is eaten separately, after it has been boiled in its own shell until quite thick.

30. They do not preserve the carapace of either description of turtle, but, having removed the flesh, place the shell over the fire, that all the remaining fat may be melted, when—with an appreciation worthy of a City alderman—they ladle it into their mouths with *Cyrena* shells, which thus serve as spoons. So great a delicacy do they consider this that the shell is finally broken up and divided, that no particle may be lost! This fat is largely used in the manufacture of *kòi·ob-*, and it may be judged how highly they prize the unguent since they are willing to deny themselves this dainty rather than allow their supply to run short.

31. Food is preserved by placing it on the small grating (*yât-leb-tâ·ga-*)[2] above the hut fire,[3] or in the following rather peculiar fashion:—having procured and cleaned a length of bamboo (*fam. sp.*), they heat it over a fire that the juices contained in it may be gradually absorbed. When this is satisfactorily accomplished, half-cooked pieces of pork, turtle, or any other food,[4] are packed tightly into it, and the vessel is again by degrees put over the fire, in order to heat it slowly, lest the rapid expansion of the meat should cause a crack; when steam ceases to issue forth, the bamboo is taken off the fire, and, after the opening has been closed by leaves, is set aside with its contents until a meal is required, when it is replaced on a fire, for, as I have remarked in another place, it is a peculiarity of these savages to eat their food in an almost boiling state.[5] As soon as the meat has been once more thoroughly baked, the bamboo is split open with an adze or other

[1] To kill a turtle they pierce the eye with a skewer or arrow (*i·dal jî·rabke*); when the flappers and belly-shell are removed (*lû·lake*), the animal is cut up (*ad·rake*) prior to distribution.

[2] *Vide* "Habitations," paragraph 6.

[3] Jean de Lery, in the account of his adventures among the Indians of Brasil (about 1557), describes the "wooden grating set up on four forked posts; . . . and as they did not salt their meat this process served them as a means of keeping their game and fish."—(E. B. Tylor's "Early History of Mankind," p. 262.)

[4] They have not acquired a liking for either beef or mutton, but are very fond of fowls, rice, dhall, sugar, and sweets of all kinds; it is strange, therefore, to find in Colonel Tickell's paper that "fish they were indifferent to, also to rice."

[5] *Vide ante* "Anatomy and Physiology," paragraph 8.

implement, and all take a share in the feast.[1] Meat thus prepared will keep good for several days.

32. I alluded just now to their method of preparing the seeds of the *Semecarpus* and *Artocarpus chaplasha* for consumption during the rains; it is as follows:—The outer husk, or skin, having been removed, a quantity of the fruit is placed on a wooden platter, and each person present renders assistance by partially sucking (!) the various pieces, which, after this preliminary process, are half boiled in water, and then wrapped up in large bundles of leaves, and buried in moist soil; no mark is made over the spot, but there appears to be no fear of forgetting it, though several weeks usually elapse before the monsoon breaks, and these decaying deposits are dug up, when the smell, as may be supposed, is most offensive to all but those who are to the manner born; by them, however, strange to relate, it is evidently highly appreciated. The next stage through which the seeds have to pass consists in freeing them in water from the decaying matter, and drying them in the sun, or over the fire, where they are left in nets (*chā·panga-*[2]) or leaves until required for use, when they are again baked. With this exception no food is dried in the sun, nor is anything salted or intentionally smoked, though this last cannot fail to be, to some extent, the result of their mode of storing food, as described in the previous paragraph.

33. Besides the various fruits already mentioned as in season during the dry months, yams and honey are very abundant; as their method of treating both fruits and yams has been already described, it now remains for me to notice the ingenious way in which they procure honey, and to name the special trees which, flowering in succession, afford ample material from whence the bees produce a more or less abundant store.

34. At the close of the monsoon one of the large jungle trees, called by them *rār-* (*Eugenia* sp.), comes into bloom, and though no honey is made from its flowers, it is said to act beneficially on the bees as a purgative, and to prepare them for the commencement of the honey season.[3] The *lē·kera-* (*Leguminosæ* sp.), blossoming a little later, is the first honey-yielding flower; the *dūrula-*,[4] *chī·lib-* (? *Diospyros densiflora*), *ōro-* (*Chickrassia tabularis*), and *chā·dak-* (*Rubiaceæ*) coming next into season, enable the bees to produce large combs, but the finest are found after the *pā-* (*Semecarpus*), *lā·ja-* (*Sterculia* (?) *villosa*), *yē·re-* (*Sterculia* sp.), *jī·dga-*,[4] have

[1] *Vide post* "Hunting and Fishing," paragraphs 90 and 91.
[2] *Vide* Appendix B, item 22.
[3] Hence *rā·rke*, (to) clean.
[4] The botanical names of these have not as yet been ascertained.

blossomed: this is considered the height of the honey season, and is called *lad'a chàu-*.[1] It appears that on moonlight nights just at this time the bees consume a great portion of their honey, so that the "jungles" declare it to be useless to go for combs, either by day or night, until the moon has sensibly waned.

35. When about to make a raid on the hives, the Andamanese procure a certain plant, believed to be of the *Alpinia* species, called *ji·ni-*, and having stripped off the leaves, chew the stem and smear the essence thus extracted over their bodies; the mouth is also filled with the same juice, and thus armed *cap-á-pie* they proceed to disperse the bees, who, on attempting to attack them, are at once repelled by the obnoxious odour of the *ji·ni-*, emitted in a fine spray from the mouths, and also attaching to the persons of their despoilers, who sometimes make further use of the chewed stalks of the offensive plant in driving off the last remaining defenders of the hive.

36. Small combs[2] of both the white and black honey are commonly obtainable till about September—*i.e.*, so long as the *Dipterocarpus lævis*, the *Pterocarpus dalbergioides*, and a few other trees continue to blossom.[3]

37. While I had charge of the homes (and probably ever since), a large sum was annually realised by the aborigines towards their support from the sale of honey thus obtained to the free residents at Port Blair. So much indeed did they collect that we were able to store it in barrels and bottles, and generally found we had sufficient to meet all demands until the approach of the following season.

FOOD.—1. Besides the articles of food from which all abstain during the *á·kà-yàp-*,[4] we have seen that there are certain fruits, edible roots, &c., which, in supposed obedience to *Pü·luga-*'s commands, are not gathered at prescribed seasons of the year,[5] and that mourners[6] (*á·kà-ōg-*) also deny themselves by refusing to partake of their favourite viands until after the *ri-tō·latnga-*;[7] but beyond these restrictions, which are of general application,

[1] *Vide* Appendix H.

[2] The combs produced from the blossoms of the under-mentioned trees—*i.e.*, *Ab·lib-* (*Croton argyratus*), *bi·la-* (*Terminalia* (?) *citrina*), and *bat·ya-* are much less plentiful, and they are smaller; this is also found to be the case with those made from the *chà·langa-* (*Pterocarpus dalbergioides*), *mà·rag-* (*Mesua ferrea*), *ka·raj-* (*Terminalia bialata*), *jà-* (*Gluta longipetiolata*), and *pòb-* (*Lagerstræmia hypoleuca* (?) *regina*).

[3] As they are not, in their savage state, in the habit of storing honey, they are without any but the black honey during a great portion of the year.

[4] *Vide ante* "Initiatory Ceremonies," paragraphs 2 and 10.

[5] *Vide ante* "Superstitions," paragraph 12.

[6] If the mourners are *ĕrem-tâ·ga-* they abstain from pork, and if they are *âryö-to-* they abjure turtle (*vide ante* "Death and Burial," paragraph 4).

[7] *Vide ante* "Death and Burial," paragraph 7.

every Andamanese man and woman is prohibited all through life from eating some one (or more) fish or animal: in most cases the forbidden dainty is one which in childhood was observed (or imagined) by the mother to occasion some functional derangement; when of an age to understand it the circumstance is explained, and cause and effect being clearly demonstrated, the individual in question thenceforth considers that particular meat his *yât-tūb-*,[1] and avoids it carefully. In cases where no evil consequences have resulted from partaking of any kind of food, the fortunate person is privileged to select his own *yât-tūb-*,[2] and is of course shrewd enough to decide upon some fish, such as shark or skate, which is little relished, and to abstain from which consequently entails no exercise of self-denial.

2. No one who has not attained the dignity of *gū'ma*,[3] by passing through the rites of initiation, is permitted to eat the flesh of either the dugong or porpoise; and further, it is necessary that the novice should be fed, on the first occasion of tasting either of these meats, by some friend or relative, who, having previously passed through the prescribed ordeal, is qualified thereby to admit others to the like privilege.

3. Except during the initiatory ceremonies, no prohibitions exist with regard to persons feeding themselves, or touching the food of others; after marriage the husband and wife only may eat together;[4] childless widows and widowers usually take their meals with the unmarried of their respective sexes.[5]

4. When an Andamanese woman finds that she is about to become a mother she abstains from pork, turtle, honey,[6] iguana, and paradoxurus; after a while her husband follows her example with respect to the two last-named meats, in the belief that the embryo would suffer were he to indulge in such food.[7]

[1] *Tūb-* can only be applied to food, and is therefore not so generally applicable as *tabu* among the Polynesians. The equivalent of *yât-tūb-* in the *Bojig-yâb* dialect is *tûm'a-tâp-*.

[2] It is believed that *Puluga-* would punish severely any person who might be guilty of eating his *yât-tūb-*, either by causing his skin to peel off (*mui'nyake*), or by turning his hair white and flaying him alive!

[3] *Vide ante* "Initiatory Ceremonies," paragraphs 1 and 9.

[4] The few birds that are ever shot for food (*vide post* "Hunting," &c., paragraph 27), are said to be, strictly speaking, *tabued* to all but *married* persons.

[5] *Vide ante* "Marriage," paragraphs 17 and 18.

[6] *Vide ante* "Initiatory Cermonies," paragraph 14.

[7] Among the Abipones, if the infant dies during the first few days, the women accuse the father of heartless frivolity, as their excesses or abstinences are believed to affect the new-born infant. Again, Peschel states that in the Antilles, the father who is expecting offspring might not eat the flesh of the turtle or the manatee, for in the first case deafness and deficiency of brain, and in the second disfigurement by small round eyes, might be apprehended for the child.

5. When a man wishes to address a married woman who is younger than himself he may not venture to do so directly, but must find some third person to be the medium of his communication; it is also not *selon les règles* for a man to *touch* his younger brother's (or cousin's) wife, or his wife's sister; and women are restricted in the same way as regards their husband's older brother (or male cousin) or his brother-in-law.

6. All titles such as *mai·a*, *mai·ola*, and *chān·a* cease to be applied after death; and inquiries ignorantly made after one who has recently died are replied to in a subdued tone, thus: *wai ālā·re* (he or she "was") or *wai ōkolī·re* (he or she "is dead"). As little allusion as possible is ever made to deceased persons, especially for the first year or so after their death, during which period they are indicated only by reference to the tree or place where their remains are, or were, deposited; after a while the word *lachí*, answering to "the late," is prefixed to their defunct countrymen's (and women's) names.[1]

Warfare.—1. Reference has already been made to their want of true courage or daring, and it has been stated that the Andamanese seldom, if ever, venture to make an attack unless satisfied of their superiority over their foes;[2] it will, therefore, be hardly necessary to enlarge upon their mode of carrying on hostilities, or to say that they are ignorant of the most elementary rules of warfare.

2. Should a dispute arise between members of different communities in the course of a visit or *jeg-*[3] the affair often grows in importance and becomes a tribal question, which may not be settled without more or less serious consequences; those wounded on such occasions generally fare badly unless speedily removed, as they stand great risk of being shot dead or receiving the *coup de grâce* in some other form; they are not, however, in the habit of mutilating the bodies of their victims, save in exceptional cases, where there has been very grave aggravation.

3. The assailants generally approach stealthily upon their enemies, and, though availing themselves of every advantage afforded by the density of the jungle, do not take further precautions or devise stratagems whereby to conceal their trail as they proceed on their way. They wear no breastplate,[4] nor do

[1] Ex.: "múnshí" *Bí·ela* (*vide* Plate II, fig. 2), whose *corpse* was *placed* on a machán beside a tree called *yol-*, was spoken of as *yol lā kā·tāng len tegí yā·te-* (he who is by the *yol-* tree); had he been *buried* he would have been referred to as *yol lā·kā·tāng len bū·guk yā·te-*.

[2] *Vide ante* "Psychology and Morals," paragraph 2.

[3] *Vide post* "Games and Amusements," paragraphs 22–27.

[4] The *jār·awa-* have been found to wear a wide belt of bark as a protection in hostile encounters.

they use shields,[1] and the idea of throwing up earth-banks, or constructing any species of defence for the better protection of their numerous encampments, does not seem to have occurred to them.[2]

4. Night attacks have been made now and again, but the favourite time is the break of day, when the unsuspecting enemy are sound asleep; or at a late hour when they are likely to be engaged in the preparation or consumption of their evening meal.

5. Women and children incur a like risk with men on these occasions, but it would not be considered a matter for boasting should any of them fall victims in the strife, while a child which might be captured uninjured would meet with kindly treatment, in the hope of his (or her) being induced ultimately to become a member of the captor's tribe.

6. The property of the vanquished is of course treated with little ceremony: everything portable is appropriated, and all else is injured or destroyed.

7. No confirmatory evidence is required to prove the truth of a statement declaring a man to have slain one or more foes, but if, in hunting, he should kill at a distance from home an animal too heavy for him to carry back unassisted, he would cut off the tail or some other portion which would afford ocular demonstration of its size, and serve as an inducement to his friends to assist him in bringing in the carcass.

Hunting and Fishing.—1. As I stated in an earlier section, the Andamanese are, for the most part, keen huntsmen, and their eagerness in the chase is one of the chief hindrances in the way of their becoming agriculturists, for a great portion of their time being thus spent, the sites of their temporary (as of their permanent) encampments are to a great extent determined by the advantages which they offer for the pursuit of their favourite pastime.

2. There do not appear to be any omens or superstitions in this connection, nor are there special ceremonies observed previous to the start or on the return of the party, save the somewhat peculiar custom, to which I have elsewhere alluded, of maintaining a glum silence for some time at the close of the day's sport.[3]

[1] Their sounding or stamping boards (*pâ-kwâ-yem-ngâ-*), used in their dances, have, in consequence of their resemblance to shields, been mistaken by more than one visitor as such.

[2] For the weapons used in warfare, *vide post* "Hunting," paragraph 5.

[3] *Vide Journ. Anthrop. Inst.*, vol. xi, p. 287. It may here be added that the only explanation which they offer to account for this practice is that they intend thereby to convey to their friends an exaggerated notion of the fatigues they have endured for the general weal.

3. Females take no part in these expeditions, and boys seldom accompany their elders until after their twelfth year.

4. If more than a few hours' absence is anticipated, besides a supply of provisions, a smouldering log is entrusted to some one member of the party, whose duty it is to prevent its extinction,[1] and to kindle it into a blaze whenever a fire is required. No immediate honours are conferred upon the successful sportsman, but stories of feats of extraordinary prowess are related, with more or less embellishment, from time to time for the benefit of the young and the edification of strangers. No record is kept of the game killed, but, as those distant tribes who are not yet possessed of dogs (or only of a very few) still retain the primitive custom of suspending the skulls of their victims from the eaves or on poles round their huts, a fair idea of their success can be formed by themselves and others from the number thus displayed.

5. Whether in hunting game or in attacking an enemy, the bow (*kā·rama-*) and arrow are employed, and these are almost[2] identical in form among all the eight tribes of Great Andaman. For spearing turtles and large fish a harpoon (*kowai·a l'ā·ko dū·tnga-*[3]) is used: as a description of this serviceable weapon and of the mode in which it is employed, has been given in Appendix B, it is unnecessary to repeat the information in this place.[4] The only other weapon in use is the pig-spear

[1] *Vide ante* "Fire," paragraph 6.

[2] The comparatively slight difference existing between the form of the five *kō·jīg* and three *gō·rama-* bows, and the wide distinction observable between both of these and the *jā·rama-* (Little Andaman) bow will be best seen by referring to Plate VI, figs. 1, 4, and 8 (*vide* also Appendix B, item 1).

[3] *Vide* Appendix B, item 10.

[4] In reference to the subject of *fish-spears* an interesting discovery was made on the occasion of the last visit (October, 1882) paid by Mr. H. Godwin-Austen, now in charge of the Andaman Homes, to North Andaman. Some six or more specimens of what, I believe, is quite an unique wooden fish-spear were seen in one or two of the *gō·rama-* culture. As one was fortunately brought away a sketch is here given of it. It reminds one somewhat of the fish-spears used by the Nicobarese (*vide* Journ. Anthrop. Inst., vol. vii, Plate XV), though very inferior, and is doubtless, like them, intended for spearing small fish. It is called *ti·rama*.

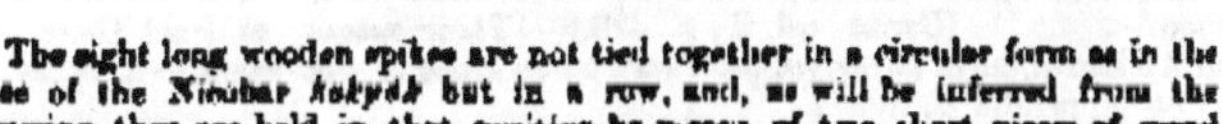

The eight long wooden spikes are not tied together in a circular form as in the case of the Nicobar *kokyōk* but in a row, and, as will be inferred from the drawing, they are held in that position by means of two short pieces of wood lashed to them at right angles: from the appearance of the lower end of this weapon, it would seem probable that it is fixed—like the *kowai·a l'ā·ko dū·tnga*—into a bamboo shaft when about to be hurled, but I have ascertained lately that this is not the case, it is merely held at the pointed end.

(*ârlā·tugu-*[1]), which is of comparatively recent introduction, its adoption being due to the abundance of iron obtainable for some time past by the *.bŏ'jig-ngī'ji-* and other tribes near our settlement at Port Blair.

6. To an untrained eye no difference is noticeable in the appearance of the weapons of similar style and construction, but the aborigines are quick in detecting individual peculiarities in the manner of knotting the strings of bows, arrows, &c.[2]

7. As has been remarked by General Pitt Rivers,[3] the bows of the Great Andaman tribes, especially those of the southern half, known to the islanders as the *.bŏ'jig kâ·rama-*, resemble those in use in Mallicollo, one of the New Hebrides, and in New Ireland, being of a "peculiar flattened S-shaped form, curved towards the firer in the upper part as held in the hand, and to a slight extent the reverse way at the bottom."[4]

8. Except in the case of boys living on or near the coast, whose toy bows are often made of the *Rhizophora conjugata*, the wood of the mangrove is rarely, if ever, used, and the bamboo *never*,[5] for they find that certain other trees,[6] are more suitable for their purpose.

9. No whalebone or sinews are used for the purpose of imparting additional elasticity to the bow, and no evidence is forthcoming to show that they ever applied poison to their arrow or spear-heads—in fact, the only poison known to them appears to be the *Nux vomica*, and this they merely avoid as a noxious or useless plant.

10. It is true that certain passages in Dr. Mouat's book[7] convey a contrary impression, for, from the observations made during his short trip round the islands, he seems to have entertained no doubt that these savages habitually applied poison to their arrow-heads;[8] but, in the sense in which I understand his

[1] *Vide* Appendix B, item 9.

[2] For an example of this *vide ante* "Communications," &c., paragraph 6 (foot-note).

[3] *Vide* Journ. Anthrop. Inst., vol. vii, p. 440.

[4] In the ethnographical department of the museum at Maidstone, I have lately observed a bow from Banks Island (*New Hebrides*), which bears a striking resemblance to the commonest form of the peculiar *.bŏ'jig* bow, for sketch of which see Plates II and VI.

[5] "Their weapons are bows and lances of iron-wood. The former are bamboo. . . . ." (Grant vol. ii., p. 378.) [Their spears, at least those of Great Andaman, have never yet been seen by us made of iron-wood.—E. H. M.]

[6] *Vide* Appendix B, item 1.

[7] Pp. 324 and 350.

[8] It may be of interest to mention in this place a curious alleged fact which has been brought to my notice by the petty officers and others connected with the homes, *i.e.*, that the wounds which are inflicted now-a-days by the iron-headed arrows of the Andamanese are not so painful or so liable to fester as they were formerly, and this they attribute to the fact that, while it has always been the practice of these savages when sharpening their blades to

remarks, I am persuaded that he has credited them with more intelligence on this point than they possess.

11. The origin of the belief appears to be traceable to the fact that they generally in former times tipped their arrow-heads with fish-bones,[1] more particularly the serrated tail-bone of the sting-ray, which, as is well known, is capable of inflicting a very serious wound in consequence of the liability of the fine brittle spikes to break off and remain in the flesh after the extraction of the arrow, thereby causing, in the majority of cases, bad ulcers, which, in the absence of skilful treatment, frequently resulted in the sufferer's death.[2]

12. The maladroitness of strangers who have failed even to bend the Andamanese bows[3] has apparently been due to their having held the wrong end uppermost, for, so far from there being any difficulty in using even their strongest bows, it has been proved that after a little practice Europeans are able to compete almost on even terms with all but the few "crack" shots among the aborigines, provided at least that the object aimed at be stationary; but they less readily acquire the skill which the Andamanese display in rapid shooting, and in discharging the arrow with the full force of which it is capable.

13. The large bows (from 5½ to 7 feet long) are constructed chiefly for ornament and presentation to friends, and are seldom used except for shooting fish and pigs along the shore. The smaller kinds are preferred in jungle expeditions, and on most other occasions, as they are more convenient and also more easily replaced in case of accident, less time and trouble being required for their manufacture.

14. One of the chief drawbacks to the bows used by these tribes is that they cannot be fired in silence,[4] in consequence

moisten them with saliva, the inmates of the homes—who are those chiefly employed as jungle police—now eat *salt* with their food, which was never the case fifteen or twenty years ago. Whether, assuming the story to be true, the effect can be accounted for by the circumstance stated, or, as seems more probable, is due to the improvement in the physical condition of the convicts since the early days of the settlement, is a question for medical authorities to decide.

[1] Writing nearly a century ago, Colebrooke mentioned that "their arrows are headed with fish-bones, or the tusks of wild hogs; sometimes merely with a sharp bit of wood, hardened in the fire, but these are sufficiently destructive." [The *fibula* (*ar-pē·ti-*) of the pig was also used for the same purpose.]

[2] *Vide* footnote to Appendix B, item 58.

[3] *Vide* Mouat, p. 321. Had Dr. Mouat's remarks applied to the Little Andaman or other *jār·awa-* bows, which are of totally different construction (*vide* Plate VI), they would have been more readily understood, for even the aborigines of Great Andaman have experienced much difficulty in shooting with the few specimens of this weapon which have fallen into their hands; doubtless, therefore, much knack and practice, as well as strength, are needed in using them.

[4] From this defect the *jār·awa-* bow appears to be exempt which is easily

of the string striking the lower or convex portion of the weapon.[1]

15. There are five varieties of arrows, viz.: the *rā·tā-*, the *tī·rlē·d-*, the *tō·lbō·d-*, the *ē·la-*, and the *ē·la l'ā·kā lū·pa-*, none of which are provided with more than one point or blade.

16. The first of these (*rā·tā-*) is used in their games, and is the first form which their fish arrows take; it consists of a shaft made of *Bambusa nana*, to the end of which is fastened a piece of hard wood, which is rendered harder and less liable to split by being gradually heated over a fire: this foreshaft also gives the necessary weight to ensure accuracy of flight, and to increase the force of penetration. The *tī·rlē·d-* is merely a *rā·tā-* with its point sharpened for use, in shooting the smaller varieties of fish. The *tō·lbō·d-* is a *rā·tā-* with an iron point, and generally a barb as well, secured to the head: it is chiefly used in fishing. The above three arrows usually measure 4 feet 6 inches to 4 feet 9 inches in length, while the remaining two, of which a sufficient description will be found in Appendix B, do not generally exceed 3 feet 6 inches.

17. The Andamanese take especial pride in keeping the bladed heads of their arrows and spears as bright as possible: the shafts are straightened by dint of pressure with teeth and fingers, but no feathers or other devices are employed to increase the velocity of flight. As illustrations of their arrows and other weapons will be found in Plates VI, VII, VIII, and IX, and as, in Appendix B, I have described their manufacture, it is unnecessary for me here to repeat the information which can be obtained by reference.

18. There are one or two points connected with the iron-bladed arrows to which, I believe, attention has never yet been drawn. I allude to the position of the barbs and the object of the seam. In the *ē·la-* the blade is so fixed as to be in a line with the seam of the fastening at the end of the shaft, and, whether provided with one or more barbs, these are always placed in a line with the blade, the seam above referred to being used as a "sight." In the *ē·la l'ā·kā lū·pa-*, which has no seam, the barb which is most in a line with the blade is used as a "sight," and accordingly placed uppermost. In forming these blades they shape them so as to allow of a small portion being inserted in the foreshaft (see fig.), and it is then fixed as firmly

accounted for by the resemblance it presents to the ordinary European pattern: this, however, appears to be the sole advantage which it possesses over the two varieties used in Great Andaman.

[1] *Vide* "Superstitions," paragraph 5, and "Religious Beliefs," paragraph 19

as possible by means of string,[1] which is protected with a coating of *kā·ngatā-būj-*.[2]

19. It is a singular fact that the mode in which the tribes of Great Andaman discharge their arrows differs from that in vogue among the *jāraw-*. While the latter are said to adopt the plan usual among ourselves of holding the nock of the arrow *inside* the string by means of the middle joints of the fore and middle fingers and drawing the string with the same joints, it is the practice among the former to place the arrow in position between the thumb and top joint of the forefinger, and to draw the string to the mouth with the middle and third fingers. The feet are only used in stringing and unstringing the bows, and never for bending the bow in shooting, as was at one time supposed to be the practice among the *jāraw-*, whose long and clumsy *kā·rama-* have puzzled the *.bō·jig-ngī·ji-*, as well as ourselves, to use with any effect.

20. In Great Andaman the waistbelt[3] *(bōd-)* or other cincture often does duty as a quiver while fishing and hunting, and the arrows are placed behind, with the heads upwards, both in order to avoid causing injury or inconvenience by hindering freedom of action, and to be readily seized and brought into position for firing.

21. Their pointed arrows carry with considerable effect to a distance of 40 or 50 yards. A *tō·lbō·d-* has been found to pierce a deal plank 1½ inch thick at the former range, and probably up to 100 yards one of these arrows is capable of inflicting a serious wound, but an accurate aim is scarcely possible beyond less than half that distance. In the case of the two varieties of pig-arrow much less can be attempted, as those ill-balanced, though formidable, missiles will not carry with certainty further than 12 to 15 yards, and if fired at wider ranges usually fly very wildly.

[1] A better method has, however, been adopted by the *jār·awa-*, viz., that of making three holes in the blade, and passing through them the string which secures it to the foreshaft, thus rendering disconnection of the parts a matter of some difficulty. The precaution thus taken against loss of the blade is evidently due to the comparative scarcity of iron in their territory, which circumstance is the natural consequence of the attitude of hostility, or of avoidance of intercourse, which has been persistently maintained towards the eight Great Andaman tribes, as well as towards ourselves, by one and all of the various scattered *jār·awa-* communities. [With reference both to this sketch and that of the *.bō·jig ē·la-* head, in paragraph 18, it should be added that these are mere sectional drawings of these objects. In the finished arrow the string-fastening is carried up to the base of the blade, and the whole of this string work is finally coated with *kā·ngatā-būj-*.]

[2] *Vide* Appendix B, item 62.

[3] *Vide ante* "Attire," paragraph 2.

22. It is not found that they have any inclination to adopt civilised weapons or tools in lieu of their own, but they have not been slow to avail themselves of the facilities afforded them in recent years for substituting iron for shell, bone, and (?) stone,[1] in the manufacture of their various implements.

23. The blow-pipe, which is used so generally by the Negritos (*Semangs*) of the Malayan peninsula, finds no place among the weapons of these savages. Its absence may be readily accounted for, firstly by their ignorance of poison, or at least of any method of utilising such knowledge as any of them may possess, and secondly by the fact that they are so well able to supply all their wants with the implements already referred to in the foregoing, that their inventive faculty has not been sharpened by the pangs of hunger to devise other or more effective means of destruction. It may be added that slings, throwing sticks, clubs, bird-bolts, or blunt-headed arrows for stunning animals or birds, are likewise not in use among them.

24. Although the pig is the object of their chase in their hunting expeditions, they invariably take a few of their pointed arrows, preferably the *tó·lbō'd-*, on the chance of coming across some smaller game, such as an iguana or paradoxurus.[2] To facilitate rapid shooting a man will often hold a number of arrows in the hand which grasps the bow.

25. From constant practice they are, as might be supposed, very skilful at shooting fish under water. Dr. Brander has correctly observed that "they seem intuitively to have calculated with great accuracy the difference of direction to be allowed for oblique aqueous refraction;" but these shots are almost always, if not invariably, made at a distance of a few yards only, and never so far as "30 yards,"[3] or "with three-pronged barbed arrows," such missiles being neither made nor used, at least by any of the Great Andaman tribes.[4]

26. Boys soon learn to practice at near objects with the small bows and arrows to which allusion has already been made, and many of them often contribute materially to the family larder by their early prowess. It is a common sight to see youths and children (and even their elders), when travelling, wantonly shoot at small passing objects, both on land and in the water, by way

[1] *Vide* Journ. Anthrop. Inst., vol. xi, p. 271.

[2] While these two animals are killed at all seasons of the year, the pig-hunts take place chiefly during the rains, when this animal is in excellent condition, and their diet, owing to the comparative scarcity of fruit and honey, less varied; even if with young the pig is not spared.

[3] The well-nigh impossibility of ever seeing from the shore or from a canoe a fish swimming at such a distance would sufficiently account for this.

[4] It is possible that Dr. Brander saw the *single* specimen of an arrow answering to this description which was obtained in 1880 from North Sentinel Island.

of practice or to display their skill. No reproach is offered by the bystanders to one who wounds an animal without killing it.

27. Pigeons, waterfowl, ducks, and flying-foxes are sometimes shot, but never while on the wing, or when perched in such a position as to risk the recovery of the arrow.

28. In addition to the bows and arrows, their hunting gear consists generally of a bone (*tá·lag-*[1]), a *Cyrena* shell (*û·ta-*[2]), an adze (*wō·lo-*[3]), and often now-a-days a spear (*ār-dū·tnga-*[4]); sometimes a knife (*chó-* or *kō·no-*[5]) is also taken, but as the blade of the pig-arrow or spear can be made to serve this purpose, it is not regarded as an essential part of their equipment.

29. They employ no stratagems for deceiving or decoying game, nor do they prepare snares or pitfalls for it.

30. When unaccompanied by dogs the hunters usually follow the pig's tracks, evincing while doing so their accurate knowledge of its habits. Immediately the object of their search is sighted they endeavour to surround it as noiselessly as possible—taking no precautions, however, against approaching it from windward—and, finally rushing forward and yelling vociferously, discharge their arrows. This practice of driving is generally adopted near the coast and in the vicinity of a belt of *Rhizophora conjugata* where the animals, becoming entangled among the roots or sinking into the soft soil, are easily captured or despatched. The ownership of the carcass is decided in favour of the person who inflicted the first serious wound, and he is exempt, if he please, from carrying home his prize or from any further trouble in connection with it; the cleaning, cooking, and quartering of the animal is undertaken by any one who chooses to volunteer his services, during which interval the day's adventures are narrated: those who have remained at home share equally with the hunters[6] in the spoil, for they are supposed to have been engaged in contributing to the general wants of the community.

31. There are, of course, some in every encampment who, from laziness or want of skill, are of very little use in this respect, but, since any ill-natured remarks at their expense would inevitably result in a more or less serious quarrel, they are rarely twitted with the circumstance, but are permitted to partake of the feast.

[1] *Vide* Appendix B, item 52; also *post* "Stone Implements," paragraph 2.

[2] *Vide* Appendix B, item 51; also *post* "Natural Forms, &c.," paragraph 1.

[3] *Vide* Appendix B, item 15; also *post* "Natural Forms, &c.," paragraph 2.

[4] *Vide* Appendix B, item 9; also *ante* paragraph 5.

[5] *Vide* Appendix B, item 77; also *post* "Natural Forms, &c.," paragraph 4.

[6] On the return of the hunting party the chief is apprised of the nature and amount of the "bags;" whatever is brought in by the married men is taken to their private huts and distributed as they please, but the spoils of the bachelors are at the disposal of the chief, and are distributed according to his orders.

32. At the conclusion of the repast, the sportsman who has most distinguished himself during a more than ordinarily successful chase is expected to entertain the company, while they dance, with an impromptu song, in the chorus of which the women join.

33. Much of the foregoing applies to the *ăryŏ·to-*, as well as to the *ĕremtă·ga-*, except of course that, with the former, hunting expeditions are less frequent than turtling and fishing operations.

34. Turtle-hunts take place during the flood-tide, both by day and night; the favourite hour of all is that between sunset and the rising of the waning moon,[1] for then, with the aid of the phosphorescent light, called *pĕrō·i-*, caused by the movements of the canoe, they are often able to discover and harpoon the turtle before it is at all aware of their approach; on these occasions they select, if possible, a rocky portion of the coast, where there is little or no foreshore, giving it as their reason that turtles frequent such places on dark nights in order to lay their eggs, and are then easily captured. At other times, the localities preferred for these expeditions are those styled *yăua·la-*, where there is a fine stretch of sand with an extensive foreshore, the reason, of course, being that every dark object is so easily seen in shallow water against a clear sandy bottom.

35. The green or edible turtle (*Chelonia virgata*), called *yă·dī-*, is hunted both by day and night, but the hawkbill (*Caretta imbricata*), called *tĕu-*, only by day, as they declare the latter is never seen on dark nights.[2] The flesh of the former is of course preferred, and no use being made of the tortoiseshell obtainable from the latter, it is treated after the feast with as little consideration as the valueless shell of the *yă·dī-*.[3]

36. The practice of capturing turtles by "turning" them when on shore is unknown among these savages; whether this be due to their regarding it as mean and unsportsmanlike, as the disdainful looks and remarks of those I questioned on the subject would lead one to suppose, or whether it be because they so thoroughly enjoy their own methods of procedure, which so fully answer their requirements, I am not prepared to determine, but it is, nevertheless, certain that although well aware, from their knowledge of the animal's habits, that it could be easily surprised

[1] This period has accordingly received a specific name, viz., *ā·kā-tig-pĕ·la-*.

[2] An average size *yă·dī-* weighs about 80 to 100 lbs., and a *tĕu-* considerably less. The heaviest specimen of the former which ever came under my notice weighed about 400 lbs. The ordinary price of a full-grown turtle at Port Blair is five rupees.

[3] These remarks do not of course apply to those living at the homes, as they have long since learnt to benefit considerably by disposing of their tortoiseshell to visitors and residents at Port Blair.

and captured when frequenting the shore, they never take advantage of the opportunities thus presented.

37. Even on the darkest nights many turtles are speared at the moment when they rise to the surface in order to breathe. The sound which they then make, though slight, is sufficient at once to attract the attention of the keen-eared *ǎryǒ'to-*[1] standing on the projecting prow, and to enable him to direct his harpoon with unerring aim; he usually jumps into the water after his victim, lest the barbed head should, in the act of dragging the line, slip out of the wound and the animal escape. When the turtle is in such deep water as to render spearing it from the canoe an impossibility, the harpooner leaps into the water feet foremost, with the spear in his hand, and frequently succeeds at once in transfixing the animal. After spearing a sting-ray, they drag it by means of the harpoon to the boat, whereupon one of the party seizes it by its tail, and holding it firmly between his *teeth*, knocks off, with a piece of wood or other instrument, the formidable spike or spikes which project from the root of the tail; after thus disarming their victim, they proceed to drag it into the canoe or to the shore.[2]

38. From the accounts of some writers respecting the prowess of the Andaman Islanders in the water, it might be inferred that they rival or even excel the "finny denizens of the deep" in their own element. This is, of course, incorrect, and due to misapprehension; the secret of their "invariably returning to the surface with some scaly prize" finds its explanation in the fact that they never think of diving[3] after a fish that has not been first transfixed (according to its size) by an arrow or harpoon.[4]

39. The art of fishing with a hook and line was unknown to, and has not found favour among them, as they are far more successful than ourselves in catching fish by their own methods,[5] which are as follow:—at low water the women and children with hand-nets capture such fish and shell-fish[6] as are left by the

[1] *Vide ante* "Tribal Communities," paragraph 5.

[2] Two or three fatal accidents have, to my knowledge, occurred in recent years on dark nights to inexperienced turtle-hunters at one or other of the homes, in consequence of their having plunged on to the back of one of these fish after harpooning it, mistaking their victim in the darkness for a turtle.

[3] "Should the fish be large some of those in the boat dive down, attacking the victim with knives and spears" (Day).

[4] They are, moreover, not in the habit of "diving for shell-fish"—except it be for a *Tridacna crocea*, which they occasionally discover in deep water—for quantities are always found in shallow water at low tide.

[5] "The present writer has seen a party of Andamanese shoot and secure nearly one hundred fish during one low tide on a coral reef, and that with no very extraordinary exertion" (*vide* "Bombay Gazette," 22nd August, 1891).

[6] The favourite time for collecting shell-fish is the low tide at daybreak occurring about the third and fourth days after new and full moon, and known to them by the name of *tö'ya-*.

receding waves in the rocky hollows on the foreshore, and at the turn of the tide the men are usually to be seen standing up to their waists in water, or poling along the shore in their canoes, and shooting with their bows and arrows at the fish as they dart past.[1]

40. The seeds of a plant called *ú·rog-*[2] are sometimes crushed and thrown into creeks where fish and prawns are likely to be, as it has the effect of driving the fish from their hiding place, and leads to their easy capture in hand-nets held in position for the purpose.

41. In former times, and even now in the more distant communities, large nets of about 80 feet in length and 15 feet in depth, with meshes of several inches in diameter, were spread at the mouths of creeks for catching turtles and big fish; but since iron has been so easily obtained and canoes and harpoons have become more numerous, the *dryô·to-* usually capture their turtles, &c., by these means in preference to the older method, which entailed much labour in the manufacture. The following is the mode employed when nets are used:—one side is sunk by means of stones, and the other is kept up by floating sticks called *tá·log-*, of the *al·aba-*[3] tree (*Melochia velutina*), to each of which a cane-leaf is attached; the ends are then drawn across such parts or creeks into which fish may easily be driven by beating the water with the bamboo shafts of their turtle spears. When any turtle or fish is driven into the net, the exact spot is at once indicated by the disturbance of one of the logs, with its tuft of leaves, whereupon they generally find little difficulty in despatching their captive.

Navigation.—1. It is a subject of surprise to all who, during the past fifteen or twenty years, have come in contact with the Andamanese, and have observed the style and capabilities of their canoes, to read the high encomiums that have been bestowed on the skill with which they are constructed, and to find that they are credited with such extraordinary speed as to distance easily a cutter, as well as a gig, manned respectively by picked crews of blue-jackets and Chinamen,[4] the former of whom "said, in their own usual exaggerated style of remark, they nearly killed

[1] The results obtained by the men are said to be inferior to those obtained by the women and children, but this is probably due to the large quantity of molluscs and crustaceans usually collected in the hand-nets.

[2] A species of *Lagerstromia*. This is similar to the custom among the Gaboon tribes described by Dr. Brown, who mentions that "at the Gaboon it is the leaves of a pretty leguminous plant, with yellow flowers . . . which is used. So rapid is the poison that if a handful of the bruised leaves are thrown into a pool the fish will almost immediately die and come to the surface."

[3] *Vide ante* "Superstitions," paragraph 7, and *post* "String," paragraph 1.

[4] *Vide* Mouat, pp. 315–321.

themselves in their effort to maintain the credit of their ship, their cutter, and their flag."

2. Nowhere on Great Andaman, at all events at the present day, have any aborigines been found capable of propelling a canoe at more than half the speed of one of the ordinary gigs in common use at Port Blair; moreover, in respect to the extreme buoyancy of their skiffs, but little κῦδος seems due to the Andamanese boat-builder, for having had, until quite lately, no other implement than a rude, though tolerably effective, adze with which to form them, he was compelled to select for his purpose the lightest and softest woods that were procurable. At the same time there is no doubt that if they possessed the requisite knowledge, and the means were available for constructing stronger and more seaworthy craft, they would lose no time in employing them; for they fully recognise the inferiority of their boats, both in regard to workmanship and speed, to those used by Europeans, or by their neighbours the Nicobarese. In one respect only do they consider that their own canoes surpass all others, and that is in the projecting prow, which enables them to spear fish and turtle with more ease than is possible in boats of a different construction.[1]

3. The current tradition[2] of the escape of four persons in a boat when the world was submerged, may be fairly considered as affording some evidence that this mode of transit is not regarded as of recent introduction.

4. Many conflicting opinions have been expressed by different writers under this head, and the form of canoe originally manufactured by the Andamanese has been much discussed. They themselves declare that the outrigger (*chà·rigma-*) was adopted immediately after the Deluge, in consequence of the deterioration of a species of *Pandanus* tree, called *màng-*,[3] of which, prior to that catastrophe, they had been able to make large plain "dug-outs." Until recently[4] the outrigger continued

[1] In the South Kensington Museum there are models of canoes made by the natives of the Andamans and Nicobars, which will give to any interested in the subject a fair idea of their relative merits, as well as of the skill of their respective makers; and it may be added that in the entrance court of the India Museum (South Kensington) a specimen of a fair-sized Andamanese canoe is now to be seen minus its outrigger.

[2] *Vide* "Mythology," paragraph 16.

[3] *Vide* "List of Trees," Appendix L.

[4] The following information was obtained from an Andamanese chief:—"We have used outrigger canoes from time immemorial. It is in recent times that we have commenced making the large plain canoes, and this we were induced to do from the facility with which we have been able to obtain iron. Owing to their large size they do not require outriggers. When the sea is rough we prefer these large dug-outs, and the small outrigger canoes when it is calm; the latter are more easily made, but do not last many months when in constant use, whereas the former will serve for a year or more."

in use, and is still to be seen in North and Middle Andaman, but the possibility of obtaining unlimited supplies of iron has enabled those living near Port Blair to return once more to the traditional "dug-out" of antediluvian times; it also seems that this description of canoe is gaining in favour among the tribes of Middle Andaman and the Archipelago, though it had not, in 1879, when I visited that part, penetrated as far as North Andaman.

5. As is correctly stated by Dr. Mouat (p. 316) the Andamanese never venture far from the coast: this was conclusively proved by their ignorance of *Barren Island*[1] and *Narcondam*, until taken past them in the settlement steamer.[2]

6. The safety of either the outrigger or "dug-out," and their adaptability for use as lifeboats,[3] is more than doubtful, while the confidence which is reposed in them by their owners may be judged from the fact that they never venture far from land, and when crossing from one island to another do their utmost to lessen the passage through deep water as much as possible by keeping close in shore and coasting along until the narrowest part of the channel is reached.

7. A glance suffices to show the most casual observer that it would be impossible[4] to preserve the equilibrium of these frail barques without their *outriggers*, which, being attached to three or four pieces of wood passing through the interior of the canoe are, moreover, not easily removable.

8. The advantages possessed by the large plain "dug-outs" over the outriggers are twofold: for in the first place they can breast a fairly rough sea, while the others are fit only for use in perfectly calm weather; and in the second place, while the former can accommodate a party of from fifteen to forty persons

[1] Visible within a short distance of the east coast of the Archipelago.

[2] Since the date of the raids committed by the *jâr'awa-* (of Little Andaman) upon the Car Nicobarese, of which mention is made (as a tradition) by Mr. G. Hamilton (*vide* "Asiatic Researches," vol. ii, p. 337, published 1801), no distant voyages appear to have been attempted by these savages in canoes.

[3] "They would make most excellent lifeboats, such, we believe, as have never yet been constructed by any of our most experienced boat-builders" (*vide* Mouat, p. 317). The returns of life-boat institutions would, however, be somewhat prejudicially affected by the adoption of this suggestion; for, as the same writer goes on to say (p. 318), "the greatest adepts in rowing, steering, and guiding our ordinary boats, find themselves completely at a loss when they get into a Mincopie canoe. When any of our men recklessly got into them, and attempted to paddle out a little way to sea, they invariably succeeded in capsizing them, receiving a thorough drenching in the water as a suitable punishment for their rash and imperfect seamanship."

[4] It is therefore difficult to understand the following allusion made by Dr. Mouat (p. 317):—"When the Mincopie go to sea in them they attach to some part of the boat an outrigger, in some respects resembling that which the Cingalese fishermen attach to their boats."

PLATE IV

the latter are seldom large enough to carry more than four or five, and usually not more than two adults.

9. The chief excellence of both these descriptions of canoes is that they cannot sink, owing to the nature of the wood of which they are constructed, and when, as not unfrequently happens, they capsize or are filled by a heavy wave, their occupants skilfully contrive, with but little delay, to right them and bale out the water, while clinging to the sides.

10. Most of the canoe-making is carried on during the months of August, September, and October, and the average time and labour expended is that of about eight men for a fortnight in hollowing out a canoe or "dug-out," and forming the much esteemed prow; for this purpose a trunk is selected varying in length from 10 to 30 feet, and when the bark has been removed the exterior of the proposed canoe, with its important prow, is shaped with an adze (*wō·lo-*[1]), afterwards the interior is scooped out with the same implement; fire is not now-a-days employed to expedite this latter process, whatever may have been the custom in past generations,[2] though I may add that there do not appear to be any traditions in support of such a theory.

11. At the bottom and water-level, canoes, though sometimes more, are never less than $1\frac{1}{2}$ to 3 inches thick, and indeed, if this were not the case, it would be impossible for them to stand, even for a few days, the rough treatment to which they are subjected, or to bear the spoils of a successful turtling expedition.

12. Though the result of the builders' labour might, by making every allowance for the rudeness of their tool, be termed "creditable," it seems passing strange that any writer should especially commend the "finish," "perfection," and "elegance" of the work, and maintain that it surpasses that which could be wrought by Chinese carpenters, whose skill in all handicrafts is so well established.

13. The Andamanese anchor consists merely of a heavy stone, or large lump of coral, fastened securely to a stout line of a few fathoms' length. Rafts are quite unknown to them at the present day, and no evidence of their use in bygone years has been discovered.[3]

14. The canoes are propelled along the shore[4] by means of the haft of the harpoon spear (*kowai·a ló·ko dū·inga-*[5]), or, in

[1] *Vide* Appendix B, item 16.

[2] *Vide* Colebrooke and Journ. Anthrop. Inst., vol. xi, p. 290, Appendix I.

[3] "They use also rafts made of bamboos to transport themselves across their harbours, or from one island to another" (Colebrooke).

[4] Except when the men are engaged in turtling, the women frequently assist in propelling the canoe.

[5] *Vide* Appendix B, item 10.

deep water, by paddles (*wā̆l·igma-*[1]), the size of which is not determined by custom, but varies according to the whim of the maker and the size of the piece of wood (generally of the *Myristica longifolia*) at his disposal;[2] all, whether small or large, are used indiscriminately, either with the outriggers or simple "dug-outs;" paddles are never made by women, to whom, however, their ornamentation with *kòi·ob-* and *kā·ngatā-bŭj-* is afterwards entrusted.[3]

Ornamentation.—1. While the Andamanese habitually ornament their various utensils, weapons, &c., they never attempt to show their talent or originality by representing natural objects, or by devising a new pattern, but slavishly adhere to those which custom has prescribed for each article.[4]

2. These designs are executed by means of a *Cyrena* shell, or are painted in *kòi·ob-*, *tā·la-ōg-*, or *kā·ngatā-bŭj-*; occasionally they content themselves with smearing the entire surface of the object with either of the two first-named pigments, but more often a background is thus formed for the better display of further embellishments.

3. These three substances supply their only colours, *i.e.*: brick-red (*kòi·ob-*), white (*tā·la-ōg-*), and brown (*kā·ngatā-bŭj-*).

4. Small land and sea shells[5] (especially the *Dentalium octogonum*), certain seeds and bones are much prized, not only for making personal ornaments, but also for the adornment of weapons and implements, as well as the human skulls and jawbones which they often wear and carry about with them.

5. It may be added that the details of ornamentation are in most cases subordinate to the general form and outline of the object in question.

6. The following is believed to be a complete list of the designs,[6] both carved and painted, which are in use:—

I. CHEVRONS (*jū·bo-tārtā·nga-*).

Painted with *kòi·ob-* or *tā·la-ōg-* on bows, buckets, canoes, and paddles.

[1] *Vide* Appendix B, item 11*a*.

[2] Dr. Mouat states (p. 310) that they are made of three sizes, and (p. 330) that "the work of making them is entrusted solely to the women and children," but I have failed in discovering any foundation for these assertions.

[3] The canoes, too, are often similarly ornamented, especially when new.

[4] Of enamelling they possess no knowledge.

[5] Beads, when offered by us, are gladly accepted for use in lieu of small shells.

[6] When it is stated that all these designs are executed by means of pointed sticks, shells, or even the finger-tips, it is scarcely necessary to add that they fall far short of the neatness and mathematical precision characterising most of these illustrations, which therefore can only be taken as representing the particular pattern attempted.

II. Cross Lines (*ig-gi·tinga-*).

Cut by means of a *Cyrena* shell on the *rō·gun-*[1] and *ij·i-gō·nga-*,[2] and painted with *tā·la-ōg-*, between parallel lines, on the sounding board (*pū·kuta-yem·nga-*[3]).

III. Cross Lines (*ig-bar·nga-*).

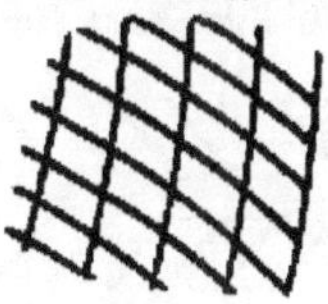

Painted on the outer surface of baskets, the vertical lines with *kòi·ob-*, and the oblique ones with *tā·la-ōg-*.

IV. Parallel Lines (*ig-ō·inga-*).

Painted with *kòi·ob-* or *tā·la-ōg-* across handle of paddle.

V. Parallel Lines and Zigzag (*jō·bo-tārtā·nga-* or *tā·nanga-*).

Painted with *tā·la-ōg-* on *rō·gun-*[4] and *ij·i-gō·nga-*.[5]

VI. Lozenge Pattern.

(*a*) *jō·bo-tārtā·nga-*

(*b*) *ig-ē·nga-*.

Painted with *tā·la-ōg-* or *kà·ngatà-bàj·*, on *rō·gun-*,[4] *ij·i-gō·nga-*,[5] *ò·do-*,[6] and *pū·kuta-*.[7]

[1] Waistbelt, worn by married women only.
[2] Chaplet, worn by both sexes.
[3] Sounding board, used in keeping time for dancers.
[4] *Vide* Appendix B, item 26.
[5] *Vide* Appendix B, item 31.
[6] *Nautilus* shell, used as a drinking vessel.
[7] *pū·kuta-yāt-māk·nga-*, wooden tray used at [illegible].

VII. Plait Ornament or Guilloche (*poliòr·nga*).

Painted with *tö·la-ög·* on bows and eating trays.

VIII. Fish-Bone (*bar·nga·*).

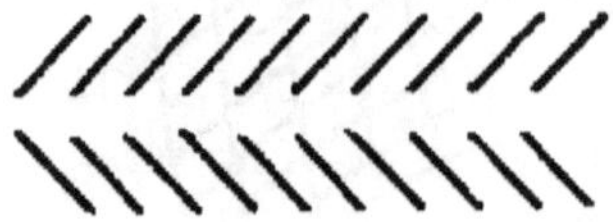

Painted on *chip·*.[1]

IX. Cross Incisions (*igû·nga·*) (? *ig-yi·tinga·*).

Cut by means of a *Cyrena* shell on bows (*kâ·rama·*), and handles of adzes (*wô·lo·*).

X. Loop Pattern (*öt-ê·nga·*).

Painted with *tö·la-ög·* on the *chi·di·*

[1] Sling or belt, worn like a sash by men and women for carrying children.
[2] *Pinna* shell, used as a plate or tray.

Plate 7

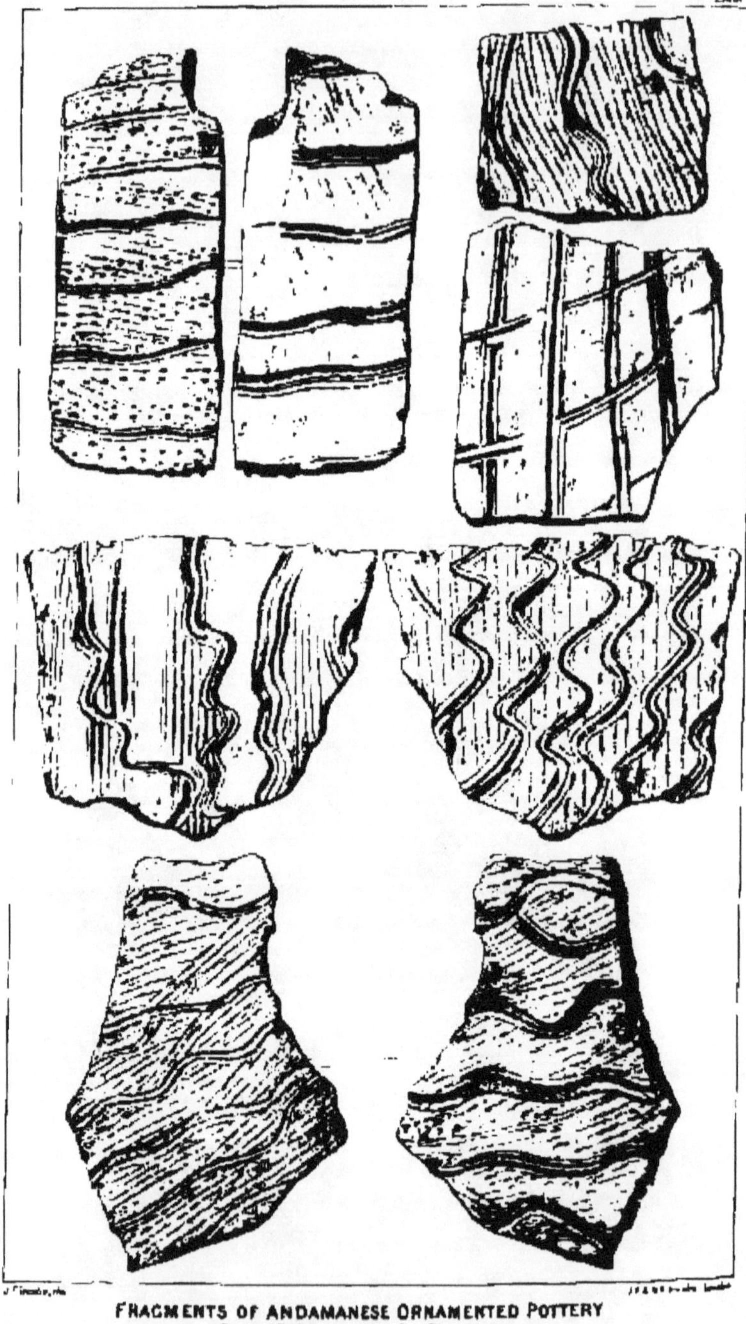

FRAGMENTS OF ANDAMANESE ORNAMENTED POTTERY
from a Kitchen Midden in Port Blair Harbour

XI. Vandykes with Scolloped Bands and Cross Lines (? *ig-pdi'ngakagn-*).

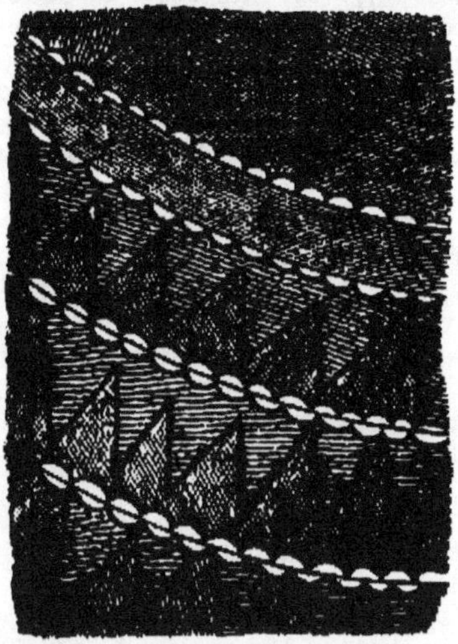

Painted with *kd'ngatd-bdj-* on *d·do-*[1]

Pottery.—1. These savages evince a superiority over the Australians, Tasmanians, Fuegeans, and many of the Pacific Islanders, in possessing some knowledge of the art of making pots.

2. It was formerly believed that they had "no vessel capable of resisting the action of fire,"[2] but careful examination of their kitchen-middens has proved, beyond all doubt, that their present manufacture was equalled—if indeed it were not surpassed—many generations ago by their ancestors; the traditions current among them on the subject may also be mentioned, in passing, as pointing to a like conclusion.

3. The late Dr. Stoliczka, in his interesting paper on the Andamanese kitchen-middens,[3] writes as follows :—"In submitting the rude fragments of pottery . . . to an archæologist in Europe, no one would long hesitate in referring them to the

[1] *Nautilus* shell, used as a drinking vessel.

[2] *Vide* Symes, who is also incorrect in adding in a footnote : "The fragments of earthenware vessels mentioned by Mr. Colebrooke were probably brought from the Nicobars or from the Continent, by the boats that often visit the Andamans for the purpose of taking the nests before mentioned" (*i.e.*, of the *Collocalia nidifica*).

[3] *Vide* Proceedings As. Soc. Bengal, January, 1870.

stone age, at least to the neolithic period; for, indeed, they are almost identical with the fragments of pottery found in the Danish kitchen-middens, though here fragments of pottery are comparatively very rare."

4. The manufacture of pots (*būj-*[1]) is not confined to any particular class, or to either sex, but the better specimens are generally produced by men, and though the result is in neither case very satisfactory as regards appearance, they yet answer the purpose for which they are intended very fairly,[2] and frequently serve as objects of barter among the various communities.

5. They invariably use, unmixed with any other substance, a particular description of clay called by them *būj-pā-*, which is only found in a few places, where, of course, the work is usually carried on: the method pursued is similar to that practised by the Kaffirs, and the only implements employed are a short pointed stick, an *Arca* shell (the variety called *pō·rma-*), and a board, which is generally either a sounding board (*pū·kuta-yem·nga-*[3]), or, if sufficiently large, an eating tray (*pū·kuta-yāt-māk·nga-*[4]).

6. As nothing of the character of a potter's wheel is known among them, the shape of the vessels depends upon the skill of the operator and upon the correctness of his eye. The first step in the process of making a pot is to remove any stones that are in the clay, which is then moistened with water and kneaded until it is of a proper consistency; several lumps are next rolled out in succession on the board, by means of the fingers and palms, into strips of about fifteen inches long and half-an-inch thick: one of these is now twisted by the artist into a cup-like shape,[5] in order to form the base of the pot, which he proceeds to build up, taking care the while to exert sufficient pressure to ensure a uniform thickness, by adding one roll above another, each one commencing where the last ended, until the required dimensions are attained; then, if it be sufficiently firm and consolidated, an *Arca* shell is carefully passed (*ngā·tanga-*) over the inner and outer surfaces, which are thus rendered smoother, and are at the same time freed from any minute bits of stone that had previously escaped observation; the serrated edges of the

[1] *Vide* Appendix B, item 16.
[2] *Vide ante* "Food," paragraphs 12, 21, and 27.
[3] *Vide* Appendix B, item 19.
[4] *Vide* Appendix B, item 72.
[5] The pots made by the *yē·rewa-* and *yār·awa-* tribes (*i.e.*, North and Little Andaman) have up to the present time been found to have a more pointed base than those of the five *bō·jig* tribes, but I believe no Andaman pot intended for cooking purposes has yet been made of such a shape as to allow of its standing. The small cup- (or sometimes saucer-) like pots (*vide* Plate VII, fig. 10*a*) are used for making and warming *kā·ngaīd-bāj-*.

shell also impart a more finished appearance to the vessel ere it is further engraved (*ō·inga-*) on both surfaces[1] in wavy, checked, or striped designs,[2] not, as has been assumed,[3] by the finger-nail, but by means of the pointed stick before mentioned. The potter then places the utensil in the sun to dry, or, if the weather be wet or cloudy, before a fire, taking care to alter its position from time to time so that all parts may be equally subjected to heat. When sufficiently hardened, he bakes it thoroughly by placing burning pieces of wood both inside and around the vessel; occasionally during this process the pot cracks, which of course renders it useless, but if this does not happen it is allowed to cool, and is then considered ready for use.

7. With good management a pot is ordinarily fit for use by the close of the day on which it is made. They may be said to be all of one quality and to differ only in size so as to be suitable for the use of a single family or a large party. The largest description is usually only to be seen in permanent encampments, the smaller kinds being taken when occasion arises for a migration, as for instance on account of a death,[4] or because arrangements have been made for an entertainment at some other place.[5] The medium size is almost invariably provided with a rough basket-work casing, which not only renders it more portable but also serves to protect it, in some measure, from the many accidents to which it is liable.

8. The pots ordinarily made will hold about nine pints, but the larger kinds possess double this capacity, while others again are no larger than half an ordinary cocoanut-shell; these last are employed in making *kā·ngatā-būj-*, and also when using it;[6] with this exception none of the vessels are reserved or manufactured for any special purpose, but serve alike for all times, whether for festivals, migrations, or ordinary occasions. No substitutes for

[1] Perhaps the original object of this practice may be explained by the conjecture contained in the following extract from Peschel's work:—"In examining the site of an old pottery manufactory of the Red Indians on the Cahokia, ... Carl Rau discovered half-finished vessels, that is to say, baskets of rushes or willow, lined inside with clay. When the vessel was baked the fire naturally consumed the external covering. . . . That the Europeans of prehistoric times also originally lined basket-work with clay, may be inferred from the decorations of vessels of the stone age. These decorations consist merely of rows of marks made with the finger-nail, as if to represent the traces left by the basket-work. When some bold individual began to shape the clay by hand, his earthen vessels were perhaps regarded as not genuine, or of inferior quality, as they had not originated in the time-honoured fashion; in order to meet these doubts he may have counterfeited the impressions of the rushes with his nail."

[2] *Vide* Plate V, for illustration of these.

[3] *Vide* de Röepstorff.

[4] *Vide ante* "Death and Burial," paragraphs 4 and 15.

[5] *Vide post* "Games and Amusements," paragraph 22.

[6] *Vide* Appendix B, item 62.

pottery are in use, as has been supposed,[1] unless the fact of certain molluscs[2] being cooked in their shells can be so described. Broken pottery is not buried in graves or beneath landmarks, but is cast aside as rubbish.

9. No kind of painting or varnishing is ever attempted, and models of men or animals are never made. They are also ignorant of glazing and of making porous pottery for cooling vessels.

Natural Forms and Miscellaneous Manufactures.—1. The natural forms of stones are employed by the Andamanese, as by other savage tribes, as anvils and hammers. Like the natives of New Guinea,[3] they always carry with them, or keep ready for use, one or more *Cyrena* shells (*ū́-ta-*), as these serve them in a great variety of ways: for example, in *dressing* and *preparing* the wooden portion of their arrows; in *sharpening* their bamboo and cane[4] knives, and the inner edge of the boar's tusk, in order to adapt it for use as a plane; as a *spoon*,[5] in eating gravy, &c.; as a *knife*, in cutting thatching leaves, &c., and in severing the joints of meat; and as a *scraper* in separating the pulp from the fibre of the *Anadendrum paniculatum* and other plants, from which they manufacture their various descriptions of string and cord; these shells are likewise employed in making the ornamental incisions in their weapons, implements, leaf-ornaments, &c.,[6] in preparing the peculiar *ŏ́j-*[7] appendage (worn when dancing); and they are also frequently used for planing purposes.[8] Indeed, I think I may fairly say that among their savage arts there is probably nothing so calculated to surprise and interest a stranger as the many and clever uses to which necessity has taught them to put this simple but highly effective tool.

[1] This refers to the following passage in the late Dr. Stoliczka's "Note on the Kjökken-Möddings of the Andaman Islands":—"I have been informed that in some parts of the island their only cooking utensils are large specimens of *Turbo marmoratus*, valves of *Tridacna gigas*, and others."

[2] Viz.:—*Cyrena*, *Arca*, *Mytilus smaragdinus*, *Cerithium*, *Patella variabilis* (limpet), and a few other small varieties.

[3] "They always carry with them a bamboo knife; . . . when required they sharpen the edge with a shell (a fresh water species of *Cyrena*), which is always carried for the purpose. . . ." (See a paper on the natives of the *Fly River*, New Guinea, by Signor L. M. d'Albertis, in the Journ. Anthrop. Inst., vol. vi, p. 215, 1876).

[4] Like the Tahitians and Fijians of former times they have also been in the habit of using bamboo knives; these are made of the outside of a piece of bamboo, are shaped into form while green, and are then dried and charred so as to render them as hard and sharp as possible.

[5] "The mussel-shell suggested the first idea of the spoon, and still performs its functions on the Atlantic shores of Morocco" (Peschel).

[6] *Vide* "Ornamentation," paragraph 2.

[7] *Vide* Appendix B, item 76.

[8] It has already been mentioned under "Food" (paragraph 8) that the *Cyrena* is also used in opening other bivalves.

2. *Arca* shells, on account of their serrated lips, serve the double purpose—when a pot is being manufactured—of removing pieces of stone from the outer surface, and of imparting a more finished appearance to the vessel. *Pinna* shells are kept as receptacles for *tá'la-ōg-*, and as plates for food, while *Nautilus* shells do duty as drinking vessels. No evidence can be found in support of Mr. St. John's statement,[1] that human skulls are used as boxes to contain small objects, for neither these nor the skulls of animals appear to have been ever so employed;[2] the former are kept and carried, as I have elsewhere explained, merely as mementoes of the departed, and the latter are stuck on poles, or hung round the eaves of their huts, as trophies of the chase. *Pinna* and other shells are said to have been used in former times as adze blades, but this is no longer the case, for quantities of iron are always obtainable. Strange as it may seem to some of my readers, there is no trace or tradition of stone having been utilised for this purpose.

3. The only instances in which these tribes appear to have had recourse to the natural defences of animals in the manufacture of their weapons are—(*a*) in the use of the serrated bone at the root of the tail of the sting-ray[3] for their fish-arrows; and (*b*) of the valves of *Perna ephippium*,[4] which were formerly—after being ground and shaped—fastened to their wooden-headed arrows, for use in hunting, and in hostile expeditions. Since, however, they have found themselves able to procure ample supplies of iron, these shell arrow-heads, like the shell adze-blades, have been discarded in favour of iron wire, nails, hoop-iron, &c.

4. The bamboo, although not employed by the Andamanese in such a variety of ways as it is by many savages, is yet in constant use in one or other of the following modes, viz:—of the ordinary medium size (male species) they form the *shafts* of their turtle-harpoons;[5] of the female species[6] they make *water-holders*, and receptacles for cooked food[7] when travelling (*gōb-*[8]); *knives* (*pō-chō-*[9]), which are narrow pieces hardened

[1] Transactions of the Ethnol. Soc., vol. v, p. 45.

[2] Very possibly the belief originated in the manner I suggested in a previous paper (*vide* Journ. Anthrop. Inst., vol. xi, p. 273).

[3] *Vide ante* "Hunting, &c.," paragraph 11.

[4] *Vide post* "Stone Implements," paragraph 5 (footnote).

[5] The shafts of their pig spear, being short are made of heavier material, viz., the thick rattan.

[6] Pieces of *Bambusa gigantea*, which have floated across from Burmah, or have reached their shores from wrecks, are much prized as buckets, none but the small ordinary bamboo being indigenous.

[7] *Vide ante* "Food," paragraph 31.

[8] *Vide* Appendix B, item 62.

[9] *Ibid.*, 69.

over a fire, and sharpened by means of a *Cyrena* shell; *netting-needles* (*pō'tòkla-*[1]) and *tongs* (*kai-*[2]), which last consist merely of a strip of bamboo, bent double, with pointed ends;[3] the slender *Bambusa nana*, called *rī'dī-*, is generally selected for forming the hooked pole (*ngā'tunga-*[4]), and it is likewise invariably employed for the shafts of their wooden and iron-pointed arrows.

5. Although there are materials ready to hand wherewith they might easily construct a few such simple musical instruments as are made and used by the Nicobarese, no attempt seems to have been made by them in this direction, for the rude sounding board (*pū'kuta-yem'nga-*[5]) can hardly be included under this head. This circumstance seems to find its explanation in the fact that though they are good timists their talent for music is (as will be presently shown,[6] on the testimony of more than one competent authority) of the lowest type.

6. A brush, suitable for painting the stripes on their baskets (*jōb-*[7]), baby-slings (*chīp-*[8]), &c., is obtained from a drupe of the small fruit of the *Pandanus Andamanensium* (*māng-*), the pulp having been first extracted by means of a *Cyrena* shell.

7. Skins of animals, thorns, or spines of trees are not made use of by these people in any way, nor do they have recourse to caves, rock-shelters, or tree-tops for their dwellings, though they occasionally, as I have before mentioned, avail themselves of the buttress-like formations of the roots of such trees as the *Ficus laccifera*, *Bombax malabaricum*, *Sterculia villosa*, &c., when travelling in bad weather, or when suddenly overtaken by a storm. Palm-leaves, as I explained when describing their habitations,[9] are employed for thatching purposes.

Leather-work.—From the last paragraph it will be correctly inferred that there is no evidence of their having ever possessed a knowledge of the art of dressing and preparing skins for use in any form: this may be due as much to the limited number and variety of those animals[10] whose hides might be turned to account in this way as to the equable temperature of the climate, which renders such, or indeed any covering unnecessary.

[1] *Vide* Appendix B, item 67.
[2] *Vide* Appendix B, item 80.
[3] A narrow and pointed piece of bamboo, bitten at the end so as to loosen the fibres, is made to serve as a brush in painting designs on their buckets, sounding boards, &c.
[4] *Vide* Appendix B, item 17.
[5] *Vide* Appendix B, item 10.
[6] *Vide post* "Games and Amusements," paragraph 26, and footnote.
[7] *Vide post* "Basket-work," paragraph 3, and Appendix B, item 21.
[8] *Vide* Appendix B, item 24.
[9] *Vide ante* "Habitations," paragraph 2.
[10] Viz., dugong, porpoise, paradoxurus, iguana, and pig.

Metallurgy.—Having been, till comparatively recent times, ignorant almost of the existence as well as of the uses of iron, it is not to be wondered at that smelting and forging have been to them unknown arts. Now that they are better informed, and are able to procure pieces of hoop-iron, keel-plate, &c., they apply them to the manufacture of their blades and adzes, reducing them to the required thinness by continually striking the cold metal with a hard smooth stone (*tai'li-bun'a-*[1]) on a rude anvil (*rä'rap-*) of the same substance; such portions of the iron as are then found to exceed the dimensions requisite for the weapon or tool under construction are placed over the edge of the anvil and broken off by dint of repeated blows: the new edge thus formed, being more or less jagged, is then ground on a hone till the blade assumes the desired shape. Many of the aborigines who have been living for some time at Port Blair have, however, advanced a stage beyond this, for, by using such old chisels as they may succeed in procuring, they contrive to make their arrow-heads and other implements much more speedily than by the old method. The pointed weapons, *e.g.*, the *kowai'a-* and *tö'lbö'd-*, are made from pieces of stout wire, large nails, &c., by dint of laborious and patient hammering on the *rä'rap-*, and grinding on the *tä'lag-*.

Stone Implements.—1. Although a great portion of the inhabitants of Great Andaman have for some time past been able through us to procure iron in sufficient quantities to substitute it for stone (not to mention bones and shells), still they can by no means be said to have passed out of the *stone age*; indeed, the more distant tribes still retain the use, with scarcely any modification, of most of the stone and other implements which served their ancestors. Even the inmates of the homes at Port Blair may still often be seen employing one or other of them, evidently therefore from choice: this more especially refers to the first three in the following list,[2] which comprises the small number of stone implements in ordinary use among the present aboriginal inhabitants of the islands:—

rä'rap-, the anvil.

tai'li-bun'a-, the hammer (probably a smooth round piece of dolerite or fine-grained basalt).

tä'lag-, the whetstone (consisting of slightly micaceous sandstone).

tö'lma lö'ko tūg-[3] (lit., *quartz tooth*), chips or flakes for shaving, tattooing, &c.

[1] *Vide* next section, paragraph 1.

[2] There are no special makers, or procurers, of these stones.

[3] These are either fragments of opaque whitish vein quartz, or of transparent rock crystal, or are obtained from pebbles of opaque bluish-white quartz with

14., cooking stones; common pebbles, about a couple of inches in diameter, which are heated, and then placed on all sides of the food which it is intended to cook.

2. When a new *whetstone* is required—as no method of cutting stone is known to them—a block of soft sandstone is chosen, which, if too large, is placed on a fire till it breaks; the piece best adapted for the purpose is then taken and shaped according to fancy, by the aid of one of the hard smooth stone hammers; after being used a short time the edges wear down, and it answers as a hone for several months.[1]

3. Chips and flakes are never used more than once; in fact, several are generally employed in each operation: those having a sharp blade-like edge are reserved for shaving, while others with a fine point are kept for tattooing or scarifying; when done with they are thrown on a refuse heap, or otherwise disposed of, lest injury should befall anyone by inadvertently treading on them. Flaking is regarded as one of the duties of women, and is usually performed by them.[2]

4. For making *chips* two pieces of white quartz are needed; the stones are not pressed against the thigh, nor are they bound round tightly so as to increase the line of least resistance to the blow of the flaker; but one of the pieces is first heated and afterwards allowed to cool, it is then held firmly and struck at right angles with the other stone: by this means is obtained in a few moments a number of fragments suitable for the purposes above mentioned. A certain knack is apparently necessary in order to produce the kind of chips which are at the time required: the smallest flakes are obtained in the same manner and never by pressure.

5. Glass chips are now generally used by all who are in communication with ourselves, in preference to those of flint, as they are sharper and more effective; the method in which they are obtained is the same, the thick lump of glass forming the bottom of beer and wine bottles being selected for the purpose, and never the thinner portions.

6. It has been stated[3] that formerly, for tattooing, a "sharpened flint bound to a stick" was used, and that the present instrument is a bit of broken bottle "inserted into the split extremity of a stick;" no instance has, however, been found confirmatory of the words quoted, and the Andamanese

fatty lustre, thin chips of which are translucent at the edges. (For this description I am indebted to Mr. F. W. Rudler.)

[1] For the mode of use *vide* Appendix B, item 52.

[2] All women can scarify and act as barbers, but only about 50 per cent. of them undertake the more difficult task of tattooing.

[3] *Vide* Dr. Day.

themselves declare that they never haft the stone chips or glass flakes, and that the former are never "sharpened," but produced in the manner already described.

7. Quartz is commonly met with throughout the country occupied by the tribes with which we are in friendly intercourse; no difficulty, therefore, is ever experienced in obtaining *it*, or, indeed, *any* of the other varieties of stone which they use. It is employed for no other purposes than those here indicated, as has been assumed,[1] and the art of producing fire by its means is unknown to them.[2]

8. The whetstone and hammer only are offered as mediums of exchange, but no great value is attached to either of these objects, nor is any superstition associated with their usage; they are therefore—when no longer serviceable—cast aside.

9. Stones are not used by them for cutting wood or bone, the latter being usually crushed by a hammer for the sake of the marrow. Before the introduction of iron, small holes were bored with bone or pieces of shell, but rarely, if ever, with stone, and no implement has been found which might be supposed to have served as a stone saw or scraper, for which purposes shells apparently have been generally employed.[3]

10. In his "Note on the Kjokken-Möddings of the Andaman Islands" the late Dr. Stoliczka also refers to a celt found in one of these refuse heaps as "a small but typical arrow-head," and describes it as of tertiary sandstone. The Andamanese, however, maintain that they never, even when iron was scarce, made arrow-heads, axes, adzes, or chisels of stone; they also affirm that the fragments which have been found in the kitchen-middens, and which have given rise to the impression of having formerly served one or other of the above purposes are merely quartz flakes or broken pieces of cooking stones or hones which, in former times as now, were thrown among the rubbish when no longer of use.[4]

11. Stones are not regarded as thunderbolts or worn as amulets; they are not placed in water previous to their being worked, and holes are never bored in them, nor is the surface ever ground or polished.

[1] "From the flint they manufactured knives . . . and arrow-heads" (de Röepstorff), and elsewhere he speaks of "flint hatchets," which not improbably were as much unknown in former times as at the present day. *Pecten ephippium* (*ē-la-*) shells were formerly sharpened and converted into arrow-heads: hence *ē-la-* has ever since been adopted as the name of the bladed (or pig) arrow, even although iron has now been entirely or very generally substituted for shell. Adze blades were, it seems, sometimes made of *Pinna* shells.

[2] *Vide ante* "Fire," paragraphs 1 and 4.

[3] *Vide ante* "Natural Forms," paragraph 1.

[4] *Vide* my remarks on this subject in Journ. Anthrop. Inst., vol. xi, p. 271.

Basket-work.—1. Among the few remaining industries of these savages on which I have a few words to say is that of basket-making: these baskets are invariably made from the best specimens of the common cane called *pī'dga-* which is similar to, if not identically the same as that ordinarily used by our basket-makers and chair-menders.

2. After removing the leaves, part of the cane is cut into lengths of 3½ or 4 feet, and the "skin" or cuticle is shredded off into strips ½ or ¼ inch wide; the remainder of the cane is split into as long pieces as possible, and the "skin" is cut into strips somewhat narrower than the others; shorter lengths of the canes form the "ribs" or "stakes," in and out of which the strips are woven or "slewed."

3. In order that the basket may stand steadily[1] it has always a "kick" like our bottles, and to construct this is of course the first object; when the stakes have been firmly secured in the centre, they are placed over a small hole scooped out of the ground, and the heel of the basket-maker is placed on them while the weaving is commenced; when it has been carried on to a breadth of 2 or 3 inches the heel is removed, the canes reversed, and the work proceeds in the ordinary way until within an inch of the required depth, where, for the sake of appearance, the interweaving is omitted: the handle is then formed out of a strip of the bark of the *Melochia velutina* (*al'uba-*); stripes of *ta'la-ög-* and *kōi'ob-* are usually added by way of ornamentation;[2] no method of rendering them waterproof is known. Baskets are not converted into moulds for pottery; but sometimes, when travelling, earthen vessels are placed in a loose wicker casing, in order to protect them, and at the same time to facilitate their removal.

4. There is a marked difference[3] between the baskets made by the five *.bō'jig* tribes and those manufactured by the *.yē'rewa-*; with the latter the work is more neatly finished, and the opening is small instead of being wide, as is the case among the former.[4]

5. Baskets are used for all sorts of purposes by men, women, and children, and, considering the rough usage to which they are subjected, last fairly well, for they seldom require to be renewed for several months: they are not used as strainers or colanders, the fine net (*chā'punga-*) serving this purpose.

String, &c.—1. The Andamanese do not produce their stout cord (*bē'tma-*), string (*bē'tma-tā-*), or twine (*mō'la-*), from animal

[1] The *.yē'rewa-* baskets are generally small at the base, and having no "kick" are not usually able to stand unless placed between logs of wood or other objects.

[2] The rim of these baskets is formed of a piece of *Uvaria micrantha* (*ō'ta-lūt-*) round which one or more strips of the cane above described are neatly twined.

[3] The reader is referred to the excellent sketch of an Andamanese basket (*vide* Plate VII, fig. 17).

[4] *Vide* Plate IX, fig. 14.

substances, but from the bark fibres of trees and shrubs, known to them by the names of *al·aba-* (*Melochia velutina*), *pī·lita-* (*Gnetum edule*), and *yō·lba-* (*Anadendrum paniculatum*). The first of these is found growing near the shore, where it seldom attains a height of 20 feet; it is from fibre obtained from the bark of this tree that their cinctures (*bē·tma-bā*), harpoon-lines (*bē·tma-*), and turtle-nets (*yō·lo-tē·pinga*) are manufactured. When any of the articles have to be made or replaced, it becomes the duty of some member of the male sex to procure a smooth clean branch—one which is also fairly straight and free from gnarls being preferred—and to remove the bark; the cellular integument is next scraped with a *Cyrena* shell (*ū·ta-*) until the fibres which it encloses are laid bare: these are then placed in the sun, or before a fire, to dry; when ready for use (*i.e.*, when thoroughly dry) the ropemaker ties several of the filaments to his toe and proceeds with his work by winding another strand spirally round them, adding a fresh length from time to time. When special strength or durability is needed, a coating of black wax (*tō·bul-pīd-*) is finally applied. The yarn thus produced is termed *bē·tma-mai·anga-*. When a long piece of this has been made (say 30 yards), a large portion of it is wound round the two cross-sticks forming the *kū·tegbo-*.[1] The operator, having then seated himself with legs outstretched, places a stick or cane between the big toes of his feet, and over this bar he passes the *kū·tegbo-*, thus enabling him to wind it continuously round the other half-length of the yarn, which, for convenience sake, he has previously placed by his right side, so that it is drawn behind his neck and over his left shoulder as the work proceeds. After the first foot or so of the cord has been thus made, the operator holds or clutches that portion with his toes. It will be understood that in employing the *kū·tegbo-* in the above manner, it becomes necessary at frequent intervals to unwind a certain quantity from that implement, in order to enable the work to progress. The cord thus made is called *bē·tma-*, and this it is of which their harpoon-lines and turtle-nets are made. The *bē·tma-bā-* (lit., small *bē·tma-*), mentioned above, is made in the same way, but of course less fibre and a smaller *kū·tegbo-* are used.

2. For making hand fishing-nets (*kād-*) and sleeping-mats (*pār·əpa-*[2]), the fibre of the *Gnetum edule* (*pī·lita-*) is used; in the preparation and manufacture of these, women exclusively are concerned; the first process is to cut a number of the trailers into lengths which are determined by the distances between the knots and joints: these are held against the

[1] "The cord (used for large nets, &c.) possesses the valuable quality of hardening in the water" (*vide* Mouat, p. 326).
[2] *Vide* Appendix B, item 65.

thigh, and the cuticle is removed by means of the *Cyrena* shell; the underlying white fibres are left for a week or ten days in the sun until thoroughly dry, when they separate readily, and are easily worked up into fine or coarse twine, as may be required by the manipulator.

3. The fibre of the *Anadendrum paniculatum* (*yō·lba-*) is chiefly used for making bowstrings, reticules (*chā·panga-*), necklaces, and twine for arrow fastenings; its manufacture is accordingly not restricted to either sex. When the bark has been stripped off, in lengths of 8 to 15 inches, the operator presses the inner portion upon his (or her) thigh, and then rapidly but carefully passes a *Cyrena* shell along the outer surface until the fibres alone remain; these are then, as in the previous cases, dried in the sun, or before a fire; when a sufficient supply of material has been thus obtained, it is made into fine twine or, if not required for immediate use, wrapped in leaves in order that it may be kept fresh. Although apparently free from any obnoxious properties, this plant, as well as the fibres obtained therefrom, until it is converted into twine or bowstrings, is believed by the Andamanese to render the flesh of a turtle uneatable if placed near it; consequently this meat, when inadvertently so contaminated, is thrown away; further, no one who has been collecting *yō·lba-*, or who has been engaged in preparing the fibre, can (for a period extending to three days) be allowed to cook a turtle, or even to accompany a party engaged on a turtling expedition! Sharks and other dangerous fish are also credited with having so wholesome a horror or detestation of this plant (and also of *Cyrena* shells!) that the aborigines are in the habit of attaching some *yō·lba-*, or *Cyrena* shells (or both), to their cinctures as a safeguard when about to swim in parts believed to be infested by these creatures.

4. The yellow skin of the root of a certain orchid, called *rā-*, which is commonly found on trees near the shore, is often seen intertwined with their *yō·lba-* string, in personal ornaments, and occasionally in the decoration of weapons, but where strength is a requisite it is of course not used.

5. Bowstrings of *pī·lita-* and *yō·lba-* are made in the manner described in the manufacture of *al·aba-* rope, but ordinary string is made in the following manner:—a few of the prepared filaments are twisted into a yarn on the thigh with the palm of the hand; when two lengths have been obtained, they are together rolled into string of the desired strength, and beeswax is smeared over it to make assurance doubly sure.

6. Twine, made from the *yō·lba-*, is used in netting the fine chains (*rāb-*[1]) and the reticules (*chā·panga-*[2]); for turtle-

[1] *Vide ante* "Death and Burial," paragraph 5, and Appendix B, item 42.
[2] *Vide* Appendix B, item 22.

nets the stronger *ol·aba-* is employed, while for the hand fishing-nets (*kūd-*[1]) string, made from the *pī·lita-*, is almost exclusively reserved. In this handicraft the Andamanese are especially skilful, and regulate to a nicety the size of the mesh by using the little or forefinger; it should be mentioned that their rude netting needles of bamboo (*pō·tōkla-*[2]) are not very dissimilar to those used in Europe. Sewing is to them an almost unknown art, but they describe needlework by the word *jd·ke*, which expresses their manner of uniting the large *kā·pa-* leaves, to form a screen, with the pliable stem of this leaf, and also their mode of repairing a canoe, holes being bored and strips of cane (*pī·dga-*) threaded above and below the crack, which has been previously filled in on both sides with *tō·bul-ptd-*.[3]

Games and Amusements.—1. And now, having passed in brief review their various arts and manufactures, I will bring my account of Andamanese life to a close with a brief description of their games and amusements.

2. Unlike many Eastern races they evince from their earliest years a partiality for active pursuits in which monotony or great bodily exertion are not entailed, and great was the delight of the children in the Orphanage when they were instructed in some of our English games, especially kite-flying, and see-saw;[4] it is at the same time curious to note that, though not borrowed from aliens, their pastimes, in many instances, bear close resemblance to those in vogue among children in this and other lands; notably is this the case with regard to those known to us as blind-man's-buff,[5] leap-frog,[6] and hide-and-seek.[7]

3. With respect to the first-named of these, large leaves, in lieu of a handkerchief, are fastened over the eyes, and the difficulties of the "blind man" are greatly increased by its being obligatory for him to catch the person who blinded him, while being pulled about and jostled by the rest of the players.

4. In "leap-frog," instead of stooping, one man squats on his heels while his companion bounds over him without touching him and takes the same position, to be in his turn jumped over.

5. Mock pig-hunting[8] after dark is another very favourite amusement; one of the party undertakes the *rôle* of the pig and, betaking himself to a distance, runs hither and thither

[1] *Vide* Appendix B, item 20.
[2] *Vide* Appendix B, item 67.
[3] *Vide* Appendix B, item 97.
[4] To this game they have given the name *ad-yē·nenga-*.
[5] Called by them *ā·i-td·pa-li·renga-*.
[6] Called by them *ōkld·r-tidi·atinga-*.
[7] Called by them *ab-ā·tanga-*.
[8] Called by them *ad-reg·igngа-*.

imitating the grunting of that animal, while his comrades shoot off harmless arrows[1] in the direction from whence the sounds proceed until one hits its intended mark.

6. Another variety of this game is as follows:—one man leaves the encampment after dark armed with *ŭ·tara-* arrows, which, on his return after a brief absence, he fires off into different huts, while the occupants hide themselves or run away screaming as if attacked by an enemy.[2]

7. Similarly in the sea they play at turtling: one end of a long line is held firmly by some one in the canoe, the other being fastened to the arm of the man who is to represent the turtle. Diving suddenly into the water, he is at once followed by the rest, who try to capture him, while he does his utmost to elude them by swimming, doubling, and diving, till fairly exhausted.

8. Sometimes, when they are assembled together in the evening, one of the men will get up and exclaim, "I will go after the Evil Spirit of the Woods" (*wai dō ĕ·rem-chāu·gala jŭ·dke*).[3] Taking nothing with him but a lighted log, he goes off into the jungle and is soon lost to sight; his friends then call to him and inquire if he has caught the demon, whereupon he begins to rush about shouting and hitting about him as if in pursuit of, or struggling with some one; he is next asked "Who are you?" (*mija ngōl?*)—apparently to suggest the idea that during his combat with the evil one he has been transformed, or rather, has lost his identity,—the reply is given in a feigned voice, "I am ——" (naming some person long since deceased) "and have come for such and such a purpose." Something being then thrown at him he threatens them with annihilation unless they desist; still remaining in his hiding-place he amuses himself, and presumably also his friends, by singing, until at last two or three of the company search him out and bring him back to the camp, where, with a view of keeping up his assumed character, he remains silent and feigns sleep, often for the rest of the evening.

9. An impromptu swing is sometimes devised out of one of the long stout creepers, commonly found overhanging a bough perpendicularly from a height of 40 to 50 feet: clinging firmly to this they swing each other[4] as far as possible, just as we swing children.

[1] Made of a soft wood called *ŭ·tara-*, of the *Alpinia* species; the points are flattened with the teeth before using.

[2] This game is called *it·i-tai·jnga-*.

[3] This game is known as *ĕ·rem-chāu·gala dĕ·pnga*.

[4] This goes by the name of *ig-lĭ·lunga-*. [During a visit paid to Rutland Island, in 1881, a *jōr·owa-* swing was seen suspended from a stout branch. It

10. Young men often compete with one another in swimming, diving feet foremost into the water from an overhanging rock or branch with shouts of delight. Sometimes they will race together in their canoes,[1] but this only happens on chance occasions, when the idea has been suddenly suggested by one of the party, and not by pre-arrangement.

11. In parts, where trees of the *Alpinia* species abound, they now and then vie in seeing who amongst them can force his way with greatest rapidity through the dense barrier of leaves and smooth stems which it presents,[2] and thus probably they acquire, in great measure, the skill which in an early section[3] I mentioned they invariably display when threading their way through the jungles.

12. At times they compete in throwing *upwards* into a lofty tree a short piece of string, weighted at each end with a stone,[4] the object of course being to see who can fling highest. Similarly *Cyrena* shells are occasionally sent skimming through the air to test their powers in throwing long distances.[5]

13. While wandering along the coast they may sometimes be seen playing at ducks-and-drakes[6] with any small flat stones they may chance to pick up.

14. They are all especially fond of showing their skill in shooting a moving object, and for this purpose select the round root of a creeper called *gō·dam-*, or the pod of the *Carapa obovata*, which they roll along the ground or down a slope, aiming at it while in motion.[7]

15. No special amusements are indulged in by women[8] whose chief delight seems to consist in the laudable endeavour to surpass one another in adorning the persons of their relatives with the best design in *tä·la-ōg-*.

16. Young boys sometimes amuse themselves with wrestling (*ad-lĕ·nga-*) on the sand, where also they may not unfrequently be observed playing at mock burials.[9] On these occasions one

resembled those used by European children, but was made of cane and was provided also with a narrow wooden seat.]

[1] This racing is termed *ar-ti·rlenga-*.

[2] This is called *ōr-lō·tolnga-*.

[3] *Vide ante* "Physical Powers and Senses," paragraph 4.

[4] This game is called *tū·lama-*

[5] This variation of the game is called *ō·ko-kē·chinga-*; when the shell is about to be thrown the convex side is held uppermost.

[6] The word to express this is *ekē·chekanga-*.

[7] This has also been found to be a practice among the *jār·awa-*.

[8] It has, however, been observed that, not unlike their fairer sisters elsewhere, they are especially fond of gathering together and chatting of the social topics of the hour; the eagerness and volubility they display in their discussions on these occasions are quite amusing to watch.

[9] These are termed *ab-nā·nga-*.

of their number has to submit to be covered with sand until the head only is visible; fire is then placed near the spot after the custom of their race; for the like reason these sports usually take place near some landmark, such as a conspicuous tree, boulder, or overhanging rock: when the semi-interred child has had enough of it he jumps out and another companion is chosen to take his place.

17. Children may also sometimes be seen diverting themselves by tying a fine string to the leg of a toad or tree-lizard;[1] this cruel sport, unless their elders interfere, is only ended by the death of the unfortunate captive.

18. They are fond of searching for small crabs and fish, and having them cooked for a sham banquet:[2] the earnestness they display in "pretending" on these occasions is irresistibly entertaining, and would be heartily appreciated by European children who have experienced the delight of preparing a "doll's feast."

19. Boys also play at seizing each other under the surface of the water, or amuse themselves with making tiny canoes and floating them towards one another; they are, as I have before mentioned, early provided with miniature bows and arrows, and encouraged to become good marksmen.

20. While the foregoing amusements are of frequent occurrence among the juvenile members of a community,[3] the chief diversion of the adults consists in entertainments resembling the Australian "corroboree," when dancing and singing are kept up for many successive hours by moonlight, or by the blaze of the camp fires.

21. Any passing event, such as a successful hunt, an unexpected visit from distant relatives or friends, the commencement of a new season, the recovery of some member of the community from illness, a marriage, and even the termination of the mourning period,[4] is made the excuse for one of these entertainments.

22. Besides these smaller festivities, large gatherings of a tribe are also organised from time to time by the head chief, who generally receives an offer, in the first instance, from the members of some far-off community to give a *jeg-* at his encampment. As these offers are only made when it is known to be convenient they are always accepted, and invitations for a certain day are at once sent to all living within an easy distance.

[1] This is called *rô-pua kâ-ll'raga-*.
[2] These are called *gah-mak'nga-*.
[3] "Cats' cradle" (called by them *ji'dra-*) is also one of their recognised amusements.
[4] *Vide* "Death and Burial," paragraph 7.

23. The intervening days are spent by the proposers of the entertainment in perfecting a song and chorus, which it is intended to perform, and which generally has been composed expressly for the occasion, by some volunteer[1] upon whom also devolves the responsibility of singing the solo and training the so-called chorus. As a considerable amount of distinction among his fellows may be gained by the manner in which he acquits himself in his onerous undertaking, it will be readily understood that the *improvisatore* spares no pains over the preparation and rehearsal of a new song, which, as he fondly hopes, will render his name, if not immortal, at all events famous for many a year. The subject is chosen in reference to some recent personal or tribal exploit or adventure, and is embodied in a distich, followed by a chorus, or rather refrain, which as often as not consists merely in a repetition of the couplet forming the solo; in this refrain women alone are instructed; the main point aimed at is apparently accuracy of time, for, as I have said in my last paper, everything, even sense, is sacrificed in their songs to rhythm.[2]

24. In order to combine pleasure with profit, sundry implements or articles, which are more common in their community than in that of their hosts, are taken by the visitors on these occasions for purposes of presentation, or, to speak more correctly, of barter.

25. It is the duty of the hosts to make all necessary preparations, to provide torches, as well as food and water, for the expected guests, and to sweep the *bū́lum-*,[3] clearing it of all rubbish, lest inconvenience or injury should be occasioned by the stones, shells, bones, &c., which gradually accumulate, in spite of the "kitchen-middens" so invariably found in the vicinity of all permanent encampments of long standing.

26. When nearing the scene of their festivity the visitors pause, for the double purpose of a rehearsal and that the women may have time to adorn the party in their holiday suits of paint, as these would have lost their beauty and freshness if donned previous to leaving home.

27. That a weird and dramatic effect should be produced on a civilised mind by one of these entertainments, especially when occurring at night, will be readily understood if one pictures the scene:—in a small clearing in the midst, or on the border of a dense jungle are gathered a hundred or even more painted

[1] A song that has proved a success at any of these festive tribal meetings is sometimes repeated by "special request" at one of the smaller gatherings; "all rights" in these productions "are reserved," and no one but the composer is at liberty to sing a song, however popular!

[2] *Vide ante* "Language," paragraph 6.

[3] *Vide ante* "Habitations," paragraph 11.

savages of both sexes; the moon sheds a soft light on all, while from each hut the lurid glare of a wood fire throws its fitful shadows across the scattered groups; on one side, seated in a row, are the women who are to join in the refrain; on the other, in dark relief within their several huts, are seen the audience, many of whom assist in marking time by clapping their hands or by slapping the hollow between their outstretched legs with their open palms. In a conspicuous position stands the composer and conductor: with one foot on the pointed end of a sounding board,[1] and supporting himself on a spear, bow, or pole, he gives the time to the singers and dancers by kicking the board with the sole or heel of the other foot; in this wearying duty he is from time to time relieved by one of his male friends and, occasionally, even by a woman. During the solo, which partakes of the character of a "recitative," all other voices are hushed, and the listeners remain motionless, but as soon as the signal is given for the refrain, a number of men emerge suddenly from the gloom surrounding the encampment, and rushing excitedly into the arena, perform their part with frantic energy, generally adding their voices to those of the women to swell the volume of sound. Save at the *ti-tö'latnga-*,[2] women only occasionally take a share in the dances, but their performances are considered by some foreigners as rather suggestive of impropriety—with what justice I am not prepared to say, for modesty, at least, is satisfied by the wearing of a larger leaf apron than usual.

28. There is now-a-days[3] but one description of dance in vogue with either sex, but it differs somewhat in the two sexes, and therefore must be dwelt upon briefly.

29. A man, when dancing,[4] curves his back, and throws all his weight on one leg, the knee of which is bent; his hands are raised to a level with his chest, and outstretched before him, the thumb of one hand being held between the forefinger and thumb of the other, while the remaining digits are separated and extended upwards;[5] he then advances by sudden jerks and hops

[1] These sounding boards (*pú·kuta-yem·nga-*) somewhat resemble in shape the carapace of a turtle, and might naturally be mistaken by a visitor (*vide* Colebrooke and Mouat) for shields, but I cannot account for Dr. Hodder's description of a "rough skin drum" (*vide* "Pall Mall Budget" of 20th April, 1877). See also Appendix B, item 19.

[2] *Vide ante* "Death and Burial," paragraph 7.

[3] From Lieutenant Colebrooke's description of the Andamanese dance of a hundred years ago, it would seem that since that date their style has undergone a great change, for he says they "dance in a ring, each alternately kicking and slapping his own breech *ad lib.*"

[4] *Vide* Plate III, fig. 2.

[5] Sometimes to heighten the effect a bow and arrow are carried in this position.

taken with the leg on which he is resting, and taps the ground after every second movement with the sole of the other foot; in this manner he crosses and recrosses the entire *bū·lum-*, joining in the chorus as he proceeds, each step being taken in time with the thuds on the sounding-board, and the singing of the refrain. When fatigued, the performer makes a little variation by marking time in a rather odd manner, for the knees are bent, and the *heels* are raised alternately off the ground, the chief point of importance being to maintain the same time throughout.

30. Women, in dancing, swing their arms backwards and forwards; at the same time the knees are bent, and they make a succession of short bobs up and down, in perfect time; every now and then a few steps in advance are taken, and then the action is repeated.

31. To convey an accurate impression of the exact step, or of the effect of the respective performances of the two sexes, is not easy, but I trust that the above descriptions will convey a fair idea of their general character and peculiarities.

32. The alternating of solo and chorus continues for many hours, and generally only ceases with the first faint streaks of dawn, when those of the hosts who have managed to keep awake during the long night revel, lead the visitors to the huts they are to occupy, and then themselves sing and dance as a return compliment.

33. To a stranger not gifted with a keen ear for music, there is at first a certain amount of attraction in the oft-repeated cadence, but it must be confessed that, after a residence in the neighbourhood of one of the homes, one learns to wish that their musical performances were characterised by a little more variety, and were rather less protracted, though some compensation may be found at night, as the steady continuance of the monotonous sounds has a most soothing and somniferous effect.

34. It seems hardly necessary to say that all their songs are sung in unison, for they have no idea of choral or part-singing, nor are they able to catch up and repeat an air. They appear, however, able to distinguish between various kinds of music, and especially to appreciate the performances of our regimental bands, but this may perhaps in part be due to the tone of the big drum, which somewhat resembles that produced on their sounding-boards.

35. Dr. Brander gives a specimen of their monotonous chant —the compass of which will be found to include only three notes—in the following stave of our musical notation :—

36. Every now and then, as the refrain ends, the soloist cries—

ō·ba abogū· bē·late,[1] (*a*)

to which the singers respond by shouting—

tēd·re-d·re-d·red,[1] (*b*)

which seems equivalent to *Tra-la-la*, for it has no meaning *per se*.

37. When the guests have sufficiently rested from their night's exertions, they visit their special friends or relatives, and, if within the prescribed limits of affinity,[2] indulge[3] in weeping together;[4] these visits are usually followed by an interchange of gifts, the hosts taking the initiative, and a *fracas* not unfrequently ensues, for donor and recipient are not always of a mind as to the respective values of their "presents." Should all, however, pass off smoothly, the assemblage breaks up into various small parties for hunting or fishing, according to the situation of the encampment.

[1] These are styled respectively the (*a*) *ārbē·datnga-*, and the (*b*) *ā-rē·nnga-* or *āryā·nnga*.

Further, in reference to their musical abilities, I would here quote from a friend, who at my request had kindly consented to test the powers of the aborigines in this particular, as I unfortunately am not qualified to do so myself.—

"I examined five women, seven men, and three young boys as to their musical abilities, and as far as I could judge, they have not the remotest idea of pitch or tune, even the chorus of their own song, *chāklā yā· lak·a māl·jrā!* started by *āb·ra-yud*, was taken up in several keys, and it was difficult to distinguish the original. I tried all the voices separately: it seemed quite accidental if they pitched on the keynote, but as for leaving it when once got hold of to go up and down the scale they *would* not! so that it was impossible for me to ascertain either the quality or the register of the voices. The boys were, if anything, a shade the best; . . . a lot of drilling may beat a few notes into their heads."

[2] *Vide ante* "Customs, Meeting and Parting," paragraph 2.

[3] "The Sandwich Islanders recognise tears as a sign of happiness" (Lubbock, p. 552).

[4] No greetings take place on these occasions between the performers and their hosts until after the entertainment (which often lasts many hours) is over.

And now, though there is, I feel, much more that might with advantage be recorded regarding this interesting race, I must bring these memoirs to a conclusion; but in doing so would mention as evidence of the results of our training that several Andamanese lads have been taught to wait at table, and prove both useful and handy at such duties, behaving with most becoming gravity, as if, indeed, they had been to the manner born! It is a somewhat absurd sight to see these jet-black imps dressed in white, with arms crossed and head thrown back, standing like statues behind their masters' chairs, watchful to fulfil any service required; as soon, however, as the meal is over, the white garment is replaced by a jacket, or, in *puris naturalibus*, the well-trained servant is transformed into a romping *gamin*, ready for any fun or frolic that may offer, and entering into it apparently with the full conviction that he deserves and has earned such relaxation by his exemplary conduct as a table servant. When a dance has been given in the settlement it has been amusing to watch them in the balconies endeavouring to vie with their masters' performances in valse, polka, and galop: I have seen them, after taking note of the step, select their partners (all boys) and set to work, thinking evidently that it is part of the sport for each couple to cannon against another!

But though the Andamanese can thus in a measure enter into and enjoy civilized employments and amusements, the instincts of savage life, with its unrestrained freedom of action, generally prove in the end too strong for them, and they are carried, by an apparently irresistible impulse, back to their jungle homes, where they resume their aboriginal customs and habits, thus verifying the old Horatian maxim—

"*Naturam expellas furcâ tamen usque recurret.*"

APPENDIX A.

ALPHABET FOR WRITING THE SOUTH ANDAMAN LANGUAGE.[1]

SIGN.	ENGLISH, &c.	SOUTH ANDAMAN.
	Oral Vowels and Diphthongs.	
a	.. idea cut	.. *ai·ōka*, *Anadendrum paniculatum*
á	.. curr (with untrilled *r*)	*bá* small, *yá·ba* not
à	.. Ital. casa	*eld·kà* region
ā	.. father	.. *dā·-ke* don't (imperative)
â (1)	fathom	.. *jâr·awa* name of a tribe
e (2)	bed	.. *ē·maj Terminalia bialata*
	chaotic	.. *pū·d·re* burn-did
ē (3)	pale	.. *ē·la* pig-arrow
i	.. lid	.. *ig-bā·dig-re* see-did
ī	.. police	.. *pī·dī* turtle, *pīd* hair
o	.. indolent	.. *bō·gali* European
ó (4)	pole	.. *jūō* basket
ò	.. pot	.. *pôl·i-ke* dwell-does
ō	.. awful	.. *tō·go* wrist, shoulder
u	.. influence	*bū·kura Diospyros sp.*
ū	.. pool	.. *pū·d·re* burn-did
ai	.. bite	.. *dai·-ke* understand-does
au	.. house	.. *chōpau·e* narrow
áu	.. Germ. haus	.. *rāūs* body
ōi	.. boil	.. *bōi·goli* European
	Consonants.	
b	.. bed	.. *bād* hut
ch	.. church	.. *chāk* ability, *mich·aku* why, *.chāk* Ross Island

SIGN.	ENGLISH, &c.	SOUTH ANDAMAN.
d	.. dip	.. *dō·ga* large
g	.. gap	.. *gāb* bamboo utensil
h	.. hay	.. *hēbo! dwīh* (*h* sounded, see note 5) stertern
j	.. judge	.. *jā·bag* bad, *ē·maj Terminalia bialata*
k	.. king	.. *kā·gal-ke* ascend-does
l	.. lap	.. *lig* navigable channel
m	.. man	.. *mō·ga* face
n	.. nun	.. *nā·n-ke* walk-does, *rō·pas* toad
ñ	.. Fr. gagner	*ūñā·ba* another, one more
ng	.. bring	.. *ngō·ji* friend, *ērāū·dang-ke* in-trees-search-does (11)
hg (6)		*hgd* more
p	.. pup	.. *pīd* hair
r (7)	rest	.. *rāō* necklace of netting, *rā·tā* wooden arrow
ṛ (8)	torrent	.. *ṛā·la* sea water
s	.. sad	.. not found (9)
t	.. ten	.. *tī* blood
t'	..	*t'ī* tear (from the eye) (10)
w	.. wet	.. *wā·lo* adze, *.bal·awa* name of a tribe
y	.. yolk	.. *yobā* a little

RULES.

The syllable under stress in any word is shown by placing a turned period (·) after a long vowel, or the consonant following a short vowel, in every word of more than one syllable.

When no stress is marked, it should be placed on every long vowel and diphthong in a word, or if there are none such, on the first syllable.

As it is not usual to find capitals cast for the accented letters, the capital at the beginning of a word *is for uniformity in all cases* indicated by prefixing a direct period, as *.bal·awa.*

Substantives, adjectives, and adverbs generally end in "*da*," which is usually dropped before postpositions and in construction; hence when I write a hyphen at the end of a word, I mean that in its full form it has "*da*."

NOTES.

(1) *â* accented before a consonant, is the English *u* in nut, as distinguished from *à*, which is the short of *ā* or Italian *a* in anno.

(2) *e* accented in closed syllables, as in bed; in open syllables unaccented, as in chaotic, or Italian padre, an ore.

---

[1] As elsewhere mentioned, I am indebted to the kindness of Mr. A. J. Ellis, F.R.S., for the improvements and additions to the list of symbols formerly employed by me. This alphabet is an extract from his able "Report on Researches into the Language of the South Andaman Island, &c.," which formed part of the President's annual address for 1882 to the Philological Society.

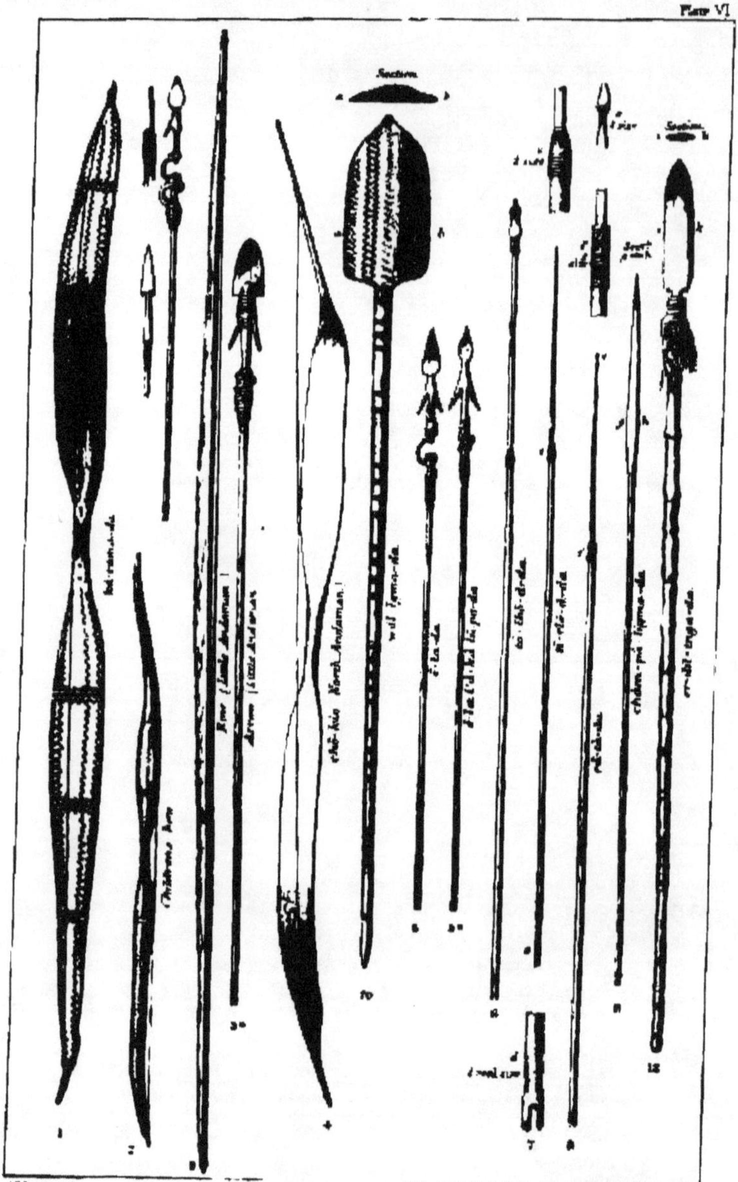

ANDAMANESE OBJECTS.

(3) No vanishing sound of *i* as in *say*.

(4) No vanishing sound of *u* as in English *know*.

(5) *h* is sounded after a vowel by continuing breath through the position of the mouth, while remitting the voice.

(6) *ñg* is a palatalised *ng*, and bears the same relation to it as *ñ* bears to *n*. To pronounce *ñ* attempt to say *n* and *y* simultaneously; to pronounce *ñg* do the same for *ng* and *y*.

(7) This *r* is soft and gentle, with no sensible ripple of the tongue, as very frequently in English, but is not merely vocal.

(8) This *r* is strongly trilled, as *r* in Scotch or Italian *r*, or Spanish *rr*.

(9) The Andamanese cannot hiss, and hence they substitute *ch* for *s*, thus *râch* for *Rôs*, the Hindi corruption of Ross.

(10) This *t'* is a post-aspirated *t*, like the Indian *th*, quite different from English *th*, and hence to prevent confusion, the Greek *spiritus asper* is imitated by a turned comma. The sound *t'*, is common in Irish-English, and may often be heard in England.

(11) When *ng* is followed by a vowel, it must run on to that vowel only, and not be run on to the preceding vowel, either as in "finger" or in "singer," thus *bē·ri-nga-da* "good," not *bē·ring-a-da*, *bē·ring-gad-a*, or *bē·rin-ga-da*. It is only when no vowel follows that *ng* is run on to the preceding vowel.

APPENDIX B.

List of Objects made and used by the Andamanese.[1]

1. *kâ·rama-*.[2] Bow of a flattened S-shaped form, as made and used by the tribes of South and Middle Andaman, and the Archipelago, viz.: *bôjig-ngîji-*, *bôjig-yâb-*, *âkà-jüwai-*, *âkà-kol-*, and *balawa-*,[3] and called by them *bôjig kâ·rama-*[4] (our style of bow), to distinguish it from the bows used by the inhabitants of North and Little Andaman: it is made of a hard wood, generally of a variety called *chai-*, or—though less frequently—of the *bad·ama-*, *yâ·ra-*, *pô·rud-*, or *chà·kak-*.[5] For hunting in the interior, the usual length of these bows, for the sake of convenience, is about 4 feet; the same or somewhat larger bows are used in the open jungle, along the coast, or when shooting fish; when made for presentation rather than for use, they are elaborately ornamented and carefully prepared in every way, and measure 6½ or 7 feet in length. It is customary to ornament

[1] In arranging this list, I have taken care to retain the numbers which are attached to each object in the Andamanese collection presented by me to General Pitt Rivers in 1878, and which is now exhibited in the South Kensington Museum. Except where otherwise specified, these objects are those used by the people of South Andaman; many of them, however, are believed to differ but slightly from such as are made by the remaining seven tribes of Great Andaman; but greater diversities are to be found among objects made by the Little Andaman and other *jâ·rawa-* tribes.

[2] *Vide* Plate VI, fig. 1.

[3] For the situation of these tribes *vide* the accompanying map.

[4] For the purposes of inflection and syntax, the termination *da*, which belongs to most substantives, adjectives, and many adverbs, is invariably dropped (*vide* Appendix A, "Rules").

[5] The botanical names of the various trees which have as yet been identified will be found in Appendix L.

both sides of every *bōjig* bow, first by cutting a rough ×-like pattern along the edge from end to end with a *Cyrena* shell, and then with grass or leaves smearing *kòiob-* (item 60) over both surfaces, to form a background, upon which they finally paint a design in *tà·la-ōg-* (item 58); the upper end, or nock, of the bow is also frequently decorated with a piece of fine netting called *rab-* (item 42); the bowstring is made of the bark fibre of the *Anadendrum paniculatum* (Andam., *yō·lba-*, item 64), to which, to increase its strength, a coating of black beeswax (*tō·bul-pid-*, item 57) is frequently applied. Children's bows[1] only are ever made of mangrove wood, and then the *Rhizophora conjugata* is usually preferred.[2]

[NOTE.—The North Andaman bows, called *chō·kio-*,[3] which are generally, if not always, made from the tree they call *bad·ama-*, differ somewhat in design from those just described; they are also more neatly made, and are never painted or otherwise ornamented, and are almost invariably of a uniform size, *i.e.*, 5 to 5½ feet in length. The Little Andaman and other *jár·awa-* bows[4] are of a totally different form, and appear to be commonly made of the wood of the tree known to them as *lō·kuma-*.]

2. *rā·tà-*.[5] The common blunt wooden-headed arrow, used when practising at an object:[6] the shaft consists of a reed-like variety of bamboo (*Bambusa nana*) called *rā·di-*, and the fore-shaft is generally a piece of the hard portion of the wood of the Areca, or less frequently of the root of the *Rhizophora conjugata*: the point is usually hardened over a fire, and straightened by means of their teeth.

3. *tirlē·d-*.[7] The ordinary fish arrow, which differs from the *rā·tà-* only in that the point is sharpened.

4. *tō·lbō·d-*.[8] Fish arrow, about 4½ feet long, made like the preceding varieties, but provided with an iron head and barb; the string fastenings attaching the same to the foreshaft are covered with *kà·ngatà-bùj-* (item 62). In former times the head of this arrow consisted of a fish-bone; the serrated bone at the root of the tail of the sting-ray (item 53) was often employed for this purpose.

5. *ē·la-*.[9] Pig arrow, about 3½ feet in length: the foreshaft consists of a triangular piece of flattened iron fastened to the end of a small stick about 4 inches in length; at the base of the

[1] *Vide* Plate VI, fig. 2.

[2] This of course is only procurable by those living on or near the coast. The bows of the *ēremtà·ga-* children are usually made of wood of the *Trigonostemon longifolius*.

[3] *Vide* Plate VI, fig. 4.

[4] *Vide* Plate VI, fig. 3.

[5] *Vide* Plate VI, fig. 8.

[6] *Vide* Part III, "Games and Amusements," paragraph 14.

[7] *Vide* Plate VI, fig. 7.

[8] *Vide* Plate VI, fig. 6.

[9] *Vide* Plate VI, fig. 5.

head one or two (rarely three) iron barbs are fixed to the stick, the end of which is fitted into a socket (*ā·kà-chā·nga-*) provided for it in the shaft; the head and shaft are connected by a flattened thong about 8 inches long, made from the fibre of the *Anadendrum paniculatum*, and which, before the arrow is fired, is always wound round the wooden portion of the foreshaft by twisting the latter when placing it in its socket; when an animal is struck the head of the arrow is retained in the flesh by the barbs (*ōrchō·ga-*), and as the foreshaft slips out of its socket by reason of the struggles and movements of the animal in its efforts to escape, the trailing shaft quickly becomes entangled in the brushwood, thereby detaining the victim and ensuring its capture.

6. *ē·la l'ā·kà kā·pa-.*[1] This, as indicated by its name, is merely a plain pig arrow, having no foreshaft like the more elaborate *ē·la-*: it is less effective than the latter, but more easily made.

7. *tō·lbōd l'ā·rtām-.*[2]

7a. *ē·la l'ā·rtām-*[3] (lit., ancient). Fish and pig arrows, headed respectively with fish bone (*nāp l'ār būl-*, item 53) and the *Perna ephippium* shell, which are said to have been used in former times when iron was unobtainable.

8. *chām-pā·ligma-.*[4] Plain wooden arrows, about 3½ feet in length, made of the wood of the Areca palm: it is said that when iron was scarce these were shaped somewhat like the *ē·la-* (item 5) or *tō·lēd-* (item 3), and used as pig and fish arrows, but now they are never so employed, being apparently made only for the "sake of auld lang syne," or to display the skill of the maker.

[NOTE.—The *jār·awa-* are only as yet known to employ the two varieties of arrows, viz., the *ē·la-* and the *tō·lē·d-*; the latter much resembles those bearing the same name and made by the eight Great Andaman tribes, but the former is a more formidable weapon, being larger and more strongly made.]

9. *ēr-dū·tnga-* or *gū·ain-.*[5] Pig spear, generally 6 or 7 feet long; the haft consists ordinarily of a piece of ground rattan (*bōl-*), and a large double-edged blade forms the head. This weapon is rarely used, the *ē·la* (item 5) being preferred.

[NOTE.—It appears that none of the North Andaman or *jār·awa-* tribes have ever been seen with such a spear; probably this is partly due to the difficulty they experience in obtaining iron.]

10. *kowai·a kō·ko dū·tnga-*[6] Turtle spear: the shaft[7] is a

[1] *Vide* Plate IX, fig. 5.
[2] *Vide* Plate IX, fig. 4.
[3] *Vide* Plate VIII, fig. 76.
[4] *Vide* Plate VI, fig. 9.
[5] *Vide* Plate VI, fig. 12.
[6] *Vide* Plate VII, fig. 24.
[7] This shaft is called *tīg-*, and is used for poling the canoe along the shore.

bamboo (male species preferred), often 18 feet or more in length; for the reception of the harpoon a socket is prepared at the small end, which is strengthened by pieces of mangrove wood, over which strips of cane are neatly tied. The harpoon consists of a strong barbed iron head fastened to a short piece of wood to which a long line (*bē·tma-*) is attached. When a turtle or large fish is struck the harpoon detaches itself from the shaft, which floats and is picked up after the capture has been effected.

[NOTE.—A harpooner almost invariably follows up a successful cast by plunging into the water, lest in the act of dragging the line the harpoon should slip out of the wound and his victim should thus escape.]

11. *rō·ko-*.[1] Generic name of the various kinds of canoes made in recent years[2] by the aborigines of South Andaman and adjacent parts, where, owing to the facility of obtaining iron tools, large dug-outs, called *gē·lyanga-*, capable of accommodating twenty to forty persons, are constructed in place of the small outrigger canoe (*chā·rigma-*) with which the other tribes have still to content themselves. They are usually made of the *Sterculia villosa* (Andam., *bā·ja-*), and are often ornamentally painted.

[NOTE.—The outrigger is called *tel-*, and is always made of the wood of *ca...* (one of the *Sterculiaceæ*), which is soft and light.]

11*a*. *wāl·igma-*.[3] Paddle: these are not made by women, nor are they of any prescribed size, this being regulated merely by the fancy of the maker, and the material at his disposal; they are frequently adorned by women with chevrons[4] (*jō·bo-tārtā·nga-*) of *kōi·ob-* (item 60) or *tā·la-ōg-* (item 58).

12. *yāto-tē·pinga-*. Turtle-net, made by men,[5] of a stout cord (*bē·tma-*), which is prepared from the bark fibre of the *Melochia velutina* (Andam., *ā·aba-*); the meshes vary in size according to the fancy or skill of the maker.[6]

13. *dā·kar-*.[7] Bucket made by the Great Andaman tribes of the wood used in constructing canoes, *i.e.*, *Sterculia villosa*, with a loop of cane to form the handle; the implement used in hollowing out these vessels is the blade of the adze (*wō·lo-*, item 15), which is detached from its handle and fastened to a straight piece of wood so as to form a sort of chisel.

[NOTE.—The Little Andaman and other *jār·awa-* buckets are made in the same manner, but are much larger and superior in every way; they are, moreover, neatly ornamented round the sides with strips of cane evenly laid on and fastened at the rim by plaiting.]

[1] *Vide* Plate VIII, fig. 69.
[2] *Vide* Part III, "Navigation," paragraph 4, and footnote.
[3] *Vide* Plate VI, fig. 70.
[4] *Vide* Part III, "Ornamentation," paragraph 6.
[5] *Vide* Plate VIII, fig. 60.
[6] *Vide* Part III, "String," paragraph 6.
[7] *Vide* Plate VII, fig. 14.

Plate VII

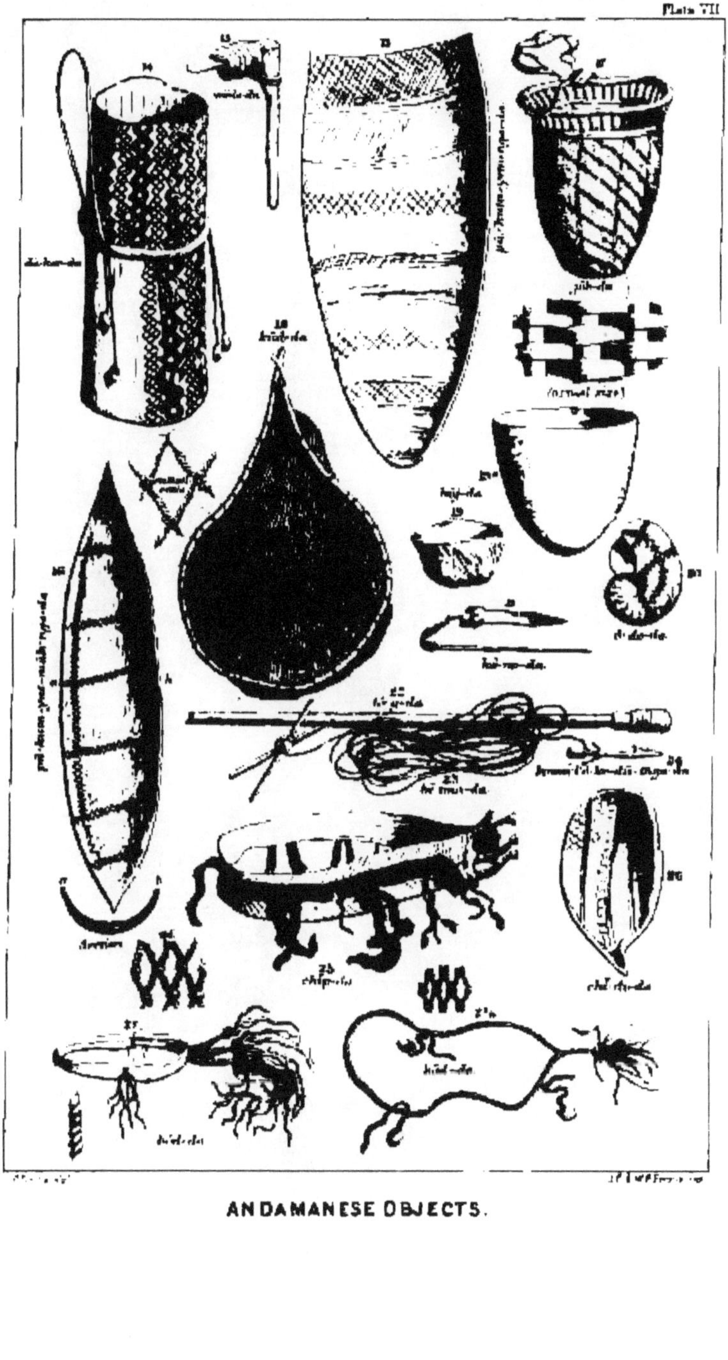

ANDAMANESE OBJECTS.

14. *ā·do-.*[1] Nautilus shells painted with *kā·ngatā-bāj-* (item 62), and used as drinking vessels.

15. *wō·lo-.*[2] Adze: this tool is used not only in making canoes, buckets, bows, &c., but in digging graves. The handle consists of an L-shaped piece of mangrove wood, *Rhizophora conjugata* (Andam., *bad·a-*), and the blade is generally made of such pieces of iron as the keel-plate of a boat; formerly *Pinna* and such like shells are said to have been used, but strange to say it does not appear that stone celts were ever so employed.

16. *lā·kā-.*[3] A long pointed stick of the *Memecylon variana*, (Andam., *pī·taing-*) or *Rhizophora conjugata* (Andam., *bad·a-*), which is used as a hoe in digging up yams and other edible roots.

[NOTE.—A similar implement is found in use among the Australians.[4]]

17. *tōg-ngā·tanga-.*[5] Pole, 12 to 15 feet long, of *Bambusa nana* (Andam., *rī·di-*), to which a short piece of bamboo is securely fastened, with a strip of cane (Andam., *pī·dga-*), or stout cord, to form a hook; it is used in gathering fruit—especially jack-fruit (*Artocarpus chaplasha*)—and is the only object of the nature of a hook *made* by the Andamanese.

18. *būj-.*[6] Cooking pot: these are made of various sizes by members of both sexes, and are shaped by the hand and eye only;[7] after being sun-dried they are surrounded with, and filled by pieces of lighted wood in order to complete the process of baking. When needed for travelling they are fitted with light wicker frames (*būj-rā·mata-*) to facilitate their removal, and to protect them from injury. The capacity of an average-sized pot is 9 or 10 pints.

[NOTE.—The *yē·rewa-* and *jē·rewa-* pots have a conical base, and in this respect differ from those made by the tribes of South Andaman.]

19. *pū·kuta-yem·nga-.*[8] Sounding-boards—used for marking time during a song or dance[9]—which are scooped out of the fallen trunks of the *Pterocarpus dalbergioides* (Andam., *chā·langa-*), the wood of which is very hard; they are always of the same shield-like shape, and are frequently as much as 5 feet long and 2 feet wide; the concave side is generally ornamented with designs in white clay (*tā·la-ōg-*, item 58). When in use the

[1] *Vide* Plate VII, fig. 20.
[2] *Vide* Plate VII, fig. 13.
[3] *Vide* Plate IX, fig. 2.
[4] *Vide* "Anthropology," p. 216, by Dr. E. B. Tylor, F.R.S.
[5] *Vide* Plate IX, fig. 1.
[6] *Vide* Plate VII, fig. 19.
[7] *Vide* Part III, "Pottery," paragraphs 4 and 6.
[8] *Vide* Plate VII, fig. 15
[9] *Vide* Part III, "Games and Amusements," paragraph 27.

convex side is uppermost; the pointed end is stuck in the ground, and kept in position with one foot; a stone is then placed under the board to enable the performer to make more noise when keeping time, which he does by thumping or kicking the board with the heel of the other foot.

20. *kūd-.*[1] Hand fishing-net constructed from the prepared fibre of the *Gnetum edule* (Andam., *pī'lita-*) by women and girls, who also by its means catch large quantities of fish and prawns, both in streams and among rocks along the coast at low tide. It is about the size of an ordinary butterfly-net; the frame is made of a length of a creeper known to them as *ō'ta-kāt-*, the ends being bound together to form a handle.

21. *jōb-.*[2] Baskets used by all the Great Andaman tribes for carrying food and various other articles: they are generally made by women.[3]

[NOTE.—The baskets made by the *.ār-yōto-* or North Andaman tribes, differ from those found among the *.bō'jig* tribes in having a wider base and a smaller mouth.[4]]

21*a*. The *jā'rawa-*[5] baskets differ from those in use among the Great Andaman tribes in having no firm base.

22. *chā'panga-.*[6] Netted reticules made and used by women for carrying small objects: the string used for this purpose is generally prepared from the fibre of the *Anadendron paniculatum* (Andam., *yō'lba-*, item 64), but as this is not always attainable the less-valued fibre of the *Gnetum edule* (Andam., *pī'lita-*) is sometimes employed as a substitute.

23. *pārepa-.*[7] Sleeping mat made by women of strips of a species of *Calamus* fastened securely in the ordinary manner with string made from the fibre of the *Gnetum edule* (Andam., *pī'lita-*, item 65). When in use the rolled-up portion of these mats—which are generally 15 to 20 feet long—serves as a pillow.

23*a*. The *.jā'rawa-*[8] sleeping mats hitherto found have always been of short lengths, but as wooden pillows similar to those in use among the Nicobarese have been found in their huts, it is probable that the specimens obtained represent full sized mats.

24. *chīp-.*[9] Sling or band made by women from the bark of

[1] *Vide* Plate VII, fig. 18.
[2] *Vide* Plate VII, fig. 17.
[3] *Vide* Part III, "Basket-work," paragraphs 2 and 3.
[4] *Vide* Plate IX, fig. 14.
[5] *Vide* Plate IX, fig. 14*a*.
[6] *Vide* Plate VIII, fig. 22.
[7] *Vide* Plate IX, fig. 15.
[8] *Vide* Plate IX, fig. 15*a*.
[9] *Vide* Plate VII, fig. 25.

the *Melochia velutina* (Andam., *alaba-*), which is worn like a sash over one shoulder by women, and sometimes by men, when carrying infants.[1]

The plain specimens are called *chip-lūpa-*.

Those ornamented with netting *chip-rāb-*.

Those ornamented with shells *chip-yīmnga-*.

25. *bōd-*.[2] Waistbelt made from the leaves of the young screw-pine (*Pandanus Andamanensium*); the bunch of leaves or tail is worn at the back.

[NOTE.—These specimens are of the kind worn by women and girls of the eight Great Andaman tribes; the females of the *jārawa-* tribes appear to go entirely nude.]

25a. *bōd-*.[3] Waistbelts of similar description, but having a less bushy tail, are worn more or less generally by men and youths of the eight Great Andaman tribes.

26. *rōgun-*.[4] Belt made from the leaves of the young screw-pine, which is worn by adult married women only.

27. *ta-chōnga-*.[5] Garters, which are frequently worn by men and youths: they are made in the same way as the *bōd-* (item 25.)

28. *tōgo-chōnga-*.[6] Bracelets, also worn by men and youths, much resembling the last-named object.

29. *garen-pāla-*.[7] Ornamental waistbelt of *Dentalium octogonum*, which is worn occasionally by both sexes.

30. *bēria-*[8] *jārawa-* waistbelts, necklets, and armlets, which are believed to be worn by men and youths only.

31. *ēji-gōnga-*.[9] Head-dress of Pandanus-leaf, worn occasionally by young men and women.

The following ten articles are worn by both sexes as ornaments either round the neck or head:—

32. *ūna-ēla-ta-*[10]	..	made of	fresh water-shells.
33. *pēr-ta-* ..	..	„	cane or wood.
34. *yādī-ta-*[11]	..	„	turtle bones.
35. *baian-ta-*	..	„	paradoxurus bones.
36. *dūkn-ta-*[12]	..	„	iguana bones.

[1] *Vide* Part III, "Social Relations, &c.," paragraph 10.
[2] *Vide* Plate VII, fig. 27.
[3] *Vide* Plate VII, fig. 27a.
[4] *Vide* Plate VIII, fig. 29.
[5] *Vide* Plate IX, fig. 9.
[6] *Vide* Plate IX, fig. 8.
[7] *Vide* Plate VIII, fig. 35.
[8] *Vide* Plate IX, figs. 13, 13a, and 13b.
[9] *Vide* Plate IX, figs. 6 and 6a.
[10] *Vide* Plate VIII, fig. 48.
[11] *Vide* Plate VIII, fig. 38.
[12] *Vide* Plate VIII, fig. 40.

37. *bī'ma-tá-* .. made of red coral.
38. *rā'ta-ō'la-tá-* .. „ small sea shells.
39. *rō'keto-tá-*[1] .. „ *Hemicardium unedo* shells.
40. *ngā'tya-tá-*[2] and *jū'mu-ta-* „ mangrove seed tops.
41. *garen len pīd-* .. „ *Dentalium octogonum* and children's hair.[3]

42. *rāb-.*[4] Fine netting, plain or ornamented with shells, worn occasionally by both sexes as necklaces, armlets, &c. Baby-slings (item 24), bows, pig-spears, &c., are sometimes ornamented with pieces of this netting.

43. *rā-.* Ornamental cord, made by men from the yellow skin of an orchid root, and worn round the waist intertwined sometimes with fibres of the *Melochia velutina* (Andam., *al'aba-*). It is also occasionally interwoven with fibres of the *Anadendron paniculatum* (Andam., *pō'the-*), in order to make ornamental fastenings for arrows, turtle harpoons, and personal adornments.

44. *chāu'ga-tá-.*[5] Human bone necklaces sometimes ornamented with *Dentalium octogonum.* These are worn as charms during illness by friends or relatives of the deceased, and may be often seen tied tightly round the part in pain; they are also worn when in health to ward off disease.[6]

45. *chāu'ga l'ōt chē'ta-.*[7] Human skull, carried *in memoriam* by relatives of the deceased.[8]

46. *chāu'ga l'ā'kā ē'kib-.*[9] Human jaw, which is carried in a similar manner.[10]

47. *pī'licha-.*[11] Boar's tusk, used for planing bows, paddles, &c., as it answers this purpose, in *their* hands, admirably, it is much valued; when required for use the inner edge is sharpened with a *Cyrena* shell.

48. *tai'li-bana-.*[12] Stone hammer, which the men now use principally in beating out iron for arrow-heads, &c., and the women when making bone necklaces.

49. *chā'di-.*[13] *Pinna* shell, used as plates for food, or as receptacles for pigments.

[1] *Vide* Plate VIII, fig. 45.
[2] *Vide* Plate VIII, fig. 73.
[3] An interesting description of these various necklaces will be found in a paper by Dr. Allen Thomson, F.R.S., Journ. Anthrop. Inst., vol. xi, p. 295.
[4] *Vide* Plate VIII, fig. 34.
[5] *Vide* Plate VIII, fig. 40.
[6] *Vide* Part I, "Medicine," paragraphs 2, 7, 8.
[7] *Vide* Plate IX, fig. 7.
[8] *Vide* Part II, "Death and Burial," paragraphs 5 and 13.
[9] *Vide* Plate IX, fig. 7a.
[10] *Vide* Part I, "Medicine," paragraph 9.
[11] *Vide* Plate VIII, fig. 65.
[12] *Vide* Plate VIII, fig. 72.
[13] *Vide* Plate VIII, fig. 26.

Plate VIII

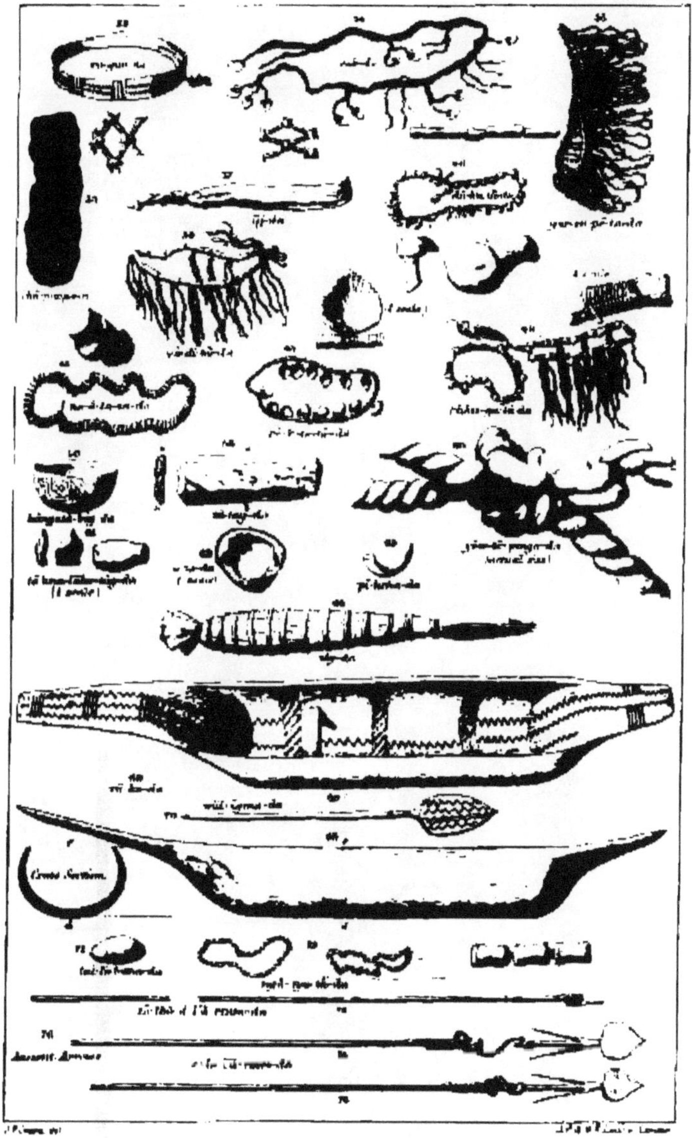

ANDAMANESE OBJECTS.

50. *ăi'ma l'ōko tūg-* and *bĭ'jma l'ōko tūg-*.[1] Quartz and glass flakes and chips used for shaving, scarifying, and tattooing.[2]

51. *ŭ'ta-*.[3] *Cyrena* shell: great use is made of this, and of other varieties of this class, viz., as knives for cutting thatching leaves, for making the ornamental incisions on bows, paddles, &c., for planing, for sharpening the boar's tusk (item 47), for dressing and preparing arrows, for making the *ūj-* (item 76), for preparing the fibres obtained from the *Melochia velutina* (Andam., *alaba-*), *Gnetum edule* (Andam., *pĭ'lita-*), and the *Anadendrum paniculatum* (Andam., *yō'lba-*); they are also used as spoons in eating the gravy of pork, turtle, &c., and are in fact so constantly in demand that a supply is always kept and carried about ready for use.

52. *tă'lag-*.[4] Hone or whetstone, which when in use is held in the right hand and applied to the edge of the blade, which is generally held over the inner side of the left foot, the operator being seated on the ground; pointed weapons are sharpened on it in the usual way.

53. *ăp l'ār bū'l-*. Serrated bone at the root of the tail of the sting-ray; in former times their *tō'lbōd-* arrows (items 4 and 7) were headed with these bones, and it is believed that the early reports of the poisoned arrows of the Andamanese are entirely due to this circumstance; for, owing to their fragile spikes, these bones are apt to cause very serious flesh wounds.[5]

54. *gar'en-*. *Dentalium octogonum* used in the manufacture of various personal ornaments.

55. *rīm-*. Resin obtained from a large tree (*Celtis* or *Gironniera*) of that name, which is used in making *kā'ngata-bŭj-* (*vide* item 62).

56. *ā'ja-pīd-*. Wax of the white honeycomb: it is one of the ingredients in *kā'ngata-bŭj-* (item 62), and is also used in the manufacture of the *chā'panga-* (item 22).

57. *tō'bul-pīd-* or *lē're-*. Wax of the black honeycomb, made by a small description of bee in the hollows of trees: it is generally procured by men, and is applied to bowstrings, arrow fastenings, and the *kŏd* (item 20) is used for caulking cracks in canoes and buckets.

[NOTE.—The honey is eaten, but is not so much relished as that from the white comb.]

[1] *Vide* Plate VIII, fig. 61.

[2] *Vide* Part III, "Stone Implements," paragraphs 3–6.

[3] *Vide* Plate VIII, fig. 53.

[4] *Vide* Plate VIII, fig. 56.

[5] "These wounds often cause great inflammation, whence a notion has been prevalent from ancient times that the sting is charged with venom, but of this there is no evidence. Other species of the sting-ray are plentiful in the warmer parts of the world, and they are everywhere dreaded. The spine is used by the savages of the South Sea Islands to point their spears" ("Chambers's Cyclop.").

58. *ta'la-ōg-.*[1] White clay, used mixed with water, for ornamental painting of the person and of various articles, *e.g.*, bows, baskets, buckets, trays, &c.: the work is done by women: when painting their relatives they spare no pains in executing neat designs with their finger-nails.

[NOTE.—Women during pregnancy are in the habit of nibbling small quantities of this substance from time to time, in the belief that it is beneficial to their condition.]

59. *ōg-.* Common whitish-grey clay, lumps of which are found somewhat plentifully in various parts of the islands. It is used, mixed with water, for smearing over the body when the heat is oppressive.[2] A lump of it is placed on the top of the forehead as a symbol of bereavement, and kept there generally until the expiration of the mourning period.[3] It is also sometimes used by way of ornament on the person, by smearing the trunk and limbs with the wash and then, before it has had time to dry, passing the outspread finger-tips over the surface so as to form some pattern.[4]

60. *kōi'ob-.*[5] Red-ochre paint, which is made by mixing red oxide of iron, *ū'pla-* (*vide* next item), with some greasy substance, the fat of the pig or turtle, sometimes of the iguana, dugong, &c., and occasionally the oil of an almond, called *ō'maj-*, is used. This pigment is applied to the person either ornamentally or otherwise. It is accredited with hygienic properties,[6] and from its mode of application it can be readily determined whether the wearer is suffering or rejoicing. The nostrils and centre of the upper lip are occasionally painted with it, as the smell of the fat is agreeable to them.[7] Before a corpse is removed for burial it is smeared over the face and neck with this paint as a mark of respect, and in order to please the departed spirit.

61. *ū'pla-.* Red oxide of iron after it has been dried and baked. It is principally used in making the pigment described in the preceding paragraph. It is also employed in the manufacture of the red wax, called *kā'ngatā-bū́j-* (*vide* next item).

62. *kā'ngatā-būj-.* Red wax, generally prepared by men, composed of *tī'ja-pīd-*, *rīm-*, and *ū'pla-* (items 56, 55, and 61); in the absence of the last-named ingredient *kōi'ob-* (item 60) is

[1] *Vide* Part III, "Painting," paragraph 7.
[2] *Vide* Part I, "Anatomy and Physiology," paragraph 5.
[3] *Vide* Part II, "Death and Burial," paragraphs 2, 6, 8, and footnote [1].
[4] *Vide* Part III, "Painting," paragraphs 5 and 6.
[5] *ū'pla-* is collected chiefly during the dry months; in its natural condition, as found, it is called *kōi'ob-chō'laga-*; in that condition it is applied to sores, and to the persons of fever-patients; it is administered internally for coughs, fevers, &c. (*vide* Part I, "Medicine," paragraphs 4 and 5).
[6] *Vide* Part I, "Medicine," paragraph 2.
[7] *Vide* Part I, "Odour."

substituted. These three substances are melted and stirred over a fire until of a proper consistency; the pigment is then poured into small pots or large shallow shells, where on cooling it soon hardens. When required for use the pot or shell is placed on the fire and the melting wax applied according to fancy. The string fastenings of fish and pig arrows (items 4, 5, and 6) the turtle harpoon (item 10), and pig spear (item 9), are protected with a coating of this wax, and it is applied ornamentally to the food trays (item 72), nautilus shells (item 14), and the outside of buckets (item 13); it is also used for closing cracks in buckets, and in canoes if not too large.

63. *chū'lnga-*. olive-coloured clay found in small springs in the jungles: in its liquid form it is applied medicinally after the manner of *kĭn'ob-chū'lnga-* (*vide* footnote [1], p. 184).

64. *yŏ'lba-*. (*Anadendrum panicalatum*), the fibre of which is much valued on account of its excellence; string made from it is used for bowstrings and arrow fastenings, for netting the *chā'panga-* (item 22), and *rāb-* (item 42), for making their various necklaces and other personal ornaments, and also for the fastenings of knives and turtle harpoons.

65. *pī'lita-* (*Gnetum edule*), from the fibre of which string is prepared and used almost exclusively by women, chiefly for the manufacture of the *bōd-* (item 20), and *pār'pa-* (item 23); it is not sufficiently strong to serve as arrow fastenings, though on an emergency it is sometimes used for this purpose.

66. *al'aba-* (*Melochia velutina*). From fibre obtained from this tree rope is made for turtle-lines (*bē'tma-*), nets, and cables, the preparation and manufacture of which devolve on men; the bark of this tree also furnishes the material of which the *chip-* (item 24) or baby-slings are made.

67. *pŏtŏkla-*.[1] Netting-needles, made in two sizes of bamboo and used in making nets.

[NOTE.—The turtle-net (item 12) is not made with netting-needles, but with two sticks called *kā'tegbo-*.[2]]

68. *pa-chā-*. Bamboo knives, which are shaped into form while green and then dried and charred over a fire to render them sharp and fit for use; formerly they were employed for cutting meat and other food.[3]

69. *wai-chā-* and *pār-chā-*. Two varieties of cane knives, but similar to item 68.

70. *tō'ug-*.[4] Torch, made by women, of resin wrapped in a large leaf (*Crinum lorifolium*); it is used when fishing, travelling, or

[1] *Vide* Plate IX, fig. 12.
[2] These are made of a light hard wood known as *bē'rwil-*.
[3] *Vide* Plate IX, fig. 10.
[4] *Vide* Plate VIII, fig. 66.

dancing by night: the resin is obtained from a large tree called by them *mait-*, which also is often employed in the construction of their largest canoes. A larger description of torch is made by men, and used when fishing by night.

71. *kā·pi-*. Gurjon wood torch, obtained from the heart of rotten logs of the *Dipterocarpus lævis* (Andam., *ā·rain-*): as these do not burn so readily as the *tō·ug-* (item 70) they are rarely used outside their huts.

72. *pū·kuta-yāt-mā·k·nga-*.[1] Food tray, made by men of some soft wood, generally of the large flat buttress roots of the trees (*Sterculiaceæ*) of which their canoes are made.

73. *ā·ra-*. Long fringe-like cane-leaf wreaths, which are made by women, and suspended from trees, &c., round an encampment or hut where a death has occurred, and round the spot where the corpse is deposited in order to warn off persons inadvertently approaching the place, which is believed to be haunted by the spirit of the deceased.[2]

74. *kā·pa-jā·nga-*. Fan-like screen, made by women, of a description of palm-leaf (Andam., *kā·pa-*), two of which are fastened together with leaf stems: it is used for many purposes, amongst others as a protection from rain and from the direct rays of the sun in hot weather; in the absence of a *pār-epa-* (item 23) it is often used as a sleeping mat, and it serves also as a wrapper for bundles of various kinds.

75. *kā·pa-*. Leaf wrappers, as described above, are employed for storing and packing the red oxide of iron.[3]

76. *āj-*.[4] Long brush-like shavings of the *Tetranthera lancæfolia*, prepared by men with the sharp edge of a *Cyrena* shell. When dancing these are often held (by both sexes) in their hands, or are stuck in their waistbelts or other personal ornaments.

77. *kō·no-*.[4] Iron knife used in cutting up food; to some a wooden or iron skewer is attached, they are then called *chām-chō-*.

78.[5].

79. *ō·bunga-*. Species of apron, consisting of one to six leaves of the *Mimusops Indica* (Andam., *dū·gota-*), which are fastened to the lowest *bōd-* by women from motives of modesty;[6] the leaves are not spread out so as to cover a wide surface, but are laid one above the other, and removed separately as each becomes stiff and shrivelled: the reason given for the selection of this

[1] *Vide* Plate VII, fig. 16.
[2] *Vide* Part II, "Death and Burial," paragraph 3.
[3] *Vide* Plate VIII, fig. 37.
[4] *Vide* Plate VIII, fig. 31.
[5] This No. is attached to "Specimens of Andamanese Hair" (*vide* footnote 1, p. 175).
[6] *Vide* Part I, "Psychology and Morals," paragraph 8, and footnote.

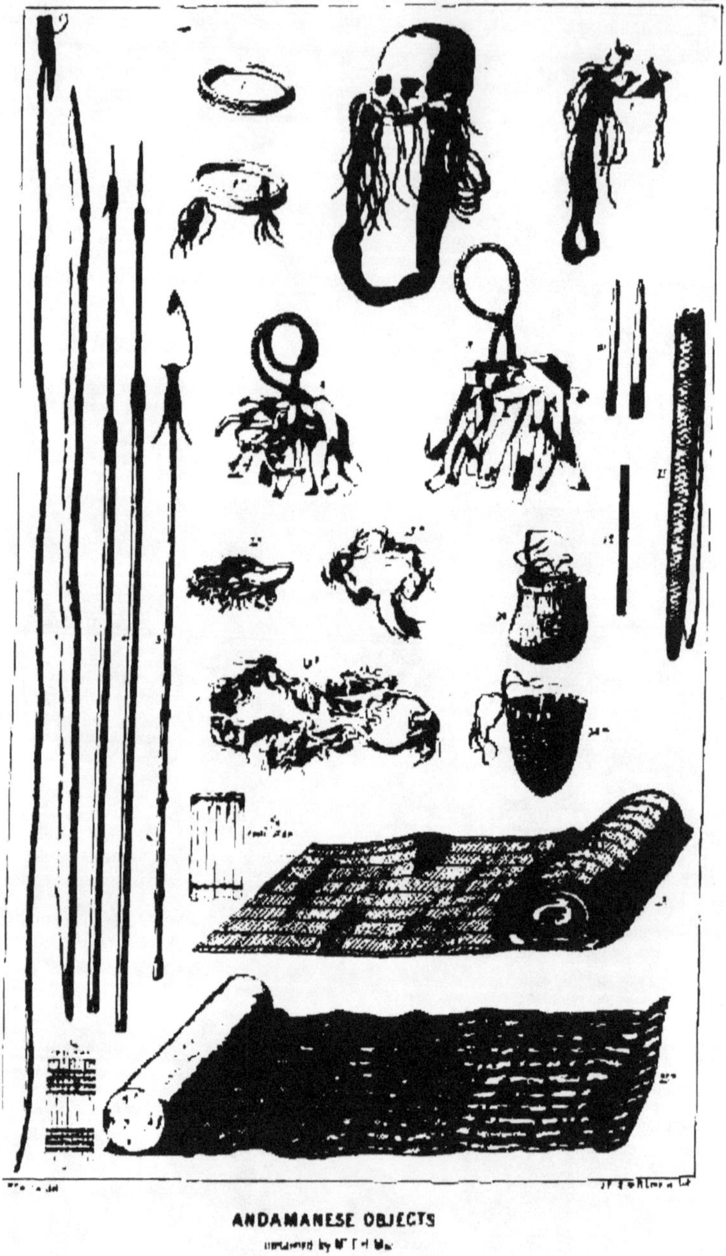

ANDAMANESE OBJECTS

obtained by Mr. E. H. Man

particular leaf is that it keeps green and fresh for a longer time than any other.

[NOTE.—The women of the North Andaman tribes, until recent years, appear to have worn no *ō·bunga*, or only in a very modified form; the change which is now observable among them in this respect is doubtless to be traced to their intercourse with the people of South Andaman.]

80. *kai-*.[1] Bamboo tongs, made by women, and used for any purpose which would involve a risk of burning or scalding the fingers, such as lifting a pot or piece of cooked food off the fire.

81. *ko·pōt-*. Bucket made from a single joint of the *Bambusa gigantea*, pieces of which are sometimes found on the coast, having floated ashore from the neighbouring continent or from wrecks; they are much valued on account of their lightness and the labour saved in making a wooden bucket (*dā·kar-*, item 13), which being, as before described, scooped out of a single piece of wood, is a laborious undertaking.

[NOTE.—The origin of the *dā·kar-* is doubtless to be traced to the *ko·pōt-*.]

82. *gōb-*. Bamboo vessel, of which there are two varieties, viz., (*a*) for use as a water-holder: this is often 4 or 5 feet long, the partitions at the joints being broken through with a spear head or other suitable instrument, the lowest one only being left to form the bottom of the vessel; and (*b*) for use as a cooking pot and food-holder: its length consists of a single joint of bamboo, into which—after it has been cleaned, washed, and dried over a fire—food is packed and cooked; as will be seen by reference to Part III,[2] these vessels are only capable of serving on a single occasion; the handle is formed with a piece of *bō·tma-*.

83. *lā-*. Cooking stones: the mode in which they are used is described in Part III.[3]

84. *kā·ta-ngā·tanga-* (*lit.*, crab-hook). An implement employed for picking up live crabs between rocks, in order to save the fingers from being nipped; it consists merely of a branch broken off the *Rhizophora conjugata*, which (unlike other trees) at once furnishes a strong hook suitable for the above purpose.

85. *ō·ra-tig-jī·rabnga-*. Tufted leaf brushes, which are used for the same purpose as the *ō·ra-* (item 73), and also by persons recently tattooed to drive away flies.

[A few other objects, omitted from this list, will be found described in Journ. Anthrop. Inst., vol. vii, pp. 457–465.]

[1] *Vide* Plate IX, fig. 11.
[2] *Vide* "Food," paragraph 21.
[3] *Vide* paragraph 27, and "Stone Implements," paragraph 2.

APPENDIX C.

TABLE OF WEIGHTS AND MEASUREMENTS OF 48 ANDAMANESE MALE AND 41 FEMALE ADULTS.

Males.

No.	Weight.	Height.	Size round head.	Round neck.	Round chest.	Round waist.	Round buttocks.	Round thigh.	Round calf.	Round ankle.	Round biceps.	Round arm.	Round fore-arm.	Round wrist.	Length of spine.	Length of arm and hand.	Length from shoulder to elbow.	From shoulder to wrist.	From ankle to knee.	From ankle to hip.	Length of foot.
	lbs.	ft. ins.	ins.	ins.	ins.	ins.	ins.	ins.	ins.	ins.	ins.	ins.	ins.	ins.	ins.	ins.	ins.	ins.	ins.	ins.	ins.
1	110½	5 3½	[illegible]	14	[illegible]	[illegible]	[illegible]	[illegible]	[illegible]	[illegible]	[illegible]	[illegible]	[illegible]	[illegible]	[illegible]	[illegible]	[illegible]	[illegible]	[illegible]	[illegible]	10
2	94	4 10	[illegible]	[illegible]	[illegible]	[illegible]	[illegible]	[illegible]	[illegible]	[illegible]	[illegible]	[illegible]	[illegible]	[illegible]	[illegible]	[illegible]	[illegible]	[illegible]	[illegible]	[illegible]	[illegible]
3	92	5 0½	[illegible]	[illegible]	[illegible]	[illegible]	[illegible]	[illegible]	[illegible]	[illegible]	[illegible]	[illegible]	[illegible]	[illegible]	[illegible]	[illegible]	[illegible]	[illegible]	[illegible]	[illegible]	[illegible]
4	[illegible]	4 11½	[illegible]	[illegible]	[illegible]	[illegible]	[illegible]	[illegible]	[illegible]	[illegible]	[illegible]	[illegible]	[illegible]	[illegible]	[illegible]	[illegible]	[illegible]	[illegible]	[illegible]	[illegible]	[illegible]
5	[illegible]	4 10½	[illegible]	[illegible]	[illegible]	[illegible]	[illegible]	[illegible]	[illegible]	[illegible]	[illegible]	[illegible]	[illegible]	[illegible]	[illegible]	[illegible]	[illegible]	[illegible]	[illegible]	[illegible]	[illegible]
6	[illegible]	4 9	[illegible]	[illegible]	[illegible]	[illegible]	[illegible]	[illegible]	[illegible]	[illegible]	[illegible]	[illegible]	[illegible]	[illegible]	[illegible]	[illegible]	[illegible]	[illegible]	[illegible]	[illegible]	[illegible]
7	[illegible]	4 11	[illegible]	[illegible]	[illegible]	[illegible]	[illegible]	[illegible]	[illegible]	[illegible]	[illegible]	[illegible]	[illegible]	[illegible]	[illegible]	[illegible]	[illegible]	[illegible]	[illegible]	[illegible]	[illegible]
8	112	5 2	[illegible]	[illegible]	[illegible]	[illegible]	[illegible]	[illegible]	[illegible]	[illegible]	[illegible]	[illegible]	[illegible]	[illegible]	[illegible]	[illegible]	[illegible]	[illegible]	[illegible]	[illegible]	[illegible]
9	118	5 0½	[illegible]	[illegible]	[illegible]	[illegible]	[illegible]	[illegible]	[illegible]	[illegible]	[illegible]	[illegible]	[illegible]	[illegible]	[illegible]	[illegible]	[illegible]	[illegible]	[illegible]	[illegible]	[illegible]
10	112½	5 0½	[illegible]	[illegible]	[illegible]	[illegible]	[illegible]	[illegible]	[illegible]	[illegible]	[illegible]	[illegible]	[illegible]	[illegible]	[illegible]	[illegible]	[illegible]	[illegible]	[illegible]	[illegible]	[illegible]
11	118	5 4½	[illegible]	[illegible]	[illegible]	[illegible]	[illegible]	[illegible]	[illegible]	[illegible]	[illegible]	[illegible]	[illegible]	[illegible]	[illegible]	[illegible]	[illegible]	[illegible]	[illegible]	[illegible]	[illegible]
12	[illegible]	4 8	[illegible]	[illegible]	[illegible]	[illegible]	[illegible]	[illegible]	[illegible]	[illegible]	[illegible]	[illegible]	[illegible]	[illegible]	[illegible]	[illegible]	[illegible]	[illegible]	[illegible]	[illegible]	[illegible]
13	[illegible]	4 8	[illegible]	[illegible]	[illegible]	[illegible]	[illegible]	[illegible]	[illegible]	[illegible]	[illegible]	[illegible]	[illegible]	[illegible]	[illegible]	[illegible]	[illegible]	[illegible]	[illegible]	[illegible]	[illegible]
14	[illegible]	4 [illegible]	[illegible]	[illegible]	[illegible]	[illegible]	[illegible]	[illegible]	[illegible]	[illegible]	[illegible]	[illegible]	[illegible]	[illegible]	[illegible]	[illegible]	[illegible]	[illegible]	[illegible]	[illegible]	[illegible]
15	[illegible]	4 9½	[illegible]	[illegible]	[illegible]	[illegible]	[illegible]	[illegible]	[illegible]	[illegible]	[illegible]	[illegible]	[illegible]	[illegible]	[illegible]	[illegible]	[illegible]	[illegible]	[illegible]	[illegible]	[illegible]
16	[illegible]	4 11½	[illegible]	[illegible]	[illegible]	[illegible]	[illegible]	[illegible]	[illegible]	[illegible]	[illegible]	[illegible]	[illegible]	[illegible]	[illegible]	[illegible]	[illegible]	[illegible]	[illegible]	[illegible]	[illegible]
17	77½	4 [illegible]	[illegible]	[illegible]	[illegible]	[illegible]	[illegible]	[illegible]	[illegible]	[illegible]	[illegible]	[illegible]	[illegible]	[illegible]	[illegible]	[illegible]	[illegible]	[illegible]	[illegible]	[illegible]	[illegible]
18	[illegible]	5 1	[illegible]	[illegible]	[illegible]	[illegible]	[illegible]	[illegible]	[illegible]	[illegible]	[illegible]	[illegible]	[illegible]	[illegible]	[illegible]	[illegible]	[illegible]	[illegible]	[illegible]	[illegible]	[illegible]
19	[illegible]	4 11	[illegible]	[illegible]	[illegible]	[illegible]	[illegible]	[illegible]	[illegible]	[illegible]	[illegible]	[illegible]	[illegible]	[illegible]	[illegible]	[illegible]	[illegible]	[illegible]	[illegible]	[illegible]	[illegible]
20	[illegible]	4 10½	[illegible]	[illegible]	[illegible]	[illegible]	[illegible]	[illegible]	[illegible]	[illegible]	[illegible]	[illegible]	[illegible]	[illegible]	[illegible]	[illegible]	[illegible]	[illegible]	[illegible]	[illegible]	[illegible]
21	[illegible]	5 0	[illegible]	[illegible]	[illegible]	[illegible]	[illegible]	[illegible]	[illegible]	[illegible]	[illegible]	[illegible]	[illegible]	[illegible]	[illegible]	[illegible]	[illegible]	[illegible]	[illegible]	[illegible]	[illegible]
22	[illegible]	4 8	[illegible]	[illegible]	[illegible]	[illegible]	[illegible]	[illegible]	[illegible]	[illegible]	[illegible]	[illegible]	[illegible]	[illegible]	[illegible]	[illegible]	[illegible]	[illegible]	[illegible]	[illegible]	[illegible]
23	101	4 10	[illegible]	[illegible]	[illegible]	[illegible]	[illegible]	[illegible]	[illegible]	[illegible]	[illegible]	[illegible]	[illegible]	[illegible]	[illegible]	[illegible]	[illegible]	[illegible]	[illegible]	[illegible]	[illegible]
24	omitted.	[illegible]	[illegible]	[illegible]	[illegible]	[illegible]	[illegible]	[illegible]	[illegible]	[illegible]	[illegible]	[illegible]	[illegible]	[illegible]	[illegible]	[illegible]	[illegible]	[illegible]	[illegible]	[illegible]	[illegible]
25	omitted.	[illegible]	[illegible]	[illegible]	[illegible]	[illegible]	[illegible]	[illegible]	[illegible]	[illegible]	[illegible]	[illegible]	[illegible]	[illegible]	[illegible]	[illegible]	[illegible]	[illegible]	[illegible]	[illegible]	[illegible]
26	[illegible]	[illegible]	[illegible]	[illegible]	[illegible]	[illegible]	[illegible]	[illegible]	[illegible]	[illegible]	[illegible]	[illegible]	[illegible]	[illegible]	[illegible]	[illegible]	[illegible]	[illegible]	[illegible]	[illegible]	[illegible]
27	106	4 11	[illegible]	[illegible]	[illegible]	[illegible]	[illegible]	[illegible]	[illegible]	[illegible]	[illegible]	[illegible]	[illegible]	[illegible]	[illegible]	[illegible]	[illegible]	[illegible]	[illegible]	[illegible]	[illegible]
28	[illegible]	5 1	[illegible]	[illegible]	[illegible]	[illegible]	[illegible]	[illegible]	[illegible]	[illegible]	[illegible]	[illegible]	[illegible]	[illegible]	[illegible]	[illegible]	[illegible]	[illegible]	[illegible]	[illegible]	[illegible]
29	104½	5 1½	[illegible]	[illegible]	[illegible]	[illegible]	[illegible]	[illegible]	[illegible]	[illegible]	[illegible]	[illegible]	[illegible]	[illegible]	[illegible]	[illegible]	[illegible]	[illegible]	[illegible]	[illegible]	[illegible]

APPENDIX C (Males)—continued.

No.	Weight.	Height.	Size round head.	Round neck.	Round chest.	Round waist.	Round buttocks.	Round thigh.	Round calf.	Round ankle.	Round biceps.	Round arm.	Round fore-arm.	Round wrist.	Length of [illegible].	Length of arm and hand.	Length from shoulder to elbow.	From shoulder to wrist.	From ankle to knee.	From ankle to hip.	Length of hand.
	lbs.	ft. ins.	ins.	ins.	ins.	ins.	ins.	ins.	ins.	ins.	ins.	ins.	ins.	ins.	ins.	ins.	ins.	ins.	ins.	ins.	ins.
30	104	4 9½	[illegible]	[illegible]	[illegible]	[illegible]	[illegible]	[illegible]	[illegible]	[illegible]	[illegible]	[illegible]	[illegible]	[illegible]	17	27	12	21½	16	31½	9½
31	108	4 11½	[illegible]	[illegible]	[illegible]	[illegible]	[illegible]	[illegible]	[illegible]	[illegible]	[illegible]	[illegible]	[illegible]	[illegible]	17	26½	13½	23½	15½	30½	9¾
32	100½	5 0½	[illegible]	[illegible]	[illegible]	[illegible]	[illegible]	[illegible]	[illegible]	[illegible]	[illegible]	[illegible]	[illegible]	[illegible]	16	[illegible]	14	24	16½	31½	9½
33	104	4 11½	[illegible]	[illegible]	[illegible]	[illegible]	[illegible]	[illegible]	[illegible]	[illegible]	[illegible]	[illegible]	[illegible]	[illegible]	17½	27	12½	23½	16	30	9¾
34	94	5 0½	[illegible]	[illegible]	[illegible]	[illegible]	[illegible]	[illegible]	[illegible]	[illegible]	[illegible]	[illegible]	[illegible]	[illegible]	16½	27	14	23	15½	30½	9¾
35	89	4 10½	[illegible]	[illegible]	[illegible]	[illegible]	[illegible]	[illegible]	[illegible]	[illegible]	[illegible]	[illegible]	[illegible]	[illegible]	17	26	12½	21½	16	32	9
36	not weighed.	5 1	[illegible]	[illegible]	[illegible]	[illegible]	[illegible]	[illegible]	[illegible]	[illegible]	[illegible]	[illegible]	[illegible]	[illegible]	18	28	14	24½	17½	30	10
37	97	4 10	[illegible]	[illegible]	[illegible]	[illegible]	[illegible]	[illegible]	[illegible]	[illegible]	[illegible]	[illegible]	[illegible]	[illegible]	19½	28½	13	22	17	31½	[illegible]
38	88	4 10	[illegible]	[illegible]	[illegible]	[illegible]	[illegible]	[illegible]	[illegible]	[illegible]	[illegible]	[illegible]	[illegible]	[illegible]	16½	28	13	[illegible]	16	32	[illegible]
39	not weighed.	5 [illegible]	[illegible]	[illegible]	[illegible]	[illegible]	[illegible]	[illegible]	[illegible]	[illegible]	[illegible]	[illegible]	[illegible]	[illegible]	18	28	12	21	15½	30	[illegible]
40	[illegible]	4 9½	[illegible]	[illegible]	[illegible]	[illegible]	[illegible]	[illegible]	[illegible]	[illegible]	[illegible]	[illegible]	[illegible]	[illegible]	16½	29½	12	[illegible]	15½	31	[illegible]
41	[illegible]	5 1½	[illegible]	[illegible]	[illegible]	[illegible]	[illegible]	[illegible]	[illegible]	[illegible]	[illegible]	[illegible]	[illegible]	[illegible]	18	[illegible]	13	[illegible]	16½	32	[illegible]
42	88	4 9½	[illegible]	[illegible]	[illegible]	[illegible]	[illegible]	[illegible]	[illegible]	[illegible]	[illegible]	[illegible]	[illegible]	[illegible]	16½	28½	12½	23	16	31	[illegible]
43	89	4 9	[illegible]	[illegible]	[illegible]	[illegible]	[illegible]	[illegible]	[illegible]	[illegible]	[illegible]	[illegible]	[illegible]	[illegible]	20½	28	12½	[illegible]	15	30½	[illegible]
44	88	4 9	[illegible]	[illegible]	[illegible]	[illegible]	[illegible]	[illegible]	[illegible]	[illegible]	[illegible]	[illegible]	[illegible]	[illegible]	18	27½	13	22	16	31½	[illegible]
45	not weighed.	4 9	[illegible]	[illegible]	[illegible]	[illegible]	[illegible]	[illegible]	[illegible]	[illegible]	[illegible]	[illegible]	[illegible]	[illegible]	16½	28	13	22½	16	31½	[illegible]
46	not weighed.	4 10½	[illegible]	[illegible]	[illegible]	[illegible]	[illegible]	[illegible]	[illegible]	[illegible]	[illegible]	[illegible]	[illegible]	[illegible]	17	27½	12½	22	16	31½	[illegible]
47	not weighed.	4 9	[illegible]	[illegible]	[illegible]	[illegible]	[illegible]	[illegible]	[illegible]	[illegible]	[illegible]	[illegible]	[illegible]	[illegible]	17	[illegible]	13	21	15	29	[illegible]
48	not weighed.	4 7½	[illegible]	[illegible]	[illegible]	[illegible]	[illegible]	[illegible]	[illegible]	[illegible]	[illegible]	[illegible]	[illegible]	[illegible]	17	[illegible]	12	21½	16	30½	[illegible]

APPENDIX C (Females).

No.	Weight.	Height.	Size round head.	Round neck.	Round chest.	Round waist.	Round buttocks.	Round thigh.	Round calf.	Round ankle.	Round biceps.	Round arm.	Round fore-arm.	Round wrist.	Length of spine.	Length of arm and hand.	From shoulder to elbow.	From shoulder to wrist.	From ankle to knee.	From ankle to hip.	Length of foot.
	lbs.	ft. ins.	ins.	ins.	ins.	ins.	ins.	ins.	ins.	ins.	ins.	ins.	ins.	ins.	ins.	ins.	ins.	ins.	ins.	ins.	ins.
1	84	4 7½	19	10	[illegible]	[illegible]	34	[illegible]	[illegible]	[illegible]	[illegible]	[illegible]	[illegible]	[illegible]	16	[illegible]	11	20	15	[illegible]	[illegible]
2	[illegible]	4 8	[illegible]	[illegible]	[illegible]	[illegible]	[illegible]	[illegible]	[illegible]	[illegible]	[illegible]	[illegible]	[illegible]	[illegible]	[illegible]	[illegible]	11½	[illegible]	15	[illegible]	[illegible]
3	[illegible]	4 9	[illegible]	[illegible]	[illegible]	[illegible]	[illegible]	[illegible]	[illegible]	[illegible]	[illegible]	[illegible]	[illegible]	[illegible]	[illegible]	[illegible]	11	[illegible]	15	[illegible]	[illegible]
4	87	4 6	[illegible]	[illegible]	[illegible]	[illegible]	[illegible]	17	[illegible]	[illegible]	[illegible]	[illegible]	[illegible]	[illegible]	[illegible]	[illegible]	11	[illegible]	[illegible]	[illegible]	[illegible]
5	[illegible]	4 10½	[illegible]	11	[illegible]	[illegible]	[illegible]	[illegible]	[illegible]	[illegible]	[illegible]	[illegible]	[illegible]	[illegible]	[illegible]	[illegible]	11	[illegible]	[illegible]	[illegible]	[illegible]
6	[illegible]	4 [illegible]	[illegible]	[illegible]	[illegible]	[illegible]	[illegible]	[illegible]	[illegible]	[illegible]	[illegible]	[illegible]	[illegible]	[illegible]	17	[illegible]	12	[illegible]	[illegible]	[illegible]	[illegible]
7	[illegible]	4 [illegible]	[illegible]	[illegible]	[illegible]	[illegible]	[illegible]	19	[illegible]	[illegible]	[illegible]	[illegible]	[illegible]	[illegible]	[illegible]	[illegible]	12	[illegible]	14	[illegible]	[illegible]
8	[illegible]	4 7	20	[illegible]	[illegible]	[illegible]	[illegible]	[illegible]	[illegible]	[illegible]	[illegible]	[illegible]	[illegible]	[illegible]	[illegible]	[illegible]	11½	[illegible]	14	[illegible]	[illegible]
9	[illegible]	4 [illegible]	19	11	[illegible]	[illegible]	[illegible]	[illegible]	[illegible]	[illegible]	[illegible]	[illegible]	[illegible]	[illegible]	[illegible]	[illegible]	12	[illegible]	14½	[illegible]	[illegible]
10	[illegible]	4 [illegible]	[illegible]	[illegible]	[illegible]	[illegible]	[illegible]	[illegible]	[illegible]	[illegible]	10	[illegible]	[illegible]	[illegible]	[illegible]	[illegible]	12	[illegible]	[illegible]	[illegible]	[illegible]
11	[illegible]	4 [illegible]	[illegible]	[illegible]	[illegible]	[illegible]	[illegible]	[illegible]	[illegible]	[illegible]	[illegible]	[illegible]	[illegible]	[illegible]	[illegible]	[illegible]	12	[illegible]	15	[illegible]	[illegible]
12	[illegible]	4 [illegible]	[illegible]	[illegible]	[illegible]	[illegible]	[illegible]	[illegible]	[illegible]	[illegible]	[illegible]	[illegible]	[illegible]	[illegible]	[illegible]	[illegible]	12	[illegible]	16	[illegible]	[illegible]
13	[illegible]	4 [illegible]	[illegible]	[illegible]	[illegible]	[illegible]	[illegible]	[illegible]	[illegible]	[illegible]	[illegible]	[illegible]	[illegible]	[illegible]	[illegible]	[illegible]	12	[illegible]	16½	[illegible]	[illegible]
14	117½	4 [illegible]	[illegible]	[illegible]	[illegible]	Pregnant.	[illegible]	[illegible]	[illegible]	[illegible]	[illegible]	[illegible]	[illegible]	[illegible]	[illegible]	[illegible]	11	[illegible]	14	[illegible]	[illegible]
15	104	4 10	[illegible]	[illegible]	[illegible]	[illegible]	[illegible]	[illegible]	[illegible]	[illegible]	[illegible]	[illegible]	[illegible]	[illegible]	[illegible]	[illegible]	11	[illegible]	[illegible]	[illegible]	[illegible]
16	[illegible]	4 10	[illegible]	[illegible]	[illegible]	[illegible]	[illegible]	[illegible]	[illegible]	[illegible]	[illegible]	[illegible]	[illegible]	[illegible]	[illegible]	[illegible]	[illegible]	[illegible]	14	[illegible]	[illegible]
17	87	4 7½	[illegible]	10	[illegible]	[illegible]	[illegible]	[illegible]	[illegible]	[illegible]	[illegible]	[illegible]	[illegible]	[illegible]	[illegible]	[illegible]	[illegible]	[illegible]	14	[illegible]	[illegible]
18	[illegible]	4 8	[illegible]	[illegible]	[illegible]	[illegible]	[illegible]	[illegible]	[illegible]	[illegible]	[illegible]	[illegible]	[illegible]	[illegible]	[illegible]	[illegible]	[illegible]	[illegible]	15	[illegible]	[illegible]
19	[illegible]	4 [illegible]	[illegible]	11	[illegible]	[illegible]	[illegible]	[illegible]	[illegible]	[illegible]	[illegible]	[illegible]	[illegible]	[illegible]	14	[illegible]	[illegible]	[illegible]	[illegible]	[illegible]	[illegible]
20	[illegible]	4 [illegible]	[illegible]	[illegible]	[illegible]	[illegible]	[illegible]	[illegible]	[illegible]	[illegible]	[illegible]	[illegible]	[illegible]	[illegible]	14	[illegible]	[illegible]	[illegible]	[illegible]	[illegible]	[illegible]
21	[illegible]	4 [illegible]	[illegible]	[illegible]	[illegible]	[illegible]	[illegible]	[illegible]	[illegible]	[illegible]	[illegible]	[illegible]	[illegible]	[illegible]	[illegible]	[illegible]	[illegible]	[illegible]	[illegible]	[illegible]	[illegible]
22	[illegible]	4 [illegible]	19	[illegible]	[illegible]	27	[illegible]	[illegible]	[illegible]	[illegible]	11	[illegible]	[illegible]	[illegible]	[illegible]	[illegible]	[illegible]	[illegible]	[illegible]	[illegible]	[illegible]
23	[illegible]	4 [illegible]	[illegible]	10	[illegible]	[illegible]	[illegible]	[illegible]	[illegible]	[illegible]	[illegible]	[illegible]	[illegible]	[illegible]	[illegible]	[illegible]	12	[illegible]	[illegible]	[illegible]	[illegible]
24	[illegible]	4 [illegible]	[illegible]	[illegible]	[illegible]	[illegible]	38	[illegible]	[illegible]	[illegible]	[illegible]	[illegible]	[illegible]	[illegible]	[illegible]	[illegible]	[illegible]	[illegible]	[illegible]	[illegible]	[illegible]
25	omitted.	4 [illegible]	[illegible]	[illegible]	[illegible]	[illegible]	[illegible]	[illegible]	[illegible]	[illegible]	[illegible]	[illegible]	[illegible]	[illegible]	[illegible]	[illegible]	[illegible]	[illegible]	[illegible]	[illegible]	[illegible]
26	omitted.	4 [illegible]	[illegible]	[illegible]	[illegible]	[illegible]	[illegible]	[illegible]	[illegible]	[illegible]	[illegible]	[illegible]	[illegible]	[illegible]	[illegible]	[illegible]	[illegible]	[illegible]	[illegible]	[illegible]	[illegible]
27	[illegible]	4 [illegible]	[illegible]	[illegible]	[illegible]	[illegible]	[illegible]	[illegible]	[illegible]	[illegible]	[illegible]	[illegible]	[illegible]	[illegible]	[illegible]	[illegible]	12	21	[illegible]	31	[illegible]
28	100½	4 10	[illegible]	[illegible]	31	[illegible]	34	[illegible]	[illegible]	[illegible]	[illegible]	[illegible]	[illegible]	[illegible]	[illegible]	[illegible]	12	[illegible]	[illegible]	[illegible]	[illegible]
29	omitted.	4 [illegible]	[illegible]	[illegible]	[illegible]	[illegible]	[illegible]	22	11	7	[illegible]	10	[illegible]	[illegible]	[illegible]	[illegible]	[illegible]	[illegible]	16	[illegible]	[illegible]
30	[illegible]	4 [illegible]	[illegible]	[illegible]	[illegible]	[illegible]	[illegible]	[illegible]	[illegible]	7	[illegible]	[illegible]	[illegible]	[illegible]	[illegible]	[illegible]	11	[illegible]	14	[illegible]	[illegible]
31	[illegible]	4 [illegible]	[illegible]	[illegible]	[illegible]	[illegible]	[illegible]	[illegible]	[illegible]	[illegible]	9	[illegible]	[illegible]	[illegible]	15	[illegible]	[illegible]	21	16	[illegible]	[illegible]
32	[illegible]	4 [illegible]	[illegible]	[illegible]	[illegible]	27	33	[illegible]	12	[illegible]	[illegible]	[illegible]	[illegible]	[illegible]	[illegible]	27	12	21	[illegible]	[illegible]	[illegible]
33	[illegible]	4 [illegible]	20	11	[illegible]	[illegible]	[illegible]	19	[illegible]	[illegible]	10	[illegible]	[illegible]	[illegible]	15	[illegible]	[illegible]	22	[illegible]	[illegible]	[illegible]
34	[illegible]	4 [illegible]	[illegible]	11	[illegible]	23	36	[illegible]	[illegible]	[illegible]	[illegible]	10	[illegible]	[illegible]	17	[illegible]	12	21	16	30	[illegible]

Appendix C (Females)—*continued.*

No.	Weight.	Height.	Size round head.	Round neck.	Round chest.	Round waist.	Round buttocks.	Round thigh.	Round calf.	Round ankle.	Round biceps.	Round arm.	Round fore-arm.	Round wrist.	Length of spine.	Length of arm and hand.	From shoulder to elbow.	From shoulder to wrist.	From ankle to knee.	From ankle to hip.	Length of foot.
	lbs.	ft. ins.	ins.	ins.	ins.	ins.	ins.	ins.	ins.	ins.	ins.	ins.	ins.	ins.	ins.	ins.	ins.	ins.	ins.	ins.	ins.
35	102	4 9½	20½	11½	29	27	30½	21	13	8	8½	9½	8½	5½	18	27½	13	22	17	34	8
36	omitted.	4 8½	21	10½	28½	29	35½	20½	12½	7½	9½	8½	8½	5½	18	26½	12	21	15	30½	8½
37	110	4 8½	20	11	29	28½	34	19½	11½	7½	10	9½	8½	5	18	26	10½	18	15	30	8
38	102	4 7	20½	11½	30	22	33½	16	12½	7	9	9	8½	5½	14	26	12	21	16	31	8
39	100	4 11½	19½	11	28	27½	33	19½	13	7½	9	9	8½	5½	19½	27½	12	21½	16½	32	8½
40	121	4 8½	19½	11½	33½	26½	35	26	12½	7½	12½	12½	10	5½	19½	26½	11½	20½	14½	29	8
41	120	4 7	20½	11½	30	25	30½	23½	13½	8½	12½	11	10½	5½	18	26	12	21	14	31	8½

Captain H. F. Taylor, late 13th Regiment, M.N.I., kindly afforded me much assistance in the preparation of these Tables.

APPENDIX D.

THE remarks contained in the following extract, from a paper by Mr. J. E. Calder,[1] on the extinct race of Tasmanian savages, have been found so applicable to the Andamanese that they are quoted at some length as affording interest in comparative ethnology :—

"Reasoning from such facts as that they went perfectly naked, were unacquainted with the simplest arts, were even ignorant of any method of procuring fire, and erroneously thought to have no idea of a Supreme Being or future condition, they were almost held to be the link that connected man with the brutes of the field and forest.

"The aboriginal's wants were indeed so few, and the country in which it had pleased the Almighty to place him supplied them all in such lavish abundance, that he was not called on for the exercise of much skill or labour in satisfying his requirements. He had no inducement to work, and (like all others who are so situated) he did not very greatly exert himself. Necessity, said to be the mother of invention, was known to him only in a limited degree, and his ingenuity was seldom brought into exercise. His faculties were dormant from the mere bounty of Providence. The game of the country and its vegetable productions would have amply supported a native population ten or a dozen times larger than it ever was. Of fruits there are, indeed, none worthy of the name; but in the vast forests of the country are to be found very many vegetables which, though disregarded by Europeans, were relished by the savage. . . . . Hence his fire, however he first obtained it, like that of Vesta, was never suffered to die out. . . . . The women appeared to great disadvantage by their fashion of shaving the head quite closely, which in their wild state was done with flints and shells, and afterwards with glass when they could get it. . . . . The shoulders and breasts were marked by lines of short raised scars, caused by cutting through the skin. . . . . The huts were the frailest and most temporary structures conceivable. They were often meant only

[1] Journ. Anthrop. Inst., iii, Feb., 1874.

for a night, and perhaps were only occupied for a week. . . . . They were great flesh-eaters but not cannibals, and never were, and some of them being incautiously asked if they ever indulged in this practice, expressed great horror at it. They never named the dead and certainly never ate them. . . . . Their condition in a land of plenty rendered an acquaintance with arts of any kind nearly unnecessary. . . . . The minds of the aborigines are beginning to expand. They have more enlarged views of their present situation, and are grateful for the favors conferred on them. They are volatile in their spirits, and are extremely facetious and perfectly under command. . . . . The natives are perfectly docile, and the greatest tranquillity exists among them."

It appears, also, that the Tasmanians, like the Andamanese, were in the habit of applying a composition of red ochre and grease to their persons, that it was the duty of the women to obtain shell-fish, that they were remarkable for their "violent dances accompanied by vociferous singing," and that "their chief amusement was hunting."

APPENDIX E.

LIST OF ANDAMANESE WORDS USED AS ORDINALS.

	Of two.	Of three.	Of four.	Of five.	Of six.	Of any greater number than six.	Remarks.
1st (of two or more, as in a row)	ō·tolō·(da)[1] ...	ō·tolō·(da) ...	ō·tolō·(da) ...	ō·tolō·(da) ...	ō·tolō·(da) ...	ō·tolō·(da)	[1] When reference is made to animate objects ārlōgu·- is often used.
2nd "	tārō·lo(da)[4] ...	ad·pu-chāli(da)[3]	ārō·lo(da)[2] ...	ārō·lo(da) ...	ārō·lo(da) ...	ārō·lo(da)	[2] Also used to denote "the next."
3rd "	...	tārō·lo(da) ...	ad·pu-chāli(da)	ad·pu-chāli(da)	ad·pu-chāli(da) }	ō·tarō·lo-ā·lepun(da) or ō·tegō·lo-āā·bapun(da)	[3] Lit., between, or in the middle.
4th "	...	...	tārō·lo(da) ...	ad·pu-chāli-tārō·lo(da) }	ō·tar·r(da) }		[4] Lit., the last.
5th "	...	...	...	tārō·lo(da) ...	ō·tar·r tarō·lo (da) }		
6th "	...	...	...	...	tārō·lo(da) }		
Last but one	...	...	...	...	...	ō·tar·r-tarō·lo (da)	
Last	...	...	...	...	...	tārō·lo(da)	

Speaking of a row or line of animate or inanimate objects:—

The first, ō·[illegible]-
" second, id·[illegible]·lo-
" next, [illegible]-
" middle one, ad·pu-chāl-
" last one, ō·[illegible]·paringo-

APPENDIX F.

SPECIMEN OF THE SOUTH ANDAMAN LANGUAGE

1. *wai dōl ōko-jū'wai ē'remtā'ga. dī'a ā'r lōt tīng*
indeed I (name of tribe) jungle-dweller. my village of name
ōtō'lo-bō'cho. jū'ru tek elarpā'lada. mī'da ē'lawdi'ngaya bēd tek toigō'ra
(name of village). sea from far. If daybreak at home from coast
len nāū'nga bē'dig tā'rik dī'la len ke'galke. mēd-ārdū'ru ō'gar jī'baba
to walking by perhaps evening in reach-will. we all moons several
ē'kan ā'r len pōl'ike āgā tārū'lolen jeg l'edā're āryō'to bī'a
own villages in live-do then afterwards dance for sake of countmen of
pai'chalen yān'gake. ō'na ā'cha nai'kan jeg'i'kke ārlalen iyal- l'edā're
midst-in go-do. when this like dance-go-do always barter for
min tō'yuke kīchī'kan reg-dam'a, ēdā'te reg-kō'ub, ēdā'te
things take-do namely pork (lit., pig-flesh), also pig's fat paint, also
rā'ta, ēdā'te yāb, ēdā'te chā'panga, ēdā'te kūd,
wooden-pointed arrows, also baskets, also reticules, also hand-nets for fishing,
ēdā'te rāb, ēdā'te tā'la-og, ēdā'te bō'ing, ēdā'te pār'epa,
also necklaces of fine net-work, also white-clay, also bones, also sleeping-mats,
ēdā'te kā'pa-jā'tnga, dōrā'h.
also leaf-screens, etcetera.

2. *mēda kē'galnga bē'dig līmanak ō'tolā' ōt'mōl-tō'yuke ōl-bē'dig*
we arriving on according-to-custom first sing-do and
kō'ke tārū'lolen ārdū'ru min iyal'ke, āgā mēd-ikpō'r
dance-do afterwards all things barter-do, then we two (*i.e.*, some of us)
dā'nga len ighā'dignga l'edā're āryō'to bī'a pai'chalen
spearing to seeing for countmen of (*i.e.*, with) possession
ē'dam len ā'kangal'ke. maraī-dī'a
bottom (of boat) in go in boat-do our rest (*i.e.*, the rest of us)
āryō'to-aplyi mī'ikanga ē'rem-dal'eke.
countmen-friends accompanying in jungle-hunt-pigs-do.

3. *ārla ikpō'r tārū'lolen mēd'a min ārdū'ru, kīchī'kan ā'la,*
days two (a few) afterwards we things all, such as pig-arrows,
ē'lata, chō, wō'lo, bī'jma, gā'dā-kō'reb,
iron, knives, adzes, bottles, turtle-unguent (red paint made with turtle-fat),
gā'dā-dam'a, ō'do, chī'di, gar'en, ēr'kata-ta,
turtle-flesh, nautilus-shells, *Pinna* shells, *Dentalium octogonum*, *Hemicardium unedo*
dōrā'h, iyal'nga len ē'rok yā'te eninga-bē'dig dā'leyā'ke āgā
etcetera, bartering in received which having-taken take-leave-do then
mō'yke.
return-home-do.

4. *igwā'ram āryō'to len (ā'rlaya) ōko-dal'nga tek, ōl-bē'dig lō'binga tek,*
Just as countmen to (always) hunting by, and poling by
ōl-bē'dig gā'i-dū'a tek ek'a-kā'chya ākā-wī'lab yā'bada, chā
and means-rest (*i.e.*, other means) by ever food-difficulty not so
mā ē'rem-tā'ga len bē'dig wāb dī'a-ē'rtak yāt ārdū'ruda.
we jungle-dwellers to also season every food all (sorts).

5. *mēd-ē'rem-tā'ga ārdū'ru gū'mul ga ē'kan bād len ā-ētiteg'ikeō'gun*
We-jungle-men all rainy season during own homes in remain-do only

rdp-wāb len yūm pi·tringa l'edā·re ēr-tāl·ke, mat ngi·ji ārdū·ru
fruit-season in rain absence because-of pay-visits-do our friends all
igbā·dīgnga l'edā·re. ō·gar ū·batā·l an ikpō·r len met·a wō·jke ēlpāg·i
seeing because-of moon one or two in we return-home-do again
bai·la[1]-wāb len kai·ta-ban[2] jū·ronga lek būd tek
(name of tree)-season in jack-fruit-seed burying for homes from
mat-tā jī·rike. ō·gar ū·batā·l len ē·kan ēr lat wō·jke.
we shift-our-quarters-do. moon one in own villages to return-home-do.

6. *mit·ig-bū·dwa len āryō·to tek ē·rem-tā·ga at-ū·baba*
Our-tribesmen among coastmen from (than) jungle-men numerous
.bā·rāi·kābit tek .tō·lo-bōi·cho bū·dinda dū·na ē·rem kaktā·r len
(name of village) than (name of village) large but jungle interior in
.tō·lo-bōi·cho tek ēr dō·ga bū·dinda mē·tat būd āryō·to lēa būd tek
(name of village) than villages many large our huts coastmen of huts than
chā·nagda tā lāb jī·baba met·a pū·i tō·pike yā·ba.
large years many we fresh thatch-do not.

7. *tā·lāb ū·ma len mat-ārdū·ru ē·kan ū·kan ēr lagū·ba yāt dū·gaga ārobe.*
Year whole in we all own own villages some food plenty find-do.
ingā·tabingā·tāk yāt tō·paga bē·dig chā·pān ārtamnalāng, mat·a āba-jā·ranga
now-and-then food getting for [illegible] children we constantly
kō·ike .ōt-bē·dig rā·mid-tō·pake.
dance-do and sing-do.

8. *ō·na mē·tat barai·j a ū·chin ōkolī·ke ūgā mat-ārdū·ru [illegible]*
When our village in any one die-does then we-all [illegible]
l'ārtū·a len jā·lake. kā·to chāng-tō·rnga[3] an dar·nga[3] len chā·ra nai·kan [illegible]
vacant to migrate-do. there but or in custom like [illegible]
ikpō·r pō·ike, thrū·laka tā ā·rakngu bē·dig ā·l-tō·latnga[4] len
few (lit., two) live-do, afterwards bones obtaining on tears-shedding (dance) for
.tō·lo-bō·cha lat wō·jke.
(name of village) to return-home-do.

9. *mō·da ūkolī·nga yā·baba mat-ē·rem-tā·ga lī·a barai·j len at-jang·gi*
If dead without we jungle-dwellers of villages in old persons
līg·ala bē·dig ā·rlalen pō·ike. ū·gun rāp-wāb len mē·tat pai·chalen aīpail
children also always live-do. only fruit-season in us with women
ī-yā·taga-bē·dig bar·mike kō·nig ā·llārdū·ru at-jang·gi
paying visits-for pass-night-away-from-home-do otherwise they-all old people
līg·ala nai·kan ē·kan barai·j len bū·duka.
children like own villages in live-do.

10. *gū·mul len reg-dal·enga l'edā·re mat kā·lo ij·i-lō·tnga ā·rla ikpō·r*
Rainy-season in pig-hunting because of we men often days few
bar·mike.
pass-night-away-from-home-do.

11. *mad-ē·rem-tā·ga āryō·to nai·kan ā·rla-rī·alok jā·langa lī·a kianwai*
We-jungle-people coastmen like constantly migrating of custom
yā·ba l'edā·re mō·hichik ā·rlalen mē·tat bē·ra ōt-bē·dig ā·kā-kī·chalng·ten
not because of we always our rubbish and food-refuse near
kā·rār yā·ba, kianchā mē·tat barai·j len ōt-da jā·bag yā·bada.
scatter-do not therefore our villages in small bad not.

[1] *Terminalia procera*, which flowers about the middle of May.
[2] *Artocarpus chaplasha.*
[3] *Vide* Part I, "Habitations," paragraphs 3 and 4, for description of these varieties of huts.
[4] *Vide* Part II, "Death and Burial," paragraph 7.

12. *mè·tat àryó·to len bè·dig barao·j l'ŭpd·r kà·to òt'òrobak iji-kì·ringa*
Our coast people among even villages few there they often
è·gar l'ŭpd·r pū·ike, ar-ot-dikra ō·ko-jòr·anga yo·lake.
means few dwell-do, their rest (*i.e.*, the rest of them) constantly migrate-do.

13. *mad-ē·rem-tā·ga ūl-bè·dig àryó·to lì·a ar lag·iba*
Us jungle dwellers and coast-dwellers of villages near
bàd-l'ā·rtdm dò·yada. jā·ru l'igrò·klik len ā·rlaya ē·rem tā·boda dò·na ē·rem
kitchen-middens many are vicinity in always jungle dense, but jungle
bakta·r len tā·bo yā ba.
middle in dense not.

14. *A·kà-.kedè lì·a ē·rem bakta·r len lì·raga-bè·dig wai dōl*
(name of tribe) of jungle middle in going-on indeed I
ē·rem-tā·ga at-ā·baba igbā·digre. med·a lū·ake ak·a kà·to mardā·ru tek
jungle-dwellers numerous see-did. we consider that there us-all than
at-ā·baba. ē·rem len dōl·u-rē·atek chā·ga-tā·banga l'idal· tek
numerous. jungle in everywhere ancestors (this side of the Deluge) time since
tinga-bā bè·ringa. wai dōl d'ichitik .bū·jig-ngi·ji ardā·ru
paths (lit., roads small) good. indeed I now (name of tribe) all
igbā·digre, ū·ig bè·dwa di·rap-tek gaba·da.
seen have, their tribesmen now-a-days few.

15. *med-ardā·ru .ā·kà.bū·jig-yū·b ōl-bè·dig .ā·kà-.bèl l'a kianna·i idai·ke;*
We all (name of tribe) and (name of tribe) of customs know-do
ka·t ak·à·ra wala·at pē·ra, at bè·dig .mò·ko-jū·wai nai·ban
their customs were similar, among-them also we (name of tribe) like
àryó·to ōl-bè·dig ē·rem-tā·ga. kà·to bè·dig ē·rem-tā·ga è·gar jī·baba
coast-people and jungle people. there also jungle-dwellers means several
dim len ō·ko-jòr·anga bè·daba l'ī·ba l'ban bād len bè·dig
heart-of-jungle in habitually dwell-do own own encampment in also
ā·riliga·ke. .ā·kà-.bū·jig-yū·b lì·a dim bè·ka l'akā·ru ka·to
remain-do. (name of tribe) of heart-of-jungle small because of there
ē·rem-tā·ga gaba·da.
jungle-dwellers few.

[A free translation of this Appendix will be found in the Journal of the Anthropological Institute, vol. xi, pp. 280–82.]

APPENDIX F(a).

PHILOLOGICAL HARP.[1]

	Denoting	Near.	Remote.	Interrogative.	Relative.	Correlative.
		This, *é'cha-*	That, *é'lla-*	Who { *mi'ja-* / *mij'ola* }; Which, *tenchá'-*	Who / Which } *á'te-* (in construction *pá'te-*)	That same, *ál-la'dig*
1	Time	Now, *á'chitik*	Then, *deki'baiya*[4]; Then (in rel. past), *dekia'baiya*	When, *tain-*	When, *á'ua-*; As much time as, *ikan-[illegible]-bakik*	Then, *ligi*; At the same time, *[illegible]-ilem*
2	Place	Here { *ká'ra-* / *ká'rin-* / *ká'min-* / *bom-* / *ká-* }	There { *ká'ta-, i'tan-* / *é'chamen-*[6] / *é'cham*[6] }	Where, *ika-*	Wherever, *ui'n-ya*	There, *ál-la'dig-ya*
3		Hither, *ineh-*	Thither, *ká'tik-*	Whither, *ichorichá-*	Whither, *ain ien*	Thither, *ig*
4		Hence { *é'chik-*[2] / *ká'rin-tek* / *ká'rik-*[3] }	Thence { *ká'ta-tek* / *é'chamek* }	Whence { *[illegible]* / *[illegible]* }	Whence, *ain tek*	Thence *ál-la'dig tek*
5	Manner	Thus, *ikan-d'ya-*	In that way, *ekd'ra-*	How, *[illegible]*	As, *[illegible]*	So, *ekd-*
6	Likeness	Like this, *é'cha-nai'-ben*	Like that { *él-nai'-ben* / *ká'ta-nai'-ben* }	Like what, *[illegible]*	Like which { *ká'a-ba-* / *kich-[illegible]* }	Like the same { *é'chuba-* / *kich-[illegible]-* / *kich-[illegible]-* / *nai'-ben* }
7	Quantity	This much or so much { *ikan-wai'-* / *it'ua-* / *bai'-* }	That much, *é'chatit'n-*	How much, *[illegible]*	As much[5]	So much[5]
8	Number	This many, *ikanchat'n-*	That many, *é'chichatil'n-*	How many { *[illegible]* / *[illegible]* }	As many[6]	So many[6]

[1] This scheme is taken from Forbes's well-known Hindustani Grammar (p. 68).
[2] Probably abbreviated from *é'cha tek* (lit., this from).
[3] Probably abbreviated from *ká'ra tek* (lit., here from).
[4] In reference to a past period.
[5] Generally used in an indefinite sense, signifying "thereabouts"; also when pointing towards an object partly hidden and not easily discernible.
[6] Hitherto unascertainable.

APPENDIX G.

THE SEVEN FORMS OF THE POSSESSIVE PRONOUNS IN RELATION TO PARTS OF THE BODY (HUMAN AND ANIMAL).

I.

dūt .. *my* ..
ngūt .. *thy* ..
ōt .. .. *his* ..
l'ōt.. .. *—'s* ..
mū·tot .. *our* ..
ngū·tot .. *your* ..
ō·tot .. *their*
l'ō·tot .. *—s'* ..

chē·ta-, *head*; mūn-, *brain*; yā-, *occiput*; kā·kà-, *scalp*; lō·ngota-, *neck*; lā·pta-, *nape*; chāl·ma-, *chest*; ā·wa-, *lung*; tū-, *prostate gland*; tū·lōpo-, *phlegm*; kūg-, *heart* (*the seat of the affections and passions*), *the bosom*; kū·ktā-ban·a-, *heart* (*the organ*).

Ex.—ōt chē·ta bō·dia-. *His head is large.*
His head large.

II.

dōng .. *my* ..
ngōng .. *thy* ..
ōng.. .. *his* ..
l'ōng .. *—'s* ..
mōi·ot .. *our* ..
ngōi·ot .. *your*
ōi·ot- .. *their*
l'ōi·ot .. *—s'* ..

kō·ro-, *hand, or finger*; kō·ro-mū·gu-chāl-, *large* (*lit., middle*) *finger*; ī·tī-pī·l-, *little finger*; kō·ro-dō·ga-, *thumb*; el·ma-, *palm of hand, also sole of foot*; tī·go-, *wrist*; kō·tur-, *knuckle*; bō·do-, *nail of finger, or toe*; pāg-, *foot*; rō·koma-, *toe*; tō·chab-, *large toe*; ī·lam-, *small toe*; gō·nlul-, *heel*; tār-, *ankle*; chāg-, *kidney*; tā·banga-, *small intestine*; tā·ga-, *peritoneum*.

Ex.—dōng kō·ro ngōng tek kī·tia-. *My hand is smaller than thine.*
my hand thy from (than) small.

III.

dā·kā .. *my* ..
ngā·kā .. *thy* ..
ā·kā .. *his* ..
l'ā·kā .. *—'s* ..
mak·at .. *our* ..
ngak·at .. *your*
ak·at .. *their*
l'ak·at .. *—s'* ..

bang-, *mouth*; dā·liya-, *palate* (*of mouth*); ā·dal-, *chin*; pai-, *lip*; pai·le-pīd-, *moustache*; ō·rma-, *throat*; ē·tal-, *tongue*; dyī·la-, *gullet*; ō·rma-bā-, *windpipe*; ē·kib-, *jawbone*; ē·kib-pīd-, *beard*; ted·imo-, *vomit*; gō·dla-, *collar-bone*; chā·ga-, *side*; tā·bal-, *saliva*; chai·ad-, *breath*.

Ex.—kā·to .bōi·goli l'ārdū·ru l'ak·at ē·kib-pīd lā·panga-.
There European all their beard long.
All those Europeans have long beards.

IV.

dab .. .. *my* ..
ngab .. .. *thy* ..
ab .. .. *his* ..
l'ab .. .. *—'s* ..
mat .. .. *our* ..
ngat .. .. *your*
at .. .. *their*..
l'at .. .. *—s'* ..

chāu-, *body*; gū·dur- *and* lān-, *back*; gō·rob-, *spine*; pō·dikma-, *shoulder-blade*; pai·cha-, *thigh* (*also lap*); gū·ke-, *groin*; chā·lta-, *shin*; chā·lta-dam·a-, *calf of leg*; kō·pa-, *elbow*; kō·pa-dam·a-, *fleshy part of fore-arm*; kū·rupi-dam·a-, *fleshy part of upper arm*; lō-, *knee*; ā·pita-, *hough*; pā·rētā-, *rib*; ā·pa-chāu-, *belly* (*abdominal walls*); ēr-, *navel*; ū·pta-, *stomach proper*; jū·do-, *entrails, bowels*; jī·ri-,[1] *supra-renal fat and omentum*; mūg-, *liver*; pī·lma-, *spleen*; ī·jnga-, *uterus*; ā·wa-, *arm-pit*; yī·lnga-, *tendon Achilles*; nō·ma-, *gall-bladder*.

[1] For a description of the *ray-jī·ri-gū·mul-*, *vide* Part II, "Initiatory Ceremonies," paragraphs 15–17.

V.

dig (*or* di) ..	*my* ..	dal-[1] *or* dōl-[1] *eye*; dal àr pïd-,[1] *or* dōl àr pïd-,[1] *eye-lash*; dal ōt ĕd-,[1] *or* dōl ōt ĕd-,[1] *eyelid*; pû'nyur-, *eyebrow*; mū'gu-, *face* (*also fore-head*); pū'ku, *ear*; chō'ronga-, *nose*; ti'mar-, *temple*; ăb-, *cheek*; ăb-pïd-, *whiskers*; tō'go-, *shoulder*; tūg-, *tooth*; gūd-, *arm*; kū'rupi-, *upper arm*; kō'pa-, *fore-arm*; gō'ra-, *biceps*; kām-, *breast*; kām l'ōt chē'ta-, *nipple of breast*; dē'riya-, *gum*; ī'ī-, *tear*.
ngig (*or* ngi) ..	*thy* ..	
ig (*or* i) ..	*his* ..	
l'ig (*or* l'i) ..	—'*s* ..	
mit'ig (*or* mit'i)	*our* ..	
ngit'ig (*or* ngit'i)	*your*	
it'ig (*or* it'i) ..	*their*	
l'it'ig (*or* l'it'i)	—*s'* ..	

Ex.—ōl ab-gō'ra dō'gada, ig gō'ra igbà'di! *He is very strong; see his biceps!*
He strong very, his biceps see!

VI.

dar ..	.. *my* ..	chāg-, *leg*; chō'rog-, *hip*; ē'te-, *loin*; mål'wit-, *large intestine*; kōl'um-, *mesentery*; gū'dwin-, *os coccygis*; ŭ'lu-, *urine*; ū'lu l'ïa ōr-, *bladder* (ōr = *shells*); ō'ta-, *testicle*; tō-, ō'no-, *and* dam'a-, *buttocks*; mā'ga-, *rectum*; tâ'mar-, *anus*.
ngar ..	.. *thy* ..	
ar ..	.. *his* ..	
l'ar ..	.. —'*s* ..	
mar'at	.. *our* ..	
ngar'at	.. *your*	
ar'at ..	.. *their*	
l'iar'at	—*s'* ..	

Ex.—mar'at chāg-, *our legs*.

VII.

dō'to ..	.. *my* ..	kī'nab-, *waist*. This appears to be the only part of the body with which this form is used.
ngō'to ..	*thy, your*	
ō'to ..	*his, their*	
l'ō'to ..	—'*s*, —*s'* ..	
mō'to	*our* ..	

N.B.—In the case of the following words, the possessive adjective peculiar to the part referred to is taken:—pïd, *hair*; ĕd-, *skin*; tā-, *bone*; ti-, *blood*; mū'rudi-, *go*; gū'mar, *sweat*; yī'linga-, *vein, muscle*; wain'ya-, *cuticle*; mūn-, *pus*; dē'kia-, *pulse*.

Ex.—mō'tot pïd-, *the hair of our heads*;
ngak'at ĕd-, *the skin of your lips*;
dig ta-, *the bone of my arm*;
ngar ti-, *the blood of thy leg*;
&c.;

i.e., the above would be understood to represent mō'tot chē'ta pïd-; ngak'at pai ĕd-; dig gūd tā-; ngar chāg ti-.

[1] These words generally take the abbreviated form, *di*, *ngi*, &c.

APPENDIX H.

List of *Proper Names*, together with a List of the "*Flower*" *Names* borne by young women during maidenhood, and until they become mothers, and a List of the various *Seasons*.

Proper names (common to both sexes).	
.bōi'ba	.kōt'-tala
.bē'ra	.bī'ra
.bē'rabi	.lī'ya
.bī'ra	.bī'bola
.bī'ala	.mī'ba
.bī'ra	.mī'bala
.bī'ruda	.bōgō-ngoda
.bōi'-lōrola	.wā'-lī
.bē'ria	.pū'rībā
.bē'ringa	.pū'tīpa
.chā'rama	.pū'wīula
.chā'tla	.pū'ngia
.dā'ra	.rī'a
.dī'lai	.rī'ala
.ī'ra	.bī'tai
.ī'rola	.lī'ra
.jī'ra	.wā'ī
.jī'pīala	.wōi'chola
.kū'la	.wī'laga
.kū'ya	.yī'ya

"Flower" name.	Name of tree (or insect) in season.	Names of the various minor seasons.
.chī'lipa ...	lī'kara- ...	lī'kara-wōdi-[1] ...
	chī'lip- ...	chī'lip-wōdi- ...
.ē'la ...	pū- ...	pū-wōdi- ...
	jīr- ...	jīr-wōdi- ...
.ē'ra ...	ē'ra- ...	ē'ra-wōdi- ...
.jī'diga ...	jī'dig-	jī'diga-wōdi-
	lā'tib- ...	lā'tib-wōdi- ...
.pū'ra ...	pū'ra- ...	pū'ra-wōdi- ...
	bē'ja- ...	bē'ja-wōdi- ...
.pū'taba ...	pū'tab- ...	pū'tab-wōdi- ...
.bai yu ...	bai'in- ...	bai'ta-wōdi- ...
.rē'cho ...	rē'cho- ...	rē'cho-wōdi- ...
	chā'dab- ...	chā'dab-wōdi- ...
.chā'lunga ...	chā'lunga- ...	chā'lunga-wōdi- ...
.chā'rapa ...	bā'tu-[5] ...	tō'pongo-wōdi- ...
	chā'rap- ...	chā'rap-wōdi- ...
.chē'ra ...	ōi'yum-[7] ...	ōi'yum- or lō'pongo-wōdi- ...
	chē'ran- ... [8]	chē'ran-wōdi- ...
.pū'lu ...	rūo- ...	rūo-wōdi- ...
	pū'lu- ...	pū'lu-wōdi- ...

Names of the principal seasons.	Remarks.
pū'para, also pū'para-wōdi- (for lī'kara-wōdi- and chī'lip-wōdi-)	The "pū'para-" commences about the middle of November, and ends about the middle of February. It comprises the cool season. [1] "wōdi-" signifies "season."
yā're-bā'-dēa, also rēgo-wōdi-[3] (for pū-wōdi- to bai'ta-wōdi-; ē'ra-wōdi- to bai'ta-wōdi- bracketed as [4])	The "yā're-bā'-dēa-" comprises the summer and autumn of the year. Honey is abundant at the commencement of this season, during the whole course of which the principal fruit trees are in bearing. This season lasts about three months, viz., till about the middle of May. [3] Lit., season of abundance. [4] This period is called "lad-wōchāt-" (dirty body) owing to their practice of smearing their persons with the sap of a plant (jī'me-) when engaged in removing a honeycomb from a hive swarming with bees.
gū'mul- (for rē'cho-wōdi- to pū'lu-wōdi-; rē'cho-wōdi- to chā'lunga-wōdi- bracketed as [6]; tō'pongo-wōdi- to pū'lu-wōdi- bracketed as [6])	This season embraces the (a) tā'lia-ting dā'rekan-fīk (fresh foliage) or spring, and (b) gū'mul-wōdi-. The former lasts about 3½ months, viz., till about the close of August. It comprises not only the spring but the first half of the rainy season. The latter (gū'mul-wōdi-) lasts about 2½ months viz., till about the middle of November, and comprises the latter half of the rainy seasons. Among the articles of food eaten at this season are (a) the bā'tu- (a slug found in rotten logs of Gurjun wood) and (b) the ōi'yum- (larva of the Great Capricorn beetle). The tails of the former are broken off and thrown away, hence tō'pongo- (breaking off).

APPENDIX L.

LIST OF TERMS INDICATING VARIOUS DEGREES OF RELATIONSHIP.

my father (male or female speaking) ..	dab mai·ola; dab chá·bil-; dar ö·dinga-.
my step-father " " ..	dab chá·bil-.
my mother " " ..	dab chá·nola; dab ĕ·tinga-; dab wĕ·jinga-; dab wĕ·jeringa-.
my step-mother " " ..	dab chá·nola.
my son (if under 3 years of age, either parent speaking)	di·a ĕ·te-.[1]
my son (if over 3 years of age, father speaking)	dar ö·dire; dar ö·di-gá·te-.
my son (if over 3 years of age, mother speaking)	dab ĕ·tire; dab ĕ·ti-gá·te-; dab wĕ·jire; dab wĕ·ji-gá·te-; dab wĕ·jerire; dab wĕ·jeri-gá·te-.
my daughter (if under 3 years of age, either parent speaking)	di·a bá·te-.[1]
my daughter (if over 3 years of age, either parent speaking)	di·a bá-.
my daughter (if over 3 years of age, father speaking)	dar ö·dire-pail-; dar ö·di-gá·te-pail-.
my daughter (if over 3 years of age, mother speaking)	dab ĕ·tire-pail-; dab ĕ·ti-gá·te-pail-; dab wĕ·jire-pail-; dab wĕ·ji-gá·te-pail-; dab wĕ·jerire-pail-; dab wĕ·jeri-gá·te-pail-.
my grandson (either grand parent speaking) .. .. ; my brother's grandson (male or female speaking) .. .. ; my sister's grandson (male or female speaking)	di·a bá·lola.
my grand-daughter (either grand-parent speaking) .. .. ; my brother's grand-daughter (male or female speaking) .. .. .. ; my sister's grand-daughter (male or female speaking)	di·a bá·lola-pail-.
my elder brother (male or female speaking)	ad-en tö·bare; ad-en tö·banga-; ad-en tö·kare; ad-en tö·kanga-.
my elder sister (male or female speaking)	ad-en tö·bare-pail-; ad-en tö·banga-pail-; ad-en tö·kare-pail-; ad-en tö·kanga-pail-.
my younger brother (male or female speaking)	dar dö·atinga-; dö·kö kám-; dar wĕ·jinga-; dar wĕ·jeringa-.
my younger sister (male or female speaking)	dar dö·atinga-pail-; dö·kö kám-pail-; dar wĕ·jinga-pail-; dar wĕ·jeringa-pail-.
my elder brothers (male or female speaking)	am-et tö·bare; am-et tö·banga-; am-et tö·kare; am-et tö·kanga-.

[1] Vide Appendix K.

my younger brothers (male or female speaking)	*mar·at dō·atinga-; mak·at kim-; mar·at mō·jinga-; mar·at mō·jeringa-.*
my elder sisters (male or female speaking)	*am-et tō·bare-pail-; am-et tō·banga-pail-; am-et tō·bare-pail-; am-et tō·kanga-pail.*
my younger sisters (male or female speaking)	*mar·at dō·atinga-pail-; mak·at kim-pail-; mar·at mō·jinga-pail-; mar·at mō·jeringa-pail-.*
my father's brother (elder or younger) my mother's brother " " my father's sister's husband .. .. my mother's sister's husband .. .. my father's father's brother's (or sister's) son .. .. my mother's mother's brother's (or sister's) son .. .. my husband's grandfather .. .. my wife's " .. .. my wife's sister's husband (if elder) .. my husband's sister's husband (if elder)	*dī·a mai·o.*
my father's sister (elder or younger) .. my mother's sister " " .. my father's brother's wife .. .. my mother's brother's wife .. .. my grandmother, my grand-aunt .. my father's father's sister's daughter my mother's mother's sister's daughter my husband's grandmother .. .. my wife's " .. .. my husband's sister (if senior and a mother) .. .. my elder brother's wife (if a mother) ..	*dī·a chā·nola.*
my brother's son (male or female speaking) .. .. my sister's son (male or female speaking) .. .. my half-brother's (or half-sister's) son, or my first-cousin's (male or female) son (male or female speaking) ..	*dar bā-.*
my brother's son's wife (male or female speaking) .. .. my sister's son's wife (male or female speaking) .. .. my half-brother's (or half-sister's) son's wife, or my first cousin's (male or female) son's wife (male or female speaking)	*dar bā lai ik-yā·te-.*
my brother's daughter (male or female speaking) .. .. my sister's daughter (male or female speaking) .. .. my half-brother's (or half-sister's) daughter, or my first-cousin's (male or female) daughter (male or female speaking)	*dar bā-pail-.*
my brother's daughter's husband (male or female speaking) .. my sister's daughter's husband (male or female speaking)	*dar bā lā ik-yā·te-.*

my half-brother's (or half-sister's) daughter's husband, or my first-cousin's (male or female) daughter's husband (male or female speaking)	*dar bā la ik-yā·te-.*
my father's brother's son, if older (male or female speaking) .. .. my father's sister's son, if older (male or female speaking) .. .. .. my mother's brother's son, if older (male or female speaking) .. .. my mother's sister's son, if older (male or female speaking) .. .. .. my elder half-brother, whether uterine or consanguine (male or female speaking)	*dar ebē·bil entō·bare; dar ebē·bil entō·bare.*
my father's brother's son, if younger (male or female speaking) .. .. my father's sister's son, if younger (male or female speaking) .. .. my mother's brother's son, if younger (male or female speaking) .. .. my mother's sister's son, if younger (male or female speaking)	*dar dō·atinga-.*
my younger half-brother, if uterine (male or female speaking)	*dā·bā kām-.*
my younger half-brother, if consanguine (male or female speaking) ..	*dar dō·atinga-; dar mī·jinga-; dar mī·jeringa-.*
my father's brother's son's wife, if older (male or female speaking) my father's sister's son's wife, if older (male or female speaking) .. .. my mother's brother's son's wife, if older (male or female speaking) .. my mother's sister's son's wife, if older (male or female speaking) .. .. my elder half-brother's wife, whether uterine or consanguine (male or female speaking)	*dar ebē·bil entō·bare lai ik-yā·te-.*
my father's brother's son's wife, if younger (male or female speaking) .. my father's sister's son's wife, if younger (male or female speaking) .. my mother's brother's son's wife, if younger (male or female speaking) .. my mother's sister's son's wife, if younger (male or female speaking) ..	*dar dō·atinga lai ik-yā·te-.*
the wife of my uterine half-brother, if younger (male or female speaking) ..	*dā-bā kām lai ik-yā·te-.*
the wife of my consanguine half-brother, if younger (male or female speaking)	*dar dō·atinga- dar mī·jinga- or dar mī·jeringa-* } *lai ik-yā·te-.*
my father's brother's elder daughter (male or female speaking) .. .. my father's sister's elder daughter (male or female speaking) .. .. my mother's brother's elder daughter (male or female speaking) .. .. my mother's sister's elder daughter (male or female speaking)	*dī·a ebē·nol ā-entō·ba-yā·te-.*

my elder half-sister, whether uterine or consanguine (male or female speaking)	*dī·a chā·nol à-entō·ba-gū te-.*
my father's brother's younger daughter (male or female speaking) my father's sister's younger daughter (male or female speaking) my mother's brother's younger daughter (male or female speaking) my mother's sister's younger daughter (male or female speaking)	*dar dō·atinga-pail-.*
my younger half-sister, if uterine (male or female speaking)	*dā·kà bēm-pail-.*
my younger half-sister, if consanguine (male or female speaking)	*dar dō·atinga-pail- ; dar wē·jinga-pail- ; or dar wē·jeringa-pail*
my father's brother's elder daughter's husband (male or female speaking) my father's sister's elder daughter's husband (male or female speaking) my mother's brother's elder daughter's husband (male or female speaking) my mother's sister's elder daughter's husband (male or female speaking) my elder half-sister's husband, whether uterine or consanguine (male or female speaking)	*dī·a chā·nol à-entō·ba-gū·te lā ik-pō·te-.*
my father's brother's younger daughter's husband (male or female speaking) my father's sister's younger daughter's husband (male or female speaking) my mother's brother's younger daughter's husband (male or female speaking) my mother's sister's younger daughter's husband (male or female speaking)	*dar dō·atinga-pail lā ik-pō·te-.*
the husband of my uterine half-sister, if younger (male or female speaking)	*dā·kà bēm pail lā ik-pō·te-.*
the husband of my consanguine half-sister, if younger (male or female speaking)	*dar dō·atinga-pail-* *dar wē·jinga-pail-* or *dar wē·jeringa-pail-* } *lā ik-pō·te-.*
my grandfather (male or female speaking) my grandfather's brother (male or female speaking) my grandmother's brother (male or female speaking) my elder sister's husband (male or female speaking)	*dī·a mai·ola.*
my husband	*ad ik-pō te-.*
my wife	*dal ik-pō·te-.*
my husband's father my husband's mother my wife's father my wife's mother my husband's elder brother my wife's brother (if older) my husband's sister's husband (if older) my wife's sister (if older[1] and a mother)	*dī·a mai mola.*

[1] Otherwise her name would be employed.

my husband's brother's wife (if older) .. my wife's brother's wife (if older) ..	dī·a ad·mola.
my husband's brother (if of equal standing) .. .. my wife's brother (if of equal standing)	dī·a ad·ma.
my son-in-law (male or female speaking) my younger sister's husband (male or female speaking)	dī·a dā·aiya.
my daughter-in law (male or female speaking) . .. . my husband's sister, if younger (male or female speaking) .. .. .. my husband's brother's wife, if younger (male or female speaking) .. .. my wife's brother's wife, if younger (male or female speaking)	dī·a bī·n-.
my step-son (either speaking)	dab aden·ire.
my step-daughter (either speaking) ..	dab aden·ire-pail-.
my adopted son " " ..	dōl ōdi·tinga-.
my adopted daughter " " ..	dōl ōdi·tinga-pail-.
my parents " " ..	dab ant-ōl-ōdi·nol.
my foster-father " " ..	dab mai ōt-ōdi·tinga-.
my foster-mother " " ..	dab chāna ōt-ōdi·tinga-.
the relationship subsisting between a married couple's fathers-in-law .. the relationship subsisting between a married couple's mothers-in-law ..	ā·kā ya bāb-.
my husband's brother (if younger) ..	dā·kā bā-bū·la-.
my younger brother's wife	dā·kā ba-pail-.
my wife's sister's husband (if younger) my husband's sister's husband (if younger)	mar, or (if a father) mai·a.
twins (whether of the same sex or not)	ōdi·dinga-.
widow	chāna urī·ba-.
widower	mai urī·ba-.

APPENDIX K.

List of Terms applied to Males and Females from Birth to Old Age in order to indicate their Age, Condition, &c.

Males.

During the first year ..	*abdē·reka-*	*ā·la-*[1]	The term *ablá·panga-* (long) is applied to a boy who is tall for his age.
During the second year ..	*abkā·tia-*	*ā·la-*[1]; *ablī·ga-*[2]	
During the third and fourth years	*abdō·ga-*	*ā·la-*[1]; *ablī·ga-*[2]	
From four till ten years of age	*dwal·agangа-* or *dwal·agare*	*ablī·ga-*[2]; *ād·la-*	Until the commencement of the probationary "fast" (as well as after its completion) he is called *bō·tiga-*.
During the eleventh and twelfth years	*ā·kā-kā·daka-*	*ablī·ga-*[2]; *ād·la-*	
From twelve to fifteen years of age (the ordinary "fasting" period)	*ā·kā - kā·daka - dō·ga-*	*ād·la-*; *abwā·ra-*[3]	During such portion of this period as he "fasts" he is called *ā·kā-gōb-*, or *ā·kā-gā·ba-*.
After breaking the probationary "fast" (for first month)	*ā·kā-gū·i-*	*abwā·ra-*[3]	He now breaks the "fast," and is called *gū·ma* until he becomes a father.
From then till he becomes a father	*ā·kā-gū·mal-*	*abwā·ra-*[3]	He is addressed as *gū·ma* from the time of his breaking the "fast" till his wife's first pregnancy, when he becomes *mai·a*. Should he never have a child he is called *mai·a* a little later in life.
Single { bachelor only ..	*abwā·ra-*		
Single { whether bachelor or widower	*kā·ga-lō·ga-*		
Bridegroom	*abdā·rabil-*		
Full grown (whether married or single)	*abwā·ra-gōī-*		
Newly married (during first few days only)	*arwā·rad- ; ōng-tāg-gū·i-*		
Newly married (during first few months only)	*ān-jā·ti-gū·i-*		Only applied to young persons.
Married (while still without a child)	*ōng-tāg-*[4]		While his wife is *enceinte* he is called *gij-jā·bag-*.
Married (having had a child)	*abā·bil- ; abā·bil-abda- ; mai·a*		During the first two or three months after the death of his child he is called *mai·a ā·kol·nga-*.
Married (more than once—not applied during widowhood)	*tarwā·ki-*		
Widower	*mai-orlē·ba-*		The *survivor* of an old couple who have been united since their youth is called *ōrō·fi-gōī-*.
Old	*abjang·gi- ; abeld·roga-*		
White-haired	*abtōl-*		

[1] Signifies testicle. [2] A child. [3] A bachelor.
[4] Their jungle-bed of leaves is called *tāg-*.

Females.

During the first year ..	*abdī'erka-*[1]	*kā'ta-*[2] (first year to fourth year)	The term *ā'kā-tā'ng-* (tree) is applied to a girl who is tall for her age.
During the second year ..	*abē'tia-*[1]	*ab'lī'ga-*[3] (second to twelfth year); *kā'ta-*[2]	As in the case of males, both before and after the probationary "fast"[4] she is called *bō'tiga-*.
During the third and fourth years	*abdō'ga-*[1]	*ab'lī'ga-*[3]; *kā'ta-*[2]	
From four till ten years of age	*ā'mal'aganga-*[1] or *ā'mal'agare*	*ab'lī'ga-*[3]; *pū'tola* (four till about sixteen years)	
During the eleventh and twelfth years	*dryō'ngi-*	*ab'lī'ga-*[3]; *pū'tola*	
From twelve till about sixteen years of age (her ordinary "fasting"[4] period)	*dryō'ngi-pū'i-*	*pū'tola*; *abjad'i-jōg-*[5]	She commences her "fast" during this period, and while so doing is called *ā'kā-yāb-*, or *ā'kā-gā be-*.
After breaking the probationary "fast" (for first month)	*ā'kā-gō'i-*[1]	*abjad'i-jōg-*[5]	As soon as she attains maturity she is called *āulā'wi-*, or *ā'kā-tā'wi-*, and then receives her "flower" name (*vide* Appendix H).
Spinster	*abjad'i-jōg-*		
Bride	*abdī'robil-pail-*		
Full grown, if unmarried	*abjad'i-jōg-gō'i-*		
Full grown, if married (but not yet a mother)	*ōng-tāg-*;[6] *ablā'ga-*		
Full grown, if married (but with no child alive)	*ablā'ga-*		
Newly married (during first few days only)	*arwē'red*;[1] *ōng-tāg-gō'i-*[1]		
Newly married (during first few months only)	*ān-jā'ti-gō'i-*;[1] *ōng-tāg-*[1]		Only applied to young persons.
Married (while still without a child)	*ōng-tāg-*[1]		While *enceinte* she is called *pij-jā'bag-*.
Married (having had a child)	*ōdā'wer*; *ōdin-ōdā-*; *ōdā'na*; *ōdā'nola-*		During the first two or three months after the death of her child she is called *ōdā'na ōroli'nga*
Married (more than once—not applied during widowhood)	*tarwā'ki-*[1]		
Widow	*ōdā-arāl'ba-*		
Old	*abjang'gi-*;[1] *abohā'raga-*[1]		
White-haired	*abtōl-*[1]		

[1] In those cases in which the term is common to both sexes, or ambiguity would otherwise exist, the word *pail-* (female) is added when a woman is referred to. Ex.: *ōng-tāg-pail-*; *abtōl-pail-*.

[2] Signifies the genitals of a female.

[3] A child.

[4] A spinster.

[5] As elsewhere explained (*vide* Part II, "Initiatory Ceremonies") this term is used merely to imply abstention, during a period varying from one to four or more years, from certain favourite articles of diet.

[6] Their jungle-bed of leaves is called *tāg*.

APPENDIX L.

LIST OF SOME OF THE TREES AND PLANTS IN THE ANDAMAN JUNGLES.

Andamanese name.	Botanical name.[1]	Remarks.
ā·baga- (a)	Dillenia pilosa.	
aia·ga-	Dipterocarpus alatus .	(Burm.) *Kanyin ngi.*
al·aba-	Melochia velutina ..	(*vide* Appendix B, item 67)
ān- (a) (e) .. .	Calamus, sp. No. 1.	
ā·para- (d) (k) .. .. Aka ā·bad-	Ptychosperma Kuhlii ..	
ā·raga-	.. ..	(Hindi.) *Palawa.* (Burm.) *Bē·bia.*
ā·rain- (m)	Dipterocarpus laevis ..	(Burm.) *Kanyin byu.* Gurjon oil tree.
bad·a- (o)	Rhizophora conjugata ..	(Burm.) *Byūma.*
bad·ar- (a)	Sonneratia tomentosa (?)	
bai·la- (a) (h) .	Terminalia procera ..	(Burm.) *Bambway byu.*
bai·ja- (g)	Sterculia (? villosa) ..	(Burm.) *Saba-basi.*
bā·lab-	.. .. ..	*vide* Part II, "Religious Beliefs," paragraph 19.
bal·ya-		
bē·rata- (g)	Caryota sobolifera.	
bē·taga- (d)	Ceriops Candolleana ..	(Burm.) *Madama.*
bē·la-	Katantium herpestes.	
bē·ma-	Albizzia Lebbek (?) .	(Burm.) *Kūk·ko*
bē·robōd-	Glycosmis pentaphylla.	
bē·rami-	Claoxylon affine (?)	
bē·bē-	Terminalia (? citrina).	
bē·riga-	Planchonia valida ..	(Burm.) *Bambwe ngi.*
bē·rēbē-		
bē·tim-	Sophora sp.	
bōl- (r)	Calamus sp. .. .	Ground rattan.
bō·ma-	Claoxylon sp.	
bō·roma- (a)	Myristica longifolia ..	(Hindi.) *Jaiphal.* (Burm.) *Zā·dipho.*
bō·ta-kō·ko- (o)	Sabia (?)	
bōb-	Ancistrocladus extensus (?)	
bē·kara- (l)	Diospyros (?) nigricans ..	Bastard ebony, or marble wood (superior variety).
bēr-		
bē·ta-	.. .. . .	Extensively used in the manufacture of arrows.
chāb- (a)	.. ..	(Hindi.) *Badām.*
chā·dak-	Rubiaceae.	
chāg·a-	Paratropia venulosa.	
chai-	.. ..	Bows made from this tree.

[1] It has been chiefly owing to the kind assistance afforded by Dr. G. King, Superintendent of the Botanical Garden, Howrah (near Calcutta), that I have been able to ascertain the botanical names of so many of the trees in this list.

Andamanese name.	Botanical name.	Remarks.
chaij- (a) (b)	Semecarpus anacardium	(Hindi.) *Bhilawa*.
chá'kan- (b)	Entada pursætha.	
chá'langa- (q)	Pterocarpus dalbergioides	(Hindi.) *Sisu*. (Burm.) *Padauk*.
chám- (f)	Areca laxa of Hamilton (a variety of Areca triandra).	
chá'mái-	Cynometra polyandra.	
chúdag'ta-	Calamus sp.	Leaves used in thatching huts, and for making the warning wreaths round a grave or deserted encampment.
chóp-	Terminalia sp.	
chó'ta-	Albizzia Lebbek (?) ..	(Hindi.) *Siris*. (Burm.) *Thit*.
chóbargo-pí'nga-	Hopea odorata	(Burm.) *Thingan*-[illegible].
chá'ur-	Leea sambucina.	
chó'-kih-	Diospyros densiflora (?)	
chó'-od-	.. ..	(Burm.) [illegible].
chó'bal-	Atalantia sp.	
chó'ngara- (a)		
chó'pa- (a)	Leguminosæ.	
chóó- (a)	Calamus sp. No. 2 ..	The fruit somewhat resembles a medlar in flavour.
chá'kaga-	Goniothalamus Griffithii.	
chó'lij-	Hypolytrum trinervium.	
chár- (i)	Celtis cinnamomea.	
dá'kar-tá'la-	Hydnocarpus (?) ..	(Hindi.) ? *Lál chini*. (Burm.) ? *Chánda*.
dá'dabla-	Xanthophyllum glaucum.	
dód-	Myristica Irya	Sometimes used for paddle making.
dó'gota- (a) (f)	Mimusops Indica (or ? littoralis)	(Hindi.) *Mówa*. (Burm.) *Kapáli thit*.
dó'ata- (p)	Guettarda speciosa.	
dó'mia-	.. ..	(Burm.) *Pinkim*.
dá'ra-	Barringtonia racemosa.	
dóla'la-		
? *ej-* (b)	Terminalia bialata.	
eng'ara- (a)	.. ..	Wild plantain.
érepoid-lát-	Strychnos nux vomica.	
gá'ube-		
gud-	Calophyllum spectabile.	
gal'dim- (a) .. .	Leguminosæ sp.	
gor'ong- (a)	Bombax malabaricum ..	(Hindi.) *Sembal*. (Burm.) *Didu*.
gá'gma-	Trigonostemon longifolius	Leaves used medicinally as a febrifuge.
í'tál- (b)	Pandanus (?)	
já- (a)	Gluta longipetiolata ..	(Burm.) *Thip-pyé*.
jó'la-	Rubiaceæ.	
jang'ma- (a)	Stephania hernandifolia.	

Andamanese name.	Botanical name.	Remarks.
jī·dga		
jī·ni- (a)	Alpinia sp.	(*Vide* Part I "Medicine," para. 4, and Part III, "Food," para. 35.)
jōr-	Odina Wodier	(Burm.) *Nabhai*.
jū·laij- (b)	Dendrolobium umbellatum	
jū·mu- (a)	? Bruguiera gymnorhiza, or Rhizophora mucronata	(Burm.) *Byubo*.
[illegible]	Ficus hispida.	
kai- (a)	Mangifera sylvatica ..	Wild mango.
kai·ta- (a) (b	Artocarpus chaplasha ..	(Hindi.) *Kathar*. (Burm.) *Toung-peng*.
kā·par- (a) (b)	Licuala (probably peltata)	
kā·rud- (a)	? Sterculia (*or* Sanadera Indica)	The fruit contains a nut which after being sucked is broken, when the *shell* is eaten and the *kernel* thrown away.
kār·ega- (a)	Diospyros sp.	
kō·kum- (r) ..	Pajanelia multijuga.	
kōn- (a)	Diospyros sp.	
kō·rīd·la-	Urceola longiflora.	
[illegible]	One of the Rubiaceæ.	
[illegible]	Dracontomelum sylvestre.	
[illegible]	Lacturia salubris ..	The fruit being large and round is often used as a moving target by being rolled along the ground or down a slope and shot at while in motion.
[illegible]	Leguminosæ sp.	
[illegible] *(a)*	Angiopteris evecta.	
[illegible]		
[illegible]	Atalantia sp.	
maū·- (r)	Sterculia (?)	(Burm.) *Ȧuk pwed*.
mang- (a) (b) (f)	Pandanus Andamanensium.	(Hindi.) *Keora*.
mō·rag-	Mesua ferrea	(Hindi.) *Sil*. (Burm.) *Gangaw*.
[illegible]	Heritiera littoralis.	
mā·tein- (a)	Anacardiaceæ.	
ngō·tya- (a)	Bruguiera sp.	
ngō·bōr- (b)	Cycas Rumphii.	
ngō·raimo-	Ficus sp. No. 1.	
ō·dag-	Eugenia sp.	
ō·durma- (a)		
ē·hi- (a)	Ficus (probably macrophylla).	
ō·lma-	.. ..	(Burm.) *Thinnatnw*.
ō·ro-	Chickrassia tabularis ..	(Burm.) *Nga·ne*.
ō·ropa- (a) (b) (c) .	Baccaurea sapida ..	(Hindi.) *Khatta phal*. (Burm.) *Kanazo*.
ōria-tāt- (a) (g)	Uvaria micrantha.	
pā- (b)	Semecarpus (?)	(Burm.) *Thitsebe*.

Andamanese name.	Botanical name.	Remarks.
pai·ua	Clausena (probably Wallichii).	
[illegible] (*b*)		
[illegible]	Lagerstrœmia regina (? hypoleuca)	(Burm.) *Pimu*.
pár-	Leguminosæ sp.	
pá·ra-		
pá·rad-	Gramineæ.	
pá·tag-	Meliosma simplicifolia ..	Leaves sometimes used as aprons by women (*vide dá·gola-*). The kernel of the seed is eaten.
[illegible]		
[illegible] (*a*)	Gnetum scandens.	
[illegible]	Memecylon variegatum	
[illegible] (?)	Diospyros sp.	Mottled ebony, or marble wood (inferior variety).
pī·dga- (*a*)	.. ..	Common cane.
pī·lita-	Gnetum edule	Fibre extensively used (*vide* Appendix B, item 62).
pī·rij-	Afzelia bijuga.	
pī·tī-	Derris scandens.	
pí- (*f*)	Bambusa Andamanica.	
pór- (*a*)	Korthalsia (or Calamosagus) scaphigera.	
pī·rud-	probably Schmeidelia glabra	(Burm.) *Kimberlin*.
pá·a-	Bambusa	Used for making the shaft of the turtle-spear, and for poling canoes.
pá·lain- (*b*)	.. ..	(Burm.) *Ngá-su sp.* No. 1.
pū·lia- (*b*)	Mucuna sp.	
pá·lka-	Memecylon (probably capitellatum).	
pú·ta- (*b*)	Nipa fruticans	Dhunny leaf palm.
ré-	Dendrobium secundum.	
rdā-	Phœnix sp.	(Hindi.) *Kajūr*.
rár-	Eugenia (?)	(Hindi.) *Chandan*. (Burm.) *Thabyé*.
rau-	Ficus laccifera	(Hindi.) *Bargat*. (Burm.) *Nyaung*.
rē·cho-	Eugenia sp.	(Burm.) *Mai dinbu*.
rog tā·bā cādi-	Polyalthia Jenkinsii.	
ri·di-	Bambusa (?)	Used for making the shafts of the *rá·ta-*, *ti·rlēd-*, and *tá·lbōd-* arrows.
ram- (*c*)	Celtis (or Gironniera) ..	(Burm.) *Thayim*.
rā·tala-	Syzygium Jambolanum.	
tā·langa-tāi-	Antiaxis calocarpa ..	(Burm.) *Gangau ogre*.
tā·lapa-	Terminalia trialata (?) ..	(Hindi.) *Chúglam*. (Burm.) ? *Ngá-su sp.* No. 2, or *Kyé ne he*

Andamanese name.	Botanical name.	Remarks.
tâu-		
tâ·par-	Erycibe coriacea.	
ta·tib- (a) (i)	Croton argyratus (Blyth)	(Burm.) *Chûsan.*
ti-		
tô·kat-	.. ..	(Burm.) *Kidintang.*
tôl-	Amomum dealbatum (or sericeum).	
tôp-	Barringtonia Asiatica.	
tô·la-	.. .. ..	(Burm.) *Pyû.*
ûd- (b)	Menispermaceæ.	
û·dala-	Pandanus verus.	
ûj- (e)	Tetranthera lancæfolia ..	(*Vide* Appendix B, item 76.)
ûl-	Carapa obovata	(Burm.) *Penlâong.*
û·tura-	Maranta grandis (or Phrynium grande).	
waiarga-		
wâ·nga-	Pterospermum acerifolium.	
wai·waga-	.. .. ..	(Hindi.) *Jangli salpan.* (Burm.) *Pûan.*
wi·lima-	Podocarpus polystachia..	(Burm.) *Thit min.*
yâ·rla-		
yôtigri-	Rubiaceæ.	
yô·ra-	Sterculia sp.	
yû·lim-	Anadendrum paniculatum.	

Additional Notes.

(a) Fruit is eaten.
(b) Seed is eaten.
(c) Heart of the tree is eaten.
(d) Pulpy portion of spathe is eaten.
(a) Leaf stems used in manufacture of sleeping mats. Leaves used for thatching purposes.
(f) Leaves used by women as aprons (*ô·bunga-*); rotten logs used for fuel (see also "Superstitions," para. 8).
(g) Stem of this plant used for the frame and handle of the hand-net (*kâd-*) (*vide* Appendix B, item 20).
(h) Leaves used for thatching, for screens (*vide* Appendix B, item 74), for bedding, for wrapping round corpse, for packing food for journey, &c., and prior to cooking.
(i) Rotten logs used for fuel.
(j) Used in manufacture of the foreshaft of the *râ·ta-*, *tô·lbôd-*, *ê·la·da-*, and *ele·ma-* arrows (*vide* Appendix B, items 2, 3, 4, 6), and sometimes also the shaves.
(k) Leaves used for thatching and for bedding.
(l) Leaves used in the manufacture of articles of personal attire (*vide* Appendix B, items 25 and 28).
(m) The middle portion of rotten logs used for torches.
(n) Rarely used for making canoes.
(o) Used for adzes, sometimes for foreshafts of arrows, and for making children's bows.
(p) Leaves used for flooring of huts.
(q) Buttress-like slab roots used for making the sounding-boards employed when dancing.

(*r*) Used for making canoes.
(*s*) Resin used in manufacture of *kā·ngaid-laj-* (*vide* Appendix B, item 62).
(*t*) Used in making the *gōb-*, *kai-*, and sometimes the *tōg-* (*vide* Appendix B, items 82, 80, and 10).
(*u*) Generally used for making paddles, and the leaves for bedding.
(*v*) Used for making shaft of hog-spear.
(*w*) Used for making buckets, fastenings of adzes, turtle-spears, torches (*tō·ug-*), and of bundles; also for suspending buckets, for stitching cracks in canoes, and in thatching.
(*x*) Used for making canoes; the resin is employed in making torches.
(*y*) Used for making canoes, pails, and eating trays.

APPENDIX M.

LIST OF SHELLS AND SHELL FISH COMMONLY KNOWN TO THE ANDAMANESE.

Andamanese name.	Scientific name.[1]	Remarks.
bad·a-ō·la- (*a*)	Monodonta (? labeo).	
bad·gi-ō·la- (*a*)	Delphinula laciniata.	
bē-	Pecten (?) Indica	Scallop.
chā·pata- (*b*)	Pterocera chiragra	Scorpion shell.
chàu·ga lūt chā·kal-	Murex tribulus.	
chej- (*alen chū·la-*)	Pinna (? squamosa)	Bouquet-holder shell.
chi·da- (*b*)	Pinna (?)	
chā·kata-	? Conus eburneus.	
chā·rom- (*a*)	Scolymus cornigerus.	
chō·mai- (*a*)	Tridacna crocea.	
chū- (*a*)	Murex (? palma-rosæ)	Rose-bud shell.
ē·la-	Perna ephippium.	
garun-	Dentalium octogonum.	
gar·en-ō·la- (*a*)	Turbo (?)	Top-shell.
ī·na-ō·la- (*a*)	Nassa (? tænia)	Dog-whelk.
jār·awa-ō·la- (*a*)	Purpura Persica.	
jī·rba-ā-	Cyrena (?)	
jō·rul- (*b*)	Cerithidea telescopium.	
jū·ru-win id·kā bang-	Solen vagina	Razor-fish.
kā·mrāj-	Trochus (? obeliscus).	
kā·rada-	Arca granosa.	
kō·nop- (*a*)	Tridacna squamosa.	
lī·do-	Turbo marmoratus	Is eaten by the *bal·awa-* tribe only.
lī·ta- (*a*)	Cassis glauca	Helmet-shell.
mā·la- (*a*)	Venus (?)	
mā·ral- (*a*)	Venus meroë	Pattern-shot Venus.
mā·ron- (*a*)	Patella variabilis	Rock-limpet.

[1] To the Rev. T. L. J. Warneford, formerly chaplain at the Andamans, I am indebted for the classical names of many of the shells in this list.
(*a*) denotes those that are cooked and eaten.
(*b*) denotes those that are cooked and eaten by *married* persons only.

Andamanese name.	Scientific name.	Remarks.
ngé·rod-	Mitra adusta	Mitre-shell.
ó·da-	Nautilus (? zic-zac).	
ó·la- (a)	Cerithium (? nodulosum).	
ó·lag-	Strombus (? pugilis).	
pai·dak- (a)	Arca (? barbata).	
pail- (b)	Mytilus smaragdinus ..	Sea-mussel.
pai·lia- (b)	Pharus (?)	
pâp-ó·la- (a)	Turbo porphyrites.	
pï·le- (a)	Circe (?)	
pî·rma- (a)	Arca (?)	
.pū·laga ida ó·lang- ..	Dolium latilabris (? also galea).	
rê·kola-	Hemicardium unedo.	
rü·kla- (b)	Cyrena (?)	
tá·ra-ó·la- (a)	Natica albumen.	
tau·big-pū·nar-	Conus (? nobilis).	
tob- (a)	Bulla naucum	Bubble-shell.
tû·bun-	Cypraea Arabica	Cowry.
"	" Mauritiana.	
"	" Talpa.	
"	" Tigris.	
"	" Vitellus	
til-	Cassis Madagascariensis (? also tuberosa)	Queen-conch.
chi·ba	Ostrea (?)	Eaten many years ago but not now.
tá·o- (a)	Trochus Niloticus.	
ó- (a)	Cyrena (?)	
ū·dup-	Conus textile	Cone shell.
ū·yo-	? Turbinella pyrum, or *Pyrula* (? ficus)	Chank shell.
mal- (b)	Spondylus (?)	Thorny oyster.
má·ngala- (a)	Arca (? granosa).	
wâp- (b)	Ostrea (?)	Oyster.
gū·di lia ē·te- (a) ..	Haliotis glabra (*also* " asininus)	Ear-shell.

APPENDIX N.

Statement showing the Earnings of the Aborigines in the Andaman Homes from 1st April, 1875, to 31st March, 1882.

The official year ending	For re-capturing runaway convicts at Rs. 5 each.	By sale of (a) sea-shells and tortoiseshell.	(b) [illegible], oysters, crabs, prawns, and turtles' eggs.	(c) honey and jungle products.	(d) bows, arrows, &c.	(e) cane mats, thatching leaves, &c.*	[illegible] a, b, c, d, and e.	Total.†	Remarks.
	Rupees.	Rupees.	Rupees.	Rupees.	Rupees.	Rupees.	Rupees.	Rupees.	
31st March, 1876 ...	130	640	240	437	29	—	—	1180	* These sales, however, represent but a fraction of the work done by the female inmates of the Homes, as upwards of Rs. 1000 worth of blankets and thatching leaves manufactured in the two years ending 31st March, 1877, were not charged for, besides large sums in the following years.
" 1877 ...	145	540	420	547	75	—	—	1543	
" 1878 ...	85	376	410	341	144	29	—	1800	
" 1879 ...	80	300	419	454	131	42	—	1367	† These amounts are exclusive of various sums—aggregating Rs. 2177 in the seven years—realised chiefly by the sale of surplus produce raised in the "Home" gardens, and by money prizes and rewards gained by the Aborigines for recovering sunken property, winning races at sports, &c.
" 1880 ...	40	270	643	303	109	80	...	1649	
" 1881 ...	25	704	540	708	240	370	—	2445	
" 1882 ...	120	802	818	826	82	850	418	3448	

INDEX.

A

Abipones, 134.
Abnormalities, 13.
Aboriginal population, xii, xiii, 2.
Aborigines, earnings of, xx, and Appendix N, 216.
Abuse, 27.
Activity, 23.
Adam, 96-98.
Adoption, 56-58.
Adze, how made, 179.
„ „ used, 73, 149.
Aëtas, 2.
Age, limit of, 11.
Agglutination, xxiv, 56.
Agriculture, 120.
Albinism, unknown, 14.
Alcoholic drinks, fondness for, xx, 119, 134.
Amusements, 163-174.
Anatomy and Physiology, 5-8.
Ancestors, 86, 96, 101.
Anchor, 149.
Andaman, possible derivation of name, 2.
Anderson (Capt. T. C.), 95, 128.
Angels, 90.
„ road of the, 118.
Anger, how expressed, 21.
Animals, training and domestication of, 121.
Animals, killed for food, 129.
„ onomatopoetic names of, 122.
„ names derived from ancestors, 102.
Arca shell, how used, 125, 154, 157.
Area of group, xii.
Asiatic, 53.
Arrows, 136, 140, 160, 176, Appendix B, 177.
Arrows, how discharged, 141.
„ not poisoned, 138.
Artocarpus, chaplasia, 108.
„ „ seeds, how preserved, 132.
Astonishment, how expressed, 20.
Astronomy, 116-118.
Attack, favourite time for, 130.
Attire, 109-111.
Attitudes, 21.
„ in sleep, 22.
Australians compared with, 47, 52, 62, 89, 123.

B

Baby-slings, 23, 109, and Appendix B, 180.
Baking with stones, 126.
„ in leaves, 129, 130.
„ in bamboo vessel, 131.
Baldness, 10.
Ball (V.), xi, xii.
Bamboo food-vessel, 124, 131.
„ how utilised, 157, 158.
„ knife, 157, and Appendix B, 186.
„ tongs, 156, and Appendix B, 187.
„ water-holder, 8, and Appendix B, 187.
Bandages of leaves, 20.
Barbe (Père), xxiii, 115, 118.
Bark-belt, 7.
Barren Island, x, 81, 148.
Barter, mode of, 180.
Basket-work, how performed, 162.
„ legend anent, 97.
Bates (H. W.), 128.
Bathing, 51.
Beards, 10.
Bêche de mer, xiv, 118, 124.
Beeswax, burning of, 89, 100.
„ as a remedy, 17.
Belcher (Sir E.), 67.
Beliefs, 83-95.
Betrothal of children, 68.
Bigamy unknown, 67.
Birds, by whom eaten, 127, 134.
„ superstition regarding, 87, 121, 122.
Birth names, 90, and Appendix H.
Birth, treatment of infant at, 18.
Blair (Capt. A.), xiv.
Blandford (T. W.), 34.
Blind man's buff, 165.
Boats, see Canoe.
„ mythical submarine, 91.
Boils, how treated, 19.
Boiling of fish, 125.
„ of pork, 91, 130.
„ of yams, 126.

Boiling water, 125.
Bones of animals, 18, 137.
„ of relations, 18, 75–77.
Bow, differences in construction, 138.
„ tradition regarding, 97.
Brains of animals eaten, 131.
Brander (Dr. E. S.), 5, 6, 11, 13, 27, 142.
Breath, 7.
Bride, 69, 70.
Bridge of invisible cane, 96.
Broca, Paul, 7.
Brown (Dr. R.), 47, 67, 71, 82, 146.
Burden, maximum of, 22, 116.
Burial of adults, 76, 77.
„ of enemies or strangers, 78.
„ of infants, 73–75.

C

Calder (J. E.), 2, and Appendix D, 186.
Campbell (Sir A.), xi.
Cannibalism, xiii, 45, 88.
Canoe, traditional form of, 97.
„ making, 140.
„ how propelled, 140, 150.
„ races, 167.
Capital punishment, 43, 48.
Carapace of turtle, how treated, 131.
Car Nicobar, xxii, 3.
Caryota sobolifera, superstition anent, 85.
Caste distinction unknown, 124.
Catarrh, how treated, 17.
Cate-nut eaten, 133.
Cat's-cradle, 168.
Centipede stings, how treated, 20.
Cerambyx heros (*v.* Great Capricornis beetle).
Ceremonies at meeting, 79.
„ at parting, 80.
„ funeral, 73–79.
„ initiatory, 61–66.
„ marriage, 67–70.
Chiefs, how chosen, 41.
„ duties of, 41.
„ death of, 41.
Child-marriages, 72.
Childless parents, 77.
„ widows, 71.
Children, how treated, 26, 100.
„ amusements of, 165–168.
„ captured in warfare, 136.
„ instruction of, 100.
„ mental capacity of, xxi, 27.
Chirography, 45–47.
Civilisation, contact with, xviii–xxiii, 2, 173.
Chips or flakes of quartz, 115, 160, Appendix B, 183.
Cicatrices, 112.
Climate of Andamans, x.
Climbing, skill in, 21.
Clothing, *see* Attire.
Clouds, forms of, recognised, 118.
Coast-men, 16, 23, 34, 36, 39, 41, 44, 119, 123, 144, 145.
Colebrook (Col. R. H.), xiv, 4, 20, 49, 79, 110, 139, 170.
Cold, how regarded, 8, 94.
Colour of eye, 7.
„ of hair, 11.
„ of race, 6.
„ of soul, 94.
„ of spirit, 94.
Communications, 45, 46.
Communities, coast, 24, 34, 36, 40.
„ inland, 29, 35, 36.
Communities, Tribal, 33.
Compass, cardinal points, how distinguished, 119.
Conjugal fidelity, 67, 107.
Conservatism, 50, 88.
Constancy, 67.
Consumption, 14.
Conti Nicolo, 2.
Cooking, care taken in, 128, 131.
„ stones, 160.
„ by whom performed, 129.
Coral reefs, xii.
Corbyn (Rev. H. F.), xviii.
Corpse, treatment of, 75–77.
„ position in grave, 76, 77.
Cough, remedy for, 17.
Council fires, 83.
Counting, method of, 32.
Courage, want of true, 24, 135.
Cousins, how regarded, 58.
Covenants, oaths, &c., 42.
Crackling, fondness for, 130.
Creator, belief in the, 89, 95.
Creation, legend regarding, 95, 96.
Creeks, legend regarding formation of, 97.
Crimes, 43, 44.
Crosses, 12.
Customs, *see* Adoption, Death and Burial Marriage, Meeting and Parting, Proper Names, Initiatory Ceremonies, Shaving, Tattooing, Tabu.
Cutaneous diseases, 15, 19.
Cyrena shell, how used, 18, 150, 158, 164, 167, Appendix B, 183.

D

D'Albertis (L. M.), 118, 156.
Dancing ground, 40.
Dancing, mode of, by men, 170.
" " by women, 171.
Dance of neophytes, 63, 64.
Dance of tears, 75.
Dante, 8, 94.
Darkness legend, anent origin of, 104.
Dawn superstition, regarding, 86.
Davis (Dr. J. B.), 4, 9, 115.
Day (Dr. F.), 10, 12, 59, 61, 69, 109, 116, 120, 125, 130, 145.
Death and Burial, 73–79.
Death ascribed to magic, 28.
" sudden, 78.
" from snake-bite, 19.
" from sunstroke, 22, 130.
Deceased persons, how referred to, 126.
Defiance, how expressed, 2.
Deformations, 115.
Deluge, legends of, 98–101.
" superstitions regarding recurrence of, 85, 127.
Demonology, 88–92.
Demons, belief in, 89, 90, 92.
" death ascribed to, 78, 89.
Dentalium octogonum used for ornament, 130, Appendix B, 182.
Depilation, 10.
Development and Decay, 11.
Dialects, their, 50–68.
" legends anent, 98, 101.
Difficulties of intercommunication, 45, 55.
Diseases prevalent, 16, 17.
Disgust, how shown, 20.
Dispersion, legend of, 97, 98, 101.
Distant (W.), 124.
Diving, 43, 167.
Divorce, 67.
Dobson (Dr. G. E.), 5, 12, 14, 36, 39.
Dogs, 119, 121, 137.
Domestication of animals, 121.
Drawing, ignorance of, 47.
Dreams, how regarded, 20, 87.
Drongist, fable of a, 105.
Drunkenness, 44.
"Ducks and Drakes," 167.
Dugongs, ceremonies connected with first eating, 134.
Dug-out canoe, 146.
" " antediluvian form of 147.
Duties of men, 107.
" women, 108, 111, 113.

E

Ear, 5.
Ear-ache, cure for, 19.
Earthen vessels, 153.
Earthquakes, recurrence of, x, xi.
Earthquakes, how regarded, 86.
East, term for, 118.
East wind, 118.
Eating meat, mode of, 124.
" gravy, 19, 125, 131.
" honey by neophytes, 65.
" turtle, 63.
Eclipse of moon, 93.
Eclipse of sun, 85, 93.
Eden, Garden of, 96, 98, 108.
Edible birds' nests, 118.
Edible roots, 126.
Education of children, 109.
Eggs (turtle), how eaten, 124, 129.
Elephants legendary, 87, 104.
Elephantiasis, 20.
Ellis (A. J.), 3, 56, and Appendix A, 174.
Emulation, spirit of, 26.
Encampments, coast, 26.
" diagram of, 40.
" inland, 34.
" permanent, 27, 39, 136.
" temporary, 38, 136.
" undefended, 126.
Endurance, powers of, 32.
Entala pursetha, superstition regarding, 68.
Entertainments, 168–172.
Epidemics, 15.
Epilepsy, 15.
Erythrism, 14.
Esquimaux, 92, 124.
Etymology, 23.
Eve, 90.
Evil spirits, belief in, 16, 29, 90, 91.
Exhumation of human remains, 74, 77.
Extinction of race, xxv, 8, 16.
Exchangeable values, &c., 119–120.
Eye, colour of, 7.
Eye-sight keenness of, 23.
Eyebrows, shaving of, 10.

F

Facial angle, 11.
Farrer, 65.
Fasting period, 63.
Fasting in mourning, 74.
Fat, excessive development of, 13.
Fearlessness, 24.
Feet, size of, 4, 5.

Fever, malarial, treatment of, 16.
Fijians, 15.
Figuier (L.), 2, 38, 56.
Fire, 82.
" how preserved when travelling, 82.
" method of rekindling, 83.
" obtained from the sky, 96.
" safeguard against evil spirits 84.
" rekindled over infant's grave, 74.
" wood collected by women, 83, 108.
Fish as an article of diet, 127.
" favourite, 125.
" cooking of shell-fish, 125.
Fish-spears, 137.
Fishing, 136–148.
" with bows and arrows, 146.
" with nets, 145, 146.
Fishing, how performed, 160.
" a fam. duty, 160.
Flood, legends of, 98–101.
Flower, (W. H.), xiii.
Flower-name, 60, and Appendix H, 201.
Food, 122–133.
" care in preparing, 123, 128, 129.
" sufficiency of, 123.
" average amount eaten, 124.
" mode of preserving, 131.
" mode of storing, 38, 131.
" variety of, 127.
" in what state eaten, 9, 129, 131.
Fonls, 47.
Form and Size, 4–6.
Foster-parents, 57.
Fowls, fondness for, 131.
Frog-stroke, 48.
Fruits, list of principal, 128.
" eaten with ashes, 128.
" eaten medicinally, 19.
" method of cooking, 128.
Future Life, belief in, 94.

G

Gaboon tribes, 146.
Galatea, Pygmalion and, 102.
Games and Amusements, 165–178.
Generosity of disposition, 25.
Geographers, Arabian, xii. 2.
Geological legends, 103, 104.
Ghosts, bridge of, 94.
Gifts, 80, 169.
Glass flakes, 160.
Government, 40–42.
Grant (Capt. J.), 172.
Gravy, how eaten, 125, 131.

Great Andaman, xi, xxiv, xxv, 111, 112.
Great Capricornis beetle, larvæ of, eaten, 123, 127.
Guests, how treated, 26, 172.

H

Habitations, 37, 40.
Hades, belief in, 87, 96.
Hair, mode of dressing, 9, 10.
" colour of, 11.
" on body, 6.
" structure of, 9.
" shaving the, 10.
" not dyed, 10.
" early rumours of a tribe with long, 10.
Hamilton (G.), 148.
Harbours, xi, xii.
Harpoon, 137, and Appendix B, 177.
Headaches, cure for, 19.
Hearing, sense of, 24.
Heat precautions against, 5.
Heaven, belief in, 88, 96.
Height of adults, 5, and Appendix C, 188–191.
Heredity, 28.
"Hide and seek," 165.
Hills, 31, 86.
Hodder (Surgeon-Major), 7, 56.
Homes established by Government, xviii–xx, xxii, 13, 36, [illegible], 111, 120, 171.
Homfray (J. N.), xviii, xix, xx, 32.
Hones, see Whetstone.
Honey-feast, 65, 66.
" mode of gathering, 138.
" when obtained from, 66, 134.
Hospitality inculcated, 26, 57.
Hostility to strangers, xiv, xviii, 2, 45, 119.
Hottentots, 14, 74, 76.
Human bones, necklaces of, 18, 76, 78, 106, Appendix B, 182.
Human skulls, 75, 78.
" " not used as receptacles, 157.
Hunting and Fishing, 136–147.
Huts v. Habitations.
Hosts, duties of, 26, 160, 172.

I

Iguana eaten, 127.
Ill-temper, how shown, 21.
Immortality, belief in, 96.
" of animals, birds, and fish, 96.

Infanticide, 109.
Infants, excessive mortality of, 11.
„ burial of, 73–75.
„ mode of carrying, 109.
„ naming of, 60.
„ pre-existence of, 87.
„ treatment of, 18.
„ shaving of, 114, 115.
Inheritance, laws of, 120.
Initiatory Ceremonies, 61–66, 180.
Inland tribes, xxv, 26, 34, 119.
Intelligence, xxi, 27.
Intercommunication, difficulties of, 45.
Intercourse with aliens, result of, xxv, 15, 24, 44.
Interments, 73–78.
Interval between death and burial, 73.
Interview Island, ix, 10, 36.
Invisible cane bridge, 94.
Iron highly prized, xxii, 119, 159.
„ legend of finding, 102.

J

Jealousy, 20, 70.
Journey, a day's, 22, 116.
Jungle life, preference for, xxi, 87; 172.
Justice, how administered, 42.
„ sense of, 25.

K

Keane (A. H.), 47.
Kidney-fat a delicacy, 62, 130.
King (Dr. G.), Appendix L, 200.
King-fisher, 99, 103.
„ legendary Prometheus, 99.
Kissing, 79.
Kitchen-middens, xxiii, xxv, 87, 126, 153, 161, 169.
Kyd Island, 47.
Kurz (S.), xii, 28.

L

Language, 40–58.
Laws, 42, 48, 120.
Leaf-apron, 26, 110, 111.
Leaf-screens, 18, 81, Appendix B, 189.
"Leap-frog," 165.
Leather-work, 153.
Legends regarding Creation, 96.
„ „ Deluge, 98–101.
„ „ dispersion, 98, 101.
„ „ diversity of dialect, 98, 101.
Legends regarding drought, 105.
„ „ elephants, 103.
„ „ formation of creeks, 97.
„ „ finding of iron, 102.
„ „ neophytes who were petrified, 102.
„ „ origin of night, 104.
„ „ origin of fire, 90.
„ „ propagation of yams, 102.
„ „ Pygmalion and Galatea, 102.
Lery, Jean de, 131.
Limbs, well-formed, 4.
„ measurements of, 5, and Appendix C, 186–191.
Limit of age, 11.
Lightning, how regarded, 85, 90.
Little Andaman, xxii, xxiv, 4, 139, 141.
Loads, mode of carrying, 23, 115.
Longevity, 11.
Long-haired tribes, supposed existence of, 10.
Lord's Prayer, translation of, 54.
Lubbock (Sir J.), 24, 30, 57, 122, 124, 172.

M

Magic and Witchcraft, 28, 29.
Magnanimity, 26.
Mohammedan travellers, 4, 5.
Mangrove fruit, how eaten, 127.
Mariage de convenance, 71.
Marriage, 67–72.
„ how brought about, 68.
„ ceremonies, 69.
„ irregularly contracted, 69.
„ not permissible between relatives, 67.
„ presents, 70.
„ second, 70.
„ errors of various writers regarding, 71, 72.
Marital relations, 67, 107, 108.
Marrow, fondness for, 131.
Measles, epidemic of, 15.
Meat, mode of eating, 124.
Medicine, 16–20.
Meeting and Parting, &c., 79–81.
Meeting between friends, 79.
„ between husband and wife, 80.
„ childless couples, 80.
Men, duties of, 107.
„ mode of carrying loads, by, 23.
Metallurgy, 159.
Meteors, how viewed, 84.
Migrations, 36, 37.

Migrations, by whom arranged, 106.
Milky way, 118.
Miller (Capt.), xxiii, 119.
Mincopie, possible origin of name, 3.
Miniature bows and arrows for children, 109, 138, 168.
Mock pig hunts, 165.
„ turtle hunts, 165.
„ burials, 167.
Modesty, sense of, 26, 56, 110.
Moon, eclipse of, 92.
„ regarded as masculine, 84, 92.
„ superstition regarding, 84, 85.
„ tradition anent, 105.
„ tidal influence recognised, 117.
Morality, 26.
„ branches of, xix, 67.
Morals, 24–28.
Mortality, rate of, 2.
„ excessive infant, 11, 13.
Motions, 11, 22.
Mouat (Dr. F. J.), xiv–xvi, 4, 7, 9, 16, 18, 20, 48, 71, 73, 83, 89, 95, 126, 130, 146, 148, 150, 163, 170.
Mourning period, 74, 168.
Mourners, 73, 75, 77, 123.
Mucous membrane, 8.
Musical ability, absence of, 171, 172.
„ instruments not made, 158.
Murder, 42.
Mutilation, 74, 115.
Myristica longifolia, 62, 150.
Mythology, 95–106.

N

Naga Hill tribes, 23.
Names, Proper, 59–61.
„ birth, 60.
„ flower, 60, and Appendix H, 201.
„ nick, 61.
„ given to natives of India, 23.
Narcondam, 31, 82, 148.
Narcotics, 44.
Natural Forms, 156–158.
Nautilus shell, 151, 153, 157.
Navigation, 146–150.
Neap-tide, 118.
Necklaces, 75, 77, and Appendix B, 181.
Negritos, xxiv, 2.
Neophytes, 62–66, 102.
Netting needles, 158, 166, and Appendix B, 186.
Netting, 163.
Nicobarese, xxii, 115, 147, 148, 158.
Night, supposed origin of, 104.
Nomadism, 35, 37.
Nudity, 109.
Numeration, 32.
„ ignorance of, 117.
Nux Vomica, 138.

O

Oaths and Ordeals, 42.
Odour, 7.
Omentum of pig eaten, 130.
Ophiophagus elaps, 19, 60, 85.
Ophthalmia, 15.
Ordinals, 32, and Appendix E, 194.
Orion's belt, 118.
Ornamentation, 150–153.
„ diagram of designs, 151–153.
Ornaments, 109.
„ made by women, 108.
Outriggers, when introduced, 147.
Oven-trees, 88.
Owen (Richard), xiii, 14, 126.
Oysters, 122.

P

Pace, average length of, 21.
Paddles, 150.
Painting, 112–114.
„ materials used in, 113, 114.
„ of weapons and implements, 150.
„ restrictions on the unmarried, 113.
„ tradition regarding, 97, 102, 112.
Palm-leaves, 38, Appendix B, 186.
Papuans, psychological affinities with, 27.
Papuans, 2, 45.
Paradise, belief in, 94.
Paradoxurus, 19, 127, 130.
Pathology, 14, 15.
Peal (S. E.), 23.
Perseverance, 25.
Portman (Oscar), 11, 59, 67, 92, 110, 111, 121, 122, 155.
Physical powers and senses, 22–24.
Physiognomy, 20, 21.
Physiology, 6–8.
Pigs, antediluvian, 96.
Pig hunts, 143.
„ most frequent during rains, 126.
„ mock, 165.
Pigs, mode of killing, 129.
„ baking of, 129, 130.
„ superstition regarding, 91, 130.
„ boiling, 91, 130.

Pig-feet, 65.
Pig, not eaten at certain times, 123, 134.
Pinna shells, how used, 157.
Pitt Rivers (General A.), 83, 138.
Poetical dialect, 50.
Poison, 87.
Polyandry, 67.
Polygamy, 67.
Porpoise, ceremonies on first tasting, 134.
Poss. pron. adj., list of, 51–44, Appendix G, 190.
Pottery, 153-156.
Potter's wheel unknown, 154.
Pottery, substitutes for, 156.
Pots, method of making, 154, 155.
Pre-existence of infants, belief in, 87.
Private property, rights of, 120.
Prognathism, 14.
Propagation of yams, 102.
Property, 118.
Proper Names, 60, 61, Appendix H, 201.
Psychology and Morals, 24–28.
Purgatory, belief in, 94.
Puris, 38.
Pygmalion and Galatea, 108.

R

Rats, rapid extinction of, 3.
Rams, canoe, 157.
Rafts, 149.
Rainbow, how regarded, 86.
Rainfall, average, x.
Rate of pulse, 6.
„ respiration, 6.
Re-adoption, 57.
Re-birth, belief in, 87.
Records of game killed, not kept, 127.
Refrain of songs, 169.
Rehearsal of songs, 169.
Religious Beliefs and Demonology, 89, 95.
Relationships, 58, 59.
Reproduction, 13, 14.
Restrictions in regard to touching or speaking to certain relatives, 135.
Resurrection, belief in, 94.
Rheumatism, treatment of, 17.
Rhythm, 50, 169.
Rice, fondness for, 131.
Ridley (Rev. W.), 60, 62.
Roasting, 129, 130.
Röepstorff (F. A. de), xxv, 122, 153, 161.
Rudler (F. W.), 160.
Rutland Island, ix, xxiii, 10, 12, 100.
Running, 23.

S

Saddle Peak, x, 30, 81, 97, 99.
Sandwich Islanders, 172.
Scarification, 17, 19.
„ a fem. duty, 108.
Scenery of Andamans, xii.
Scent, sense of, 23.
Scorpion sting, how treated, 20.
Second sight, belief in, 28.
Second marriages, 70.
Seers, 25, 29, 98.
Self-denial, 26.
Self-respect, 56.
Semangs, 2, 142.
Semecarpus, how preserved, 132.
Senses and physical powers, 22–24.
Sham feasts, 168.
Shaving, 114, 115.
„ of eyebrows, 10.
„ infants, 115.
„ duty of women, 10, 108.
„ with quartz or glass flakes, 115, 159.
Shell-fish, mode of opening, 125.
„ „ cooking, 125.
Sexes, relation of, 107.
Shields not used, 160.
Shooting, skill in, 139, 142, 143, 167.
Sight, keenness of, 22.
Silence after hunting, 126.
Singing, 171, 172.
Silence enjoined on neophytes, 60, 65, 66.
Size and Form, 4–6.
Skiffs, buoyancy of, 147.
Skin, colour of, 6.
Skulls of deceased relatives, 78.
„ deformation of, 115.
Sleep, attitude in, 22.
„ loss of, 8.
„ forbidden to neophytes, 63, 66.
Smoking, injurious effect of, xix, 46.
Snakes (sea) eaten, 123.
Snake bites, cure for, 18.
„ death from, 19.
„ superstition regarding, 87.
Sneezing, how regarded, 87.
Social Relations, 107.
Social status, on what dependent, 41.
Somali, 48.
Songs, how composed, 169.
Soul, 91.
Sounding board, 130, 151, 169, Appendix B, 179.
Spirits, dread of evil, 29, 84, 90, 91.
Spirit combats, game of, 166.
Spirits of the departed, 86, 91.
Stars, 92.

St. Andrew, St. John, R. F., 157.
Stone Implements, 159–161.
Storms, superstition anent, 85.
Stoliczka (Dr. F.), xxv. 126, 153, 150, 161.
Stratagems not used to decoy game, 148.
Stratagems not employed in warfare, 135.
String, how made, 163.
Strings, 162–164.
Suicide, 43.
Sun regarded as fem., 92.
,, eclipse of, 85.
Sun-dial, 117.
Superstitions, 84–88.
Surprise, how shown, 80.
Suttee unknown, 73.
Sweets, fondness for, 131.
Swimming, 47, 65, 167.
Swinging, 166.
Symes (Col.), 55, 96, 166.

T

Tabu, 133–135.
Tamils, 59.
Tangi, 79.
Tanna, New Hebrides, 28.
Tasmanians, 2, 9, 82.
Taste, sense of, 23.
Tattooing, 110, 111.
,, coloured pigments not used, 113.
,, legend of origin of, 102.
,, mode of execution, 112.
,, tribal differences in regard to, 112.
,, reason for, 111.
,, performed by women, 108, 111, 112.
Teeth, general excellence of, 6, 18.
Telugus, 59.
Temple (Lieut. R. C.), 53, 56.
Tears sign of happiness, 80, 172.
Tears, dance of, 75.
Thomson (Dr. Allen), 9, 77.
Threefold constitution, belief in, 94
Thunder, how regarded, 85, 90.
Throwing competitions, 167.
Tickell (Col.), 50, 131.
Time, mode of reckoning, 116.
Tid-bits, 122, 128.
Tobacco-smoking, xix, 44.
Topography, 30, 31.
Trade, Exchangeable Values, &c., 114–120.
Traders, malpractices of, xiv, 119.
Training of animals, 121, 122.
Transmigration, past belief in, 93, 122.
Tribes linguistically distinguished, xxiv, 30, 51.
Tribes, rumours of long-haired, 10.
Tribal communities, 33–36.
Tribal distribution, 30.
Tribal marks, xxiv, 112.
Turtle hunts, 144, 145.
,, mode of killing, 131.
,, -blood, mode of cooking, 131.
,, eggs sometimes eaten raw, 129.
,, not eaten during mourning, 74, 133.
,, -fat esteemed a delicacy, 131.
Twins, 13.
Tylor (E. B.), 10, 96, 131.

V

Visual powers, 23.
Voices, 2.
Volcanoes, 81, 82.

W

Wallace (A. R.), 2.
Warfare, 135, 136.
Wax 17, 29, 74, 88.
Water, how boiled, 125.
Weapons used in hunting, &c., 137.
Wedding presents, 70.
Weeping sign of joy, 80, 172.
Weights and measures, 116.
Weight of adults, 5, and Appendix C, 188–191.
Whetstone, how made, 160.
,, medium of exchange, 161.
Widows, 71.
Winds, names for, 118.
Wood (Rev. J. G.), 67, 71.
Women, duties of, 88, 108, 115.
,, mode of carrying loads by, 28, 115.
Wounds, cure for, 19.
Wounded foes, how treated, 135.
World, belief respecting form of, 93.
World, belief respecting end of, 90.
Wrestling games, 167.

Y

Yams, how cooked, 126.
,, legend of propagation of, 108.
,, when in season, 132.
Yorubas, 68.
Yule (Col. H.), 2, 82.

HARRISON AND SONS, PRINTERS IN ORDINARY TO HER MAJESTY, ST. MARTIN'S LANE

REPORT

OF

RESEARCHES INTO THE LANGUAGE

OF THE

SOUTH ANDAMAN ISLAND.

ARRANGED BY

ALEXANDER J. ELLIS, F.R.S., F.S.A.,

TWICE PRESIDENT OF THE PHILOLOGICAL SOCIETY,

FROM THE PAPERS OF

E. H. MAN, Esq.,

ASSISTANT SUPERINTENDENT OF THE ANDAMAN AND NICOBAR ISLANDS,

AND

LIEUT. R. C. TEMPLE,

OF THE BENGAL STAFF CORPS, CANTONMENT MAGISTRATE AT AMBALA, PUNJAB

(Reprinted from the Eleventh Annual Address of the President to the Philological Society, delivered by Mr. Alexander J. Ellis, F.R.S., F.S.A., on his retiring from the chair, 19 May, 1882, and contained in the Transactions of that Society for 1882-3-4, pp. 44-73. The original pagination is retained.)

ON THE LANGUAGE OF

THE SOUTH ANDAMAN ISLAND.

Proceeding from Sumatra northwards into the Bay of Bengal, we find first the Nicobar, and then the Andaman group of islands. The latter is composed of the North, Middle, South and Little Andamans, with numerous smaller ones adjacent. In 1858, Port Blair, an inlet on the south-east of South Andaman, was selected as a penal settlement for the Sepoy rebels, and it was there that the Indian Viceroy, Lord Mayo, was murdered by a fanatic prisoner in 1872. Mr. E. H. Man went to the Andamans officially in 1869, and in July, 1875, was put in charge of the Andamanese Homes, which threw him into immediate and close connexion with the natives, and gave him an opportunity of studying their language, habits and customs. In several most interesting communications to the Anthropological Institute this year. Mr. Man has described the physical and social condition of these tribes. I may mention in passing that the Andamanese are almost entirely naked[1] and totally uncivilised, but seem to have many good qualities, and are very moral in respect to marriage, being strictly monogamous. They are dwarfish in stature, the average height of men being 4 ft. 10¾ inches and of women 4 ft. 7¼ inches.[2] The accounts

[1] The women *always* wear an *ō·bun-gada* or apron, consisting of one or two leaves of the *mimusops Indica*, in front, as well as a *bō·da* or girdle with an appendage behind like a bustle, and the men *sometimes* wear a waistbelt and girdle of shells (*Dentalium octogonum*). Both men and women also frequently paint their bodies with white and red in patterns, and tattoo themselves more or less, and wear necklaces and other ornaments.

[2] The maximum and minimum height of men are 5 ft. 4½ in., quite a giant, and 4 ft. 5½ in. respectively. Those of women being 4 ft. 11¼ in. maximum, and 4 ft. 4 in. minimum. The average weight of men is 98½ lbs. or 7 stone, and of women 93½ lbs. or slightly over 6½ stone.

of travellers in former times were not only very meagre, but have been found to contain important inaccuracies both as respects the language and customs of the natives, (p. 47, n. 1).

The Andamanese have no means of writing, and no notions of religious worship. The tribes which inhabit the Andaman group are Negritos and seem to have all descended from a common source. They are entirely distinct from the inhabitants of the Nicobar Islands, who are allied to the Malays. There are at least nine Andamanese tribes speaking mutually unintelligible languages, all of which are, however, formed after a common type of construction, and although in two of them an occasional resemblance in roots can be traced, the relational words and particles, postpositions, prefixes and suffixes which form the principal peculiarity of the language, are totally different for the different tribes.

Between July, 1875, and April, 1876, Mr. Man had prepared a vocabulary of from 1800 to 2000 South Andaman words, with numerous illustrative phrases, and this he had intended to incorporate with his report to Government. But before doing so, about May, 1876, Lieutenant R. C. Temple, who was at that time in the 1-21st Fusiliers, was transferred from the head-quarters of his regiment in Burmah, to do duty with a detachment then stationed at Port Blair. Mr. Temple had already worked at the Burmese language, and published a transliteration of it.[1] Hence, on becoming acquainted with Mr. Man's collections, he took the greatest

[1] Notes on the Transliteration of the Burmese Alphabet into Roman Characters, to which is attached a Note on the Vocal and Consonantal Sounds of the Peguan or Talaing Languages. By Lieutenant R. C. Temple, 21st R.N.R. Fusiliers. Rangoon, printed at the Central Jail Press, 1876; folio, pp. viii. 21. iv. In this transliteration Mr. Temple endeavours to combine "literal" with "phonetic" transcription on the basis of Sir William Jones's system for Sanscrit as modified by Dr. Hunter. But as Burmese has the sound of English *th* in *thin*, as well as the postaspirated *t* or *t'* as here written, and has a postaspirated *s* or *s'*, but not English *sh* in *she*, Mr. Temple employs *hk*, *ht*, *hp*, *hs* for the postaspirates, which would here be written *k'*, *t'*, *p'*, *s'*, the ' representing the Greek spiritus asper. He also uses *aw* for the sound of unaccented English *au* in *authority*, and *aw* for the accented *aw* in *awful*. He likewise distinguishes *e* in *met*, *è* in French *père* (which he identifies with *ai* in English *pair*) and *é* in French *fête*. He also uses *ou* for the English sound of *ou* in *sound*. These are his chief deviations from Dr. Hunter's Indian system, and it will be seen by a subsequent note (p. 48, n. 1) that he bases his Andamanese system upon this, although, not having a native orthography to deal with in the present case, he has modified it in part.

interest in them, and proposed an improved system of spelling, which Mr. Man adopted, and they then agreed to work together. One consequence of this was that Mr. Man translated the Lord's Prayer into South Andamanese—a natural but rather an unfortunate selection perhaps, as the Andamanese have scarcely a proper word for God,[1] and could only call prayer 'daily repetition'[2] from observing the habits of the imported Musselmans—while Mr. Temple wrote a comment and introduction, based entirely on the facts furnished him by Mr. Man. The result was published in Calcutta and London (Trübner, 1877), in a little book of 81 pages, called "The Lord's Prayer translated into the South Andaman Language by E. H. Man, with preface, introduction, and notes by R. C. Temple." The preface is dated September, 1876, only four months after Mr. Temple had become acquainted with the language. To have written such a précis in so short a time (seriously diminished by his being engaged in studying for the higher standard examination in Hindustani, which he passed while at Port Blair) evinces great powers of appreciation and coordination in Mr. Temple. It was the first book which gave any trustworthy account of this language, the nature of which I shall endeavour to explain in this report.

Messrs. Man and Temple then determined to work together for the purpose of compiling a complete grammar of the language, Mr. Man collecting the data, and Mr. Temple

[1] *Pū·luga* (the system of spelling will be explained on p. 49) "is," says Mr. Temple, "as near an equivalent for 'God' as can be found in the language, and conveys nearly all the ideas we attach to the word 'God' likely to occur to a savage mind. *Pū·luga* is a spirit, who dwells in *mō·ro*, the sky (*Pū·luga l·a ā·rda mō·ro kōktā·rien*, P. of dwelling-place sky middle-in, and *Pū·luga mō·ro kōktā·rien pōl·ike* P. sky middle-in dwell-does); he is the Creator of all things and supreme over all, he was not born, has existed from time immemorial and cannot die; his house is of stone (*i.e.* of the most magnificent materials) and invisible; he is the cause of rain, of thunder, of natural death (*Pū·luga l·a mai·chalak* (or *ā·rlok*) *yū·mla pō·ke*, P. his lap-from (or house-from) rain falldoes, *Pū·luga ijirē·ībe*, P. angry-is! (an exclamation used when it thunders). *Pū·luga* is distinctly the embodiment of *goodness* and *power* . . . in contradistinction to the idea of evil embodied in *Ē·rem-chāu·gala*, the Evil Spirit of the jungles or land," (*ē·rem* jungle, *chāu·gala* ghost).—Lord's Prayer, p. 48.

[2] Hence 'the Lord's prayer' is translated as *Pū·luga l·a ā·rlatikyab·ō*, P. of daily-repetition, from *ā·rla* day, *t* euphonic, *ikyab·ō* repetition, where *yāb* means speak, and *ik* or *ig* is a modifying prefix, thus *ōl yā·buga l·igyab·o* that word repeat!

arranging the results. Mr. Man also endeavoured to obtain as much information as possible respecting the other tribes. On account of the narrow limits to which I must necessarily confine myself, and the fragmentary nature of these latter collections, I shall deal exclusively with the South Andaman language, at which these gentlemen principally worked. But the arrangements for joint authorship were unfortunately interfered with by Mr. Temple's being ordered off on duty to different stations in India in Oct. 1876, so that all the manuscript and all correspondence between him and Mr. Man had thus to pass through the post, entailing great delay, and preventing the possibility of personal communication, which would have been so valuable. Nevertheless, in the two years ending July, 1878, when Mr. Temple (who was then in the 1st Goorkhas) was ordered off on active service, and all papers were returned to Mr. Man, Mr. Temple contrived to put together and make a fair copy of a very copious grammar, of which a short specimen of 11 pages, containing the first section, "On Nouns," was printed for private circulation at Calcutta in 1878. On the MS. being sent back to Mr. Man, he went over it carefully, to bring it up to his advanced knowledge in a series of voluminous notes. These and the MS. were returned to Mr Temple after the war. But he was then appointed a Cantonment magistrate in the Panjáb, and the great press of business prevented him from obtaining privilege-leave, and thus having an opportunity to correct his grammar by the help of these additional notes. In the vain hope, however, that he might find time to do so, he retained the MSS. till July, 1881, when, with great regret and reluctance, he returned them to Mr. Man, who was at the time on leave in England. The "specimen" and the "Lord's Prayer" are the only papers that they have printed on the South Andaman language. Those which Mr. Man has read before the Anthropological Institute only touch incidentally upon it.[1]

[1] It would be really more correct to say that these are the only papers that have been printed on any Andaman language. For Colebrooke's vocabulary (*Asiatic Researches*, iv. 393-4), quoted by Crawfurd, is certainly unintelligible

In January of this year Mr. Man was introduced to me through Mr. Brandreth, a member of our Council, in order to settle the alphabet before printing it in his Anthropological papers. I was then quite ignorant of the facts just detailed, and merely endeavoured to complete the alphabet on the lines which Mr. Man had used. These had been laid down, as we have seen, by Mr. Temple, and were to some extent Anglo-Indian, especially in the use of *a*, not only for *a* in *America*, but for *a*, *u*, *o* in the colloquial pronunciation of *assumption*. A minimum of change was thus produced. The alphabet was extended to the Nicobarese language, which has all the Andamanese sounds and several others, and among these a peculiar double series of nasal vowels. The following is the alphabet finally settled by Mr. Man and myself, with examples in Andamanese and Nicobarese. This scheme is found to work well, and will be employed in all Andaman words used in this report.[1] It will be observed that the South Andaman language is very rich in vowel sounds, but is totally deficient in the hisses *f*, *th*, *s*, *sh*, and the corresponding buzzes *v*, *dh*, *z*, *zh*. Of course this alphabet has been constructed solely upon Mr. Man's pronunciation of the languages, and hence the orthography might require modification on a study of the sounds as produced by the natives themselves. This refers especially to the distinctions *ä á*, *á à*, *au áu*, *o ò*, *ô*, and the two senses of *i*, *e*, according as they occur in closed or open syllables. But as the natives understand Mr. Man readily, his pronunciation cannot be far wrong.

to six of the Andaman tribes; Tickell's (*Journal of Asiatic Society of Bengal*, No. II. 1864), though referring to South Andaman, is curiously incorrect, translating, for instance, '*yád dá*' as 'much fish,' and giving separately *yád* 'much,' *dá* 'fish,' in place of *yád* 'fish,' *dó·gaya* 'much'; and de Röepstorff's is also full of error. See Mr. Temple's preface to "The Lord's Prayer."

[1] In the following comparative list Mr. Temple's symbols stand first (and, with one exception, are roman), those here adopted stand second (and are all in italics). a *a*, a *ā*, â *á* and *á*, â *á* and *à*, e *e*, ê *ē* and *e*, è *è*, i *i*, î *ī* and *ĭ*, o *o* and *ò*, ô *ō* and *o*, ò *ò*, aw *ó*, u *u*, û *ū* and *u*, ai *ai*, au *au*, âû *áu*, oi *òi*, b *b*, ch *ch*, d *d*, g *g*, h *h*, j *j*, k *k*, l *l*, m *m*, n *n*, ng *ng* ñ *ñg*, p *p*, r *r* and *ṛ*, t *t*, ṭ *t'*, w *w*, y *y*. In Mr. Temple's writing, short *ă e i o u* in open syllables were not distinguished from the long sounds, and the position of stress was rarely marked. I adopted his short *a e i o u* and made the long of them *ā*, *ē*, *ī*, *ō*, *ū*. Then adopting his 'â, ò,' I made their short and long sounds respectively, *á*, *à*, and thus got rid of the exclusively English symbol *aw*.

Alphabet for writing the South Andaman and Nicobar Languages.

SION.	ENGLISH, ETC.	SOUTH ANDAMAN.	NICOBAR.
		Oral Vowels and Diphthongs.	
a	*idea* cut	*al·aba* kind of tree	*yang* without
ă	cur (with untrilled r)	*bă* small, *yŭ·ba* not	?
á	Ital. casa	*dá·ka* region	
â	father	*dâ·-ke* don't (imperative)	*kâa* wife
ā (1)	fathom	*jār·awa* name of a tribe	*lā·āt* [illegible]
e (2)	bed	*e·maj* name of a tree	*angé·h* (h heard, see note 8) after (in time), *heng* day, sun
	chaotic	*pŭ·ré-re* burn-did	*le·hare* book
é (3)	[illegible]	*é·la* pig-arrow	*le·ang* word
i	[illegible]	*ig-ba·dig-re* see-did	*ifu·* sweep
ī	[illegible]	*pī·di* turtle, *pid* hair	*ol* make
o	[illegible]	*.bōi·goli* European	*yō·kolai* bathe
ō (4)	pole	*jō* basket	*larō·m* Pandanus Mellori
ó	pot	*pōl·i-ke* dwell-does	*aantō·m* all
ô	[illegible]ful	*tō·go* wrist, shoulder	*lôre* cloth
ö	Germ. könig	not found	[illegible]
u	influence	*bu·tura* name of a tree	[illegible] landing place
ū	pool	*pŭ·ré-re* burn-did	*hū·ga* egg
ü	Germ. über	not found	*chü·a* I
ai	[illegible]	[illegible]-*ke* understand-does	[illegible] cocoanut shell cup
ău	[illegible]	[illegible] narrow	[illegible] a charm
öu	Germ. [illegible]	[illegible] body	[illegible] vomit
ōi	[illegible]	*.bōi·goli* European	[illegible] wallow
		Nasal Vowels and Diphthongs.	
aṅ	Fr. an	not found	[illegible] spinster, [illegible] (8) word
āṅ	(6)	not found	[illegible] spear having prongs, [illegible] two pronged spear, [illegible] guava
eṅ	Fr. vin	not found	*keá·ke* otherwise, [illegible] harpoon spear
iṅ	Port. sim	not found	[illegible] scrape, [illegible] (5) rain
oṅ	Fr. on	not found	[illegible] stalk game
ôṅ	(6)	not found	*shin-kōk·-hata* knock down, [illegible] fuel
aiṅ	(7)	not found	[illegible] five, *teiá·ye* white
hoiṅ	(7)	not found	[illegible] tobacco
		Consonants.	
b	bad	*bād* hut	*le·hare* book
ch	church	*chák* ability, [illegible] why, *.rŭch* Ross Island	[illegible] fan, [illegible] misturition
d	dip	*dŏ·ga* large	[illegible] rainbow
f	fen	not found	*ifē* you (said of three or more), *fap* thick
g	gap	*gŏ* bamboo utensil	*hōg·nare* be off !
h	hay	*hĕ* ho! *dorāh·* (h sounded, see note 5) etcetera	*hū·ga* egg, *poiyū·h* married or widowed person
j	judge	*jŭ·bug* bad, *é·maj* name of a tree	*chij* abstain
k	king	*kă·gal-ke* ascend-does	[illegible] last quarter of moon
l	lap	[illegible] navigable channel	*le·ang* word
m	man	*mŭ·ga* face	*aantō·m* all
n	nun	*ada-ke* walk-does, *rŭ·gun* toad	*nôt* pig
ñ	Fr. gagner	[illegible]·*ba* another, one more	[illegible] exorcist

SIGN.	ENGLISH, ETC.	SOUTH ANDAMAN.	NICOBAR.
ng	*bring*	*ngi·ji* friend, *irhi·dong-ke* in-trees-search-does (14)	*yang* without
ñy (9)		*ñyi* more	not found
p	*pap*	*pi·d* hair	*paiyü·h* (8) married or widowed person
r (10)	*rest*	*rà* necklace of netting, *rà·ta* wooden arrow	*karu·* large
ṛ (11)	torrent	*ṛà·ta* sea water	not found
s	*sad*	not found (12)	*sè·la* anvil
sh	*she*	not found	*sho-hö·ng* want
t	*ten*	*tì* blood	*tö·ak* toddy
t'		*t'ì* tear (from the eye) (13)	not found
v	*veil*	not found	*hen-vehö·ve* ashes
w	*wet*	*wò·lo* adze, *.bal·awa* name of a tribe	*wòt* don't (imperative)
wh	*what*	not found	*hen-whö·on* ashes
y	*yolk*	*yubë* a little	*yang* without

STRESS.

The syllable under stress in any word is shown by placing a turned period (·) after a long vowel, or the consonant following a short vowel, in every word of more than one syllable.

As it is not usual to find capitals cast for the accented letters, the capital at the beginning of a word is for uniformity in all cases indicated by prefixing a direct period, as *.bal·awa*.

NOTES.

(1) *è* accented before a consonant, is the English *e* in met, as distinguished from *é*, which is the short of *ê* or Italian *e* in *uno*.

(2) *e* accented in closed syllables, as in *veil*; in open syllables unaccented as in chaotic or Italian *padre*, *amore*.

(3) No vanishing sound of *i* as in English *say*.

(4) No vanishing sound of *u* as in English *know*.

(5) Where *ah* is written, as in *aih*, *rah*, the nasal is followed by nasalised breath, remitting the voice, but retaining the position of the vocal organs.

(6) In *ai* the sound has more of the *a* in it, than the French *an*, and in *oi* it has more of the *o* than the French *on*.

(7) In the diphthongs *aui*, *ōui*, the nasality principally affects *a* and *ō*, but it is retained through the whole diphthong, that is, the nasal passages remain open.

(8) *h* is sounded after a vowel by continuing breath through the position of the mouth, while remitting the voice.

(9) *ñy* is a palatalised *ng*, and bears the same relation to it as *ñ* bears to *n*. To pronounce *ñ* attempt to say *n* and *y* simultaneously; to pronounce *ñy* do the same for *ng* and *y*.

(10) This *r* is soft and gentle, with no sensible ripple of the tongue, as very frequently in English, but not merely vocal.

(11) This *ṛ* is strongly trilled, as *r* in Scotch or Italian *r*, or Spanish *rr*.

(12) The Andamanese cannot hiss, and hence they substitute *sh* for *s*, thus *Rūsh* for *Rūs*, the Hindi corruption of Ross.

(13) This *t'* is a post-aspirated *t*, like the Italian *th*, quite different from English *th*, and hence to prevent confusion the Greek *spiritus asper* is imitated by a turned comma. The sound *t'* is common in Irish English, and may often be heard in England.

(14) When *ng* is followed by a vowel, it must run on to that vowel only, and not be run on to the preceding vowel either as in 'finger' or in 'singer,' thus *bì·-ri-nga-da* 'good,' not *bì·-ring-a-da*, *bì·-ring-ga-da*, or *bì·-rin-ga-da*. It is only when no vowel follows that *ng* is run on to the preceding vowel.

All the papers mentioned above have been placed in my hands for the purpose of drawing up this report, and Mr. Man has also given me much personal instruction and looked over the whole of what I have written to guard against any error of fact or language. I have examined the grammar drawn up with such care and acuteness by Mr. Temple, and the vocabulary of Mr. Man, and I shall endeavour to give an account of the results at which they have arrived.

The following, written by Mr. Temple in July, 1881, on finally returning the MSS. to Mr. Man, sums up his opinion of the nature of the South and other Andaman languages:

"The Andaman languages are one group. They are like, that is, connected with no other group. They have no affinities by which we might infer their connexion with any other known group. The word-construction (the 'etymology' of the old grammarians) is two-fold, that is, they have affixes[1] and prefixes to the root, of a *grammatical* nature. The general principle of word-construction is agglutination pure and simple. In adding their affixes, they follow the principles of the ordinary agglutinative tongues. In adding their prefixes, they follow the well-defined principles of the South African tongues. Hitherto, as far as I know, the two principles in full play have never been found together in any other language. Languages which are found to follow the one have the other in only a rudimentary form present in them. In Andamanese both are fully developed, so much so as to interfere with each other's grammatical functions. The collocation of words (or 'syntax' to follow the old nomenclature) is that of the agglutinative languages purely. The presence of the peculiar prefixes does not interfere with this.

[1] Mr. Temple, following the usual unetymological definition given in dictionaries, here uses *affix* in place of *suffix*. In what follows I shall adopt the practice of Prof. S. S. Haldeman in his "Affixes in their origin and application," Philadelphia, 1865, p. 27. "*Affixes* are additions to roots, stems, and words, serving to modify their meaning and use. They are two kinds, *prefixes*, those at the beginning, and *suffixes*, those at the end of the word bases to which they are affixed. Several affixes occur in long words like *in-com-pre-hen-s-ib-il-it-y*, which has three prefixes and five suffixes." Affixes also include *infixes* (or, as Prof. Haldeman calls them, *interfixes*), where the modifying letter or syllable is introduced into the middle of the base, as in the Semitic and other languages.

The only way in which they affect the syntax is to render possible the frequent use of long compounds almost polysynthetic in their nature, or, to put it in another way, of long compounds which are sentences in themselves. But the construction of these words is not synthetic, but agglutinative. They are, *as words*, either compound nouns or verbs, taking their place in the sentence and having the same relation to the other words in it, as they would were they to be introduced into a sentence in any other agglutinative language. There are, of course, many peculiarities of grammar in the Andaman group, and even in each member of the group, but these are only such as are incidental to the grammar of other languages, and do not affect its general tenor. I consider, therefore, that the Andaman languages belong to the agglutinative stage of development, and are distinguished from other groups by the presence in full development of the principle of prefixed and affixed grammatical additions to the roots of words."

The South Andaman language, called by the natives *bō·jig-ngī·jī-da*,[1] consists in the first place of a series of base forms, which Mr. Temple reduces to roots. These forms may answer to any part of speech, and in particular to what we call substantives, adjectives or verbs. These forms do not vary in construction, and are not subject to inflexion proper. Hence there is nothing resembling the grammatical gender, declension or conjugation of Aryan languages; but the functions of such Aryan forms are discharged by prefixes, postpositions, and suffixes. It is only in the pronouns and pronominal adjectives that there is anything which simulates declension. And it is only by the use of the prefixes that anything like concord can be established.

The Andamanese have of course words which imply sex,

[1] The word *bō·jig* appears to mean our-make-of, according to our habits. Mr. Man only knows it in the names of the tribes *bō·jig-ngī·ji-* and *bō·jig-yā·b-*, our-make-of friends, our make of speech, and in such expressions as *bō·jig kā·rama-* our make of bows to shoot with, *bō·jig dā·kar-* our make of buckets, *bō·jig bū·j-* our make of cooking-pots, etc. The *bō·jig-yā·bda* inhabit the Southern portion of Middle Andaman, and most closely resemble the South Andamanese in speech.

but they are in general quite unrelated forms; thus: *dbū·lada* man, *dpai·lda* woman; *ākdkā·dakada* boy, *aryō·ngida* girl; *drō·dingada* father, *dbē·tingada* mother. 'Male' and 'female' are represented even for animals by the above words for 'man' and 'woman,' without the affixes, which are usually omitted in composition,[1] as *bā·la, pail*, and when the animals are young by the names *abwō·reda* bachelor, or *abjad·ijō·gda* spinster, rejecting the affixes as *wō·ra, jad·ijō·g*, see letter to *Jam·bu*, p. 63, sentences 15 and 16. Even in the Aryan languages 'gender,' the Latin 'genus,' means only a 'kind,' and as it so happened that the kind with one termination included males, with another females, and with a third sexless things, the time-honoured names masculine, feminine and neuter arose. But the classification thus formed has, properly speaking, nothing to do with sex, as may be seen at once from sentinel being feminine in French (*la sentinelle*) and woman neuter in German (*das Weib*). We may see from the discussions in Grimm's grammar how difficult, or rather impossible, it is to recover the feeling which led to that grouping in German, and the same difficulty is felt in other languages. The Andamanese grouping which takes the place of gender is, on the contrary, clear enough in the main. The Andamanese consider, first, objects generally, including everything thinkable. Then these are divided into animate and inanimate. Of course the vegetable kingdom is included in the latter. The animate objects are again divided into human and non-human. Of the human objects there is a sevenfold division as to the part of the body referred to, and this division is curiously extended to the inanimate objects which affect or are considered in relation to certain parts of the body. These group distinctions are pointed out by prefixes, and by the form assumed by the pronominal adjectives. So natural and rooted are these distinctions in the minds of the Andamanese that any use of a wrong prefix or wrong possessive form occasions unintelligibility or surprise or raises a laugh, just as when we use

[1] This expression includes both prefix and suffix, see foot-note, p. 51. The suffix *-da* is occasionally retained at the end of clauses, p. 64, l. 15.

false concords in European languages. I shall give examples on p. 57, which have been drawn up for me by Mr. Man. These prefixes are added to what in our translations become substantives, adjectives, and verbs, and which for purposes of general intelligibility to an Aryan audience had better be so designated. But we require new terms and an entirely new set of grammatical conceptions which shall not bend an agglutinative language to our inflexional translation. With this warning, that they are radically incorrect, I shall freely use inflexional terms, as Mr. Temple does throughout his grammar, meaning merely that the language uses such and such forms to express what in other languages are distinguished by the corresponding inflexional terms, which really do not apply to this.

Substantives, adjectives, and adverbs, generally end in *-da*, which is usually dropped before postpositions and in construction; hence when I write a hyphen at the end of a word, I shall mean that in its full form it has *-da*. Subs. and adj. also occasionally end in *-re* for human objects, and this *-re* is not dropped before postpositions. This same suffix *-re* is also extensively used in verbs, for our past tense active, or past participle passive. A common termination is also *-la*, which as well as *-re* implies human, and *-ola*, which is also honorific. What answers to our verbal substantives denoting either actor or action, is expressed by the suffix *-nga* added to verbal bases, both active and passive. What corresponds to the Aryan declension is carried out entirely by postpositions, as in fact it might be in English by prepositions, if we had a preposition to point out the accusative as in Spanish. In Andamanese those postpositions are generally *ia* of, or more usually *lia* of (where the *l*, as very frequently, is merely a euphonic prefix to vowels); *len*, to, in (but *len* also frequently marks out the object); *lat* to, towards; *lek* from and by; *la* by means of (instrument).

The plural is expressed by the addition of *lō·ng-kā·lak*[1] to the singular, when the distinction is considered necessary,

[1] Here *lōng* is probably 'their,' 4th person, see Cl. 5, p. 52. *kā·lak* is apparently no longer found separately.

which is not often, as the plural is left to be implied by the context, or is indicated by a prefix. Abstract subst. are formed from adj. by adding *yō·ma-* quality, or property, as *lā·pangada* long, *lā·panga-yō·mada* length. Negative subst. are formed by adding *ba*, an abbreviation for *ya·ba*, as *abli·gada* child, *abli·gaba* not a child, but a boy or girl.

Active verbs use the suffixes *-ke* for our gerundial form of infinitive,[1] for our pres. part., pres. ind., and occasionally future; *-re* for past time, *-ka* imperfect, *-ngabo* for future, *-nga* for verbal subst., actor and action; with numerous auxiliaries answering to our 'may, might, shall, should, will, would.' Passive verbs use *-nga* for the gerundial infinitive, the future, and verbal substantive, *-ngaba* for pres. and imperf. indic., *-ngata* for perf. and *entō·ba—ngata* pluperf., and *-re* for past participle.[2] Certain verbs distinguish the subject and others the object, as human and non-human, by change of prefix, but no rule can be given as to when a verb does one or the

[1] In his glossary Mr. Man uses the form in *-ke* (just as we say gerundially 'to exist') to shew that he means a verbal form. He says that if you ask an Andamanese the name of any action which you shew him, he will give you the form in *-ke*. But it remains to be established that this corresponds to our gerundial infinitive, at least I have not detected it in any example which Mr. Man has furnished, nor could he recall one. In Latin dictionaries *audio*, *amo*, are Englished 'to hear, to love,' which they certainly do not mean. But as it is usual to give Latin verbs in this form, so it may be usual to give Andamanese verbs in the form in *-ke*, which would be like using *audit*, *amat* in Latin. Our gerundial or supine infinitive answers to the Latin *ad audiendum*, *auditum*. Dr. Morris prefers calling it the "dative infinitive" (Hist. Outlines of Engl. Accidence, 1872, p. 177). It is frequently used for the pure infinitive in English. The pure infinitive is properly only a verbal subst., and most nearly corresponds to one of the senses of the Andamanese form with the suffix *-nga*, but in point of fact there is nothing in Andamanese identical with the Aryan infinitive.

[2] Mr. Man 'conjugates' a verb thus, using the inflexional names. I translate the suffixes *-ke* do, does, *-ke* -ing -was, *-re* did, etc., as the nearest inflexional representatives, but they do not give the true feeling of the original, to which we have nothing which corresponds in English.

ACTIVE. Inf. *ma·mi-ke* sleep-to. Pres. *dōl ma·mi-ke* I sleep-do. Imperf. *dōl ma·mi-ke* I sleep-ing-was. Perf. *dōl ma·mi-re* I sleep-did (I slept). Pluperf. *dōl entō·ba ma·mi-re* I already sleep-did. Fut. *dōl ma·mi-ngabo* I sleep-will. Imperative *dō ma·mi-ke* me sleep-let, *ma·mi* sleep!, *ō ma·mi-ke* him sleep-let, *ma·cho ma·mi-ke* us sleep-let. Optative *dōl ma·mi-nga kō·gak* I sleep-(verbal subs.) might. Continuative participle, *ma·mi-nga bē·dig* sleep-(verbal subs.) while = while sleeping.

PASSIVE. Inf. *kō·p-nga* scoop(ed)-to-be. Pres. *kā·rama dō·l-la kō·p-ngaba* bow me-by scooped-is-being. Imperf. *kā·rama dō·l-la achī·baiya kō·p-ngaba* bow me-by then scooped-was-being. Perf. *kā·rama dō·l-la kō·p-ngata* bow me-by scooped-has-been. Pluperf. *kā·rama dō·l-la entō·ba kō·p-ngata* bow me-by already scooped-had-been. Fut. *kā·rama dō·l-la kō·p-nga* bow me-by scooped-will-be.

other, so that this is a mere matter of practice. There are also reflective verbs formed by pronouns.

The greatest peculiarity of the language is the treatment of the personal and possessive pronoun. All the pronouns are sexless, but the forms used for the so-called dative seem to vary with the group. The normal form is that for the third person, 'he, she, it,' for which I will use 'it' only for brevity, and 'they' for the plural. We have then sing. *òl* it (subject). *ia* of it, *en, ūl, at, ik, eb* to it, in different forms, *en* it (object), and in it; pl. *òl·òichik* they, *ò·nta* of them, *et, ū·lat, at·at, ò·ntat, ò·llet, eb·et* to them, in different forms, *et* them, *ò·llet* in them. These relations may also be expressed by the postpositions answering to case. Then for the first person *d-* sing. and *m-* plur., and for the second *ng-* sing. and plur., are prefixed to these forms; as *òl* it, *dòl* I, *ngòl* thou, *mòl·òichik* we, *ngòl·òichik* you. There is also what Mr. Temple calls a "fourth person," obtained by prefixing *l* to those forms of the third person, which are not the subject of the sentence, and these give common postpositional forms, as *li·a* of a or the (or English possessive 's), *len* to or in a or the, and also the object of a verb, *lat*, *leb* to a or the.

These preliminary explanations will serve to make intelligible the following examples which have been furnished by Mr. Man, and will show the structure of the language better than a long series of grammatical explanations. Observe that in all these examples a hyphen at the end of a word means that the suffix *-da* (applied to all things) may be added, but that it is omitted in construction, and heard only in isolated words or at the end of a clause. The hyphens between parts of a word separate the prefix, the suffix, the postposition and the parts of which the word is compounded, and are used merely for the purpose of assisting the unaccustomed reader, generally they should all be written together in one word without hyphens, just as in German *ereifern* and not *er-eifer-n*, though the latter shews the approximate composition.

Prefixes Illustrated.

Cited as No. 1, 2, etc.

No. 1. *bē·ri-nga-* good (animate but non-human, or inanimate).

No. 2. *jā·bag-* bad (ditto).

No. 3. *ā-bē·ri-nga-* good (human).

No. 4. *ab-jā·bag-* bad (ditto).

No. 5. *ad-bē·ri-nga-* well, that is, not sick (animate).

No. 6. *ad-jā·bag-* ill, that is, not well (ditto).

No. 7. *ōn-bē·ri-nga-* clever (that is, hand-good, *ōn* referring to *ōng* its, applied to *kō·ro-* hand, see Cl. 5, p. 59).

No. 8. *ōn-jā·bag-* stupid (that is, hand-bad, ditto).

No. 9. *ig-bē·ri-nga-* sharp-sighted (that is, eye-good, *ig* its, being applied to *dal-* eye, see Cl. 4, p. 58).

No. 10. *ig-jā·bag-* dull-sighted (that is, eye-bad, ditto).

No. 11. *ā·kā-bē·ri-nga-* nice-tasted (that is, mouth-good, *ā·kā* its, applied to *bang-* mouth, *ā·ka-ga-* palate, see Cl. 3, p. 58).

No. 12. *ōn-tig-bē·ri-nga-* good "all round" (that is, *ōn* hand and *ig* eye, good, *t* being euphonic).

No. 13. *ōn-tig-jā·bag-* a "duffer" (that is, hand and eye bad).

No. 14. *ōt-bē·ri-nga-* virtuous (that is, head and heart good, *ōt* its, applied to *chā·ta-* head and *kūg-* heart, see Cl. 6, p. 59).

No. 15. *ōt-jā·bag-* vice, evil, vicious (that is, head and heart bad).

No. 1–15. Example: *ā·rlām Jū·ra ab-jā·bag l'edā·re, dōna ā·chitik ā-bē·ri-nga* (or *ā-bē·ri-nga-ke*). Free translation: Dū·ra was formerly a bad man, but now he is a good man. [Analytical translation: *ā·rlām* formerly, *Jū·ra* name of man, *ab-jā·bag* (human)-bad, *l'edā·re* exist-did, *dō·na* but, *ā·chitik* now, *ā-bē·ri-nga-* (human)-good [or *ā-bē·ri-nga-ke* (human)-good-is]. The 'is' generally unexpressed, in *l'edā·re* the *l'* is the common euphonic prefix, *edā·* v. exist, *-re* past time; which may be expressed as 'exist-did,' the verb being always put in the infinitive (properly unlimited, undefined) form, and the suffix *-re* being expressed by 'did,' as *-ke* may be by 'does,' etc., as the simplest way of expressing present and past time, see the conjugation of the verb in note 2, p. 55; the simple copula is never expressed, but in the second form *ābē·ringa* is treated as a verb, and *ke* being added makes it present, so that there is an apparent expression of the copula. Mr. Man believes the termination *-ke* as applied to anything which exists, to be derived from the partially obsolete v. *edā·* exist.

No. 16. *ōn-lā·ma-* one who misses striking an object with *hand* or *foot*, see Nos. 7 and 8 above.

No. 17. *ig-lā·ma-* one who fails to *see* or *find* an object such as honey, a lost article, etc., see Nos. 9 and 10 above.

No. 18. *ōt-lā·ma-* one who is wanting in *head*, that is, *sense*, see Nos. 14 and 15 above.

No. 19. *ab-lā·ma-* one who is a "duffer" at getting turtles after they are speared, that is, by diving and seizing them, where *ab* his, refers to *chā·u* body, see Cl. 1, below.

No. 20. *ā·ko-lā·ma-* applied to a weapon which fails to penetrate the object struck through the fault of the striker.

No. 21. *ā·kā-lā·ma-* who uses a wrong word to express his meaning (*ā·kā* its, being applied to *bang* mouth, and *tig·ik* voice, see Cl. 3, p. 58).

This will suffice to show the curious action of the South Andaman prefixes, which it will be seen presently refer especially to the different forms of the possessive pronoun when applied to different parts of the human body. The following table was drawn up by Mr. Man, and has only been slightly rearranged.

The forms of possessive pronouns are arranged according to the alphabetic order of the word signifying *his*, *her*, or *its*, singular and plural, from which the forms for the first, second, and so-called fourth person, can be deduced by prefixing *d*, *ng*, *l'* for the singular *my*, *thy*, —'*s*, and *m*, *ng*, *l'* for the plural *our*, *your*, —*s'*.

The Seven Forms of the Possessive Pronouns in relation to Parts of the Human Body.

(*Cited as Cl.* 1, 2, *etc.*)

Class 1. Sing. *ab*, pl. *at*.

chāū- body, *gū·dur-* or *lūm-* back, *gōrob-* spine, *pai·chā-* thigh, leg, *chū·lia-* skin, *chū·lia-dama·a-* skin (fleshy part), calf, *pū·ke-* groin, *kō·pa-* elbow, *kō·pa-dama·a-* fore arm-(fleshy part), *kū·rugi-dama·a-* upper arm-(fleshy part), *lō-* knee, *ā·pila-* hollow of knee, *pū·rola-* rib, *ō·r-* navel, *ā·pa-chāu-* belly, abdominal walls, *ū·pla-* stomach proper, *gū·dā-* entrails, bowels, *[illegible]-* liver, *[illegible]-* spleen, *[illegible]-* gall-bladder, *[illegible]-* womb, *[illegible]-* [illegible] fat and omentum, *[illegible]-* armpit, *pā·dik-ma-* shoulder-blade, *[illegible]-* tendon of Achilles.

Class 2. Sing. *ar*, pl. *ar·at*.

chāg- leg, *chā·rag-* hip, *ī·ta-* loin, *gūd-win-* os coccygis, *mū·ga-* rectum, *tū·mur-* anus, *ū·la-* urine, *ū·la-lī·a-ō·r-* bladder (urine-of-abode), *kōt·nan-* mesentery, *mat·rit-* large intestine, *ā·ta-* testicle, *tā-*, *ō·na-*, or *dama·a-* buttocks. Example: *meta* (or *mol·ichik*) *jār·awa l'ar·at chā·glen ab·lū·re*, we saw the legs of the *jār·awa*. [*met·a* we, a contracted form frequently used instead of the regular *mol·ichik*. *jār·awa* the South Andaman name for a tribe inhabiting Little Andaman, and having settlements in South Andaman, where they are much feared by the natives. *l'ar·at* (*l* euphonic) their, agreeing with *chāg* legs, which is made plural by the preceding plural form *l'ar·at*. *len* marks the object on to which the action passes. *ab-lū·re* (human)-see-did, the 'human' *ab* 'agrees' with the 'human' subject 'we.']

Class 3. Sing. *ā·ka*, pl. *ak·at*.

bang- mouth, *dē·li-ga-* palate, *ā·dal-* chin, *pai-* lip, *pai·-la-pī·ā-* moustache, that is, lip-(*la* euphonic)-hair, *ē·tal-* tongue, *dē·ta-* gullet, *ō·rou-* throat, *ō·rou-bā* wind-pipe, i.e. throat-small, *tal·ime-* uvula, *ē·kib-* jaw-bone, *ē·kib-pī·ā-* beard, that is, jaw-bone-hair, *pē·ā-la-* collar-bone, *chā·ga-* side, *tū·bal-* saliva, *chai·ad-* breath.

Class 4. Sing. *ig*, pl. *it·ig*, contracted to *i*, *it·i* with the words marked *.

**dal-* **dāl-* eye, **dal·-ar-pī·ā-* and **dāl·-ar-pī·ā-* eyelash, that is, eye-its-hair, **dal·-it-ē·ā-* or **dāl·-it-ē·ā-* eyelid, that is, eye-its- (*i.e.* belonging to the head)-skin, *pū·ngur-* eyebrow, *dū·ri-ga-* gum, *mū·ga-* face, forehead, *pū·kū-* ear, *chū·ro-nga-* nose, *ād-* cheek, *ā·ō-pī·ā-* whiskers, that is, cheek-hair, *tī·mar-* temple (of head), *tūg-* tooth, *tō·go-* shoulder, *gūd-* arm, *kū·rugi-* upper arm, *kō·pa-* forearm, *gū·ru-* biceps of upper arm, *kām-* breast, *kām l'it chī·ta-* nipple of the breast, that is, breast-its-head, see *it*, Class 6, *ē·k-* tear (of the eye).

Class 5. Sing. *ông*, pl. *ôt·ot*.

kô·ro- hand or finger, *el·ma-* palm of the hand and sole of the foot, *kô·ro-mū·gu-chil-* middle finger, that is, hand-(third of five), [the fourth of five is *mūrgurkal tārū·le*; the first is *ū·tolū·-* and the second (general) *ārū·le-*, but (animate) *ā·rtonlu·-*; the last but one *ū·tol·r-tārū·le-*; and the last *tārū·le*; there are only two cardinal numbers *ū·ba-tū·l-* one, and *ī·kpō·r-* two, beyond that they can in general only tap their nose with their fingers, commencing with the little finger, or say *ārdū·ru-* several, 10 to 20, *jeg·rhāu-* (human) many, say 50, *jī·baba-* very many, *ū·baba-* (non-human) but *ak-ū·baba* (lower animals) and *ota·baba-* (human) countless, a few of the most intelligent natives, however, occasionally use words for numbers up to 7, though different speakers differ as to their precise meaning.] *i·ti-pī·l-* little finger, *kô·ro-dō·ga-* thumb, that is, finger-big, *tô·ga-* wrist, *kū·tur-* knuckle, *bō·do-* nail of finger or toe (in this sense the *ō* of *bō·do* is immoderately lengthened, to distinguish it from *bō·do* sun, in which the *ō* is rather of medial length than long, hence we may distinguish *bō·do-*, nail, and *bō·do-* sun), *pag-* foot, *rō·kama-* toe, *tū·chab-* great toe, *t·kon-* small toe, *gū·chal-* heel, *tār-* ankle, *chāg-* kidney, *tā·pa-* peritoneum, *tā·ba-nga-* small intestine. Example: *dông kô·ro ngô·ngtek kā·tin-*, my hand is smaller than thine. [*dông* my, *kô·ro* hand, *ngô·ng-tek* thy-from (that is, thy hand-from = than thy hand, corresponding precisely to the ablative case after comparative in Latin), *kā·tin-* small in size (not in quantity, for which *kī* or *dō·paba* not much, is used). No mark of second degree of comparison is added, as that is implied by *tek*.]

Class 6. Sing. *ôt*, pl. *ô·tot*.

chô·ta- head, [illegible] the bosom, the heart, *kū·kta-bana-* the heart itself. Example: *mō·da l'ôt chô·ta kō·dia-* Moda's head is large. [*mō·da* a man's name, *l'ôt* his, *chôta* head, *kō·diada* large.]

Class 7. Sing. and pl. *ô·to*.

kī·nab- waist, this is apparently the only part of the body for which this pronoun is used; it also means 'narrow,' see 43, p. 58.

From this determinate use of possessive pronouns arises the custom of omitting the name of the part of the body referred to after a possessive pronoun, where it is clear what it must be. This is especially the case when the word could refer to many parts of the human body, sufficiently distinguished by the form of the possessive pronoun, as *pid-* hair, *tô-* skin, *tā-* bone, *tī-* blood, *mū·ruk-* gore, *gū·mar-* sweat, *yī·linga-* vein, muscle, *wai·nya-* cuticle, *dī·kia-* pulse, *mūn-* pus. When any doubt is felt, the full phrase is used.

Examples.

(Cited as Om. 1, 2, etc.)

Omission 1. *ad·tot chô·ta pid-* the hair of our heads. [*ad·tot* our, see No. 6 above, and hence *chô·ta* heads must be taken as plural, *pid-* hair.] This is contracted into *ad·tot pid-*, as out of the Class 6 above, it is only the head to which *pid-* hair applies.

Omission 2. *ngek·ot pua tô-* the skin

of your lips [*ngok·at* your, plural in Class 3, *pai* lip must therefore be pluralised, *ód-* skin], might be contracted to *ngok·at ód-*, but this would be slightly ambiguous, as *á·dal-* chin belongs to this class.

OMISSION 3. *dig güd tá-* the bone of my arm [*dig* singular of Class 4, *güd* arm, *tá* bone], might be contracted, but not with much certainty, except the arm were stretched out, to *dig tá-*.

OMISSION 4. *ngar chág ti-* the blood of thy leg [*ngar* thy, in Class No. 2, *chág* leg, *ti* blood], might be contracted into *ngar ti-* with considerable risk of ambiguity, unless the leg had been previously referred to, or was otherwise indicated.

As it is neither possible nor desirable to expand this report into a treatise on the South Andaman language, I looked about for some genuine native utterances, not translations, which might illustrate the natural speech of the country. Fortunately, Mr. Man was able to furnish me with precisely what I wanted. When he was sent officially to the Nicobar Islands, he took with him several young native Andamanese,[1] and in order to [illegible] their connection with their friends, and especially with [illegible] *jam·bu* (as he was always called, though that was not his real name), Mr. Man wrote letters for them at their dictation. He had to treat them quite like children for whom one writes letters, suggesting subjects, asking what they would say if they saw *jam·bu*, and so on. It was laborious work, which, however, Mr. Man did not regret, as it often furnished him with new words or phrases. These letters were then sent to the British officer in charge of the Homes at Port Blair, who did not know the language, but, from an explanation furnished, read the phonetic writing to *jam·bu*, sufficiently well to be understood, but to assist this officer Mr. Man furnished a free and an interlinear translation. I give two of these letters, which certainly, if any exist, are genuine specimens of South

[1] Their names and nicknames (in parenthesis) were *.i·ra* (*.kó·ro-* hand), *.bi·ela* (*.i·dal-* eye, as he had large saucer eyes), *.ló·ra* (Henry, his name when at the Ross orphanage), *.wó·i* (Tom, the name Mr. Man gave him when he first came to Viper Island), *.i·ra* (*.jó·dó-* entrails, so called from his protuberant belly when a child). These names may be preserved as those of the unwitting originators of Andaman literature. One other name of a native should be added, although he was not taken with Mr. Man to the Nicobars, on account of illness, and indeed he died shortly after Mr. Man left. This was *.bi·a* (*.pá·g-* foot, so called from his large feet). He was the elder brother of the above-named *.ló·ra* (Henry). All the time that Mr. Man was in charge of the Andaman Homes, about four years, *.bi·a* worked with him. He was the most intelligent and helpful native Mr. Man met, and was his principal informant throughout. Mr. Man often told him that he would bring his name to notice, and thus redeems his promise.

Andaman literature, but to make them as instructive as possible in showing the nature of the language, I divide them into numbered sentences, putting the text first, the free translation next, and afterwards, in square brackets, an analytically literal translation in the order of the original, in which, with the help of Mr. Man's translation, vocabulary and personal assistance, I endeavour to shew or explain the meaning and composition of each word and its parts, and its grammatical connection, occasionally adding other notes.

First Letter to *jam·bu*.

Cited by the simple numbers of the sentences.

1. *.maia ,jam·bu.* Worshipful *jam·bu* [*maia* is a term of respect by which chiefs or head men are addressed, perhaps 'honourable' or 'your honour' would be a nearer translation. *jam·bu* was only a nickname, but as he was always so called, Mr. Man cannot recollect any other. See his song below, p. 70].

2. *Med' ardū·ru adbī·ringa.* We are all in good health. [*med'* we, a contraction for *med·a*, the final *-a* being lost before the following *a* of *ardū·ru* all. The full form for 'we' is *mōl'ōichik.* For *ad-bī·ri-nga* well, see No. 5.]

3. *bī·ma-chā·lana tārā·lo tek mij·i at yed yā·ba.* Since last steamer no one has been ill. [*bī·ma* funnel, *chā·lana* ship, not one of their own boats; the Andamanese prefer if possible making a new word to adopting a foreign one, the present compound is more original than the modern Greek ἀτμόπλοιον, which is a mere translation of 'steam vessel.' *tārā·lo* last, see Cl. 5 under *bī·ra-mū·gu-chāl.* *tek* from, since, postp. *mij·i at* a contracted form of *mij·a at*, properly a plural possessive interrogative, 'whose?' but used idiomatically in negative sentences, for an indefinite personal pronoun, corresponding to English 'any.' *yed* sick or ill. *yā·ba-* not, always placed at end of a sentence.]

4. *.mar ,lō·ra ā·chitik igbā·dignga-len āā·kar-bō·dia mai·kan.* Master *.lō·ra* is now like a tub in appearance (so fat is he). [*.mar* applied to a young unmarried man, or a man who remains childless for the first 4 or 5 years after marriage, after which time, he is called *mai·a*, the ordinary name for a married man who has children, of which the honorific form *mai·ola* is applied to chiefs only. *.lō·ra* (Henry) the name of the youth. *ā·chitik* now, *ārla·baiya* then. *ig-bā·dig-nga-len* appearance-in, see Nos. 9 and 10. (This is one of the verbs which change the final letter of the base according to the suffix, but the law of change is not yet fully ascertained. In this case *g* is apparently inserted before *-re* and *-nga*, but on the other hand it may be simply omitted before *-ke*). *āā·kar* a tub or bucket. *bō·dia* big. *āā·kar-bō·dia*, big as a tub. (There are five words for big, 1. *bō·dia-* which when 'human' becomes *ābō·dia-*, but here has no prefix on account of being in composition, 2. *dō·gu-*, 3. *chā·nag-*, and 4. *tā·ba-nga-*, which are 'humanised' by *ab*, 5. *rī·ghoda-* 'humanised' by *a*. Without the prefixes *bō·dia-*, *dō·gu-*, and *chā·nag-* are applied to any non-human objects, and *rī·ghoda-*, *tā·banga-*, to animals only.) *mai·kan* like.]

5. *Ngā·ba ō·lien ed·a dud·darya yā·ba.* He as yet has had no fever. [*ngā·ba* as yet, *ngā* simply meaning 'then.' *ō·len* him-to, the 3rd pers. pron. with postpos., *len* to. *ed·a* ever. *dud·darya* fever, that is, ague, trembling. *yā·ba* not, see 3.]

6. *.mar .ar·i ār-arlā-tan-jnga tā·ga-ya.* Master *.ar·i* is a great flying-fox shot. [*.mar* see 4. *.ar·i* the name of

a youth (about 16 years old), of the tribe that the South Andamanese call *.Abo-jūr·wai-da*, who came in a canoe from Middle Andaman to Port Blair, where he made an important statement concerning the manners and customs of his tribe, which was reduced to writing by Mr. Man, and is published, chiefly in English, in the Journal of the Anthropological Institute, vol. xi. pp. 390–2. When he arrived at Port Blair, his language was unintelligible to the natives there, but he quickly learned their language, and as he was a very nice fellow, he was induced to remain by marrying him to a pretty girl (second in 20), who was still very young. As they had at that time no family, he was still called [illegible] or *ark* in combination, [illegible] shoot with an arrow. [illegible] verbal subst. The whole word is, therefore, skilled shooter of flying foxes. *tā·paga* excellent (human only), marks superlative degree.]

7. *ar·at dal·a dī·laga ā·kārd·ranga bā·dig, il yī·lō būd lāng-pal·len wōt lab ā·rbī-dangka.* While the others are finishing their evening meal with dainty morsels, he goes alone and searches among the trees for flying foxes near the hut. [*ar·at* their, see Cl. 2. *dal·a* rest or remainder. *dī·la-ga* evening-at. *ā·ka* referring to palate, see No. 11. *rā·r-nga* tasty things, which conclude a meal, from *rār*, v. taste, determine flavour of. *bā·dig* while or during, as a postposition to the whole preceding clause, so that it means: the rest of-them in-the evening tasty - bits - finishing while. *il* 3rd pers., hence 'he' in this case. *yī·lō* alone, unaccompanied. *būd-* an occupied hut, *ār-* an unoccupied hut. (*ad·rūbā-* hut belonging to a married couple; *bōkī·ga-* bachelor's hut; *chāng-* hut, or roof, for the huts are almost all roof, *chāng-tā·pinga-* best kind of hut, with well plaited roof, to last 2 or 3 years; *chāng-tā·rnga-* next best hut, formed of leaves bound together with cane, lasting a few weeks or months; *chāng-dar·enga-* a temporary shed, roof of loose leaves, to last a few days. The species of palm leaf ordinarily used for these roofs is called *chāng·ta-*). *lāng-pal·len* near an inanimate object. (Other terms are *ā·kā-pal·len* or *ōt-pai·cha-len* near to an animate object; *ab-ā·r-tog-lia* near a tree or post; *paga·len* near as one place to another, *ga* giving indefiniteness of object, compare *bā* and *yabā·* little.) *wōt* flying fox. *lab* for, postp. *ār-bō·dang-ke* search in-tree-does, (*ā·rem* jungle), *ā·ta* v. search on the ground for an inanimate object, *ab-ā·ta-* v. for an animate object.]

8. *en tā·nga bā·dig il lā·baki·ke yā·bada.* On seeing one he does not miss it. [*en* it. *tā·-nga* see (verbal subst.)=seeing. *bā·dig* while, consequent on, see 7. *il* he, *lā·bakit·-ke* (euphonic *l*, Cl. 3), miss-does. *yā·bada* not, see 5, where final *da* is not added to *yā·ba*.]

9. *kā·rin chā·wai rō·chobada.* There are enormous clams here. [*kā·rin* here. *chā·wai* clam, the plural is not inflected. *rō·chobada* big, applied to [illegible], see *bō·dia* in 4. This shell-fish [illegible] is the *Tridacna* [illegible] 3 or 4 feet in length [illegible] only the small [illegible] and *T. squamosa*.]

10. *ū·bada·galen yāt ate·abada dā·rumada.* There is sufficient food in one for a great number of persons. [*ū·ba-dō·ga-* one, *ū·ba-tū·l-* is also used, but *ū·ba-dō·ga-* is the emphatic form like our 'a single one,' see Cl. 5, under *mā·ya-chāl-*. *len* in, postp. *yāt* in construction, *yāt-* final, food. *at-ū·baba* countless numbers, see Cl. 6. *lab* for, postp. *dā·rumada* sufficient.]

11. *ngō·da ngōl mat attad·inga lā·ake, .pā·dri chāb .rūch-ya pōl·i yā·te bā·dien lī·rnga bā·dig, ā·kā-ta igbā·di-da.* If you don't believe us, go to the Padre sāhib's house at Ross, and see the shell (we are sending). [*ngō·da* if, *ngōl* you, *mat* us, obj. pl. *at-tad·i-nga* (human)-lie-telling-(verbal subst.). *at* is plural *ab*. *lā·a-ke* consider-do (present time), *lā* v. look or see. *.pā·dri* Italian padre, father, but applied as "Rev." to all clergymen, here the chaplain was meant. *chāb* Andamanese attempt at pronouncing the Hindī *sā·hib*. *.rūch* Andamanese attempt to say *Rūs*, the Hindī corruption of Ross, an island at the entrance of the inlet of Port Blair. *-ya* at, postp. *pōl·i* dwell. *yā·te* that, the relative. *būd* hut, see 7, but here meant for house. *len* postp. to. *lī·r-nga* go, verbal subst. *bā·dig* while, or consequent upon, see 7. The phrase means: upon going to the house of the chaplain

who dwells at Rome. *â·bi* see No. 11, in relation to taste or mouth, *tâ* bone, that is, taken together, *â·kâtâ* bone covering food *i.e.* shell. *ig-bâ·dá-bo* see-will, see 4, pres. for fut.]

12. *ngôl ö·len igbâ·di yâ·te wai·ken ngab-pat·inga bûch·âken-wai·ken tôr-rô·bo; bâ·i ö·cha â·kâtâ·da!* On seeing it we are sure you will slap your side and exclaim: what a whopping big shell! [*ngôl* you. *ö·len* it, obj. *igbâ·di* see, see 4. *yâ·te* who, see 11; that is, you who-see it. *wai·ken* certainly. *ngab* your, see Cl. I and Obs. 4 for the omission of *châu-* body, or some such word. *pat·i-nga* slap (verbal subs.) = slapping. *bûch·âken* and *wai·ken* both mean 'like' and together, 'just like.' *tôrrô·-bo* say-will. *bâ·i* exclamation of surprise. *ö·cha* this. *â·kâtâ* shell, see 11.]

13. *mei· ârdû·ru ,pâ·lo-pilâw· él-â·r-jana bûd lâ·yaba yâ·te len â·kongai·ra.* We all went to *,pâ·lo-,pilâw·*, which is a village a long way off to the north. [*mei·* *ârdû·ru* we all, see 3. *,pâ·lo-pilâw·* name of a place in the [illegible] Islands. [illegible] (appearing face) [illegible] [in these words *el* stands for *ér-* country), *târ-mû·gu-* (disappearing face) west. *bûd* hut, village. *lâ·yaba* distant. *yâ·te* which. *len* to, postp., affecting the whole phrase, which means: to P. P. which is a distant village to the north. *â·kon-gai·* go a short journey by water, *â·to-jâ·mo* is used for a long journey. *-re* past time.]

14. *kâ·to â·rla jî·baba pâi·ire.* We stayed several days there. [*kâ·to* there. *â·rla* days, plural indicated by the following word. *jî·baba* several, very many, see Cl. 5. *pâi·i-re* dwell-did, see 11.]

15. *chorkâ·r lab rô·go jad·ijô·g ârdû·ru lpai·re dî·ru mê-to-kûklî·re yâ·bada.* We bargained for a lot of young female pigs for Government, but did not forget ourselves. [*chorkâ·r* Andamanese attempt to pronounce the Hindi *sarkâr* government. *lab* for, postp. *rô·go* pigs, plural indicated by the following *ârdû·ru*, *rô·go-* is a female pig, *reg-* either male or female. *jad·i-jô·g* spinster, implying a full-grown sow-pig which has not littered, see the mode of expressing sex mentioned on p. 58. *ârdû·ru* several (see Cl. 5) or all, as in 3. *lpai·-re* barter did. *dî·ru* but. *mê·to* ourselves. *kûklî·re* forget-did. *â-to-kûklî·-ke* oneself forget-does (*mê·to* is only the form of the first person plural, see p. 58), was one of the new words discovered by Mr. Man from the dictation of these letters to *,jam·bu*. The common verb for forgetting is *ôt-kûklî·ke*, which is reflective, as *dâ d' ôt-kûklî·re*, I forgot, where *dâ d'* or *dôl d'* answers to French *je me* (in *je m'en souviens*) and similarly *ngô ng'* or *ngôl ng' ôt-kûklî·re* you forgot. The relation of *â·to-k.* and *ôt-k.* is similar to that in *ö·râ·jke* defend-does, *â·torâ·jke* oneself defend does. 'Selves' is also expressed by *ö·kan* See examples in 40. *yâ·bada* not, see 7.]

16. *kianchâ· reg-ârdû·ru gôi jî·baba mê·yuet-tê·mar lab â·nare.* We accordingly fetched several prime young male pigs for our own use. [*kianchâ·* therefore. *reg* pigs, either male or female, see 15. *ârdû·ru* bachelor, young but full grown, see p. 53. *gôi* fresh, and hence in good condition. *jî·baba* several, properly 'very many,' see Cl. 5, but as there were really only five or six, Mr. Man translated the word 'several' at the time; he supposed that the young man wished to surprise their friends at Viper by leading them to suppose by this term that they had got many more pigs than was actually the case. *mê·yuet-tê·mar* ourselves, the meaning of the separate words is not known, but we have *dô·yuru-t.* myself, *ngô·yuru-t.* thyself and *ö·yuru-t.* himself, *ö·yuet t.* themselves, *ngô·yuet-t.* yourselves. *lab* for, postp. *â·nare* fetch-did.]

17. *mei·a â·ya·bâ maiâ·nga-bo yâ·te len chî·igâke.* Those we have not eaten yet we are fattening. [*mei·a* we. *â·ya·bâ* as yet, see 6. *maiâ·-nga* eat- (passive participle, p. 55, n. 2) = eaten. *bo* not. *yâ·te* which. *len* postp. pointing out object, meaning: we are fattening those which have not been eaten as yet. The construction, though common, is somewhat involved, and would be, in English order, as boys "construe" Latin: *mei·a* we, *chî·igâke* are fattening, *len* (mark of accusative relation), *yâ·te* (those) which, *â·ya·bâ* as yet, *maiâ·nga-bo* (are or have been) eaten-not.

18. *â·kâlî·dongalen mei·a â·kâ-jai·lgale tôrô·bolen ûchi·ba rô·go lô·inga lô·dig ,dui·pur len mirik-î·kâr.* Them we will slaughter one by one, and

afterwards get some more pigs to take with us to Viper. [*á·kà-tō·do-nga* one by one, idiomatic expression, origin unknown. *len* postp. marks the object. *mol·a* we. *á·kà-jai·ñg-ke* slaughter-do, this expression is used for pigs only. *tārā·lo-len* last-to, afterwards, see Cl. 5. *ōt-ñd·la* other in addition to the former, see Cl. 6 for *ōt*, this prefix also occurs in *ōt-poig·i* once more. *rō·go* pig, see 15. *bī·i-nga* get-(verbal subs.) = getting. *bō·dig* while, or consequent upon; meaning: afterwards on getting additional pigs. *.bai·per* Andamanese mispronunciation of Viper, an island within the inlet of Port Blair. *lat* to, postp. *mal·ik* in company with us, *m-*[illegible], [illegible] in company with, [illegible] take away-will, see [illegible].]

19. [illegible] *pij len jā·bag lā·la-tim·re*, [illegible] [illegible] has tonsured Master [illegible] very badly. [*.mar* see 4. *.īra-jā·do* is the subject of the verb. *.wā·i lōt pij* is the object, as *.wā·i*'s hair. *lōt* his (head understood), see Cl. 6, and Om. 1. *pij* hair, the usual form of *pid* in construction, thus *ōt-pīj-yā·ba-* his (head)-hair-not = bald. *len* postp. obj. *jā·bag* badly. *tā·la-tim·-re* tonsure-did. This shaving of the crown of the head is the business of the women and especially of the wife, but in this case the women were left behind. The razors used are extremely fine chippings of glass.]

20. *mō·da .ī·ra-.bī·ela ab-ī·k-yā·te ā·chitik ig-bā·dike ñgā wai·kan āt-jī·r-nga-len igyod·ike ōt-bō·dig ab-tō·gake.* If .*wā·i's* wife *.ī·ra-.bī·ela* were now to see him, she would certainly box the barber's ears and abuse him. [*mō·da* if. *ab-ī·k* (female)-take away, *yā·te* who, that is, who is wife. For *ik* see end of 18, where, but for the *mit·ik*, there would have been the prefix *ab* in *abī·ke* take-away-does (present), an animate object. But *ōn·i* is to take, as *ab-lī·ga lā·ka-bang tek yaip en·ke* child its-mouth from pipe take-do = take the pipe from the child's mouth, *-ke* being also used for the imperative. Now in marrying, the chief who unites the couple *tō·t-yā·p-ke* their (persons, Cl. 6) -speak-does, the man *ad-en·i-ke* (animate, see No. 6) -take-does, the woman *ab-ī·k-ke* (human, No. 4) -take-away-does. The husband is spoken of as *ad-ī·k-yā·te-*, and the wife as *ab-ī·k-yā·te-*, as here. For the first few weeks the young couple are called *ing-tag-gō·i-* their-bed-of-leaves-fresh, and after that for the first year *ōn-jā·ti-gō·i-*, where *ōn* refers to the hands, No. 7, and *gō·i* is fresh, but *jā·ti* is not known. *ā·chitik* now, see 4. *ig-bā·di-ke* see-does, see 4, pres. time, though in English it becomes past subjunctive, after *mō·da* if. *ñgā* then, see 5. *wai·kan* certainly. *ōt-jī·r-nga* his (head understood, see Om. 1) -shave-(verbal subst.), that is, his head's shaver. *len* postp. marking object. *ig-yod·i-ke* face (see Nos. [illegible], 10 and 17, and Cl. 4), [illegible] slap (see 12) will, *ar-yod·i-ke* would be, 'leg (see Cl. 2) -slap-will,' as women do when delighted. *ōt-bō·dig* it-while or it-after, used for 'and.' [illegible] as well as,' *ab-tō·go-ke* (human [illegible]) [illegible]-will.]

21. [illegible] *bō·dig pij-gō·i* [illegible] Master .*wā·i* is [illegible] that he is losing [illegible] [*ōt-tek·ik-nga* for-his-head (Cl. 6), -ashamed-(verbal subst.), *tek·ik* be ashamed, but *t·ē·kik* weep. *bō·dig* consequent on, see 11. *pij-gō·i* hair-fresh. *len* postp. marking object. *en-ōt-jī·r-ke* cause-head-shave-does, *en* prefixed gives a causal signification to the verb = causes his head to be shaven. *yā·ba* not.]

22. *mol·a yāt bā ngōl itità·n yā·te len ō·rokre.* We duly obtained the few presents you sent. [*mol·a* we. *yāt* properly fish, food, see 10, here presents. *bā* few, little, a father or mother having one or more little ones is called *ā·bā·da*. *ngōl* you. *itità·n* send away any animate or inanimate thing, *entità·n* send away a human object, *entità* throw (v. refl.), *itā·n* permit. *yā·te* which. *len* postp. marking the whole phrase as an object. *ō·rok-re* obtain-did.]

23. *ngōt pai·chalen min ārdū·ru ōt-jey·nga l'edā·re ñgā itità·nga yā·bāken mol·a mā·tol-kūkjā·bagire.* As you have so much in the "go-down" (store), we were much disappointed at your not sending more. [*ngōt* your, Cl. 6. *pai·cha-len* lap-to, that is, in your possession. *min* thing, plural only indicated by following word. *ārdū·ru* several, see 15. *ōt-jey·-nga*, Cl. 6, collection of shell-fish, meat, jack-fruit seeds, iron, flint, or anything in a heap, but *ōt-pōy·-nga* is used for honey, fruit,

yams, fibre, and *ar-ngai-j-nga* for bows, arrows, and other implements or ornaments, and also animate objects. *l'edá-re* because of, i.e. because of your having many things collected in your possession. *ñgá* more (see 5), as well as 'thee' (see 6). *itità-nga* sending, see 22. *pŭ-ba-len* not-to, without. *med'a* we. *med-tot-kūk-jŭ-bag-i-re* our (poss. from Class 6) -heart-bad-was, we were disappointed, *i* seems to be a euphonic insertion to separate *g* and *r*.]

24. *tit'ik be-rmo-chă-lewa kē-gal pō-le ñgal min mat d-kāwă-rke.* Perhaps the incoming steamer is bringing more things for us. [*tit'ik* perhaps. *bō-rma-chă-lewa* steamer, see 3. *kē-gal* arriving, this and *yū-boli* are said of the arrival of a boat or ship only, or of going to an elevated spot. *pō-le* which. *ñgal* more, see 23. *min* thing, see 23. *mat* to us, one of the forms answering to the dative of pers. pron. *ó-kū*, see Cl. 3. *d-kā-wă-r* and *ōn-lār-tag-i* are said of conveying any animal or inanimate objects by boat only; [illegible] conveying either by land or [illegible] distinguished from present.]

25. *med'a tārtī-t idai-re ūā-a d-chitik ngōl beraij-bā-la lī-a dyar-barda.* We have learnt that you are now the head-"boss" at the Brigade Creek home. [*med'a* we. *tārtī-t* news. *idai-re* know-did. *ūā-a* that, conjunction. *d-chitik* now. *ngōl* you. *beraij* old-established encampment, whether occupied or not, otherwise *ēr-*, *ēr-drlu-a-* are unoccupied, and *bud-*, *bōd-larda-re* occupied encampments. *a-bō-le-* is a human orphan, omitting the prefix *beraij-bō-le-* is an orphan encampment, or one of which the old chief is dead and the new chief not yet appointed. This was the case with the Brigade Creek Andaman Home, which is also said here meant. *lī-a* of, postp. *dā-yā-bar-da* head (Cl. 6) -chief, from *yā-bar* govern.]

26. *kā-to ngōng jō-bo lā-kē-dig kā-rapta chā-pikok!* May no snakes or centipedes bite you there. [*kā-to* there. *ngōng* your, Cl. 4, one of the words in that class being understood. *jō-bo* snake, plural unindicated. *lā-kā-dig* and, see 22. *kā-rapta* centipedes, from *kā-rap* bite as a stinging insect. *chā-pi* bite in any way. *kok* would-that-they-may-not, *ab-ko* and *ngā-ke* are used as the imperative don't! *kā-to ōyu lō-r-kok* them permission go-I hope may not = I hope they won't let you go there; *ngō pā-kok* I hope you won't fall. As to the wish expressed see the farewell in 29.]

27. *dī-rapiek ñgá pā-kaga pū-ba.* There's nothing more to say at present. [*dī-rap* lately, *tek* from, postp., the whole meaning, 'at present.' *ñgá* more, see 23. *pā-k-aga* say, verbal subst. = saying. *pū-ba* not.]

28. *med'a drdā-ru len ġrimā-gu-ēn-nga itità-nke.* We send salaam to all. [*med'a* we. *drdā-ru* all. *len* to, postp. *ġ'i* a common prefix, implying apparently 'separation,' but its signification in compounds is lost, it is frequently omitted in this word. *mā-gu* face. *ēn-i-nga* take-(verbal subst.). The natives mean by the word to bend the head and touch the forehead, that is, to salaam, as they were taught to do by the Rev. Mr. Corbyn, the first person who had charge of them; it is a case, then, of a new word, which may be advantageously compared with the Greek *ἀποσκυνεῖν* to play the dog in; sometimes *shālā-m*, a mispronunciation of salaam, is used. *itità-n-ke* send-do, see 22.]

29. *kaw wai mā-ichik!* Good-bye! [*kaw* here. *wai* indeed. *mā-ichik* we, full form. The ceremony of taking leave by word of mouth is rather long. The host accompanies his visitor to the landing-place, or at least to a considerable distance. On parting, the visitor takes his host's hand and blows upon it; after the compliment is returned, the following dialogue ensues. DEPARTING VISITOR: *kaw wai dōl*, here indeed I. HOST: *ō ayu* (a contraction for *ō-ne* yes), *ō-chat wai* ... house indeed ..., *tōn ik-lik kach ... pā-ke?* when again hither come wilt? = very well, go, when will you come again? DEP. VIS.: *ngō-tek ... ngat ... ... thee-from (presently) I for-you thing take-away-will = I will bring away something for you one of these days. HOST: *jō-bo la ngōng chā-pikok!* snake (euphonic *la*) you bite-may not = I hope no snake will bite you, compare 26. DEP. VIS.: *wai do kagā-lapke*, indeed I on-the-head (*ōr*) -watchful-be-will. They then repeat the ceremony of blowing on each other's hands, and part shouting invitations and promises for a

future date until beyond sunshot. There are no Andaman words of greeting. Relatives on meeting throw their arms round each other and weep for joy. When any other persons meet, they simply stand looking at each other in silence for a long time, sometimes as much as half an hour, before one of them ventures to speak.]

Second Letter to *jam·bu.*

The sentences are numbered in continuation of the former.

30. *.mám .jam·bu.* Worshipful Jumbo [see 1].

31. *mad' ardü·ru adbi·ringa.* We are all in good health [see 2].

32. *tigal·kal mar'dü·ru tek o'gun .mar .lí·ra abyed·re yā·ba.* Up to the present Master *.líra* is the only one of us who has not been ill. [illegible] *mar'dü·ru* [illegible] *ardü·ru* one (Class 2) [illegible] of us. *tek* from, postp. *ō'gun* [illegible] *.mar .lí·ra* see 4. *ab-yed·-re* human (No. 4) -sick-was. *yā·ba* not.]

33. *ōl kichikaché· iloli·leire meda tádi·nga-ba, telek yát mākinga dō·ga l'edi·re.* We don't know how he has escaped (being ill), perhaps it is because he eats so much. [*ōl* he. *kichikaché·* how, in what manner. *ilo-lā·-lai-re* (Cl. 7) escape-did. *med'a* we. *tádi-nga-ba* know-(verbal subst.)-not = we are knowers not; *ba* at the end is a contraction for *yā·ba*, and never becomes *bā* (meaning 'small'), but is kept short and unaccented. *telek* perhaps, see 24. *yát* food, see 10. *mák·-nga* eat -(verbal subst.) = eating, see 17. *dō·ga* much. *l'edi·re* by reason of, 23.]

34. *mar-at dil·u abyed· yā·to ā·chitik ē·tolā wai·kan āpā·leda.* The rest of us who have been ill, are now in as good condition as before. [*mar-at* our, Cl. 2. *dil·u* remainder, see 7. *abyed·* (human, No. 4) -sick. *yā·to* who. *ā·chitik* now. *ē·tolā* first, see Cl. 6. *wai·kan* like. *āpā·la-da* (animate, No. 3) -fat-(thing generally). The natives grow rapidly thin when ill, hence to grow fat is to regain health.]

35. *ō·gar l'ōdikē·ire med'a kāt·chal len yā·bali·re.* Last month we visited Katchall Island. [*ō·gar* moon, *ō·gar-ō·rola-yabā·* -moon-baby-small, or new moon, *ab-ō·rola-* human baby, *ō·gar-ō·rola-* the moon two or three days old. *ō·gar-chā·nag-* moon-big, first quarter, *ō·gar-chāu-* moon-body, full moon, (so *bōdo-chāu-* sun-body, is noon, and *gū·rug-chāu-* night-body, is midnight), *ō·gar-kī·mak-* moon-thin, last quarter, *ka-ral·nga-nga-* waxing, *kir-ō·dori-nga* waning. *l'ō-* human, No. 3, with euphonic *l*, because apparently they regard the moon as a male, *.mai'a ō'gar,* Mr. Moon, and seem to look upon it as more like a man than any other inanimate object. The *sun* is regarded as female, and is hence called *.chān·a-* [illegible] Mrs Sun. So also in German [illegible] the moon is masculine [illegible] *yā·ba·re* [illegible] *gra·bali-* [illegible] *med'a* we. [illegible] one of the Nicobar group. *len* to or at, *yā·bali-re* disembark-did, see 24.]

36. *kā·to ā·rla ikpō·r len pā·linga bō·dig reg l'ardü·ru ēkā igal·re mā·rgi bē·dig.* During the few days we stayed there, we bartered for a lot of pigs and fowls. [*kā·to* there, see 30. *ā·rla* day, pl. indicated only by the following word. *ikpō·r* really two, but often used for a few, especially with *ā·rla*, see Cl. 5. *len* to or for, postp. *pā·li-nga* dwelling, see 11. *bō·dig* consequent on, see 11. *reg* pigs, male or female, see 15 and 16. *l'ardü·ru* several. *ēkā* for, postp. *igal·re* barter-did, see 15, the subject is *med'a* we, in preceding sentence. *mā·rgi* fowls, an adopted Hindustani word. *bē·dig* also, when placed last, see *bē·bē·dig* in 22.]

37. *kā·to ēpā·dura-lūngkā·lak bē·ringa-l'igā· ardü·ru ūnē·ada.* The people of that part are the best of all, they are all liberal. [*kā·to* there, *ig-* Nos. 9, 10, 17. *bē·dura* dweller in a hut or village, fellow-countryman, see 7. *lūng-kā·lak* sign of plural, used because there is nothing else in the sentence to indicate plurality. *bē·ringa* good. *l'igā·* (*l'* euphonic) used alone means 'distinct,' but when joined to a word of quality it shews the highest degree, superlative, most good, best, *mai'a igā·-* head chief. *ardü·ru* all. *ūn-ē·d·a-da* (Nos. 7, 8, 12, 13, 16) liberal.]

38. *.mar .wō·i, .ī·ra-jū·do bē·dig kō·to rag yā·ta igbā·digaga bē·dig mūr·gam len pōi·chatuga l'edā·re rag-gū·mul lō·re.* While there, Master .wō·i and .īra jū·do, seeing the fat pigs for which their stomachs craved, broke their pig-feast. [*bē·dig* also, see 36. *rag yā·ta* pig fat, that is, fat pig, not pig's fat, see 34. *ig-bā·dig-nga* seeing-(verbal subst.), see 11. *bē·dig* consequent on. *mūr·gam* inside or belly, *ikmūr·gam* beneath. *len* to, postp. *pōi·chat-nga* fond of (any kind of food) -(verbal subst.). *l'edā·re* because of (see 23), *i.e.* feeling fond of food to their inside. *rag-gū·mul* pig-ceremony. We have no corresponding word to *gū·mul*, it belongs to the peculiar institutions of the Andamanese. Mr. Man says: "Although .wō·i had been recently induced to marry, he was only a youth of about 16, and had not yet gone through the ceremony of 'young man making' known as *gū·mul lō·ke* (*gū·mul* devour-done), when the young neophyte who has for some time past evinced his powers of self-denial, and thereby, in a measure, his fitness to enter upon the cares and trials of married life, is enabled after a course of three ceremonies (known as *yā·di-gū·mul-* turtle ceremony, *ā·ja-gū·mul-* honey ceremony, and *rag-yī·ri-* or simply, as here, *rag-gū·mul-* pig's kidney-fat or simply pig ceremony), which take place at intervals with a degree of external ceremony, to resume the use of these favourite articles of food. *lō·re* devour-did. These ceremonies apply to the young of both sexes before reaching puberty. After this period the individual is said to be *bō·tiga-*, which implies that he or she may indulge in any kind of food at pleasure. During the period (lasting sometimes 2 or 3 years) of their abstention they are called [illegible] *ā·kā-yū·ba-* and the [illegible] is termed *ā·kal-yā·ba-*".]

39. *[illegible] [illegible] yā·bada.* They have suffered no ill consequences thereby. [*[illegible]* last—to, that is, afterwards, see 15. *at-yed·re*, *at* is the plural form of the human prefix *ab* (see 11), *yed* be sick, *re* past time, that is, men were sick. *yā·ba-da* not. They fancy that to break the *gū·mul* (see 38) will entail serious consequences, the fact being that they then generally gorge themselves with these rich articles of diet, and hence make themselves ill.]

40. *mer·a ā·chikik ī·kan lab rē·ga ikpō·r mō·to-pōi·chalen chī·ljnke.* We are rearing a few pigs for ourselves. [*mer·a* we. *ā·chikik* now. *ī·kan* selves. *lab* for. *rē·ga* pig. *ikpō·r* two, that is, a few; as two is the largest number for which they have a name, they use it indefinitely, see 36. *mō·to* our own, *pōi·cha* lap, *len* to, that is, 'in our midst.' *dō·to* s. *mō·to* pl. *ngō·to* and *ō·to* s. and pl. are the reflective forms of *dōl* s. *mō·tol* pl., *ngōl* and *ōl*, etc., as *ōl dōl jō·rke* he my-hand share-does, but *dōl dō·to jō·rke* I my-own-hand share-do. *chī·lyu-ke* fattening-are, see 17.]

41. *ta·rolī·ka mar·dū·ru ōtpāg·i kāt·cha len yā·ngare.* The day before yesterday we all went again to Katchall. [*tār* probably 'beyond.' *dī·lea* yesterday. *mar·dū·ru* we all, see 32. *ōt-pāg·i* again, *ig-pag·i* is also used, see *ōt*, *ig*, in Nos. 14, 16, and 9, 10. *pāg·i* repeat. *kāt·cha* Katchall. *len* to, postp. *yā·ngo-re* go-did, used for going to a particular place, otherwise *for* is used.]

42. *kā·to ō·gun ā·rla ā·bartī·l bar·nāre*, (but) spent only one day there. [*kā·to* there. *ō·gun* only. *ā·rla* day. *ā·ba-tū·l* one, see Cl. 4, and also 10 and 43. *bar·nā-re* spend-did, passing the night there, as on a visit.]

43. *mī·kan lab rē·ga ā·ba-dī·ga mō·ryi jī·baba bē·dig ā·tāre.* We fetched a pig and very many fowls for our own consumption. [*mī·kan* ourselves, see *ī·kan* in 40. *lab* for, postp. *rē·ga* pig. *ā·ba-dī·ga* one, or rather only one, an emphatic form of *ā·ba-tū·l*, see 10. *mō·ryi* fowl, see 36. *jī·baba* very many. *bē·dig* also. *ā·tā-re* fetch-did, see 16, *ū·ya-re* bring-did.]

44. *jō·ruten yā·di chū·ag drū·ru bē·dig igbā·digre, dī·ma dā·rre yā·bada.* On the way we saw several turtles and porpoises, but speared none. [*jō·ru* sea. *len* to or in, postp. *yā·di* turtle. *chā·ag* porpoise, both rendered plural by the following word. *drū·ru* several. *bē·dig* also. *ig-bā·dig-re* see-did. *dī·ma* but. *dā·rre* spear-did. *yā·bada* not. The usual way to catch turtles is to harpoon them with a spear called *kowai·a lā·ka dū·t-nga-*, consisting of the *ēlā-*, or a long bamboo haft, at one end of which a socket is provided for the *kowai·a-*, which is a short pointed and notched iron harpoon; these are connected by a long line,

bi·tmo-. The thick end of the *tög-* is called *ar-bi·rud-*, and the socket end *â·kâ-châng·-*.]

45. *mol·a di·lia ê·rem-len wai·i l'â-ka-tâng ol·lia-yô·iga igbâ·digre; kian-chal- â·chitik bô·rin tö·ng pâ·ke.* Yesterday for the first time we saw a wai·i tree in the jungle; we can therefore make torches here. [*mol·a* we. *di·lia* yesterday. *ê·rem* jungle. *len* in, postp. *wai·i* name of a kind of *Sterculia* tree. *l'â·kâ-tâng*, *l'* euphonic, *â·kâ* No. 11, *tâng* topmost part, this is any kind of tree, a fruit tree is *â·kâ-tâ·la-*, which may be from the same root. *ol·lia-yô·iga*, possibly a contraction of *ol-a-li-a-yô·iga* ever-afresh, quite the first. *igbâ·dig-re* see-did. *kian-chal-* therefore. *â·chitik* now, *bê·rin* here. *tö·ng* torch, consisting of the resin of the *wai·i* tree wrapped in leaves, and principally used when fishing and turtling at night, full name *tö·ng-pâ·t-nga-*. *pâ* make, only said of this torch. *ke* future time. The word for 'making' varies with different things made, thus, *wâl·igma-châp* make an oar, *bûdû·i* make a house or hut, *kôp* make a canoe, bow, etc., *tê·pi* make anything with cane, bamboo, etc., as in thatching, weaving, said also of a bee constructing its comb, *tâm·i* make a pail, *tât* make a cooking-pot, *mâr* make waistbelts, wristlets, or garters with pandanus leaves and string, *tâ·i* make arrow heads by hammering out pieces of iron, see 46, *ma·a* make string by twisting the strands with the fingers.]

46. *.mauji·la ê·rlâm â·rlaba chit·i yi·tike, ta·bâtal mol·a ê·la dâ·gagu tâ·ike.* The former .mauji·la is always writing, meanwhile we are making lots of pig-arrows. [*.mau-ji·la* Home-chief, a word coined since the Andaman 'Homes' were established, and used in addressing the officer placed in charge of them. The first syllable appears to be a form of *mâm* (see 1), and the whole word is an abbreviation for *mâm-mai·ola* worshipful chief, of which some persons suppose it was first an English corruption, afterwards adopted by the natives. In this letter Mr. Man himself is referred to, as he seemed to be in charge of the 'Homes' when he was transferred to the Nicobars. *â·rlâm* old, applied to animate or inanimate objects, but here it only means 'former,' for Mr. Man was not aged. *â·rla-len* day-in, always. *chit·i* letter, a Hindustani word. *yi·ti-ke* tattoo-does. They have applied the word 'tattoo' to writing, as it were, scratching, scribbling. *tâ·ba-tal* meanwhile, compare *ontô·ba* already, before, *tô·baba* wait a little, *dama·bârr* elder brother. *mol·a* we. *ê·la* pig-arrows, pl. indicated by next word. *dâ·gaga* many. *tâ·i-ke* make-do.]

47. *mô·tat par·ekalen â·chitik dal·ta ê·to-chô·nga ji·baba.* We have now got very many bundles of arrows in our possession. [*mô·tat* our. *par·eka-len* lap-in, in our possession, see 23. *â·chitik* now. *dal·ta* arrows, generic name for all arrows except the *ê·la-*, which is more of an ornament or toy. The several kinds are: *ra·ta-* with blunt wooden point for play, or before conversion into a *tî·rlâ-*sharp wooden-pointed, for shooting fish; *tê·lbâ-* with [illegible] with or without barb, for [illegible] and small animals, etc.; *ê·la-* with movable [illegible] blade-head, for shooting pigs and other animals, etc.; *ê·la tâ·kâ la·pa-* with fixed iron blade-head, for the same purposes. *ê·to-chô·nga* bundle of arrows or bows (see *ê·to* in Cl. 7, it is often used as a prefix to verbs), *chô* bind, as a parcel with string. *ji·baba* very many.]

48. *.malai lê·a chê·rigma ôt-lô·binga len jû·bagda; ût-mû·gu kî·nab l'edâ·re ât tôg len tâk·lake.* The Nicobar outrigger canoe is ill-suited for turtling; the narrowness of the bows prevents one from making full use of the spear. [*.malai* Malay, meaning Nicobarese, who are probably remotely Malays, and are quite different from the Andamanese. *lê·a* of. *chê·rigma* outrigger canoe, the generic name for all canoes is *rôko-*, those in the neighbourhood of Port Blair are generally without outrigger, and much larger than the *chê·rigma-*. *ôt-lô·bi-nga* (No. 14) hunt for turtles along the shore by poling-(verbal subst.). *len* for, postp. *jû·bagda* bad. *ût-mû·gu* (No. 14) bow of boat, *ig-mû·gu-* face. *kî·nab* thin, that is, narrow. *l'edâ·re* because of, that is, because of the bow being narrow. *ât* it. *tôg* turtle-spear, see 44. *len* for. *tâk·la-ke* inconvenience-does.]

49. *kianchal· lô·binga bê·dig mat ôn-tô·lat-ke.* The consequence is that in poling the canoe we (frequently) fall. [*kianchal·* therefore. *lô·bi-nga* hunting the turtle by poling-(verbal subst.). *bê·dig* while. *mat* us. *ôn-tô·-*

lat-ke cause-fall-does; *tô·lat* is to drop, and is here made causative by prefixing *en*, = makes us fall, see *en-ūt-pī·rke* in 21.]

50. *mō·da ngōl bi·rma-chī·lewa len min ardâ·ru ngā·na yā·te ititā·nke yā·ba, mōl·ōichik kūkjā·bagike.* If you don't send us by the (incoming) steamer all the things we asked for, we shall be very disappointed. [*mō·da* if. *ngōl* you. *bi·rma-chî·lewa* steamer, see 3. *len* in, postp. *mīn* things, see 23. *ardâ·ru* all. *ngā·na* v. beg, ask for, *yā·te* which we asked for, but there is no indication of person or time. *ititā·nke* send, see 23. *yā·ba* not. *mōl·ōichik* we. *kūk-jā·bagi-ke* heart-bad-are see 23, euphonically inserted *i* before *-ke*.]

51. *kâ·rin ūgā tārti·t yā·ba.* There is no more news to tell you. [*kâ·rin* here. *ūgā* more. *târti·t* news. *yā·ba* not.]

52. *med·a ngōlī ardâ·ru tek tārti·t bi·ringa igā·rike.* We are longing to have good accounts of you all. [*med·a* we. *ngōl-la* you. *ardâ·ru* all. *tek* from, postp. *târti·t* news. *i-gā·ri-ke* long-for-do, *i* prefix, an abbreviation of *ig*, Nos. 9 and 10.]

53. *ūgā·kā pūm bā lepā·re.* But little rain has fallen up to the present time. [*ūgā·kā* as yet, see 5. *pūm* rain. *bā* little. *le-pā-re* (euphonic *le*, frequently prefixed to verbs), fall-did.]

54. *kam wai mōl·ōichik.* Good-bye. [See 29.]

The above examples show the mode of thought of the natives, and what most occupies their attention. They are some of the very few expressions of genuine untutored barbarians which we possess. The analytical translation which I have been enabled to give, by the help of Mr. Man (who has very carefully revised the whole), shews not only the meaning of the parts of the words and the method of construction, but the great depth to which Mr. Man has been able to penetrate, entirely from oral instruction, into the genius and vocabulary of the language.

The agglutinative nature of the language tends directly to the detection of basic forms, and Mr. Temple has very acutely pursued this into the theory of roots. He conceives that the roots are all properly monosyllabic, and generally end with a consonant, but that these monosyllables are frequently extended by the addition of a vowel or diphthong, or the same preceded by a consonant, in which the real meaning lies in the first syllable, though it has now been lost, while the expansions serve as modifications. Occasionally the roots are of three syllables. This chapter in Mr. Temple's grammar is one of the longest and most carefully studied, but his materials were too scanty, and, as the vocabulary increased, Mr. Man found it necessary to suggest such multifarious points for reconsideration, that it would be obviously premature to give the lists which Mr. Temple has furnished. It is to be hoped that the fuller vocabulary (which has now about 6000 entries of the English-Andamanese part only), and the corrected grammar will be published in course of time. They are obviously of great importance to the Indian Government, on account of its penal settlement at Port Blair, and are well worthy of its patronage.

The Andamanese have poetry, and that of a most remarkable kind. Their only musical instrument is a stamping board to keep time, and to this rhythm everything seems to be sacrificed. The words, their order, the prefixes, the suffixes, the postpositions, are all more or less changed, the order of the words suffers, in short the poetical language requires a special study, which is the more difficult to give, as songs are always impromptu, and not, as a rule, sung again after the one occasion for which they were composed, and then only by the composer. Of the music Mr. Man regrets to state that he is unable to give any information, as he is, unfortunately, totally unacquainted with the subject. The following specimen of a song composed by the *jam·ba*, to whom the above letters were addressed, after his liberation from a six months' imprisonment, about 1865, for having shot down a sailor whom he found taking liberties with his wife, was given to Mr. Man by the author.

I. As it was sung.

Solo. *ngô·do kûk l'àrlâ·lagi·ka,*
mô·ro el·ma kâ igbâ·dàla
mô·ro el·mo lê aden·yard
pô-tôt lâh.

Chorus. *aden·yard pô-tôt lâh.*

II. Literal Translation of the Poetry.

thou heart sad
sky surface there look-at
sky surface of ripple
bamboo spear.

III. Prose Andamanese Version by Mr. Man.

ngōl kūk l'ārtā·lagike
mō·ro el·ma len kā·to igbā·dignga bēdig,
mō·ro el·ma li·a en·yar len igbā·dignga bēdig
-pō-tōg len lāg·imike.

IV. Literal Translation of Prose Version.

thou heart-sad-art
sky-surface to there looking while,
sky-surface of ripple to looking while,
bamboo spear on lean-dost.

V. Free Translation of Prose Version.

thou art sad at heart;
gazing there at the sky's surface,
gazing at the ripple on the sky's surface,
leaning on the bamboo spear.

The rhythm, as read by Mr. Man, was:

– ⏑ | – ∸ | – ⏑ | – –
– ⏑ | – – | ∸ | – ⏑ ⏑
– – | – ⏑ | – – | – ⏑ ⏑
– | – | – |

The syllables marked ∸ were of medial length. There were two short syllables at the end of the second and third lines. The three long syllables in the fourth line were very long and slow, each filling up a whole measure. Strange as some of the changes and omissions were, this is one of the least altered of the songs in Mr. Temple's grammar. We must suppose the man to be standing before his companions after liberation from prison, gazing sadly at the sky again and resting on his bamboo spear, and then the action would make the words intelligible.

An important question arises as to the durability of the

language. The English have been there for so short a time (only twenty-four years), and the only trustworthy vocabulary, that of Mr. Man, has been made for so much shorter a time, that there is no proper record by which the past can be contrasted with the present state of the language. But there are some names of places in the neighbourhood of Port Blair which cannot be explained. The Andaman names of places are all significant, and this shews that some words have entirely dropped out of use, or have become unrecognisably modified since such places were named. There will also be found in the examples I have given many evidently compound words of whose parts Mr. Man had not succeeded in obtaining any explanation. This therefore leads us to suppose that the words may alter rapidly, while the constructions may remain. The difference of words and sameness of construction in the various Andaman tribes might be accounted for on the principle of independent development, owing to little intercourse, during many hundreds of years. The ease with which young *.wō·i*, an *.ōko-jū·waida*, or native of South Middle Andaman, learned the South Andaman language, may be mainly explained by the similarity of construction. It is not so much the words of a foreign language which puzzle us as the native method of putting those words together, for this depends upon an original divergence in the lines of thought, which soon become impossible to reconcile. When, therefore, the construction remains the same, the shifting from one set of words to another is comparatively easy. At the same time, this example may serve to shew with what ease any one of these languages may change its words. If Messrs. Man and Temple succeed in getting their vocabulary and grammar of the South Andaman tongue officially recognised, and books come to be printed in accordance with them, and used in the Andaman Homes, and finally over all those parts of the South Andaman and Rutland Islands which are in the occupation of the *.bō·jigngi·jīda* (isolated parts of these islands are in the possession of the *.jār·awada*, who own Little Andaman, the Sentinels, and small intermediate islands), and the people themselves do not die out (as is unfortunately quite possible, for the deaths much exceed the births, and the 1500 South Andamanese that are estimated to have been there when we took possession of the islands in 1858 have dwindled down in 24 years to less than 500), then the change of the language may be arrested, a literary or book language may be acknowledged as that used at Port Blair, and the speech of the other islanders recognised as provincial. Even if the present South Andamanese died out, the language would remain that of government, and be adopted by the natives of other islands who naturally come to Port Blair. In the mean time, thanks to the two gentlemen whose papers I have been entrusted with, a very fair notion of this language as it now exists can be formed, and its position in the whole family of human speech, as laid down by Mr. Temple in the observations with which I began, can be duly appreciated by philologists. Even if the language become extinct before the end of the present century, the researches of Messrs. Man and Temple, as preserved in their manuscripts, would retain their philological value. Exceptional opportunities, well utilised, have resulted in a thorough, practical, and trustworthy exposition of a remarkable agglutinative language, as yet almost entirely free from external influences. The excellent memoirs on the people, their habits and customs, which Mr. Man has read before the Anthropological Institute, and are published in its Transactions, complete one of the most satisfactory accounts of an uncivilised tribe which we possess. I beg in conclusion to tender the thanks of the Philological Society to Messrs. Man and Temple, and especially to Mr. Man, without whose presence in England and unstinting personal explanations the present report could not have been drawn up.

www.ingramcontent.com/pod-product-compliance
Lightning Source LLC
Chambersburg PA
CBHW020501270326
41926CB00008B/691